Space Law in a Networked World

Studies in Space Law

VOLUME 19

The titles published in this series are listed at *brill.com/slaw*

Space Law in a Networked World

Edited by

P.J. Blount and Mahulena Hofmann

BRILL
NIJHOFF

LEIDEN | BOSTON

The Library of Congress Cataloging-in-Publication Data is available online at https://catalog.loc.gov
LC record available at https://lccn.loc.gov/2022054994

Typeface for the Latin, Greek, and Cyrillic scripts: "Brill". See and download: brill.com/brill-typeface.

ISSN 1871-7659
ISBN 978-90-04-52726-3 (hardback)
ISBN 978-90-04-52727-0 (e-book)

This book is printed on acid-free paper and produced in a sustainable manner.

Contents

SECTION III
Data Processing

Preface

Access to and uses of space technology have changed dramatically over the past 10 years. Traditionally, access to space capabilities required dedicated receivers and significant investment. This has changed with the advent of new information technologies that incorporate and disseminate the benefits of space directly to users. This new seamless delivery of space capabilities, from navigation and position to data flows of various types, means that it can be difficult to disentangle space capabilities from other information infrastructures. This also means that the legal structures developed to govern space technologies are being forced into contact with a variety of other legal structures. As new markets, innovative technologies, and increased data access emerge, legal questions abound as the *lex specialis* of space accommodates these trends. This book investigates how traditional space law is developing as space technology enters the daily lives of individuals everywhere, and how other bodies of law adapt to their interfaces with space technology.

The discourse on space law has lagged behind the swift march of technology. For example, the potential for the delivery of broadband Internet through broadcast satellites was first demonstrated in 1996.[1] Only recently, however, have scholars begun to seriously address how network technologies affect the assumptions that underlay the legal framework for space. This book seeks to fill gaps in the literature by examining legal issues that arise from the embedding of the space segment into the networked world at large. Separated into three sections, it includes interdisciplinary chapters from leading and emerging scholars that detail legal issues that result from the risks and opportunities of the digital networking of space technology.

Section 1 focuses on the issue of cybersecurity for space assets and the needs of a legal practitioner overseeing cybersecurity in the space domain. Cybersecurity has become a dominant risk for space operations of all types. While much of the cybersecurity enterprise is purely technical, law and legal processes play an important role in defining how organizations pursue cyber secure space operations. This section examines the interplay of the technical and legal aspects of cybersecurity in the space domain. Section 1 opens with a Chapter titled "A Network of Governance," in which *P.J. Blount* reflects on the nature of the governance systems that often underlay or supplement legal

1 Horst D. Clausen, Hilmar Linder, and Bernhard Collini-Nocker, "Internet over Direct Broadcast Satellites," *IEEE Communications Magazine* 37, no. 6 (1999): 146–51.

systems. He argues that the trend of rapidly changing technology, and specifically cyber and network technologies, result in a situation wherein legal practitioners must be more adept in navigating broader governance frameworks that contextualize the content and application of the law. He uses cybersecurity for space assets as an example of this phenomenon that illustrates the rise of governance with legal practice. He concludes that, as a result, space law can no longer remain as an isolated branch of the international legal system, and it will soon be part of a network of governance that extends far outside the bounds of space activities. *Andre Adelsbach et al.* present a technical assessment of the cybersecurity risks posed to space architecture. Specifically, they survey known cyber-incidents in the space domain and show how changes in network technology have increased those risks. Through an examination of the notions of cybersecurity and risk, they evaluate the various attack vectors and actors that place networked space infrastructures at risk of cyber-exploits and attacks. *Sébastien Bonnart et al.* give a broad picture of the hostile cyber operations by mapping the cybersecurity threat surface and examining both legal and technical solutions to these challenges. They differentiate between various levels ranging from unauthorized access to classified information to the outage of critical infrastructure. They describe the attributability process and discuss the means of implementing the 'States of origin' principle and the transit of States responsibility. They argue that any generalization of legal consequences is difficult, and that rather the specifics of incidents – motives, target and actors – are the operable variables in determining the applicability of already existing national and international legal systems. In the final chapter of this section, *Rada Popova* rightly observes that space law does not at all mention cyberspace, but some of its norms might be applicable to the cybersecurity of space technology and space activities. The existing cyber-related elements in international law as well as in some regional legal instruments do not offer a specific normative body to ensure that space assets are legally regulated and protected from cyber interference. Thus, for the time being, the law does not provide legal solutions to the challenges posed to space operations generally and to New Space technologies.

Section II explores the trends of connectivity and accessibility that have been enabled by a number of advances in space technology. The section seeks to engage with the opportunities made possible by developing technologies and examines the role the law plays in ensuring that the space segment is maintained as a critical part of the global network contributing to connecting the world. *Simona Spassova* explores the difference between harmful interference – a degradation of signal in radiocommunication service – and cyberattacks based on the transfer of electronic communication under the Radio

Regulations of the International Telecommunication Union (ITU). Her analysis focuses on the fact that the cyber-environment has a non-physical dimension and is ruled by human-made laws such as computer code. This stands in contrast to the electromagnetic spectrum, which consists of the range of frequencies of electromagnetic radiation and is ruled by the law of physics. This difference is critical in understanding how ITU rules apply to these types of interference. *Marco Crepaldi et al.* concentrate on CubeSat operations and the implications software design for liability. They explain that while hardware standardization of cubesats has progressed, the standards for software are not fully developed, and that some common software could have dependability issues. The authors suggest that launching States of cubesats should consider including in their authorization processes measures for ensuring that the critical software does not excessively increase the risk associated with their operations thereby mitigating the risk of malfunction and potential liability. *Elina Morozova* analyses the outcomes of the WRC-19 in regard to non-GSO systems, especially to large constellations of small satellites. She notices that in the process of ITU registration, the critical condition is the obligation to bring the frequency assignments used by a large constellation into use in the seven years prescribed by the Radio Regulations. This is problematic for large constellations due to the time it takes to build up orbital capacity. She discusses a potential remedy for these systems in the new ITU milestone approach which allows for the deployment of satellites in three phases offering more flexibility for both operators and the ITU.

Finally, Section III examines the legal issues associated with data collection from, data transmission through, and data processing in space in light of increasingly powerful computing technologies. The starting point of the chapter written by *Leopold Mantl* is the fact that big data from space contributes to a range of human activities in the contemporary networked world. One of the most common uses across society is that of geographical information systems (GIS), which facilitate an array of functions such as environmental monitoring, land use analysis, and disaster management. The meshing of Global Navigation Satellite Systems (GNSS) into these networks presents novel applications for usage of space derived data, including automated transport. It seems, however, that the space origins of the data generated by these structures does not define the legal framework for data generation and distribution. Rather, at the service level, the role of the service provider and the place of service provision are decisive factors for shaping the liability and data protection areas. The amount of data being produced by space assets is constantly increasing, but new computing techniques, such as cloud computing, are keeping pace and offering new ways to store, transfer, and process this data, and these phenomena have important legal consequences. *Ingo Baumann and Erik Pelander* focused on the legal aspects of storage, access, and processing of Earth observation (EO) data through cloud infrastructures. They enumerate the main open issues related to this activity – the security of data, privacy, and ownership of the data. The authors observe that the expansion of EO cloud platforms is slowed by untransparent contractual terms, which remain highly individualized and complex. Concerning the plans to launch satellite constellations for satellite-based cloud servers, they see as justified the doubts that the use of such systems may have extra-jurisdictional impacts, enforced by the high-level analysis of ownership and privacy concerning the data stored or used in such clouds. European Union data protection in relation to space activities is the focus of *Laura Keogh*. She notes that space activities such as remote sensing can produce personal data and fall within the scope of the legal norms designed to protect individual rights in personal data. However, the recognition of privacy by the space sector should not pose a problem if the space architecture is designed with the goal of protecting the privacy of individuals. *Sandra Cabrera Alvarado* investigates the question of the mechanism of access to data of the European Union Copernicus programme. Her chapter delves into the legally mandated "open data" policy and seeks to define its major elements of 'full,' 'free,' and 'open,' and how these are manifested through the Copernicus distribution mechanisms enshrined in various levels of binding or non-binding documents.

In this place, the editors would like to thank all authors for their valuable contributions, as well SES and the University Luxembourg for their continuous support.

Mahulena Hofmann
P.J. Blount

Figures and Tables

Figures

Tables

Notes on Contributors

André Adelsbach
is the VP Group Information and Cyber Security at SES and responsible for defining and executing SES' Cyber Security Strategy and continuously enhancing SES' security framework. Since joining SES in 2010, André is leading and developing SES' Information and Cyber Security function, which covers all aspects of information and cyber security, including security governance, security risk management, security engineering and security operations across SES. Before joining SES, André headed the Security, Audit and Governance Services team of Telindus – Belgacom ICT in Luxembourg, where he oversaw the development and delivery of strategic security services in the governmental, financial, communications, insurance and space sector. André is a cyber security enthusiast, who has been working in information and cyber security for more than 20 years. He authored more than 40 international publications and served as a program committee member and reviewer for various information security conferences and journals. André Adelsbach earned a PhD for his research in information security and cryptographic copyright protection at Horst Görtz Institute for IT Security and a master's degree in computer science from Saarland University. André is certified CISM, ISO 27001 Lead Auditor and Lead Implementer, GCFA and GREM. He is a member of the GIAC Advisory Board and served on the board of the OWASP Luxembourg Chapter.

Sandra Cabrera Alvarado
Her international studies focused on space policy and law leaded her to develop an international work experience. Currently she works at the European Association for Remote Sensing Companies-EARSC leading space projects funded by the European Commission. In 2016 she joined the University of Luxembourg with a scholarship to do her PhD studies on the legal and political analysis of the EU Copernicus' open data policy. Prior to her studies she worked in Mexico at the Mexican Space Agency (AEM) in 2013. Before that, in 2011 Sandra joined the analyst team of the U.S. telecommunications consultancy firm Northern Sky Research. In 2009, she worked as a consultant at the Science Sector at UNESCO supporting the Space for Heritage initiative projects for developing countries. She obtained an international relations degree from the Americas University in Mexico in 2003 and later pursued her master studies at the International Space University in 2007 followed by a second master in Space and Telecommunications Law at the Paris-XI Jean Monnet

University in Paris, France. She holds a Law PhD degree from the University of Luxembourg, Luxembourg.

Ingo Baumann

is partner of BHO Legal, a boutique technology law firm based in Cologne, Germany and one of Europe's leading space law firms. Ingo has more than 20 years of professional experience in the space industry. He wrote his PhD at the Cologne Institute of Air and Space Law on the international law of satellite communication. Before establishing BHO Legal, he was legal adviser within the German Aerospace Centre (DLR), becoming later the Head of the DLR Galileo Project Office, and CEO of DLR GfR mbH, the operating company of DLR for the German Galileo Control Centre. Ingo is advising ministries, space agencies, research organisations, universities and companies of all types involved in large public space programmes as well as commercial space activities across all application areas. His expertise covers international and national space law, international and national telecommunication law, procurement law, R&D law, IT law and all types of space industry contracts. Over the years, Ingo has been involved in numerous large public space programs such as Galileo, Copernicus, EDRS, SatcomBW2 and he is closely supporting several NewSpace companies in their business development. Ingo is member of the International Institute of Space Law (IISL), the European Centre for Space Law (ECSL), the Space Law Committee of the International Bar Association (IBA) and various other professional space industry organisations. He is co-editor of the upcoming Routledge Handbook of Commercial Space Activities, column editor of "GNSS & the Law" in InsideGNSS and regular speaker at space industry conferences.

P.J. Blount

(Ph.D., M.S., Global Affairs, Rutgers University; LL.M., King's College London; J.D., University of Mississippi; B.A./A.B.J., University of Georgia) is a Lecturer in Law in the School of Law and Politics at Cardiff University. He has also serves as an adjunct professor for the LL.M. in the Air and Space Law at the University of Mississippi School of Law. Previously he has served as a Research Fellow at SES, a Postdoctoral Researcher at the University of Luxembourg, an adjunct professor at Montclair State University, and a Visiting Scholar at the Beijing Institute of Technology School of Law. Blount's primary research areas are legal issues related to Space Security and Cyberspace Governance. He has published and presented widely on the topic of Space Security Law and has given expert testimony on Space Traffic Management before the U.S. House of Representatives' Subcommittee on Space. He is an editor of the Proceedings of the International Institute of Space Law and was formerly the Editor-in-Chief of the Journal of Space Law. He currently serves as the Executive Secretary of the International Institute of Space Law and is a member of the State Bar of Georgia (USA).

Sébastien Bonnart
is an aerospace professional and a cybersecurity hobbyist. After graduating from INSA Lyon as a telecommunication engineer 10 years ago, Sébastien occupied various positions within a leading integrator of ground stations. This provided him with a comprehensive knowledge of design, maintenance and use-cases of complex satellite antenna systems all over the world. As a teenager, he learned programming and was always determined to push the limits of computers and programs. After graduation, he decided to pursue space as a career and to keep cybersecurity as a hobby. Nowadays, Sébastien is developing his binary exploitation skills, complemented by playful and intense Capture-the Flag cybersecurity competitions (including Hack-A-Sat finals in 2021). His passion for space led him to join volunteers of the Space Generation Advisory Council. Here, he takes part in the publication of conference papers to raise awareness on chosen space related topics and he provides technical contributions to the Space&Cybersecurity, as well as the Small Satellite project groups. Sébastien believes that it is essential to address cybersecurity issues in outer space because over the last few decades, space and cybersecurity technologies have been evolving independently at incredible rates. It is now time for space to integrate a cybersecurity culture. However, space has particularities that will challenge digital norms until both industries cooperate and achieve a true "space cybersecurity."

Andrea Capurso
is a member of the SGAC Space and Cybersecurity Project Group. He is a PhD candidate in International Law at LUISS University in Rome, where he is conducting his research on domestic laws related to private space activities. At the same time, he works as Junior Associate at Studio Legale Guarino, a law firm based in Rome and specialized in Administrative Law. He has previously worked for Telespazio and the European Union Agency for the Space Program (EUSPA) and holds an Adv. LLM in Air & Space Law from Leiden University. The focus of his publications is on space law and cyber law. In particular, he addressed issues related to cyber operations and satellite insurance, ASAT tests and military uses of outer space, national authorizations of space missions and property rights on celestial bodies. His paper titled "The non-appropriation principle: a Roman interpretation" was awarded in 2018 by the International

Institute of Space Law (IISL) with the "Diederiks-Verschoor Award" for best paper presented at the Institute's Colloquium.

Antonio Carlo
is currently working for an international organisation in the security and defence field. He is also a PhD candidate at the Tallinn University of Technology specialising in space and cyber, particularly in defence. Antonio holds two Master degrees with honors in International Relations and Political Science from La Sapienza University of Rome. In addition to his second Master's, he studied at the Pontifical Institute for Arabic and Islamic Studies (PISAI) where he strengthened his understanding of Arabic culture and language. He is a member of the Space Generation Advisory Council, the International Institute of Space Law, and the European Centre for Space Law.

Marco Crepaldi
is an independent researcher focusing on the ethical issues of new technologies. He is interested in space activities, artificial intelligence and the governance of cryptonetworks from the legal and regulatory perspective. Following law school, he obtained an interdisciplinary doctorate in law, science and technology from the University of Bologna in co-tutelle with the University of Luxembourg. Before pursuing his research independently, Dr. Crepaldi held appointments at the University of Luxembourg in the Faculty of Science Technology and Medicine and at KU Leuven within the Centre for IT and IP Law.

Thea Flem Dethlefsen
is currently working as a Policy Officer at the European Commission. She holds a Bachelor and Master in law from University of Copenhagen and an advanced LL.M. in Air and Space Law from the Leiden University. Previously, she worked as a Contracts Officer under the Young Graduate Traineeship Programme at the European Space Agency and was the Programme Assistant during the International Space University's 2018 Space Studies Programme. She is the co-founder of the Space and Cybersecurity Project Group under the Space Generation Advisory Council and previously co-lead. She is part of the Membership Committee of the International Institute of Space Law and is the recipient of the 2019 Diederiks-Verschoor Award.

Mahulena Hofmann
is holder of the SES Chair in Space, SatCom and Media Law at the University of Luxembourg. Since 2016, she serves as director of the Master Program in

Space, Communication and Media Law. At the same time, she is lecturing international law at the Charles University in Prague. In 2016, she was head of an international team which analysed the framework of space resources activities; afterwards, she has been working on a Draft general space legislation of Luxembourg. Regularly, she is member of the Luxembourg delegation to the Legal Sub-Committee of the UN COPUOS. Between 2017 and 2019, she was representing the University in The Hague International Space Resources Governance Group. M. Hofmann is member of the International Astronautical Academy, and of the Board of the International Institute of Space Law which awarded her a Distinguished Service Award in 2020. She is author of more than 100 articles and seven books; in 2019, she published an "Introduction to Space Law" with Tanja Masson-Zwaan. In 2020, she supported the UNOOSA in the preparation of an online e-learning course in space law. Her main areas of interest are space law and international telecommunication law.

Ross Horne
is a research fellow in computer science at University of Luxembourg. He played a role setting up the Space Informatics direction of the Interdisciplinary Space Master Program on behalf of the Faculty of Science Technology and Medicine. His research centres around harnessing fundamental advances in logic to improve methods for evaluating security and privacy problems. He is also interested in communicating emerging privacy vulnerabilities to stakeholders, where the legal context can strengthen arguments in support of improving the privacy of citizens. Educated in the UK at Oxford University, and University of Southampton, Dr. Horne has spent several years in Asia, holding a senior research position at Nanyang Technological University, Singapore, and has held an associate professorship developing teaching and research at emerging universities in Kazakhstan.

Laura Keogh
achieved her bachelors from Trinity College Dublin and her masters from Edinburgh University. She is a graduate of the International Space University's 2016 SSP, where she has subsequently given workshops on the intersection between data protection and space law. She is the author of "Data Protection Compliance, A Guide to GDPR and Irish Data Protection Law," published by Clarus Press. Laura formally trained as a barrister-at-law in Ireland and currently works as data protection in house legal counsel at Meta in Ireland.

Mclee Kerolle
is a graduate of the International Institute of Air and Space Law at Leiden University where he wrote his Masters thesis on the regulation of commercial

spaceports worldwide. While his thesis was inspired by Spaceport America, it specifically focused on proposed spaceports in Hawaii and Curacao. During his time at Leiden, Mclee worked at the International Association for the Advancement of Space Safety (IAASS) where his responsibilities focused on researching third party liability issues associated with commercial human spaceflight. He also served as the Executive Secretary for the Space Generation Advisory Council (SGAC) and is currently an active member of their Diversity Action Team and Effective and Adaptive Governance for a Lunar Ecosystem (E.A.G.L.E.) Action Team. His work with E.A.G.L.E. resulted in a Lunar Charter Report being presented at the United Nations' Office of Outer Space Affairs Legal Subcommittee in the summer of 2021. Mclee also serves as the Deputy Executive Director for the Space Court Foundation, a 501(c)(3) that specializes in promoting space law and policy education. In addition, Mclee is the Program Director for the Caribbean Space Society, a working group of the Institute of Caribbean Studies that aims to establish a unified Caribbean Space Agenda.

Jonathan Lim
is an Australian lawyer, geopolitical analyst, and cyber security analyst. He is the Project Co-lead with Jus Ad Astra – focused on exploring intersections between international human rights law and outer space affairs. He is an individual Member of the International Institute of Space Law, Researcher with the Institute for Internet and the Just Society, Research Advisor with Tod'Aers, Member on the Legal Council with For All Moonkind, and serves as Special Advisor to the SGAC Space & Cybersecurity Project Group. His qualifications include a Bachelor of Arts and Juris Doctor with Monash University, Graduate Diploma of Legal Practice and Master of Legal Practice with the Australian National University, Graduate Certificate in Cyber Security with RMIT, and Graduate Certificate in Cyber Security with Charles Sturt University. As a space lawyer he has contributed his perspectives on space legal and policy affairs before the UN Office For Outer Space Affairs, International Astronautical Congress, COSPAR, Australian Institute of International Affairs, Room – The Space Journal, and contributions to Australia's 2020 Cyber Security Strategy.

Leopold Mantl
is a member of the Legal Service of the European Commission, responsible for budgetary law and financial rules of the EU. He advises the Commission on legal aspects of the multiannual financial framework of the EU and its annual budget, and on financial issues concerning Union spending programmes, including the European Defence Fund and the Union Space Programme. Previously, he was a deputy Head of Unit in DG BUDGET and DG GROW of the Commission, where he supervised the development and follow-up of the

policy in connection with the legal, financial and institutional management of the EU GNSS programmes, negotiated delegation agreements amongst others with the European Space Agency (ESA) and managed complex procurement procedures for Galileo and EGNOS. He also worked on legal aspects of the Copernicus programme of the EU. Before joining the European Commission, he was a lawyer in the Legal Department of ESA, where he gave legal and regulatory advice concerning the European launchers and the International Space Station, and in an Italian telecoms company, where he focussed on legal issues concerning satellite communication handsets, including product liability, preparation of distribution contracts and software license contracts, and co-ordination of IPR issues. He is a member of the International Institute of Space Law.

Sjouke Mauw
is full professor in computer science at the University of Luxembourg. He is head of the Department of Computer Science, head of the Security and Trust of Software Systems (SaToSS) research group and faculty member of the Interdisciplinary Centre for Security, Reliability and Trust (SnT). Until 2007 he was associate professor in computer science at the Eindhoven University of Technology (Netherlands), with a part time secondment as senior researcher at CWI (Center of Mathematics and Computer Science) in Amsterdam. Sjouke Mauw has performed research in a range of areas, such as visual specification languages, concurrency theory, algebraic specification, term rewriting, domain specific languages, testing, and distributed algorithms. His current research focuses on the application of formal methods in the area of information security. His topics of interest include: security protocols, security assessment, privacy, trust, e-voting, attack trees, network security, distance-bounding, and social networks.

Elina Morozova
is an expert in international space law and policy, management of radio frequency spectrum and satellite orbits, and satellite telecommunications. Ms. Morozova earned two master's degrees in International Law and World Economy from the All-Russian Academy of Foreign Trade under the Ministry of Economic Development and Trade of the Russian Federation and holds an LL.M degree in International Business Law from the University of Manchester. Elina Morozova is Executive Director of the Intersputnik International Organization of Space Communications, an intergovernmental satellite telecommunication organization headquartered in Moscow. At Intersputnik, she is responsible for relations with Member States and the UN system, including the Committee on

the Peaceful Uses of Outer Space and the International Telecommunication Union, and manages the International and Legal Service. She also takes part in the work of the Expert Committee of the CIS Interparliamentary Assembly – Regional Commonwealth in the Field of Communications. Ms. Morozova combines her career at Intersputnik with research. She teaches a course on international space law and telecommunications law at St. Petersburg University and participates in the activity of space-related non-profit organizations, including as a member of the Board of Directors of the International Institute of Space Law, Advisory Committee of Secure World Foundation, and Global Future Council on Space of the World Economic Forum. She is Co-Editor and Core Expert of the McGill Manual on International Law Applicable to Military Uses of Outer Space (MILAMOS) and a member of the editorial boards of Acta Astronautica, Annals of Air and Space Law, Space: Science & Technology. She authored or co-authored about forty publications on satellite communication and other aspects of space activities in Russian and English.

Erik Pellander

is a Research Fellow at BHO Legal – a boutique technology law firm based in Cologne, Germany, with focus on international, European and national public high-technology programmes in Air, Space, Security and Defense, R&D, Information and Communication Technology and Geospatial sectors. He has more than 10 years of experience in the space sector. Before joining BHO Legal in 2011, he was working at the Institute of Air and Space Law, Cologne, as well as at the legal department of the German Space Agency (DLR). Erik supports the BHO Legal's space practice since years in all relevant study and consultancy projects. He studied law at the University of Cologne and was a Scholarship student of the German Academic Exchange Service (DAAD) at the National Law School of India University in Bangalore. He further is the winner of the 2010 European Regional Round of the Manfred Lachs Space Law Moot Court Competition. Erik is a member of the European Centre for Space Law (ECSL) and authored several publications in the area of space law, international environmental law, as well as international private law.

Aaron Pickard

is a proud member of the Space Generation Advisory Council (SGAC) Space & Cybersecurity Project Group, and has contributed to this volume in that capacity. His research interests include the relationship between computing and the commercialization of both near-earth and cislunar space. Aaron also participated in the SGAC Mentorship Program in 2020. Aaron works as a Systems Test Engineer at Tyvak Nano-Satellite Systems, a Terran Orbital Corporation.

He studied computer science at Columbia University and Talmud at the Jewish Theological Seminary, and earned Bachelor of Arts degrees from both institutions in May 2020. In 2019, Aaron interned at OneWeb through the Matthew Isakowitz Fellowship Program; in 2018, he interned at NASA Langley Research Center. Aaron held leadership roles in the Columbia Space Initiative, a chapter of Students for the Exploration and Development of Space (SEDS). SEDS USA honored him with the Jeff Bezos Award in 2019. He participated in the Lucy Student Pipeline Accelerator and Competency Enabler (L'SPACE) Mission Concept Academy and NASA Proposal Writing and Evaluation Experience Academy in 2020. He was also a finalist in Revolutionary Aerospace Systems Concepts Academic Linkage in both 2017 and 2018. In his free time, Aaron enjoys cooking, playing Kerbal Space Program, and maintaining a SatNOGS ground station.

Rada Popova
is a graduate of the Law Faculty of the University of Vienna, did her Ph.D. at the University of Cologne and has been a research scholar at the Centre of Excellence at The Hague Academy of International law. Since 2021, she is the General Counsel of Isar Aerospace Technologies, the first fully privately funded developer of launchers in Europe. Previously, Rada worked as a Senior Research Fellow and Lecturer in Law at the University of Cologne. As a lawyer and legal advisor, she has provided expertise in various aerospace-related projects with the European Space Agency, the German Aerospace Center and private industry in Germany, France, Italy and Spain and actively contributes to the work of the International Institute on Space Law and the International Law Association. She has published numerous journal articles and book chapters on the regulation of space activities and regularly lectures in universities in Europe and Asia.

Antonia Russo
is a PhD Candidate in Information Engineering at the University Mediterranea of Reggio Calabria, Italy. In 2018, she obtained her Master's Degree in Telecommunication Engineering with honours. Her research interests include information security, privacy, and social network analysis. During the last year of her PhD, she has been appointed a Visiting Researcher at the European Space Agency in collaboration with the Radio Navigation Systems and Techniques Section, Directorate of Technology, Engineering and Quality (TEC-ESN). Since 2020, she has co-led the Space Generation Advisory Council's Space and Cybersecurity Project Group. In 2021, Antonia won one of the three ASI-SGAC awards addressed to Italian PhD students allowing her to present her research

and the projects she is carrying out during IAC2021 and SGC2021. She is part of the Space Newsletter Editorial Staff: an editorial project that encourages interest and passion towards space, especially the next generations. Antonia has been involved in several educational projects, such as Coding Girls and STEM2020, to empower young female students and help them pursue a STEM career.

Thomas Schaefer
has a background in Business Information Systems and fell in love with cyber security over 15 years ago. Since then, he has been working in various positions in IT Audit and Information Security, currently as VP Information Security Management at SES, a globally leading satellite communications provider. Thomas holds a range of Cyber Security certifications and is member of ISACA and ISC^2 associations. He has given guest lectures at universities and talks at various academic and industry conferences on Governance, Risk and Compliance topics. Currently, Thomas is super excited about everything around cloud security and finding innovative ways to manage cyber risk in an ever-changing world.

Simona Spassova
is a lecturer in space and satellite communications law at Sofia University St. Kliment Ohridski. She holds a PhD in International Law and her doctoral thesis focused on the problem of harmful interference with satellite communication. It was conducted within the framework of a public private partnership between satellite operator SES and the University of Luxembourg. Her research interests focus on the legal framework of the International Telecommunication Union, Cybersecurity in Space, and Human Rights. Dr. Spassova also holds an LL.M in Financial & Banking Law (University of Luxembourg) and a MA in Human Rights and Democracy (University of Bologna and University of Sarajevo). She is also working as a consultant for the International Finance Corporation (IFC, World Bank Group) in the Transaction Advisory Services Department.

George Tountas
has a background in Computer Science and holds an M.Sc. Information Security from University College London. He has been working on Cyber Security and IT Audit for more than 12 years. He is passionate about the topic and loves to collaborate with teams to get the best and most secure solutions. Currently he is a Senior Manager in Information Security Management at SES, a global satellite communication provider. He is CISA and CISSP certified and has co-authored a published paper on securing CAPTCHAS in VoIP protocols.

Laetitia Cesari Zarkan
is a doctoral researcher in Space Law and Cyber Law at the University of Luxembourg. She is also currently working for the United Nations Institute for Disarmament Research (UNIDIR). Her primary research areas are legal and political issues related to space safety, security, stability and sustainability, as well as cyber security and satellite telecommunication. Laetitia Cesari Zarkan previously worked in the space industry for a satellite operator. She holds a Master 1 in Business law from the University Paris 1 Panthéon-Sorbonne, a Master 2 in Air and transportation law from the University Toulouse 1 Capitole and a LLM in Space, Communications and Media Law from the University of Luxembourg. Laetitia Cesari Zarkan is Director of Programming at the Space Court Foundation, Co-lead of the SGAC Space and Cyber security Project Group, Member and Webmaster of the International Institute of Space Law, Member of the Jeunes de l'IHEDN and of the Société française pour le droit international. Laetitia Cesari Zarkan is also Mentor with the UNOOSA Space4Women Network and with the SGAC.

SECTION I

Cybersecurity for Space Assets

CHAPTER 1

A Network of Governance

P.J. Blount

1 Introduction

The idea of governance has become increasingly important in contemporary scholarship that examines how global processes work. This can clearly be seen in the emergence of the concept of 'global governance' in the field of international relations[1] – a concept different from international law in that it seeks to examine the myriad processes and activities that contribute to government like functions at the global level.[2] Wherein legal analysis engages in an examination of the text of the law to draw conclusions about bare legality or illegality, governance seeks to uncover processes that are hierarchically below the law, but contribute to the overall regulatory power of the law. Governance engages with a tapestry of texts and norms that structure a system, which of course includes law, but is not limited to the 'black letter' texts.

This paper will argue that as technology continues to evolve and implicate itself in human life and activities governance will become an increasingly important concept for those that have been traditionally concerned with the law. Specifically, this paper will address this phenomenon in the context of space and cyber technologies and posit that both space law and cyber law are increasingly marked by governance structures that are non-legal in nature yet contribute to the overall regulation of these technologies. The goal herein is to bring a deeper understanding of what constitutes regulatory force from a legal perspective at the crossroads of law and technology.

This chapter will first address the idea of governance and examine how the concept has been used in both space and cyber technologies. Next, this chapter will investigate how governance of technology functions by examining the

1 "Global governance encompasses the totality of institutions, policies, norms, procedures and initiatives through which States and their citizens try to bring more predictability, stability and order to their responses to transnational challenges." UN Department of Economic and Social Affairs, Global governance and global rules for development in the post-2015 era (June 2014) *available at* https://www.un.org/en/development/desa/policy/cdp/cdp_publications/2014cdppolicynote.pdf.

2 Lawrence S. Finkelstein, "What Is Global Governance?," *Global Governance* 1 (1995): 367–72.

 | DOI:10.1163/9789004527270_002

interface between space and cyberspace using the example of cybersecurity to illustrate the complex nature of these processes. Finally, this paper will reflect on what the proliferation of governance processes and documents means for the development of legal knowledge. This section will continue to focus on cybersecurity law as an example of how capacity building is needed to improve our understanding of law and technology governance.

2 Governance

The idea of governance is an ambiguous one. It is not law nor is it government. It is a "fuzzier" term, and as one commentator has stated, "we say 'governance' because we don't really know what to call what is going on."[3] The dictionary tells us that governance is "the act or process of governing or overseeing control and direction of something."[4] Governance, then, is about governing, controlling, regulating, and steering, and it implies that these processes occur outside of an anarchic system, but not necessarily within a hierarchical system. This is, of course, why the term has gained favor within the international relations discourse as it recognizes that a broader set of circumstances actually contributes to the behavioral choices of the actors involved.

Law is most often a product of text,[5] and lawyers and judges often see their role as one of examining and interpreting the legal text to draw conclusions on the rights and obligations of the subjects of the law. Text in this case serves as a frame that bounds actors in a unique way as the text itself creates substantive rules that structure a given society. Governance, on the other hand, goes beyond the text of law and seeks a broader perspective on what creates restraints and opportunities for the actors in a given system. The law, naturally, plays an important role in governance, but as will be argued herein so too do numerous other processes and texts that may not directly create substantive or enforceable rights and obligations, but nevertheless affect the behavior of the actors in a system. This is an important feature at the international level, where law is often sparsely elaborated (as compared with domestic regimes)

3 Finkelstein at 367–368.

4 Merriam-Webster, "Governance," (2021) https://www.merriam-webster.com/dictionary/governance.

5 Within the international legal system, the notion of customary law represents a significant exception to this statement. International customary law is unwritten norm-based law that results from the intentions and behavior of states. *See* Martin Dixon, *Textbook on International Law*, 7th ed. (Oxford University Press 2013) 32–42.

and legal hierarchies are malleable or nonexistent. Governance can play an important interpretive role in determining what the content of the law is and what is expected of the subjects of the law. This is not to say that the idea of governance usurps rules of textual interpretation, such as those found in the Vienna Convention on the Law of Treaties, but rather that the content of the law is often *de facto* constructed through the contextual placement of the law within ongoing and iterative processes. A potent example of this is customary international law, which is distinctively law not based on text, but based on the opinion of states that there is a legal obligation that is followed in practice.[6] In order for this law to be wielded though, there must be some proof of what the non-textual rule is. As a result, lawyers must divine the law by examining the documents and statements found in the broader system of governance as evidence of a rule. Specifically, diplomatic statements and actions by state officials – which fall in the discipline of international relations – may be indicia of the nature of rights and obligations that may arise under customary international law. Indeed, it could be argued that in order to prove a customary international norm, a lawyer must prove that the norm is supported by the larger governance structure in the international system. This is confirmed by the International Court of Justice's practice of considering nonbinding UN General Assembly resolutions as potential indicia of customary international law.[7] Indeed, similar methods can be used whenever there is ambiguity or contested meaning in the text of international law.[8]

The concept of governance looms large in areas where the law is partial or incomplete. This is particularly true in the area of technological development. As this author has argued in the past, law presents a specific problem

6 Dixon, *Textbook*, 32.

7 *See* Statement of H.E. Mr. Abdulqawi Ahmed Yusuf, President of the International Court of Justice, before the Sixth Committee of the General Assembly (1 November 2019): para. 20, https://www.icj-cij.org/public/files/press-releases/0/000-20191101-STA-01-00-EN.pdf. This statement emphasizes the role of the UNGA as "a world forum where all States could express their views and present their perspectives on the content of rules of international law," but that emphasis is connected the ease with which a UNGA resolution can be used to evince custom. *Id.* The observation can not be read as exclusive, and it clearly displays the role of governance in establishing unwritten rules of law.

8 For example, Reisman's 'international incidents' approach to international law seeks to evaluate the content of the law through an examination of the international relations that unfold with the context of international incidents. *See,* W. Michael Reisman, "International Incidents: Introduction to a New Genre in the Study of International Law," *Yale J. Int'l L.* 10 (1984): 1. This approach is also adopted for ambiguity in treaty interpretation, which allows for "subsequent practice" to have weight in the act of interpretation. Vienna Convention on the Law of Treaties (1969) Art. 31(3)(b).

in technological areas, because law can have unexpected outcomes as technology develops.[9] This is due to the simple fact that law written for the technology of the present is often inadequate for the technology of the future. This is why lawmakers often choose to adopt broader principles in the text of the law and push more specific constraints to lower levels of the regulatory stack. The regulatory stack refers to the hierarchical nature of legal systems, which often flow downward from Constitutions to legislation to regulation to policy documents with each layer downward in the stack becoming less rigid in terms of application or binding nature. This can clearly be seen in the law of cybersecurity, which to a large extent lacks legal definition.[10] Cybersecurity is an enterprise that must be tailored by the actor to the specific systems employed and the risks that those systems face.[11] The legislative process is ill equipped for this particular task due to the speed of change in cyber technologies. In other words, if the law adopts a specific technical requirement, which later becomes insecure, then organizations are faced with the choice of insecurity through compliance with the law or security through violation of the law. Laws in general refrain from prescribing specific technical solutions that should be implemented to be cybersecure. Rather cybersecurity is the result of a network of governance through which actors may select the proper controls and implementations to manage their own cybersecurity requirements. If a question of liability results from a cybersecurity incident, then the text of the law will not be used to determine whether the actor was sufficiently cybersecure. Instead, the court will look at the security measures the actor implemented and the extent to which that represented a reasonable practice within the framework of cybersecurity governance. In other words, the text of the law does not prescribe the technical characteristics of a cyber secure operation, but the arbiter of the law must make a determination as to whether an organization was adequately cyber secure within the context of cybersecurity governance.

This move towards governance structures can be observed in both the law governing cyberspace and space technologies. It has been a more prominent theme in cyberspace, which developed for decades outside of formal legal

9 P.J. Blount, "Innovating the Law: Fifty Years of the Outer Space Treaty," at 32, in Mahulena Hofmann & P.J. Blount, eds., *Innovation in Outer Space: International and African Legal Perspective* (Nomos 2018).

10 *See generally*, Jeff Kosseff, "Defining Cybersecurity Law," *Iowa L. Rev.* 103 (2017): 985.

11 In generally, cybersecurity from an organizational perspective is seen as a risk management process that is "a holistic activity that affects every aspect of [an] organization." NIST, *Risk Management Framework for Information Systems and Organizations: A System Life Cycle Approach for Security and Privacy*, SP 800–37, rev. 2 (Dec. 2018) 6.

structures. Indeed, many of the technical decisions made on how cyberspace should function were made outside of formal lawmaking processes, yet nonetheless create conditions that enable or constrain the user. One of the starkest examples of this is the Internet Engineering Task Force (IETF), which is a group that develops and adopts the core standards that allows the Internet to function. The IETF is an association that has no legal personhood and adopts standards through a "rough consensus" process.[12] The documents that the IETF adopts form key governance structures for the development of cyberspace and affect every user of the Internet, but these standards have no legal value. These standards influence the way in which code is developed and code also structures the governance of cyberspace, or in Lessig's famous maxim: "code is law."[13] Governance in cyberspace includes the outputs of nongovernmental organizations, technical standards and specifications, computer code and protocols, as well as laws and regulations. Governance as a term is a core theme in structuring how the Internet and Cyberspace work. The civil society Netmundial Initiative released principles for "multistakeholder governance" of the Internet in 2014, which focused on the diversity of actors and processes that govern how the Internet works.[14] This document was followed by the so-called ICANN transition, in which the US government announced that it would cede its oversight control over the Internet Corporation for Assigned Names and Numbers' (ICANN) Internet Assigned Numbers Authority (IANA). ICANN manages the Domain Name System (DNS) via the IANA process. The DNS is a root file system that allows web addresses to resolve to the proper server, or in other words, it creates the conditions through which a web address is resolved to the unique numerical identifier attached to a specific server on the Internet.[15] This process was initiated by the US National Telecommunication and Information Administration (NTIA), and was intended to turn this authority over "to the global multistakeholder community."[16]

12 *See* Paul Hoffman, ed., "The Tao of IETF: A Novice's Guide to the Internet Engineering Task Force" (IETF, 2012), https://www.ietf.org/tao.html and Harald Alvestrand and Hakon Wium Lie, "Development of Core Internet Standards: The Work of IETF and W3C," in *Internet Governance: Infrastructure and Institutions*, ed. Lee A. Bygrave and Jon Bing (Oxford: Oxford University Press, 2009), 126–46.

13 Lawrence Lessig, *Code 2.0* (Basic Books, 2006).

14 "NETmundial Multistakeholder Statement," (April 24, 2014).

15 For a basic introduction to the DNS see David G. Post, *In Search of Jefferson's Moose: Notes on the State of Cyberspace* (Oxford; New York: Oxford University Press, 2012) 142–162.

16 NTIA, "NTIA Announces Intent to Transition Key Internet Domain Name Functions," (March 14, 2014).

One of the most interesting things about this phenomenon, specifically within the context of Internet governance, is the emergence of a new class of international actor. The Global Multistakeholder Governance Community does not fit into previously established categories of international actors such as states, multinational corporations (MNC), Intergovernmental Organizations (IO), or non-governmental organizations (IGO). Instead, multi-stakeholder governance seems like an amplification and enhancement of the nebulous category of civil society. The goal here is not to investigate the rise of a new category, but to use this example to illustrate the rise of "governance" as an international process that is emerging, among other places, from within Cyberspace.[17] Governance in this context is networked, meaning that it flows from different nodes at different layers within a regulatory stack rather than from a top-down legalistic approach. This is not to say that formal law no longer matters or has lost its power, but instead that the law itself is part of a larger structure of governance.

The turn to governance can also be seen in the world of space law. Notably, the term has been used in the titles of recent initiatives to elaborate on future space endeavors. For instance, the McGill's Institute of Air and Space Law engaged in a wide ranging *Study on Global Space Governance*, which includes "ways forward in terms of new technical or safety standards, international codes of conduct, transparency and confidence building measures (TCBM), possible national or regional model laws, and collaborative efforts within governmental and nongovernmental bodies."[18] Also of note is the Hague Space Resources Governance Working Group, whose purpose was to help establish a framework for space resource activities with engagement from governments, industry, and civil society.[19] Neither of these initiatives pushed forward ideas for new treaty mechanisms within the space domain, but instead sought to elaborate ways in which governance mechanisms can help support the treaty regime.

17 For a more complete discussion of multi-stakeholder governance structures see P.J. Blount, *Reprogrammming the World: Cyberspace and the Geography of Global Order* (e-International Relations Press 2019) 115–133.

18 Ram Jahku & Joseph N, Pelton, "Global Space Governance: Key Proposed Actions" (Institute of Air and Space Law, McGill University 2017) 4, https://www.mcgill.ca/iasl/files/iasl/global_space_governance_-executive_summary_and_key_proposed_actions.pdf.

19 "The Hague International Space Resources Governance Working Group," (International Institute of Air and Space Law, Leiden University n.d.) https://www.universiteitleiden.nl/en/law/institute-of-public-law/institute-of-air-space-law/the-hague-space-resources-governance-working-group.

Beyond specific efforts at elaborating the idea of governance, within the field of space law there is growing emphasis on soft law, standardization, good practices, and similar concepts.[20] This is indicative of a significant shift in which the discourse has sought to bolster formal law mechanisms through an elaboration of a wider governance system that affects space activities. This trend seems to be increasingly recognized as a way to "accommodate change" within the space law which "suppl[ies] a framework for answering the governance questions that inevitably arise over a treaty's lifetime with the advent of capabilities and activities not expressly addressed by the treaty."[21] This is, of course, not to say that the law itself has diminished in importance, quite the contrary. Formal law and regulation are critical parts of any governance structure, but they exist and function in a context that is also marked by a variety of other texts that contribute to the normative aspects that affect how actors behave. Indeed, this is not unique to space law, and can be viewed in numerous other areas of international law.[22]

Under this new direction in scholarship on space law, there is an emphasis on the full structure of mechanisms that help to shape the rights and obligations within the space domain. It is an expansion from the bare text of the law into an analysis normative fabric of governance. The idea of governance is important when contemplating how cybersecurity concerns will be addressed within the context of space activities. Naturally, it is important to understand the cybersecurity enterprise through the lens of and within the bounds of hard law, but this analysis will be shallow at best. This is because both space and cybersecurity are influenced by a variety of non-legal texts – which accomplish many of the same goals as the legal texts – due to the nature of changing technology. Law lacks flexibility to adapt to technology, and thus norms related to changing technology are often non-legal in nature yet are of critical importance to the legal analysis. The turn to governance presents a valuable pathway for evaluating not just the hard structure of legal norms, but of an entire network of normative content that affects how actors within these respective domains behave.

---

20 For example, Irmgard Marboe, ed., *Soft Law in Outer Space: The Function of Non-binding Norms in International Space Law* (Böhlau Verlag, 2012); P. J. Blount, "Renovating Space: The Future of International Space Law," *Denv. J. Int'l L. & Pol'y* 40 (2012): 515–686; Paul B. Larsen, "Space Traffic Management Standards," 83 *Journal of Air Law and Commerce* 359–387; and Brian Israel, "Treaty Stasis [Agora: The End of Treaties?]," *AJIL Unbound* (blog), May 8, 2014, https://www.asil.org/blogs/treaty-stasis-agora-end-treaties.

21 Israel, "Treaty Stasis," at 64.

22 *See generally*, Kenneth W. Abbott and Duncan Snidal, "Hard and Soft Law in International Governance," *International Organization* 54, no. 3 (2000): 421–56.

3 Cybersecurity Governance in Space

Digitization and network technologies have had a dramatic impact on the world. Indeed, this may be an understatement, as it is arguable that these technologies will be the most important driver of the structure of the world in the near, mid, and possibly long term. As these technologies have proliferated there has been increasing concern with the various security aspects across domains and disciplines. As cyber capabilities have matured so too have the capabilities of those that would exploit these technologies for gain, destabilization, or even fun. This section will give a brief overview of how cybersecurity as an enterprise plays out in the space domain.

Cybersecurity is a problematic term in that it means different things to different actors.[23] Here the term is used broadly to mean the security of networked assets, including their stored data of all types, and the methods that are implemented to protect those assets. The cybersecurity process for any entity is a risk management process that weighs potential risks against potential mitigation strategies and adopts a risk management plan that responds to a potential risk in an adequate way.[24] It is important to remember that cybersecurity is an enterprise focused on risk management rather than absolute security. No system is ever truly secure from external actors, and entities pursuing cybersecurity goals have limited resources to allocate against a proliferation of threat vectors.

As a simple example, take an average internet user sending and receiving email. For this actor, there is potential risk that their email may be intercepted by a third party, thus the user must balance the gains from email use and implement a plan to mitigate the risk from a third party. One way to do this would be to use email encryption, which would require the user and the receiver to go through extra steps to ensure the security of the email. In a world where email is the norm for daily interactions and your average user sends and receives tens to hundreds of emails a day, this solution may become quite burdensome and lead to email becoming a less useful form of communication. A more reasonable strategy would be to only implement the encrypted email solution when sensitive information needs to be sent via email. This strategy maintains the benefit of email with a reasonable approach to the costs of encryption. In

---

23 *See generally*, Jeff Kosseff, "Defining Cybersecurity Law," *Iowa L. Rev.* 103 (2017): 985 & ENISA, *Definition of Cybersecurity – Gaps and overlaps in standardization* (2016) https://www.enisa.europa.eu/publications/definition-of-cybersecurity.

24 NIST, *Risk Management Framework for Information Systems and Organizations: A System Life Cycle Approach for Security and Privacy*, SP 800–37, rev. 2 (Dec. 2018) 6.

short, the user has managed their risk through the adoption of a risk mitigation plan that best allocates the user's resources. Notably, the plan adopted here is both technical (that is, encryption to protect email) and policy driven (that is, the user will monitor their content to determine when the technical solution should be used).

Despite the straightforwardness of the underlying principle of cybersecurity, it can become very difficult as modern entities take advantage of a wide range of network technologies to meet their goals. Cybersecurity requires a broad assessment of capabilities to identify risk and then the implementation of both technical and policy mechanisms to mitigate risk. For instance, many enterprises use standards such as the International Standards Organization's (ISO) 27001 standard on information security management systems.[25] Such standards are used to help identify risks and select proper controls for managing risks within the context of the particular enterprise. These mechanisms require a holistic view of information security that engages both with technical architectures and with adopting policies that educate and inform how individuals within the organizations engage with information security.

Cybersecurity in space is essentially no different: space operators must assess their risk and implement appropriate mitigation in light of their resources and overall goals. Though the process of cybersecurity in the space domain is the same, space does add another layer of complexity to the cybersecurity enterprise. This is for two reasons.

First, space is a strategic domain, and every actor in the space environment must take this into account when making security assessments. A consistent theme in the discourse on space security is that any satellite with maneuverability is a potential anti-satellite weapon (ASAT) as it could be moved into a collision course with another satellite for destructive purposes. Of course, it should be acknowledged that these types of maneuvers are not technically easy and would be dependent upon a number of factors. Regardless, the potential for using a third-party's satellite to interfere with other states' space activities is certainly a capability that many states would see as valuable. Cyber interference in satellite operations, either direct or indirect, presents a tempting counter-space capability that could potentially be obtained by states that lack advanced space capabilities necessary for more conventional on-orbit weapons. With the contemporary trend of states turning to cyber-interference tactics, space as a strategic domain heightens the cybersecurity requirements of

25 ISO/EAC 27001:2013 Information technology – Security techniques – Information security management systems – Requirements, https://www.iso.org/standard/54534.html.

all space actors, not just those operating national security payloads. This influences the risk assessment by potentially heightening the risk to space systems due to their operation in an environment, thereby making the risk assessment and management process more complex.

Second, the space industry does not have much in the way of industry specific standards to choose from when implementing cybersecurity for their systems. The ISO 27001 standard mentioned above is a general standard that is designed to be applied to information security across industries, and for this reason, while ISO 27001 is holistic, it is high-level and allows information security managers to choose implementations that best fit their specific circumstances. Industry-specific standards are important tools for maintaining cybersecurity within particular enterprises. The space industry is not very developed in this sphere. There are few examples of industry specific cybersecurity standards for space.[26] The most significant of these is the Space Overlay developed by the US Committee for National Security Systems (CNSS).[27] An overlay is a standard that is used to adapt a more general standard to a specific purpose. The CNSS Space Overlay is an important touchpoint for developing cybersecurity for space systems, but as it is geared towards national security systems it is likely overly restrictive for most operators. To this end the CNSS overlay builds on the framework established by the US National Institute of Standards and Technology (NIST) and identifies the relevant controls from the control list in NIST Special Publication 800-53.[28] Indeed, at present space operators are in the position where they must adapt more general standards such as ISO/IEC 27001, the NIST Risk Management Framework, or the Aerospace Industries Association's NAS9933 to the space context.[29] As recent research on eavesdropping on GEO satellite information flows has shown, though, space changes the context of the systems and information that are being protected.[30]

26 Brandon Bailey, et al., *Defending Spacecraft in the Cyber Domain* (Aerospace Corporation, Nov. 2019) 3https://aerospace.org/sites/default/files/2019-11/Bailey_DefendingSpacecraft_11052019.pdf.

27 CNSS, Space Platform Overlay, Attachment 2 to Appedix F of CNSSI No1253 (2014) and CNSS, *Cybersecurity Policy for Space Systems used to Support National Security Missions* (CNSSP no. 12, 2018).

28 NIST, *Security and Privacy Controls for Information Systems and Organizations*, rev. 5 (SP 800–53, Sept. 2020). It should be noted that the CNSS overlay has not yet be updated to reflect the changes in the most recent 800–53 revision.

29 NAS 9933: Critical Security Controls for Effective Capability in Cyber Defense (Aerospace Industries Association, 29 November 2018).

30 James Pavur, et al. "Secrets in the Sky: On Privacy and Infrastructure Security in DVB-S Satellite Broadband," WiSec '19, Miami, FL (2019) https://dl.acm.org/doi/10.1145/3317549.3323418.

The development of industry specific standards and best practices will be an important tool in creating resilience and security in the space domain. There has been some recent movement in the United States. The Trump Administration issued Space Policy Directive 5, which calls for the "adoption of deliberate cybersecurity best practices."[31] Additionally, the United States Space Force is implementing an Infrastructure Asset Pre-assessment program (IA-Pre), which will be applicable to commercial satellite communication solutions used by the US military.[32] IA-Pre requires commercial providers to undergo an independent audit to be included in an approved provider list before they can compete for procurement contracts. This audit assesses implementation of a defined set of controls adopted from the NIST 800–53 list of controls.

As argued above, the problem of cybersecurity in the space domain is the same yet different from cybersecurity in other domains. Like other domains, cybersecurity is a risk-based approach that requires risk identification, risk analysis, and risk mitigation. As in other fields, this approach must be adapted to the specific industry. Currently, this is where the space domain is lacking. The unique features of the space environment, including both physical attributes and geopolitical attributes, means that operators must identify, assess, and mitigate a unique set of risks. The geopolitical context in particular is often overlooked within the space context.[33] As a strategic domain, space operators likely have increased exposure to Advanced Persistent Threats, or in other words nefarious state and quasi-state actors pursuing a variety of national security goals through cyberspace.

It seems that much of what is missing from cybersecurity in the space domain is baseline knowledge on how to identify and manage risks across the diversity of operations, rather than the risk-mitigation techniques. Indeed, much of the literature on risk assessment in satellites is focused on internal or design risks rather than external risks emerging from third parties.[34] Some initiatives have

---

31 Space Policy Directive 5: Cybersecurity Principles for Space Systems (4 September 2020) 4(b)(iv).

32 USSF, IA-Pre Memo (2020) (on file with author). *See also* USSF, "USSF Commercial SATCOM Office announces development of new security program" (24 June 2020), spaceforce.mil/News/Article/2230831/ussf-commercial-satcom-office-announces-development-of-new-security-program/.

33 *See* James Pavur and Ivan Martinovic, "The Cyber-ASAT: On the Impact of Cyber Weapons on Outer Space," 11th International Conference on Cyber Conflict (NATO 2019) and P.J. Blount, "That Escalated Quickly: The Cyber-ASAT Conundrum," 701–708 in P.J. Blount et al., eds, *Proceedings of the International Institute of Space Law 2018* (Eleven 2019).

34 *For example*, there is a rich literature on risk management in SmallSats that does not address external cybersecurity risk, Fabio Santoni, "Risk Management for Micro-Satellite Design," *Acta Astronautica* 54, no. 3 (2003): 221–28; Katharine Brumbaugh Gamble and E. Glenn

begun to address these issues through information sharing, primary among these is the US led Space Information Sharing and Analysis Center (Space ISAC).[35] Despite these efforts, there is a deep need for more open-source literature to guide the industry. This is particularly so in light of the innovation bloom currently being experienced in space, which is challenging traditional technological implementations and markets. One of the features of this shift in the space industry is a host of small companies and start-ups that are entering the space marketplace. These smaller companies will lack the resources of more established companies and specifically in the field of compliance. Yet at the same time, a small space operator with on-orbit assets can create risk for numerous other operators in the proximity of those assets. So, while specialized knowledge that can be obtained from the Space ISAC, the cost of entry to this information may be beyond the means of a smaller start-up, with the basic Space ISAC membership plan costing $10,000 annually and the "platinum" plan costing $50,000 annually.

4 Developing the Governance Knowledge

The concept of 'cybersecurity law' is an elusive one. The idea of cybersecurity itself is subject to a variety of definitions that are often context specific.[36] Further, there are few laws or regulations that set out the requirements for what it means to be cybersecure. At the same time, we intrinsically know that cybersecurity is an area in which the lawyer has a role. The question then is how to define a lawyer's role in an area that lacks clear regulatory grounding? This of course brings us back to the idea of governance.

It is, indeed, a misstatement to say that cybersecurity is devoid of law completely. There are certainly laws and regulations that define cybersecurity in a variety of contexts, such as the United States' series of statutes that address federal management of information,[37] the European Union's information security

Lightsey, "CubeSat Mission Design Software Tool for Risk Estimating Relationships," *Acta Astronautica* 102 (2014): 226–40; and Xibin Cao, "Flexible Platform Based Micro-Satellite Design Method," *Aerospace Science and Technology* 53 (2016): 162–68.

35 https://s-isac.org/.

36 *See generally*, ENISA, *Definition of Cybersecurity: Gaps and Overlaps in Standardisation, v. 1.0, 2015*, https://www.enisa.europa.eu/publications/definition-of-cybersecurity/at_download/fullReport.

37 *For example*, Federal Information Security Management Act of 2002, Pub. L. No. 107–347, title III (2002).

regulation,[38] or China's cybersecurity law, which does apply to network operators.[39] In addition to these more formal sources of law, cybersecurity law flows from a number of different sources. For instance, there is a developing common law principle that corporate boards have a duty to shareholders to maintain information security[40] and trade law in the United States treats data breaches as potentially unfair business practices.[41] Similarly, laws that require security of types of information, such as the US International Traffic in Arms Regulations[42] or the European Union's General Data Protection Regulation,[43] create cybersecurity obligations relevant to specific data types.

Another important source of cybersecurity law is private law. Contracts between companies and their customers and supply chain entities should contain clauses that define the cybersecurity obligations of the parties to the contract. The idea of contract law is important, because beyond forming rights and obligations of the contracting parties, contracts implicate the law after-the-fact. That is, the legal resolution of tort and contract disputes that result from cybersecurity incidents that happen within the scope of the agreement. This means that the cybersecurity lawyer must be able to produce in cases of disputes a body of evidence showing that the organization maintained adequate levels of cybersecurity. Indeed, the same is true of tort actions and criminal or administrative prosecutions.

This is where the idea of governance comes into play. While there may be a lack of legal sources for identifying what constitutes adequate cybersecurity, there are a number of governance sources that help to create the body of evidence that is needed in a potential dispute or enforcement action. This includes many of the document types already addressed in this chapter such as policies, standards, and technical specifications. Together, with the law, these documents create an ecosystem or framework in which to pursue the cybersecurity enterprise from a legal perspective.

---

38 EU Directive 2016/1148, Concerning Measures for a High Common Level of Security of Network and Information Systems across the Union (2016).

39 Jyh-An Lee, "Hacking into China's Cybersecurity Law," *Wake Forest L. Rev.* 53 (2018): 57 and Liudmyla Balke, "China's New Cybersecurity Law and U.S.-China Cybersecurity Issues," 58 *Santa Clara Law Review* 137 (2018).

40 Lawrence J. Trautman & Peter C. Oremond, "Corporate Directors' and Officers' Cybersecurity Standard of CCare: The Yahoo Data Breach," 66 *American University Law Review* 1231 (2017).

41 Jeffrey Kosseff, "Positive Cybersecurity Law: Creating a Consistent and Incentive-Based System," 19 *Chapman Law Review* 401 at 407–411 (2016).

42 International Traffic in Arms Régulations, 22 C.F.R. 120–130 (2020).

43 EU Regulation 2016/679, General Data Protection Regulation (2016).

At the moment there is an urgent need to build capacity within the cybersecurity governance framework applicable to the space industry. As already noted, there is currently a dearth of laws, technical standards, and well-defined best practices with regards to cybersecurity for the space industry and in particular the space segment. This knowledge base needs to be built so that the industry can ensure safe and secure operations. Within the framework of cybersecurity as a risk management process, this means that in the near term there needs to be development of some core knowledge bases. Risk identification, assessment, and mitigation all need to be customized to the space context. Risk identification is, in particular, needed. At present, the work on cyber-risks for the space segment seems to be very generalized or very specialized. What is needed in the industry though are guidelines for identifying and assessing risks and vulnerabilities of space systems that can serve the diversity of actors in executing the assessments. This type of knowledge building is needed in order to help satellite operators recognize the risk factors associated with different components of space system architecture and assess how those risk factors affect the overall risk profile of the space system. Baseline guidance in risk identification and assessment is needed to ensure that operators can properly engage in cybersecurity of space systems. This type of guidance recognizes that a one-size fits all approach does not work and goes a step further by providing the means for evaluating the risk profile of the particular system at hand.

The next step is to develop good practices with regards to control implementation to mitigate the risks that space systems face. This is an essential step in the cybersecurity enterprise, as the implemented controls help to bolster the body of evidence that is needed to show that an organization was adequately cybersecure. Just as the industry is lacking in baseline guidance on risk factors for space systems, so too are there a lack of indicators of what types of controls should be in place with regards to different types of space systems. The space industry should get a similar treatment to industries such as finance or maritime transportation, which have received regulatory and/or standardized guidance on what constitutes sufficient cybersecurity or information security management. Of course, control lists will likely flow from different sources such as international organizations, governments, or industry groups, but these lists should grow from a common understanding of what makes a space operation cybersecure.

5 Conclusion

All of this is connected to capacity building in the space industry. The time is gone in which space infrastructure operated in seclusion from the networked world. There is growing concern for cybersecurity in the space industry and an increasing number of initiatives are seeking to fill the knowledge gaps needed to secure these assets. It is important to remember that cybersecurity in space is not necessarily a risk born by a single actor, any interference with a space asset has the potential to create risk for other operators and organizations.

From a legal perspective one of the keys to understanding the management of cybersecurity risk is grappling with the network of governance that creates a framework that constrains an organization's actions. This network of governance often sits beyond the bounds of formal law and regulation, but nonetheless implicates the role of the lawyer as the overseer of compliance within an organization. To the extent that cybersecurity risk creates a risk of liability, either civil or criminal, the lawyer will need to have a firm understanding of how larger governance structures intertwine with the law and contribute to its content and meaning. Quite naturally, as space activities continue the law in this area will continue to grow, but the nature of the intersection between law and technology will require that legal practitioners be adept at navigating larger frameworks that affect the legal situation of the organizations they represent.

Importantly, this is not an issue that is relegated to cybersecurity alone. This chapter has chosen to use cybersecurity as a salient example for understanding how governance networks are implicated into the space domain, but these ideas apply across a range of activities. For example, the discourse on space traffic management is significantly influenced by governance processes in light of the lack of formal legal structures. As space applications become more data rich and more network connected the governance frameworks around both the opportunities and the risks will become an implicit part of space law in a networked world.

CHAPTER 2

New Space Architectures – Connectivity and Cyber Security

André Adelsbach, Thomas Schaefer and George Tountas

1 Introduction

Recently, there is rarely a day where cyber security attacks do not make headlines. Similar to other business areas, cyber security gained critical importance in the space sector over the past 30 years. The race to space is also turning into an arms-race threatening space infrastructures.[1] New players are entering the domain with new MEO/LEO orbits, resulting in additional or changing (e.g., physical) threats. Satellites have evolved to crucial enablers for various types of critical services, from TV and news distribution, space exploration, earth observation, and navigation to connecting people anywhere on earth with broadband data services. Many aspects of day-to-day life critically depend on satellite-based services.

Set in this overall context, the current chapter investigates cyber security risks in the space sector and what stakeholders can do to protect their assets and services. After introducing key concepts, an overview is provided on historic attacks against space services and the main threat actors are discussed, including their intent and typical attack types. A review of the main classes of attack vectors is performed, followed by a reflection on the changes many space-enabled services providers are undergoing as they transform from infrastructure and satellite capacity providers to full end-to-end service providers. Trends like supply chain and ransomware attacks are highlighted and mapped to space-enabled connectivity services.

With relevant threat actors and attack types laid out, security challenges of space architectures are reviewed. Starting from common weaknesses, the discussion extends into new challenges including legal and regulatory aspects, imposed by recent technology and market evolution. The chapter closes with

1 Todd Harrison, Kaitlyn Johnson, & Thomas G. Roberts, *Space Threat Assessment 2018* (Center for Strategic and International Studies, 2018).

 | DOI:10.1163/9789004527270_003

an outlook on concepts and guidelines to tackle the evolving challenge, where recent policies and upcoming regulations like Space Policy Directive 5 (SPD-5), Infrastructure Audit-Preassessment (IA-Pre), and Revised Directive on Security of Network and Information Systems (NIS2) play a key role.

Throughout the chapter specific terminology and concepts related to cyber security risks will be used, which are introduced in the following section.

1.1 *Concepts and Definitions*

1.1.1 Cyber Security

While the term "cyber security" has emerged earlier,[2] it gained wider popularity in the last decade compared to "computer security," "IT security," or "information security." It has become part of the domain terminology of subject matter experts and professional bodies.[3] However, there are different, at times even conflicting interpretations and nuances to cyber security which can hamper meaningful discussion as shown by Schatz et al.[4] For the purpose of this paper, we will use their proposed definition, synthesizing the most common aspects of other definitions:

> The approach and actions associated with security risk management processes followed by organizations and states to protect confidentiality, integrity and availability of data and assets used in cyber space. The concept includes guidelines, policies and collections of safeguards, technologies, tools and training to provide the best protection for the state of the cyber environment and its users.[5]

This definition points out the key elements of implementing measures ("controls") like "technologies, tools and training" in order to "protect ... assets" from relevant threats, thus managing security risks.

2 B. von Solms & R. von Solms, "Cybersecurity and information security – what goes where?" *Information and Computer Security*, v. 26(1) (2018): 2–9, https://doi.org/10.1108/ICS-04-2017-0025.

3 ENISA, *Definition of cybersecurity – gaps and overlaps in standardization* (2016) www.enisa.europa.eu/publications/definition-of-cybersecurity.

4 Daniel Schatz, Rabih Bashroush, & Julie Wall, "Towards a More Representative Definition of Cyber Security," *Journal of Digital Forensics, Security and Law*, v. 12 (2017).

5 *Id.*

1.1.2 Cyber Security Risks

A cyber security risk can commonly be defined as "exposure to harm or loss resulting from breaches of or attacks on information systems."[6] To reduce negative impact stemming from this, organizations perform cyber security risk management. This is a comprehensive process[7] that requires organizations to:

1. identify risks (that is, establish the context for risk-based decisions),
2. assess risks,
3. respond to risks once determined; and
4. monitor risks on an ongoing basis.

Managing risks to information systems is considered fundamental to effective cyber security.[8]

Generally, risks associated with any attack depend on three factors: threats (who is attacking), vulnerabilities (the weakness being exploited), and impacts (what the attack does from a technical and business perspective). Depending on these, different risk management strategies can be applied, e.g., risk transfer through insurance contracts or risk mitigation through implementation of security controls.

The following example based on the space domain shall illustrate this and put key terminology in context, including threat agents, attack vectors, weaknesses, security controls, as well as technical impact and business impact.

As satellites provide critical services, such as communication, navigation, or Earth observation services, they are targeted by different *threat agents* around the world. Consider a fictitious example, illustrated in Figure 2.1, where a cyber terrorist group (*threat agent*) may want to permanently disrupt a specific satellite service (*business* impact) that supports a military activity against this terrorist group.

In order to achieve this *business impact*, the threat agent has a multitude of choices of different *attack vectors* to exploit specific *security weaknesses* and to bypass mitigating *security controls* in order to cause a *technical impact*, which results in its final objective, the *business impact*.

6 RSA, *Cyber Risk Appetite: Defining and Understanding Risk in the Modern Enterprise* (2016) https://www.rsa.com/content/dam/en/white-paper/cyber-risk-appetite.pdf.

7 E. Fischer, *Cybersecurity Issues and Challenges: In Brief* (Washington, D.C.: Congressional Research Service 2014) https://www.fas.org/sgp/crs/misc/R43831.pdf.

8 Lindsey O'Donnell, "RSA Conference 2019: The Sky's the Limit for Satellite Hacks," (6 March 2019) https://threatpost.com/rsa-conference-2019-the-skys-the-limit-for-satellite-hacks/142541/.

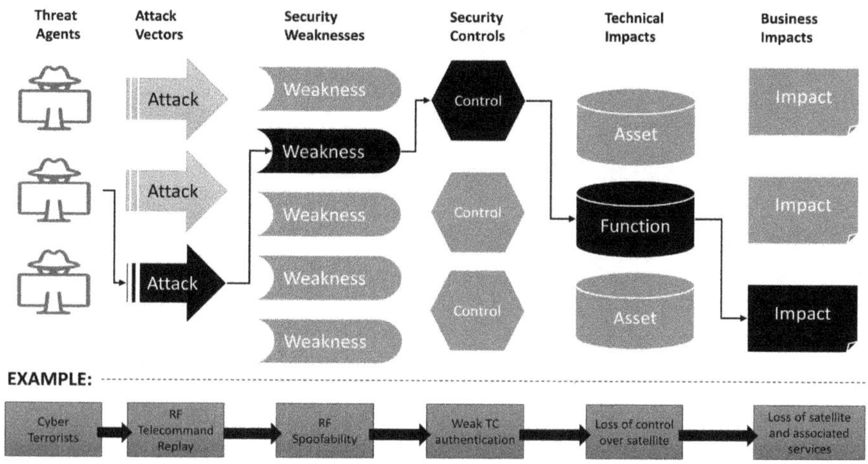

FIGURE 2.1 Illustration of cyber security risk terminologies

Applying these concepts to complex systems and infrastructures results in many permutations of attack vectors and weaknesses, which highlights the challenge for cyber security defenders, making this a multi-dimensional chess game.

One attack vector the cyber terrorist group may use could be to record a legitimate telecommand signal and replay it. This attack vector would exploit a security weakness in the RF communication channel, which could be the receiver (satellite) not being able to distinguish a legitimate from an illegitimate RF signal and sender.

To compensate for this weakness of RF communication, the satellite may be equipped with a security control known as Telecommand Authentication, which would allow the satellite to detect and reject a replayed telecommand based on some cryptographic checksums.

However, the terrorist group captured design documents in a previous attack that shows the use of a weak cryptographic algorithm in the Telecommand Authentication, which allows the terrorist group to tweak the signal to bypass the cryptographic check, that is, the satellite will ultimately accept the replayed telecommand. That command could be launching a satellite thruster, maneuvering the spacecraft into an uncontrollable and unrecoverable state (*technical impact*). This *technical impact* will ultimately lead to the *business impact* of disrupting the satellite communication service.

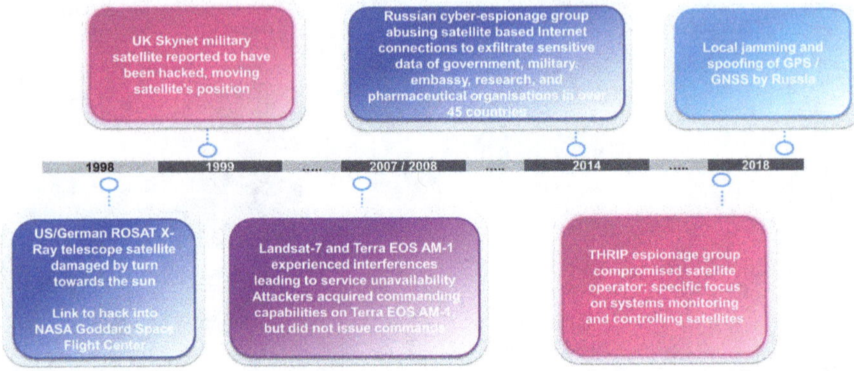

FIGURE 2.2 Timeline of a noteworthy variety of attack types and potential impacts on satellites and satellite-enabled services

While this is a hypothetical scenario, there is broad empirical evidence of attacks targeting satellite-based infrastructure and services,[9] some of which will be reviewed in the following section.

1.2 *Selected Publicly Known Attacks*

There are many reported attacks against satellite-based systems in the news and literature. The following timeline (Figure 2.2) illustrates a noteworthy variety of attack types and potential impacts.

The first documented attacks reach as far back as 1998, when attackers allegedly gained control over *ROSAT*, an X-RAY telescope satellite. By turning the satellite's X-ray payload towards the sun, attackers were able to damage *ROSAT*'s payload.

In 1999, there were news reports[10] that attackers managed to take over control of a UK Skynet satellite and were able to move the satellite to another position, demanding money in exchange for returning control over the satellite.

Later in 2007/2008 Earth observation satellites *Landsat-7* and *EOS AM-1* experienced service unavailability when attackers managed to gain commanding capabilities over the satellites via a ground station in Norway. According to a report to the US Congress, the attacks were attributed to China.[11]

9 Harrison, et al., *Space Threat Assessment 2018*.

10 Lev Grossman, "Did Hackers Hijack a British Military Satellite?" *Time* (1 March 1999) http://content.time.com/time/magazine/article/0,9171,20673,00.html.

11 Jim Wolf, "China key suspect in U.S. satellite hacks: commission," *Reuters* (28 October 2011) https://www.reuters.com/article/us-china-usa-satellite/china-key-suspect-in-u-s-satellite-hacks-commission-idUSTRE79R4O320111028.

In 2014, the Turla hacking group was found to misuse design flaws in satellite-based Internet services in order to exfiltrate sensitive data from several victim organisations without being traceable.[12] While this is not a direct attack against the satellite-based service itself, these attacks confirmed prior research that design deficiencies in satellite-based services can be leveraged and misused by attackers to misuse the satellite capabilities to perform attacks with perfect receiver anonymity.[13]

In 2018, Symantec revealed that an attacker group called THRIP compromised a satellite operator and its systems responsible for the monitoring and control of satellites. Symantec highlighted the motive may go beyond spying and towards disruption of services.[14]

At Blackhat US 2018, a security researcher proved the feasibility of compromising a VSAT modem on board of an aircraft from the ground, as parts of the VSAT modem management interfaces were exposed to the Internet and not sufficiently protected. The researcher then showed that the compromised modem provides the initial entry into the more complex service infrastructure and can then serve as a pivot point to attack other systems to intercept communications and to manipulate antenna positioning.[15]

In recent years there has been an increasing number of reported local jamming and spoofing attacks against GPS/GNSS services in different geo-political contexts, potentially to support military operations and to protect high-ranking politicians.[16]

All these instances of attacks against satellites and satellite-based services underline that cyber security threats against satellite-based services and

12 "Turla Hiding in the Sky: Russian Speaking Cyberespionage Group Exploits Satellites to Reach the Ultimate Level of Anonymity," Kaspersky (9 September 2015) https://www.kaspersky.com/about/press-releases/2015_turla-hiding-in-the-sky-russian-speaking-cyberespionage-group-exploits-satellites-to-reach-the-ultimate-level-of-anonymity.

13 Ulrich Greveler, Andre Adelsbach, & Sven Löschner, "Anonymous Data Broadcasting by Misuse of Satellite ISPs," *Proceedings of 22C3 Chaos Computer Club (CCC) Congress* (2005) https://www.nds.ruhr-uni-bochum.de/research/publications/anonymous-data-broadcasting-misuse-satellite-isps/.

14 "Thrip: Espionage Group Hits Satellite, Telecoms, and Defense Companies," *Symantec Enterprise Blog* (19 June 2018) https://symantec-enterprise-blogs.security.com/blogs/threat-intelligence/thrip-hits-satellite-telecoms-defense-targets.

15 Ruben Santamarta, "Last Call for SATCOM Security," Blackhat US (2018) https://ioactive.com/wp-content/uploads/2018/08/us-18-Santamarta-Last-Call-For-Satcom-Security-wp.pdf.

16 Matt Burgess, "To protect Putin, Russia is spoofing GPS signals on a massive scale," *Wired* (27 March 2019) https://www.wired.co.uk/article/russia-gps-spoofing.

infrastructures are a fact since more than 20 years. The interested reader may refer to Malik for further examples of known attacks.[17]

2 Threat Actors and Vectors

After laying out the general concepts around cyber security risks in Section 1.1, these concepts shall now be reviewed specifically in the context of the space domain. In line with the model introduced in 2.1, the following chapter will analyse first threat actors ("who"), then attack vectors ("how"), and finally corresponding weaknesses, which together might lead to severe business impacts as indicated by the real-world cyber-attacks presented in Section 1.2. Below this chapter will categorize the Threat Actors based on certain distinctive criteria, namely motivation, capabilities, and potential impact. Afterwards, this chapter will examine trending attack vectors prevalent in recently observed attacks. More specifically this chapter will highlight examples of Destructive Malware (Ransomware) as well as supply chain attacks.

2.1 *Threat Actors – Motivation, Capabilities and Impact*

The following section focuses on the three main classes of threat actors with different motivations, capabilities and potential impact (see Table 2.1). The list is not meant to be exlusive, however it does illustrate the key Threat Actor categories and their respective motivations, capabilities and typical attacks that are observed.

2.1.1 Organized Crime

The first type of threat actors are *Organized Crime* actors. These groups are financially motivated and have medium level capabilities. They perform predominantly opportunistic attacks for financial gain. As such, most of the time they do not even target one specific organisation. They launch large scale attempts and mainly go after the easy victims. They generally utilize attacks on victims that can be easily cashed out; they focus on mass-attacks with little tailoring. Cybercriminals are becoming more agile, exploiting new technologies with lightning speed, tailoring their attacks using new methods, and cooperating with each other in ways we have not seen before.[18] Most commonly the

17 William J Malik, "Attack Vectors in Orbit," RSA Conference (2019).

18 Interpol, "Cybercrime" (accessed 24 January 2021) https://www.interpol.int/en/Crimes/Cybercrime.

TABLE 2.1 Summary of threat actors

	Organized crime groups	**Hactivists / Cyber terrorists**	**Nation state actors**
Motivation	Financial	Ideological	National interests
Capabilities / Resources	Medium	Medium	High
Types of attacks	Opportunistic	Targeted	Targeted
Examples of attacks and potential intent	– CEO Fraud – Extortion, leveraging infections with ransomware and data theft – Cyber Espionage: theft of Intellectual Property with the aim to monetize or contract work – Crypto-coin mining	– Disruption of media and playout services – Affect specific military or military-supporting organizations and missions	– Cyber Espionage: monitor communications or steal strategic information – Cyber Warfare: compromise, disrupt or destroy critical communication infrastructure

organized crime groups would use CEO frauds or extortion schemes leveraging ransomware and data theft.

As it can be seen in Figure 2.3 the number of attacks by Cyber Crime actors is significantly larger than the other categories mentioned below, and is only set to increase in the future, as the criminals become more agile and sophisticated, allowing them to turn bigger profits to fuel their activities.[19] Ransomware attacks specifically, have become a major indirect threat for space, as they may impact ground infrastructure required to control space assets.

2.1.2 Hacktivists and Cyber Terrorists

The second class of threat actors are *Hacktivists* and *Cyber Terrorists*. This threat actor group, contrary to the previous one, is not financially but ideologically

19 *Id.*

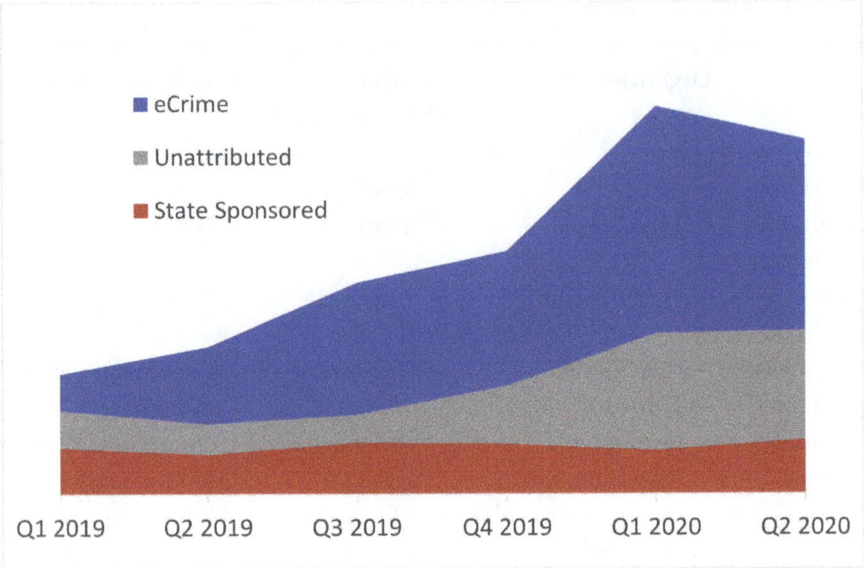

FIGURE 2.3 Distribution of intrusion threat types based on number of attacks observed from Q1 2019 to Q2 2020
SOURCE: CROWDSTRIKE, *NOWHERE TO HIDE: 2020 THREAT HUNTING REPORT* (2020) HTTPS://WWW.CROWDSTRIKE.COM/RESOURCES/REPORTS/THREAT-HUNTING-REPORT-2020/

motivated, and, in general, have medium level capabilities and resources available. However, they are potentially even more dangerous due to their intent/objective. That is because their motivation leads them to perform more targeted and determined attacks against specific organisations and with specific goals. In addition, their motives may lead them to more destructive practices since damage is the ultimate goal. In practical terms, this means that whereas a cyber criminal will perform widespread opportunistic attacks, which will eventually allow an organization to return to business after a ransom has been paid, a hacktivist may persist for a long time targeting one organization to cause permanent damage to its systems and services.

Satellite-based service providers may not necessarily be the primary target for these attackers, however they can (and have) become a secondary one. These threat actors may attack them as intermediaries to achieve their main objective: cause chaos, destabilization, and impact military or governmental operations relying on satellite-based services. Furthermore, there is the potential objective to disrupt or spoof media and playout services or affect specific missions of satellite customers, potentially leading up to loss of life.

2.1.3 Nation State Threat Actors

The third, and most capable class are *Nation State Threat Actors*, which are supporting nation state financial and geo-political interests. These threat actors are highly skilled, resourced, and organized. They have an arsenal of cyber weapons at their disposal, essentially allowing them to bypass many security controls. Nation State Actors are able to launch targeted Cyber Espionage and Cyber Warfare attacks against satellite-based service providers. This can serve one or multiple purposes, such as:
- to steal strategic and high-tech intellectual property support national economy or space programs;
- to monitor communications and locations of governmental or military users of satellite communication services; and/or
- to establish cyber warfare capabilities to support traditional warfare and geo-political conflicts by compromising, disrupting or destroying critical communication infrastructure.

Nation state attacks do not target organisations on a daily basis, but they have established the capabilities over the last years and are prepared to attack any target at any point in time, should national interest require so. For Cyber Terrorists or Nation State actors, satellite-based service providers may often be only an intermediate target to achieve their main objective. However, the collateral damage may still be extremely high.

2.2 *Attack Vectors*

Attackers can leverage a large variety of attack vectors against space-based infrastructures and services. We are going to give a short overview over specific attack vectors against space-based assets but also general attack vectors that must be considered in complex systems in general.

2.2.1 Physical Attacks

Satellite-based infrastructures and services still rely in most cases on a complex ground-based infrastructure, including communication gateways, TT&C sites and satellite operations centers, which may be directly targeted by conventional kinetic weapons or indirectly via supporting systems (power and telecommunications provider, and suchlike). For a long time, physical attacks against satellites seemed to be extremely unlikely and cost prohibitive. However, with space evolving as another military domain, anti-satellite weapons have become a reality and an attack vector that has to be considered for highly critical services with use-cases in governmental and military operations. In addition to kinetic anti-satellite weapons, like missiles or satellites itself, non-kinetic weapons like laser, micro-waves or electro-magnetic pulses exist that can physically harm satellites.[20]

2.2.2 Electronic / RF Attacks

Many satellites communication links rely on RF communication and therefore on its uplinks and downlinks for both payload communication and telecommand/telemetry to command the satellite and its payloads. These communication signals can be subject to jamming attacks, signal replay, or spoofing of different types of uplink/downlink signals and may impact the availability of the communication link, used to eavesdrop communication or to inject commands or wrong telemetry information. When applied to payload links, these attacks can be used to hijack TV broadcasts, eavesdrop on data communication or to distort navigation services.[21]

2.2.3 Cyber Attacks

Cyber-attacks have significantly increased over the past decade and attackers can leverage a large arsenal of known cyber-attack vectors ranging from buffer overflows, network-based attacks (sniffing and spoofing), web application attacks as well as social engineering attacks to obtain user's passwords or inject malware into IT systems. All these cyber-attack vectors can be applied also to all system components of satellite-based service infrastructures, ranging from satellites and Ground Infrastructure, including Ground Control Systems, Operations Support Systems (OSS), and Business Support Systems (BSS), terrestrial networks, user terminals, and so on. One of the most pre-dominant cyber-attack types today are phishing attacks.

2.2.4 Phishing Attacks

Phishing is when attackers attempt to trick users into doing 'the wrong thing', such as clicking a bad link that will download malware or direct them to a website tricking users in disclosing their passwords.[22] Phishing can be conducted via a text message, social media, or by phone, but the term 'phishing'

---

20 It should be noted that the growing number of satellites in different orbits also poses a growing risk for satellites by itself, due to potential collisions and resulting space debris that may trigger a chain reaction and impact several satellites and make orbits unusable. While collisions can happen by accident, they could also be human made, e.g., by leveraging RF or cyber-attacks.

21 Ruben Santamarta, "Last Call for SATCOM Security."

22 National Cyber Security Centre, "Phishing attacks: defending your organization" (2019) https://www.ncsc.gov.uk/guidance/phishing.

is mainly used to describe attacks that arrive by email. Phishing emails can reach millions of users directly and hide amongst the huge number of benign emails that busy users receive. Attacks can install malware (such as ransomware), sabotage systems, or steal intellectual property and money. In a targeted campaign, the attacker may use information about the employees or company to make their messages even more persuasive and realistic. This is usually referred to as spear phishing.

2.3 *Trending Attack Vectors*

2.3.1 CEO Fraud

CEO fraud is a specific type of phishing attack, where attackers send fake emails in the name of the CEO/CFO from fake addresses or compromised email accounts, trying to convince company accountants or delegates to make urgent payments to support a confidential business transaction. Even though this is not a new type of attack, it has become a typical weekly event for most organizations.

2.3.2 Ransomware Attacks

Another attack that is very prominent in the recent years is Ransomware. This is an attack whereby the attacker successfully compromises the network of an organization (for example through phishing) and encrypts many critical systems and data with malicious encryption software (Ransomware). After they have successfully encrypted a large amount of critical data, they extort the victim organization for a ransom in order to provide the cryptographic keys to recover the systems or data. Often, these attacks are paralyzing for the victim organizations and the only way to recover is to pay the ransom, often with financial support by a cyber security insurance. It is worth noting that, while cyber insurance helps the affected organisations short-term, paying ransom at a broader scale fuels these threat actors.[23]

Unfortunately, there are plenty of examples in the recent past, where ransomware attacks caused significant damage. In June 2017, in what has been characterized as one of the most catastrophic malware attacks, many companies where infected by the ransomware NotPetya causing substantial losses.

23 Interestingly, ransomware had been discussed in the research community more than 15 years ago – *see,* Adam Young and Moti Yung, *Malicious Cryptography: Exposing Cryptovirology* (John Wiley & Sons, Inc. 2004) – but its hype started only with the rise of crypto currencies that enabled attackers to safely collect and cash out ransom payments. Trends like cyber security insurance and anonymous crypto currencies are currently fueling their business models and they are posing a considerable risk.

For example, the global logistics company Maersk was infected and resulted in the loss of 49,000 laptops destroyed, and the company estimating its total losses upwards of $300,000,000. Almost at the same time, FedEx, after being infected by the same ransomware, reported losses of more than $400,000,000. It is estimated that the total economic impact of the NotPetya ransomware was more than $10 billion.[24]

2.3.3 Supply Chain Attacks

A supply chain attack is an attack that attempts to inflict damage to a company by exploiting vulnerabilities in its supply chain network. A supply chain attack entails continuous network compromise or infiltration processes to gain access to a firm's network in order to cause disruptions or outages, which ultimately harm the target company. In other words, the attackers are compromising suppliers with lower security postures than their actual targets and use that as the infiltration path to their actual victims. This is particularly important for satellite service providers since these are often important suppliers to governments, military, critical infrastructure providers, and as such they are becoming an even more attractive target.

Supply chain attacks are being used more and more often by the perpetrators. Only recently, many aerospace companies including SpaceX and Lockheed Martin, fell victim to a malware called "DoppelPaymer." In this case, the attackers did not attack directly these companies. Instead, they compromised a precision parts manufacturer that supplies the automotive, aeronautics, and aerospace industries. That company, Visser Precision, LLC, is based in Denver, Colorado, and counts Lockheed Martin, SpaceX, and Tesla among its customers. Through that supplier, they managed to infiltrate the target companies. It is suspected that the malware was encrypting and exfiltrating data.

Similarly, in an attack that became public during the end of 2020, a provider of a very prominent IT monitoring tool, Solarwinds, revealed that they had been the victim of an attack. In that case, the perpetrators managed to infiltrate the IT software provider 2 months earlier and installed malicious code on their software product. This in turn gave the perpetrators access to all the customers that were using the affected software product.

---

24 Andy Greenberg, "The Untold Story of NotPetya, the Most Devastating Cyberattack in History," *Wired* (22 Aug. 2018) https://www.wired.com/story/notpetya-cyberattack-ukraine-russia-code-crashed-the-world/.

2.4 *Traditional Challenges ("Weaknesses") Are Driving Cyber Security Risks*

The space industry has a unique combination of characteristics that could lead to an increased risk of compromise, even compared to other similar industries. In this section we will analyse these elements and how they affect the risk profile of the satellite service providers.

2.4.1 Broad Use of Proprietary Systems

Satellite service providers have built most of their infrastructure (space and ground) using highly specialized and proprietary systems. More often than not, these systems are not fully compatible with modern standard security technologies (for instance anti-malware) or good security practices (like patching or hardening of the system configuration).[25] It is not uncommon that attempts to secure the equipment may lead to loss of supplier support or warranty or may affect their functionality.

Furthermore, these systems are usually built by a multitude of specialized, small manufacturers – some with limited resources and expertise in secure product development. As a result, some systems are insecure by design, increasing the risk of compromise and leaving system owners with limited built-in protection options. In such cases, system owners must apply compensating security controls "around" these systems, ending up with a fragile system surrounded by a secured perimeter.

2.4.2 Long System Lifetimes

In most industries, companies are able to renew their systems on a regular basis (for example every 5 years). On the contrary, ground infrastructure of satellite systems is usually certified by the manufacturer based on a specific hardware, operating system, and application version. This means that hardware and software upgrades require significant adaptations of the control application, including a full re-test and re-certification of the full system. As this is extremely costly and resource consuming, often the only viable option is to not do major upgrades on the hardware or operating system. This results in satellite operators needing to maintain stock of replacement hardware to replace failed hardware. More importantly though, it obliges the operators, in certain cases, to run end of life operating system software, that does not receive security patches anymore or even has known vulnerabilities with public exploits.

---

25 Configuration hardening is the process by which a company reduces the attack surface of a system, by limiting the system functionality to only the absolutely necessary, as well as by applying security measures and good practices during maintenance.

This increases significantly the risk for these operators who need to resort to other countermeasures to limit their exposure.

For the same reasons as above, there are systems in use that have been designed and implemented more than ten years ago, which are of course based on security principles and standards of that time. These systems may not resist modern threats or adversaries. For example, those systems may employ cryptographic algorithms, which are considered weak today (for instance, RSA 1024-bit, MD5 hash function, and so on), and can be breached. Or as another example, the systems may be designed with a "security perimeter"[26] architecture, which is an outdated security operating model, instead of the "defense-in-depth"[27] approach.

2.4.3 Conflicting Priorities

Lastly, the availability of space-based infrastructures is usually of paramount importance, as it could lead to the loss of space assets. Anything that could potentially conflict with operational safety is scrutinized and subject to risk/reward tradeoffs. For example, sometimes even having basic controls such as individual, nominal accounts, or complex passwords or even locking screensavers are perceived as conflicting with operational safety, as they could potentially inhibit quick intervention in case of emergency. This is not to say that these controls are not implemented, it does highlight however, that even simple controls which would otherwise be part of the standard baseline, need to be closely examined to determine the risks/rewards.

All the previous factors highlight why the operator and providers of satellite-based infrastructure face risk environment with many challenges which cannot necessarily be mitigated by traditional or prevalent security countermeasures and which require tailored security concepts.

3 Evolution Brings New Challenges

As we have seen in previous sections, there is a large variety of threat actors, with different motivations, intents and capabilities, that target potential

26 Perimeter security refers to an approach in which a series of security mechanisms and controls (e.g., firewalls) are placed across the system or network perimeter to stop any attacker from getting access to a company's data.

27 Defense in Depth refers to an information security approach in which a series of security mechanisms and controls are thoughtfully layered throughout a computer network to protect the confidentiality, integrity, and availability of the network and the data within.

security weaknesses of space-based infrastructures and services via different attack vectors. In the last years, the space ecosystem has been undergoing a tremendous evolution and this trend is continuing and is going to accelerate further along different dimensions.

3.1 *Space Evolves as a Critical Infrastructure*

As space is becoming an enabler for more and more critical services for our societies, including navigation, earth observation, communication services, video distribution, and emergency communication platforms, the global value of space is increasing. The potential impacts of cyber-attacks are increasing accordingly, and space is evolving as a critical infrastructure. New threat actors may enter the scene, targeting space systems to impact critical services enabled by these.

The more critical the space-enabled services become, the more appealing they become for threat actors and the more those will be willing to invest into attacks. With more complex and sophisticated attacks arising against space-enabled services, defences must become more robust. It is to be expected, that more elements of space infrastructures and services will be formally declared as critical infrastructure and regulated accordingly. For instance, both the United States and the European Union have frameworks for addressing the cybersecurity of capabilities that fall within the category of critical infrastructure, which heighten the security requirements for these capabilities.[28] This is even more applicable in situations where satellite services themselves constitute critical parts of disaster recovery/relief solutions because of their ubiquitous nature and short time to deploy with low local infrastructure dependencies. It is obvious that such services, being the backup for standard communication services, need to meet highest levels of robustness and security in order to serve their purpose in potential large-scale emergency situations or even military conflict. While setting out worthwhile security objectives aiming for higher standards across the space domain, a plethora of critical infrastructure policies issued by individual nation states will pose a challenge to comply with for global space service providers. Similar challenges have been observed in previous research, for example Fischer identifies more than 50 statutes addressing various aspects of cyber security in the US alone.[29] From a legal and regulatory perspective

---

28 For the United States see Homeland Security Presidential Directive HSPD-7: Critical Infrastructure Identification, Prioritization, and Protection (17 December 2003) and NIST, *Cybersecurity Framework 1.1* (2014). For the European Union see European Commission, Communication from the Commission on a European Programme for Critical Infrastructure Protection, COM(2006) 786 final (12 December 2006).

29 Fischer, *Cybersecurity Issues and Challenges*, 7.

there could be significant gain in alignment and convergence of critical infrastructure security policies across key regulating entities for the space domain. This may serve as an area for future research.

3.2 *Growing Complexity and Attack Surface of Infrastructures*

As space and ground segments are becoming more complex to facilitate new services and applications, the attack surface and potential security weaknesses are increasing exponentially, giving attackers more potential attack vectors. space infrastructure and services are increasingly dependent on IT (Information Technology), OSS (Operational Support Systems), and BSS (Business Support Systems). Any successful attack impacting one of these support systems may have the potential to impact dependent systems and services or at least may serve as an attack vector to attack more critical parts of the infrastructure. Digital transformation initiatives are a critical enabler for novel services and driving efficiency by integrating systems and automating processes along the value chain. At the same time, higher integration also means breaking down traditional system security boundaries by opening interfaces to customers and partner organisations. OSS and BSS system interfaces are exposed to customers and partner organisations, often via the public Internet, for example to enable new data services and self-service provisioning of network capacity or managing satellite payloads via Internet-facing interfaces. Traditional security concepts, largely relying on the physical or logical network level isolation of these critical systems, are often not viable anymore. Therefore, defending future space systems and space-based services pose new security engineering challenges for systems that traditionally relied on perimeter security and complete isolation. This requires advanced concepts and a rethinking across the whole ecosystem to ensure cyber defense capabilities that can keep pace with cyber threats while remaining economically viable.

3.3 *Interdependencies in a Complex Eco-system*

With the evolution to full end-to-end services and novel use-cases, a complex eco-system is evolving with several stakeholder operating parts of the highly interconnected and interdependent service infrastructure. Market demand is driving the development of end-to-end connectivity services as well in space communications. In the past, satellite operators typically provided bandwidth and transponders on their satellites for customers to build their connectivity on, thus limiting the responsibility of the operator. Today's data connectivity services often feature a deeper vertical integration level as illustrated in Figure 2.4, with operators offering end-to-end services, for instance up to the Wifi-access point on an airplane, where passengers can connect to for their internet access. Such higher integration levels imply additional layers of responsibility for the provider with respective increments in attack surface.

Whether provided by a single operator as a more integrated service or by multiple players creating the value chain together, threat actors are well-versed in identifying the weakest link in complex systems as shown in the section Supply Chain Attacks. As the overall security posture of space-enabled services is only as strong as its weakest link, it requires a concerted effort of all involved stakeholders to design, implement and operate the overall services securely.

To illustrate the growing interdependency and its implications, consider HTS and MEO/LEO satellite systems as an example, that require more complex ground infrastructure, including ground systems, TT&C sites and additional gateway and monitoring sites. Such global space systems with their infrastructure spanning numerous countries with their own regulatory frameworks and individual legislation inevitably leads to further compliance challenges due to differing, at times conflicting policies and requirements as identified in Baylon.[30] Managing and tracking this, in turn, may dilute or divert the resources organizations have available to counter cyber risks. Hence, well-intended individual regulations to strengthen cyber security resilience in the space domain may at some point turn counter-productive if stacked without alignment between regulators. Operators of global space systems may have to comply with different national compliance frameworks and, therefore, maintain multiple sets of compliance documentations or may be audited by several national regulators. Beyond challenges instilled by global distribution directly, often third- party sites are used in those global systems. Physical security considerations of hosted critical ground system infrastructure are becoming even more important then, but also more difficult and more expensive to achieve. Careful system design and risk management are crucial and the flow-down of security requirements to third parties is critical to provide security assurance for the overall service. In the context of an increasingly complex eco-system of stakeholders with operational responsibilities for different parts of the overall service infrastructure, and the overall service security depending on the security of various sub-systems operated by different service providers, security failure/compromise of one sub-system may impact the security of another system and, ultimately, the security of the overall service.

30 C. Baylon, *Challenges at the Intersection of Cyber Security and Space Security: Country and International Institution Perspectives* (2014) http://www.chathamhouse.org/publication/challenges-intersection-cyber-security-andspace- security-country-and-international.

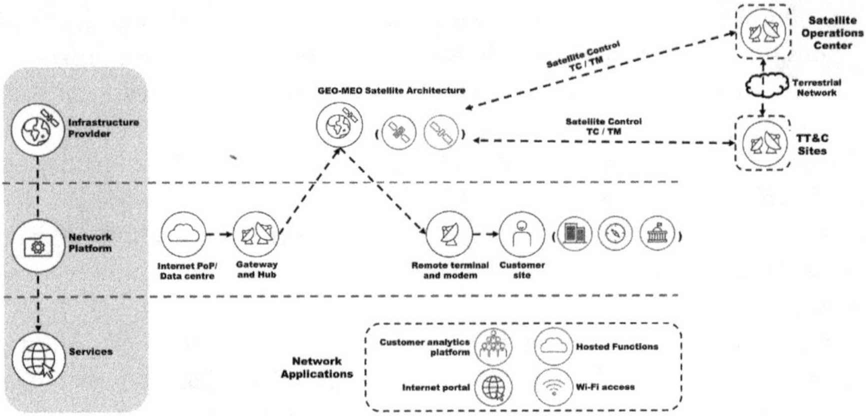

FIGURE 2.4 Infrastructure vs. Service provider

Joint initiatives, such the Space-ISAC (Information Sharing an Analysis Center),[31] founded in 2019, are instrumental in the overall security of the space ecosystem and services being delivered by this ecosystem.

4 Conclusion

Cyber attacks against space services are a fact for the past twenty years. This chapter reviewed several types of threat actors and attack vectors as well as analyzed ransomware and supply chain attacks as the critical emerging attack vectors in light of their specific relevance for satellite-based services.

Space has evolved to a critical infrastructure, essential for the functioning of our societies since it is enabling critical services like navigation and emergency communication services. As such, it is evident that the potential impacts of cyber-attacks are increasing accordingly.

Protecting satellite-based services against advanced cyber attacks always had to overcome unique challenges, such as widespread use of proprietary systems, with minimum security features, very long system lifetimes and systems that cannot be upgraded or hardened and, therefore, may suffer from unsupported operating systems with inherent easily exploitable vulnerabilities or outdated security protections. At the same time, their operational criticality often supersedes any other priorities, in the fear that in-line protection

31 Space ISAC (Information Sharing and Analysis Center), https://s-isac.org/.

measures may add additional complexity and points of failure, thus hinder availability.

Adding to traditional challenges, the space ecosystem is undergoing a tremendous evolution. This significantly enhances space-based services and enables new service models. At the same time, this evolution introduces additional challenges. Infrastructures and systems become more complex and interconnected which increases its overall attack surface substantially. Consequently, protecting space systems and space-based services in the future will require further innovation and change in the security architecture, to defend systems that traditionally relied on perimeter security and complete isolation.

In addition to all the above, growing interdependencies between infrastructure operators, service providers and various third parties create an ever-increasing complexity of the ecosystem. In the face of those challenges, organizations must design their systems carefully and manage their risks. Equally importantly, they need to flow-down their security requirements to third parties to achieve security assurance for the overall service and deter any supply chain attacks.

The protection of space-based services requires concerted efforts by organizations across the whole service value chain. Organizations and the space ecosystem will have to overcome these challenges and complexities if they want to remain competitive in the future. Cyber security teams will have to find new ways to protect the organizations and the respective communities from attackers, while keeping operational impact of security measures to a minimum on the infrastructure.

In this context, drawing experience from current policies and identifying potential synergies with existing regulations can benefit the regulating entities for the space domain. Regulators around the world started recently to address growing security concerns in this ecosystem with recent and upcoming policies and directives, such as IA-Pre,[32] SPD-5[33] and NIS2,[34] which will help

32 USSF Commercial SATCOM Office announces development of new security program, https://www.spaceforce.mil/News/Article/2230831/ussf-commercial-satcom-office-announces-development-of-new-security-program/.

33 Memorandum on Space Policy Directive-5 – Cybersecurity Principles for Space Systems (4 September 2020) https://trumpwhitehouse.archives.gov/presidential-actions/memorandum-space-policy-directive-5-cybersecurity-principles-space-systems/.

34 Revised Directive on Security of Network and Information Systems (NIS2), European Commission (December 2020) https://ec.europa.eu/digital-single-market/en/news/revised-directive-security-network-and-information-systems-nis2.

setting minimum standards and raising awareness about the importance of securing critical space-based services.

Law and regulation play a critical role in setting minimum standards upon which organizations can build their own cybersecurity plans and frameworks. Complementary to regulations, joint initiatives, such the Space-ISAC (Information Sharing an Analysis Center),[35] will help foster an open exchange on cyber security threats and vulnerabilities, thereby raising awareness and fostering collaboration by the space ecosystem to take on cyber security as a joint responsibility.

35 Space ISAC (Information Sharing and Analysis Center), https://s-isac.org/.

CHAPTER 3

Cybersecurity Threats to Space: From Conception to the Aftermaths

Sébastien Bonnart, Andrea Capurso, Antonio Carlo, Thea Flem Dethlefsen, Mclee Kerolle, Jonathan Lim, Aaron Pickard, Antonia Russo, and Laetitia Cesari Zarkan

1 Introduction*

Invisible to the human eye, up beyond the atmosphere, a cloak made of satellites, signals, and data fluxes mantles our planet. It is intertwined with the surface of the Earth through antennas, receivers, and other ground segments that elaborate and distribute the services provided from outer space. Understanding how hostile cyber operations are put in place and what consequences they produce is a crucial need for all involved in space activities. In today's interconnected context, underestimating the risks that come from the cyber domain may expose space infrastructures and the services depending on them resulting in irreparable damages.

For this reason, this chapter aims to provide a general overview of hostile cyber operations and their effects on space activities, from the start to the aftermath. Section 2 addresses the attack surface for hostile operations through a survey of hardware, software, space and ground segments, and the radio frequency spectrum. It identifies where space assets are vulnerable and sets the ground for the second section, which outlines the different strategies for protecting those vulnerabilities. Section 3 starts with the IT governance strategies a company or organization can implement. Improving IT governance mechanisms concerning space-related technologies is vital to encourage positive cyber behaviors, improve top-level decision making, reduce the possibility and effect of catastrophic incidents, and enable better strategic planning vis-a-vis cybersecurity matters. Section 3.2 presents an overview of the technical strategies to be adopted in space systems to mitigate risks related to cyberattacks. Section 4 exemplifies the consequences of previous hostile cyber operations

* The opinions expressed are those of the author and do not reflect the official opinion of the European Commission.

 | DOI:10.1163/9789004527270_004

against space assets. It addresses the impact and effects of hostile cyber operations, including the long-term or short-term consequences of the different nature and purposes of the targeted system and the kind of attack perpetrated against the system/satellite. Consequences range from unauthorized access to classified information and the outage of critical infrastructure. Section 4.2 addresses the subsequent reconstructing and incident response at both an organizational and international level. Section 5 and 6 deal with the legal implications of hostile cyber operations. Section 5 addresses the challenges of applying public international law, as Section 5.1 examines the political ambiguity over how the existing legal regime is applied, Section 5.2 looks at the technical challenges of attribution, and finally Section 5.3 looks at the legal boundaries that exist for target precision for a hostile cyber operation when it comes to collateral victims. Section 6 examines the private international aspects of a hostile cyber operation, including incidents where the perpetrators and victims are non-state actors. Section 6.1, therefore, addresses the contractual provisions that may cover a cyber operation, Section 6.2 the private arbitration and Section 6.3 the courts that can settle possible disputes relating to a breach can be solved. Section 6.4 explores how private actors can protect themselves through insurance. Finally, Section 7 provides a conclusion.

2 Overview of Cyber Geography

The first section of this chapter presents the cyber-geography of space missions. Section 2.1 starts by defining the mission components and maps the attack surface,[1] from ground segment, space segment to the orbits. Section 2.2 outlines how these systems communicate through for example satellite telecommunication and the architecture of the networks that transmit data. The purpose of this section is to provide an overview of the structure of space systems and how the different segments are interconnected which will be used to understand the weaknesses of the systems that will be explored further in Section 3.

1 "Attack surface" is defined as "[t]he set of points on the boundary of a system, a system element, or an environment where an attacker can try to enter, cause an effect on, or extract data from." Ron Ross et al, *Developing Cyber Resilient Systems: A Systems Security Engineering Approach*, NIST Special Publication 800–160, v. 2 (2019) https://nvlpubs.nist.gov/nistpubs/SpecialPublications/NIST.SP.800-160v2.pdf.

2.1 *Space Mission Anatomy*

2.1.1 Ground Segment

The ground segment is the part of a space system located on earth. It is usually the largest part of the system in terms of mass, volume, and power consumption. The main components of a traditional ground segment are the user segment, the ground station, spacecraft control and payload control.[2] The user interface or user segment can have multiple forms depending on the mission. It allows users to benefit from the space service directly through the spacecraft or through the payload control. This can, for instance, take the form of a GPS guidance system, a satellite phone, or TV antenna.

The ground station is the ground segment subsystem used to communicate with the spacecraft. It features an antenna, a transmitter, a receiver, amplifiers, and a steering mechanism, all coordinated by an antenna control system.

The spacecraft control subsystem, also referred to as the mission operations center, is interfaced with the space segment through ground stations, and maintains the spacecraft bus in operational conditions.[3] The spacecraft control subsystem monitors on the ground telemetry received from the sensors aboard the spacecraft. The spacecraft control subsystem also issues necessary commands such as collision avoidance maneuvers, sends configuration/software updates. and enables the payload aboard the space segment to operate.

The mission is accomplished by the space segment's payload, which is commanded from the ground by the payload control center. Similar to the spacecraft control subsystem, the payload control is connected with the spacecraft through antennas and controls the instruments in order to ensure completion of the mission and satisfaction of the users. The nature of the payload's operation depends on the mission.

A ground segment may be composed of more than one instance of each of these components,[4] either to provide redundancy or due to the mission's characteristics. For instance, an earth observation mission may have a spacecraft control center co-located with a payload control center, as well as multiple antennas to control the spacecraft and payload. Moreover, there can be a distinct set of antennas for direct payload data reception at the end user's

---

2 Consultative Committee for Space Data Systems, *Mission Planning and Scheduling*, Report CCSDS 529.0-G-1 (2018) https://public.ccsds.org/Pubs/529x0g1.pdf.

3 Gail A. Johnson-Roth, Geraldine A. Chaudhri, & William F. Tosney, *Ground Segment Systems Engineering Handbook*, Technical Operating Report TOR-2016–01797 (The Aerospace Corporation 2016) https://apps.dtic.mil/dtic/tr/fulltext/u2/1067478.pdf.

4 Consultative Committee for Space Data Systems, *Security Architecture for Space Data Systems, Recommended Practice* CCSDS 351.0-M-1 (2012) https://public.ccsds.org/Pubs/351x0m1.pdf.

facilities. A web interface may allow customers to order images via the payload control center through the Internet.

2.1.2 Space Segment

The space segment is composed of the spacecraft and its subsystems. The largest part of the space segment is the "bus." The bus includes the vehicle's structure, power generation, communications, attitude determination and control, avionics, and other mission-specific systems.[5] The payload is entirely mission dependent, providing the fulfillment of the mission's purpose using the resources provided by the bus. It is common to have a dedicated communication system as part of the payload. The space segment from a mission can range from being a single sub-system hosted by the International Space Station (ISS) to a large constellation of inter-connected satellites.

2.1.3 Orbits

The majority of space systems are orbiting the earth. The four main categories of orbits are: low earth orbit (LEO), medium earth orbit (MEO), geosynchronous equatorial orbit (GEO), and highly elliptical orbit. For the purpose of this chapter, this section will offer a brief overview on the commonly used orbits of low earth orbit and geosynchronous equatorial orbit. LEO characterizes spacecraft orbiting at altitudes between 100 km and 2000 km. These spacecrafts complete a full revolution in about 90 minutes. Key uses of LEO are new communications constellations, earth observation satellites with both scientific and military purposes, modern crewed spaceflight, as well as parking orbits used by spacecraft heading to more specialized orbits. Orbital parameters affect the visibility of the satellite from any particular point on Earth, and therefore the accessibility of ground users to the spacecraft. Not all spacecraft in LEO are visible from everywhere on Earth during an orbit. If the latitude of a point is extreme enough and the orbital inclination of an object is low enough, the object may never be visible from a particular point. As an example, a satellite in a circular orbit with an altitude of 820 km never offers visibility windows longer than 15.5 minutes at a time.[6] If visible, it will appear to move across the sky. A fixed omnidirectional antenna or a directional antenna with azimuth and elevation control may communicate with it.

5 NASA, *State-Of-The-Art Small Spacecraft Technology* (2020) https://www.nasa.gov/smallsat-institute/sst-soa-2020.

6 Shkelzen Cakaj et al., "Communications Durations with Low Orbiting Satellites," 4th IASTED International Conference on Antennas, Radar, and Wave Propagation (2007) https://publik.tuwien.ac.at/files/pub-et_12772.pdf.

GEO, also called geostationary orbit, describes the orbits of some spacecraft at an altitude of about 36000 km in a circular orbit over the Earth's equator. At this altitude, the revolution time for the satellite around the Earth is exactly the same as the one rotation of Earth. This orbit is heavily used by broadcast and telecommunication services. An object in GEO is either always visible or always invisible from any particular point on Earth. Satellites in GEO appear with a fixed position in the sky for an observer on Earth, and ground stations can use directional antennas that do not move to communicate with them.

Spacecraft may also orbit or land on other celestial bodies. Such operations, as well as any others where the vehicle is more than 2 million kilometers from Earth, are considered by the International Telecommunication Union to be in "deep space," as opposed to "near Earth space."[7] This has technical implications for the spacecraft's design, as well as how it transmits data back to Earth. An object in deep space's visibility from the Earth varies, based on what celestial body it is orbiting or landed on, and where that body is relative to the Earth – typically in the reference frame of the Sun. Now that the space mission components have been identified, this section continues by addressing the interconnections and attack surface they offer.

2.2 *Data, Links and Networks*

Having presented the main components of space missions, the next step is to demonstrate how they communicate together. Space missions use two main data fluxes. One is telemetry and control (TM/TC), which goes both ways between the satellite and the control center. The other is payload data that, depending on the mission, can be from space to ground (for instance, earth observation or navigation data), or both ways (such as telecommunications data).[8]

Telemetry contains the data allowing mission control to assess the health state of the spacecraft. After immediate analysis, data is archived in the mission control center for long term study of the satellite behavior. Telecommands are orders from the mission control center to the satellite.[9] These can be parameter

7 Marc Siebert et al., "Developing Future Deep-Space Telecommunication Architectures: A Historical Look at the Benefits of Analog Research on the Development of Solar System Internetworking for Future Human Spaceflight," *Astrobiology*, 19, no. 3 (6 Mar 2019): 462–477, https://www.liebertpub.com/doi/10.1089/ast.2018.1915 and ITU, *Handbook on Space Research Communication* (2014) https://www.itu.int/dms_pub/itu-r/opb/hdb/R-HDB-43-2013-OAS-PDF-E.pdf.

8 Consultative Committee for Space Data Systems, *Mission Planning and Scheduling*.

9 P. Soerensen et al., "The Flight Operations Segment," *ESA Bulletin*, n. 106 (2001) 88–95, http://www.esa.int/esapub/bulletin/bullet106/bul106_7.pdf.

adjustments for subsystems from the bus, collision avoidance maneuvers, and switching to redundant subsystems. Some telecommands have immediate effect, while others can be triggered at a specific time or by an event. For instance, some critical actions are split into several distinct commands before the satellite applies them in order to reduce the risk of an accidental activation of the action. Similar to telemetry, telecommands are also archived at the mission control center.

Payload data and its archiving are completely mission dependent. Following confidentiality principles, data should be encrypted all the way between mission, payload controls, and spacecraft. Data should also be encrypted between spacecraft and user terminals without decoding at ground station level.[10]

Missions rely on ground storage as much as possible to keep onboard storage for short-term memory. The reason for this is that storage onboard is much more expensive and unreliable than on the ground. One explanation is due to how space radiation affects the spacecraft memory, which requires expensive memories and redundancies. To put this in perspective, in 2020 the cost of a LEO launch ranged between 1,500 and 30,000 USD/kg.[11]

2.2.1 Satellite Telecommunications

The ground segment and space segment are typically connected via two-way radio links. The connection requires either a line of sight between a particular spacecraft and its ground station or additional satellites to relay data between the ground and space segment. The Institute of Electrical and Electronics Engineers (IEEE) has categorized the Radio Frequency spectrum into bands, many of which are used in space applications.[12] Spectrum allocation occurs at the national level as every country determines who is permitted to transmit on which frequencies. Frequency coordination between nations occurs through the International Telecommunication Union (ITU) Radiocommunication Sector, a division of a United Nations agency that also assists with satellite orbit deconfliction.[13]

---

10 James Pavur, "Whispers Among the Stars," Presentation at DEFCON Safe Mode (2020) https://www.youtube.com/watch?v=kuoQ_Wey4Ko.

11 Thomas G. Roberts, "Space Launch to Low Earth Orbit: How Much Does it Cost?" *CSIS Aerospace Security* (2020) https://aerospace.csis.org/data/space-launch-to-low-earth-orbit-how-much-does-it-cost/.

12 NASA, "What Are the Spectrum Band Designators and Bandwidths?" (2018) https://www.nasa.gov/directorates/heo/scan/communications/outreach/funfacts/txt_band_designators.html.

13 ITU, "Space Services Department (SSD)" (2021) https://www.itu.int/en/ITU-R/space/Pages/default.aspx.

The authority of national governments to regulate the airwaves in their territory has important legal ramifications. Satellite operators must obtain and maintain authorization from every national government in which they want to operate. Access to the radio frequency spectrum has been a topic of contention among satellite operators in the recent past, with threats of litigation,[14] actual litigation,[15] protests to government agencies,[16] and requests for regulatory action.[17] This trend of using the legal and regulatory mechanisms to attack and defend the finite resource of radio frequency spectrum seems likely to only increase. This is primarily due to the fact that access to space is becoming less technologically complex and demand for bandwidth is increasing.

Student and amateur-radio satellites tend to use VHF and UHF frequency bands, though there is a trend towards the S-band.[18] Now many LEO satellites operate in the S-band for Telemetry and Telecommand (TC) and X-band for high data-rate downlink.[19] The developing trend is to move TM/TC to X-band and the payload downlink to Ka-band to enable more satellites to transmit data without interference and higher data rates.[20]

Global Navigation Satellite Services (GNSS) such as GPS and Galileo provide users with signals on L-band frequencies.[21] GEO satellites transmit data on a variety of frequencies, typically in the C-, K-, Ku-, and Ka- bands.[22]

Optical communications, the transmission of data using lasers, is emerging as a supplement to traditional radio communications links. Laser

---

14 Theresa Hitchens, "Iridium Publicly Threatens Lawsuit to Overturn FCC'S Ligado Vote," *Breaking Defense* (2020) https://breakingdefense.com/2020/07/iridium-publicly-threatens-lawsuit-to-overturn-fccs-ligado-vote/.

15 Caleb Henry, "SES Files $1.8 Billion Claim against Intelsat over Splitting C-Band Alliance," *Space News* (2020) https://spacenews.com/ses-files-1-8-billion-claim-against-intelsat-over-splitting-c-band-alliance/.

16 Todd Feathers, "Spacex is Lobbying against Amazon's Internet-Beaming Satellites," *Vice* (2019) https://www.vice.com/en/article/5dmzyx/spacex-is-lobbying-against-amazons-internet-beaming-satellites.

17 Jeff Foust, "Viasat Asks FCC to Perform Environmental Review of Starlink," *Space News* (2020) https://spacenews.com/viasat-asks-fcc-to-perform-environmental-review-of-starlink/.

18 VHF is defined as 30–300 MHz. UHF is defined as 300–3000 MHz. S-band is defined as the 2.5 GHz band. ITU, *Nomenclature of the Frequency and Wavelength Bands used in Telecommunications.* (2015): TABLE 4, https://www.itu.int/dms_pubrec/itu-r/rec/v/R-REC-V.431-8-201508-I!!PDF-E.pdf.

19 X-band is defined nominally as 8.5–10.5 GHz. *Id.*

20 Ka-band is defined nominally as the 30 GHz band. *Id.*

21 The L-band is defined nominally as the 1.5 GHz band. *Id.*

22 The C-band is defined nominally as the 4–6 GHz band. The K-band is defined nominally as the 20 GHz band. The Ku-band is defined nominally as the 11–14 GHz band. *Id.*

communications terminals have low volume, mass, and power requirements, which may make them easier to mass-produce.[23] Optical communications have the potential to increase the efficiency of space-to-space and space-to-ground communications by improving the signal-to-noise ratio and transmitting at higher data rates.[24] Furthermore, a satellite with an optical communications system is able to target a ground station on Earth much more precisely than one with a radio transmitter because optical frequencies' wavelengths are much smaller than radio frequency wavelengths. While it is more difficult for others to passively intercept these transmissions by deploying an antenna in the footprint, a space-based optical transmitter must be pointed at the intended ground station much more precisely than a radio transmitter. At this point, the technology is not yet developed enough for mass production, and it is not likely to completely replace radio communications in the near- or medium-term. However, the technology is viable and has been adopted by enough government and industry partners that a forward-looking approach to space-based cybersecurity must consider the unique opportunities and risks posed by this technology.[25]

2.2.2 Networks

2.2.2.1 *Classical Architecture*

In the traditional architecture, the four entities consisting of user segment, ground station, spacecraft control, and payload control are separate subsystems, with potential for each to have its own internal network.[26] Most of the equipment of each entity is connected to the internal network. Both spacecraft control and payload control are also each connected with at least one ground station.[27] This means that the ground station has at least one piece of

23 Rudolf Saathof et al., "Optical Satellite Communication Space Terminal Technology at TNO," *Proceedings Volume 11180, International Conference on Space Optics – ICSO 2018* (2018) https://www.spiedigitallibrary.org/conference-proceedings-of-spie/11180/111800K/Optical-satellite-communication-space-terminal-technology-at-TNO/10.1117/12.2535939.full.

24 Suzana Sburlan, "Introduction to Optical Communications for Satellites," Keck Institute for Space Studies (2016) https://www.youtube.com/watch?v=zDjuRg5aNf4.

25 NASA, "Low-Cost Transceiver Will Allow First Laser Mass Communication," *NASA Spinoff* (2019) https://spinoff.nasa.gov/Spinoff2019/it_4.html.

26 Consultative Committee for Space Data Systems, *CCSDS Guide for Secure System Interconnection*, Report CCSDS 350.4-G-2 (2019) https://public.ccsds.org/Pubs/350x4g2.pdf.

27 Wilfried Ley, Klaus Wittmann, & Willi Hallmann, *Handbook of Space Technology* (Wiley 2009) 461.

equipment connected to spacecraft control equipment and one piece of equipment connected to payload control equipment (it may be the same device).

Ground stations can use copper or fiber optic cables to interconnect networks. Data can sometimes be transmitted over a dedicated line but more frequently a virtual private network (VPN) or equivalent over the Internet. VPNs are technologies insulating the ground segment networks from the Internet using a layer of cryptography and security protocols. This makes the Internet insulation system a potential entry point for a capable outsider with an Internet connection.

When the user segment offers a service through the Internet, this service is also a privileged entry point for attackers, as it is connected to the ground segment and accessible from anywhere.

2.2.2.2 *Co-location*

When several parts of the ground segment are co-located, this reduces the reliance on the Internet, and may even make the system completely independent if all parts of the ground segment are co-located. This architecture is more protected from a cybersecurity perspective as it removes the Internet as an entry point, but also severely constrains the system. This allows for no reliance on external services, no remote connection with users, and limits to a single antenna location – which reduces opportunities for redundancy.

2.2.2.3 *Ground Station in the Cloud*

Using emerging third-party cloud based ground station services allows for multiple new architectures from the traditional three networks. This external service can provide a full range of services from antenna rental only to a fully integrated service where ground station, mission control, and payload control are all hosted in the same provider's cloud. Some of the hybrids are already covered by our description of the co-located architecture. Proposing satellite communication services allows for historical cloud services providers to be directly interfaced with the satellites and pushes forward their own services for distribution, archiving, or performing machine learning on the data exchanged with space.[28] These are cost attractive opportunities for new functionalities that also come with potential new threat exposures due to the outsourcing of more activities, resources sharing, and multiplying interconnections between

---

28 AWS, "What is AWS Ground Station?" (2019) https://docs.aws.amazon.com/ground-station/latest/ug/what-is-aws-ground-station.html.

the satellite control and the outside world.[29] Third party ground station services come with an increased attack surface, but also with embedded cybersecurity features that improve auditability and resiliencurthermoremore, shared antenna resources could potentially be leveraged by an attacker for denial of service by booking all visibility slots between the target satellite and the ground stations provider's antennas. Consequences of not being able to communicate with a satellite for too long may cascade up to the loss of the mission. Space awareness may also benefit from analyzing the availability slots of the shared antennas and trying to deduce which satellites are using the service.

2.2.2.4 *Space Networks*

Communication buses inside a satellite constitute internal communication network infrastructures that could be used by attackers to laterally move to compromising other satellite parts. Another potential entry point is the inter satellite links (ISL). Whether there are relay satellites such as EDRS/TDRS or a constellation of satellites each communicating with one another, their routing functionality could potentially be exploited as an entry point. One can imagine a hostile cyber operation spreading from satellite to satellite using these inter-satellite networks.[30] As these new networks develop, extra-care should be taken at the engineering stage as experience from the ground teaches that any kind of interoperability and legacy protocol support constitutes an additional attack surface.

Section 2 described the complexity and characteristics of space missions from main components to their interconnection. Despite – and because of – their importance for States, military forces, commercial entities, and the public society space systems are often targeted by hostile cyber operations. Section 3 addresses these threats and some of their consequences.

3 Space Cyber Threats and Their Consequences

Following the overview of the main components of space missions and how they communicate together in Section 2, Section 3 provides a description of the type of attacks. The section sets off by defining cyber operations and provides real-life examples under Section 3.1. Section 3.2 gives an overview of the

29 Cloud Security Alliance, "Security Guidance for Critical Areas of Focus in Cloud Computing v4.0" (2017) https://cloudsecurityalliance.org/artifacts/security-guidance-v4/.

30 Jacob G. Oakley, *Cybersecurity for Space: Protecting the Final Frontier* (Springer 2020).

different entry points for hostile cyber operations to space systems, ranging from hardware to software and their supply chains. Section 3.3 proposes a tool to identify threats and their components, providing the reader the keys to understanding the mitigation strategies that will be the subject of the next section.

3.1 *Type of Operations*

3.1.1 Electronic vs. Cyber Operations (Jamming/Spoofing/Hacking)

Electronic warfare such as jamming and EMP are generally not considered cyberattacks.[31] Defined as attacks leveraging the use of direct energy, these can sometimes be associated with physical attacks, because the electronic warfare radio wave is effective because of its power.[32] On the other hand, cyberattacks are performed at the information level – the cyberattack is effective because of the data it carries.

3.1.2 Systems and Infrastructure Disruptions, Unauthorized Data Collection, and Falsification: Stage of the Operations

Cyberattacks are not a new threat to the space industry, and previous targets span from the ground segment (either through ground stations or space agencies) to the use of radio signals. The following provides examples of hostile cyber operations against space systems.

In 2008, a passenger unintentionally introduced malware to the International Space Station through a USB drive.[33] Satellites used for navigation signals have been targeted, as seen in the Black Sea incident, where the US Maritime administration reported that 20 vessels in the Black Sea area had experienced GPS "spoofing" in which a false signal confused a GPS receiver, potentially misdirecting the ship.[34]

China has also been suspected to be behind satellite related attacks, such as the 2014 hack of a US weather satellite, thereby blocking essential data that was

---

31 Julian Turner, "The New Battlefield: The Race to Integrate Cyber and Electronic Warfare," *Global Defence Technology* (2021) https://defence.nridigital.com/global_defence_technology_special/the_new_battlefield_the_race_to_integrate_cyber_and_electronic_warfare.

32 Sam Cohen, "Integrating Cyber and Electronic Warfare," AFCEA (2018) https://www.afcea.org/content/integrating-cyber-and-electronic-warfare.

33 Connor Simpson, "Russian Cosmonauts Occasionally Infect the ISS with Malware," *The Atlantic* (2013) https://www.theatlantic.com/international/archive/2013/11/russian-cosmonaut-accidentally-infected-iss-stuxnet/355150/.

34 Dana Goward, "Mass GPS Spoofing Attack in Black Sea?" *Maritime Executive* (2017) https://www.maritime-executive.com/editorials/mass-gps-spoofing-attack-in-black-sea.

used for disaster planning and transportation interests.[35] The nature of two attacks on US satellites in 2007 and 2008, which gained control of command over the satellite in 2008, through a ground station in Norway also links China as the perpetrator.[36] Although no damage was done, the attack was alarming. Space agencies themselves can also be targeted as seen with DLR in 2014, which fell victim to a form of Trojan software, enabling hackers to maintain unauthorized access for several months to confidential information without detection.[37] In 2018 hackers gained access to NASA JPL's Deep Space Network array of radio telescopes and many of their systems. A report indicates that the breach was due to a failure to adopt basic "security 101" measures.[38]

After having described space missions, their components and their communications, we will now develop their exposure to cyber-attacks. The next paragraphs present the diverse nature of cyber threats, detail their components, propose a tool to analyze them and visual examples.[39]

3.2 *Main Entry Points*

In a globalized world, a complex space operation uses sub-systems, pieces of hardware, and software from dozens of countries and a fully developed supply chain pool of thousands of companies. Every software system relies on hardware. If the hardware is compromised, so too is the system running it. Starting at an integrated circuit level, it is feasible to embed a backdoor, and stealthiness increases with the scale of the subsystem.

It does not take intent from the supplier to introduce a cybersecurity breach, because each supplier's information system may be attacked, and its production discreetly modified by hackers in order to embed a vulnerability. While nothing guarantees that a backdoor in a chip will indeed be accessible from the board where it is integrated, the threat exists nonetheless. The more

35 Tony Capaccio and Jeff Bliss, "Chinese Military Suspected in Hacker Attacks on U.S. Satellites," *Bloomberg* (2011) https://www.bloomberg.com/news/articles/2011-10-27/chinese-military-suspected-in-hacker-attacks-on-u-s-satellites.

36 Jim Wolf, "China Key Suspect in U.S. Satellite Hacks: Commission," *Reuters* (2011) https://www.reuters.com/article/us-china-usa-satellite-idUSTRE79R4O320111028.

37 Pierluigi Paganini, "German Aerospace Center Hit by Serious Malware-Based Attack," *Cyber Defense Magazine* (2014) https://www.cyberdefensemagazine.com/german-aerospace-center-hit-by-serious-malware-based-attack/.

38 Davey Winder, "Confirmed: NASA Has Been Hacked," *Forbes* (2019) https://www.forbes.com/sites/daveywinder/2019/06/20/confirmed-nasa-has-been-hacked/?sh=210f5129dc62.

39 Consultative Committee for Space Data Systems, *Security Threats Against Space Missions*, Report CCSDS 350.1-G-2 (2015).

advanced the integration level of the compromised subsystem, the more likely the hostile cyber operation will succeed. Nevertheless, suppliers of higher-level subsystems are addressing cybersecurity threats more carefully.

Software also constitutes a potential entry point into a space mission that can be a target in a hostile cyber operation. Unlike hardware, where once a chip is manufactured its design is set, modern spacecraft software is often designed to be updated as needed in support of spacecraft builders, testers, and operators. An example of this at the component level is the Software Defined Radio.[40] This technology's modifiability complicates the software of a space system and makes it a potential entry point for attackers. On the one hand, as it is subject to updates, a vulnerability that is present today may disappear tomorrow if it is identified and closed. On the other hand, a new vulnerability may be introduced by a software update.

There are two paradigms for software as an entry point to the space system. First, there are exploited "bugs," or errors in the software. Simply put, software is a microcosm of the spacecraft, in that it takes an infinite amount of effort to design it correctly.[41] Cyber operators are skilled at identifying flaws and exploiting them to support their objectives. The second paradigm for a hostile cyber operation involves no known flaw in the software itself, but leverages the known behavior of software to render the target operationally ineffective. A classic example of this sort of hostile cyber operation is a denial of service attack.[42]

The supply chain is unquestionably a vector for hostile cyber operations, based on historic examples such as NotPetya and the SolarWinds US government data breach.[43] Outsourcing any element of the supply chain – software or hardware – or support activities, like facilities, maintenance, launch vehicle, and human resources, invites cyber risk.[44] This risk can be avoided if a decision

40 Mamatha Maheshwarappa, Marc Bowyer, & Christopher Bridges, "Software Defined Radio (SDR) Architecture to Support Multi-Satellite Communications," *2015 IEEE Aerospace Conference* (2015) https://ieeexplore.ieee.org/document/7119186.

41 Dave Akin, "Akin's Laws of Spacecraft Design" (n.d.) accessed January 31, 2021, https://spacecraft.ssl.umd.edu/akins_laws.html.

42 Qijun Gu & Peng Liu, "Denial of Service Attacks" (2007) https://s2.ist.psu.edu/paper/ddos-chap-gu-june-07.pdf.

43 Joe Panettieri, "Solarwinds Orion Security Breach: Cyberattack Timeline and Hacking Incident Details," *Channele2e* (2021) https://www.channele2e.com/technology/security/solarwinds-orion-breach-hacking-incident-timeline-and-updated-details/.

44 Paul Ashcroft, "Reducing Outsourcing Cyber Risks," *Today's CPA* (March/April 2018) https://www.tx.cpa/docs/default-source/communications/2018-today's-cpa/marchapril/techissues-march-april2018-today'scpa.pdf.

is made at the strategic level not to outsource anything, and to do everything in-house. This means vertically integrating the designing, building, testing, and operation of both the space and ground segments. SpaceX is notable as having taken this approach more than any other non-government institution in the space industry. However, this method has costs in terms of both time and money that may not be justifiable in all organizations that need to operate satellites. A more middle-of-the-road approach might involve limiting outsourcing to those elements of the supply chain or support work that an institution lacks the knowledge base to execute in-house, conducting security audits, and requiring outsourcing providers to maintain cybersecurity certifications. In short, "Trust, but verify."[45]

3.3 *Characterizing Space Cyber Threats*

One of the issues in computing, and in security in particular, is the visualization of abstract concepts, especially when they have a very broad scope. In "*The Mission as a Tree: A Novel Approach to Identifying Cyber Threats to Satellites*" the authors attempt to resolve this for missions within the scope of their paper. They map the Open Threat Taxonomy to uncrewed spacecraft.[46] This leads to a visualization of cyber threats to space missions that looks similar to a data structure that software developers call a tree. The paper provides a framework for conversations at a high level about the technical characteristics of cyber threats to a space mission. This is a necessary first step to an analysis of the domain from legal and policy perspectives.

The first subtree of the threat tree is the Threat Agents Tree (Figure 3.1). It is populated with all the individuals and institutions who might wish to harm a mission through cyber means and have the capabilities to do such harm. Threat agents need to be identified before any of the other subtrees because their capabilities and limitations will constrain the development of the other subtrees. For example, a British national security satellite like Skynet does not need to worry about commercial competitors' cybersecurity threats, whereas foreign states likely present much more substantive and credible threats to it.

The next subtree is the Threat Target Tree (Figure 3.2). This tree visualizes all the elements of the mission through which a cyber-attack could be introduced.

45 Ronald Reagan, "Remarks on Signing the Intermediate-Range Nuclear Forces Treaty," Ronald Reagan Presidential Library & Museum (8 December 1987) https://www.reaganlibrary.gov/archives/speech/remarks-signing-intermediate-range-nuclear-forces-treaty.

46 Sébastien Bonnart et al, "The Mission as a Tree: A Novel Approach to Identifying Cyber Threats to Satellites," International Astronautical Congress 2020: CyberSpace Edition (2020).

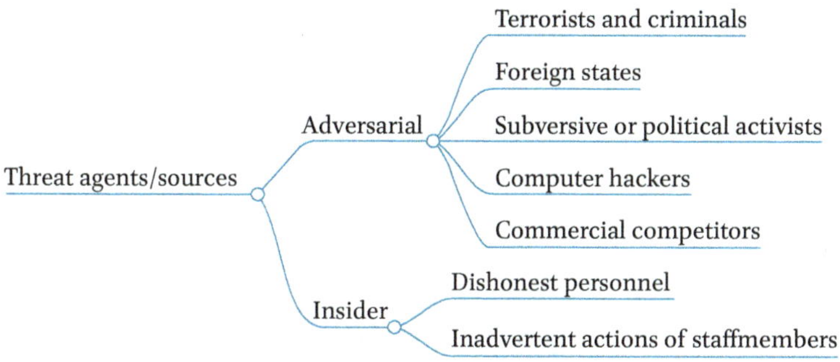

FIGURE 3.1 Illustrative threat agents tree from Bonnart et al., "The mission as a tree"

This includes places where mission- or security-critical data is stored, media by which it is transmitted, and personnel who have the authority to access it. A thorough Threat Target Tree considers hardware, software, process, systems, and human vulnerabilities that the identified Threat Agents have the capability to compromise. This subtree presents unique difficulties because its development requires an honest and self-critical assessment not just of the mission, but of each individual and institution that supports the mission – from the processors in components to nontechnical support staff at the prime contractor to cybersecurity and access control measures in place at the machine shop where mechanical components are fabricated.

The third subtree is the Threat Action Tree (Figure 3.3). This maps out all the ways that a Threat Agent could compromise a Threat Target in the cyber domain. The four most common types of cyber-attacks in general are interruption of connectivity, interception of data, modification of data, and fabrication of data. Each of these actions can be done in different ways, depending on the Threat Target. Threat actions to spacecraft in the cyber domain will be discussed in more detail in the next section.

The Threat Consequences Tree (Figure 3.4) considers the possible effects of each leaf of the Threat Action Tree on the mission. The consequences of cyber attacks to spacecraft will be discussed in more detail in the next section.

Mission planners can quantify the likelihood of a threat agent taking a threat action against each possible threat target for that action, and the probability of any relevant threat consequence arising from that action. This allows mission planners to easily identify what the likely cybersecurity risks to their architectures are and efficiently allocate more resources to mitigate the more likely threats.

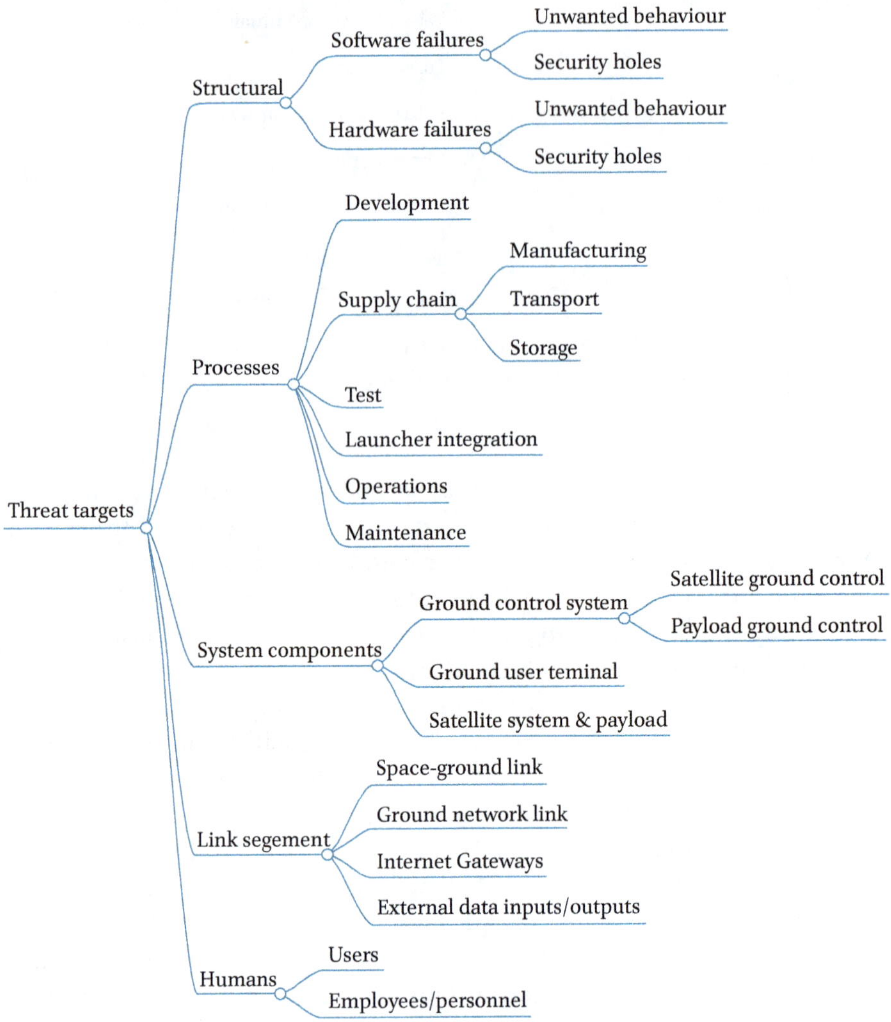

FIGURE 3.2 Threat target tree from Bonnart et al., "The mission as a tree"

The Threat Consequences subtree, however, will likely be the most difficult to quantify, because cyber-attacks have, relative to electronic or kinetic attacks, much more aleatory risk. Unlike mainstream cybersecurity where one would assume that the attacker crafted his action using a copy of the software[47] or hardware, it is currently expected not to be the case for most assets

47 E. Kenneth Hong Fong, David A. Wheeler, & Amy E. Henninger, *State-of-the-Art Resources (SOAR) for Software Vulnerability Detection, Test, and Evaluation* (IDA 2016)

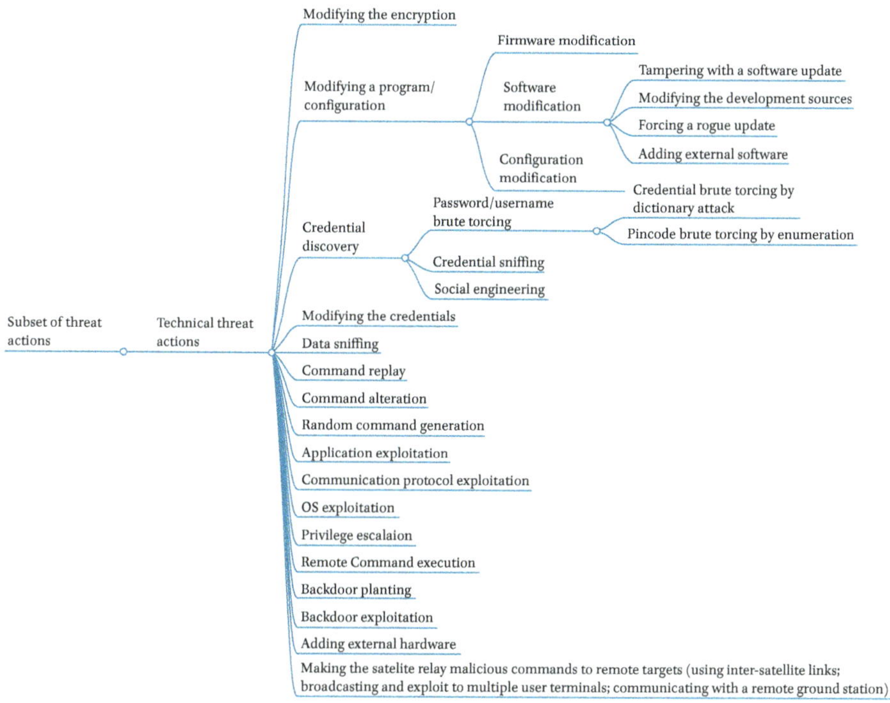

FIGURE 3.3 Illustrative sub-section of a threat action tree from Bonnart et al., "The mission as a tree"

in space. The unknown unknowns make it more difficult for a threat agent to anticipate precisely how their actions will affect their threat target. If a threat agent cannot understand in advance the effects of their attack, it must be that much more complicated for the mission operator to plan for the effects of cyber-attacks. This planning, however, may well be crucial to ensure that the mission can recover from an attack. The expected confidentiality of the hardware and software is presented here as a hypothesis and could be countered by the attacker through the possibility of initial successful ground-based attacks revealing onboard software, hardware designs, and documentation.

This section presented an overview of previous hostile cyber operations against space systems and outlined possible entry points for an attack and

---

https://www.ida.org/research-and-publications/publications/all/s/st/stateoftheart-resources-soar-for-software-vulnerability-detection-test-and-evaluation-2016.

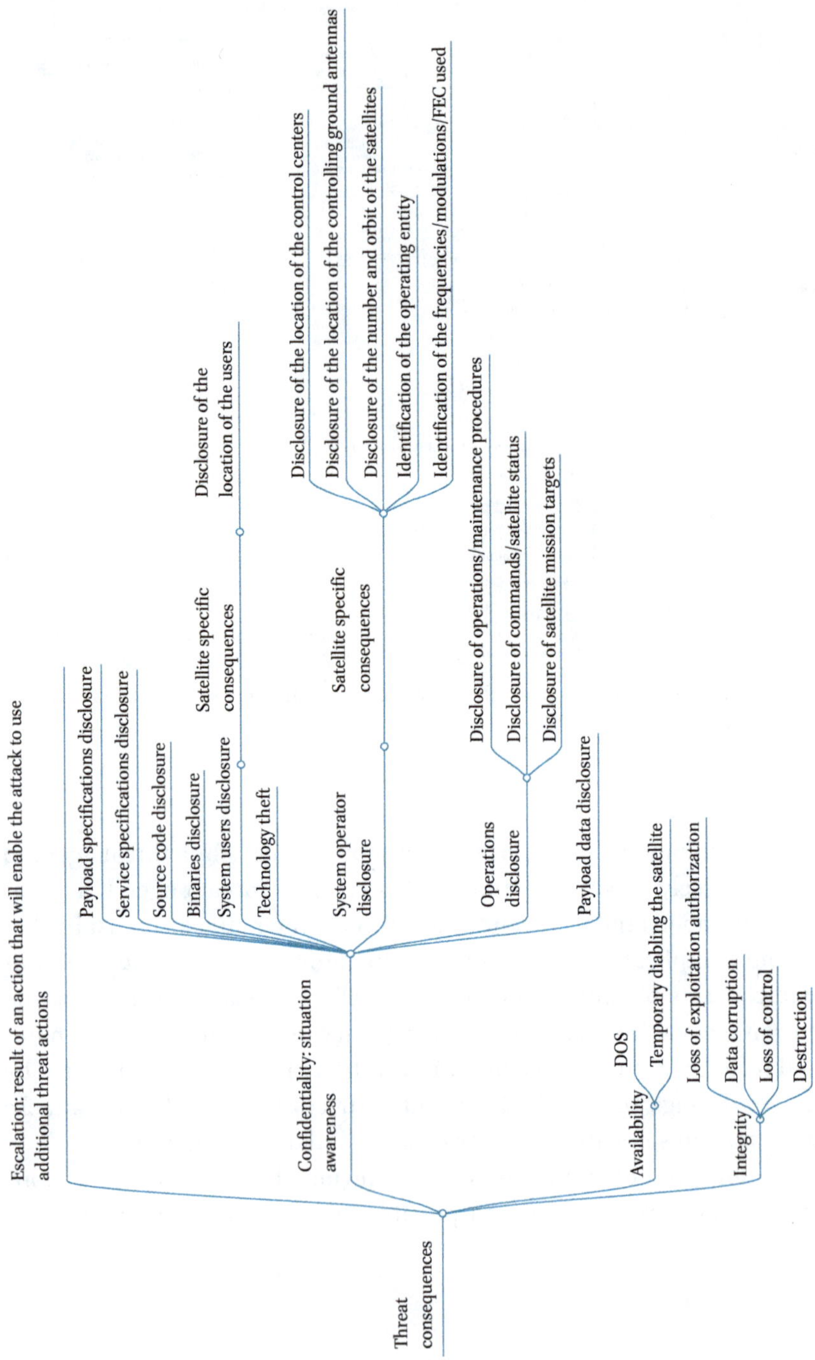

FIGURE 3.4 Illustrative threat consequences tree from Bonnart et al., "The mission as a tree"

concluded by presenting the use of trees in order to inventory and visualize threats.

4 Protective Measures to Boost Cyber Resilience of Space Assets

After having described the space environment and space mission's cyber threats, Section 4 shows how they can be analyzed as risks. Section 4.2 addresses the processes of reconstructing a system after a breach and the potential for response through international collaboration. Section 4.3 outlines IT governance frameworks, which is part of corporate governance. These frameworks facilitate means of specifying decisions, rights, and accountability tied to an organization's use of technology. Finally, Section 4.4 proposes technical strategies that an entity can adopt to mitigate the risks, including *inter alia* methods to assure software and to protect its integrity.

4.1 *Impact and Effects of Hostile Cyber Operations*

4.1.1 Long-Term Consequences on the Activities, Relationships, and Environment

Given the ultra-hazardous nature of outer space, every hostile cyber operation can have an impact on space activities. The unforgiving space environment presents a concerning likelihood of increased risk/impact due to constraints on recovery abilities and limitations on resilience. The impact of these operations might have long-term or short-term consequences based on the different nature and purposes of the targeted system and the kind of attack perpetrated against the system/satellite.

In order to define the impact and effects of hostile operations, it is important to estimate the risk related to an event. This is defined by two parameters: the first is the likelihood of the event occurring, while the second is the severity/impact of the event's consequences. By crossing these two parameters, a matrix can be created through which five categories of risk can be identified, namely: 'extreme,' 'major,' 'moderate,' 'minor,' and 'incidental.'

This "heat map" matrix (Figure 3.5) allows for the two-dimensional identification of the potential risk impact that every hostile operation can create.[48]

Assessing space activities allows for a better comprehension of the risk and therefore a better comprehension on how to diminish the impact or the

48 Patchin Curtis & Mark Carey, *Risk Assessment in Practice* (Committee of Sponsoring Organizations of the Treadway Commission, 2012).

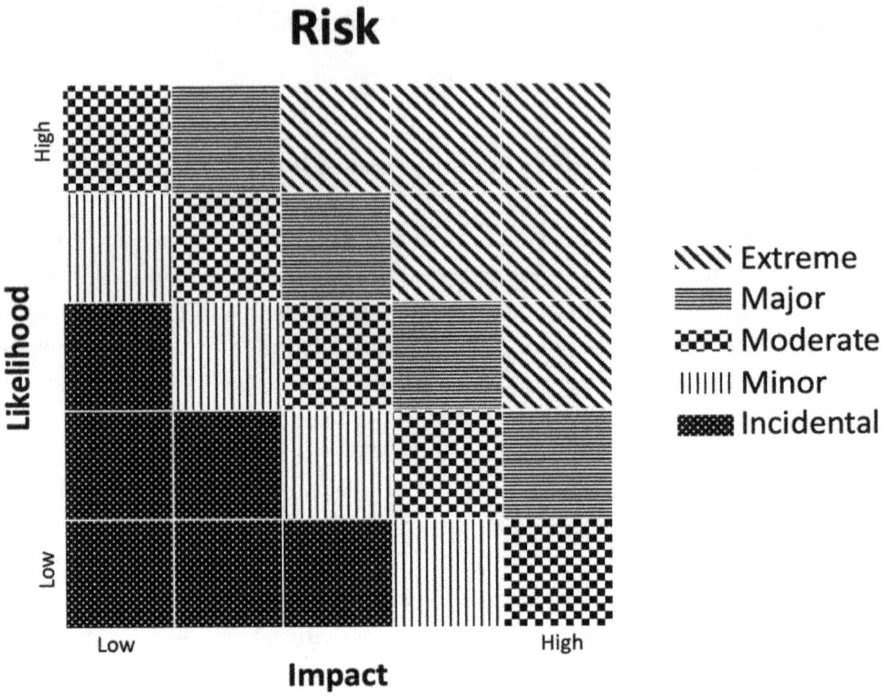

FIGURE 3.5 Illustrative heat-map

likelihood of an event. By doing so, it is possible to create a more stable system that conducts activities in a safer and more resilient structure.

Space capabilities provide a wide range of applications such as earth-observation, communication, exploration, and positioning, navigation, and timing (PNT).

- Earth-observation satellites provide information services based on Earth observation data from orbit. These systems provide land monitoring, emergency management, atmosphere monitoring, maritime environment monitoring, climate change, and security applications. These services can be used both for military and civil purposes. Civilian Earth measurable benefits from Earth Observation activities range from agriculture yields improvement, disaster risk management, famine prevention, water management, weather forecasting, to plane travel time forecasting.
- Communications satellites (SATCOM) relay and amplify radio telecommunications signals. These satellites provide telecommunications, broadcasting, and data communications services over wide areas of the globe.

- Exploration satellites aim to provide information on outer space or on celestial bodies. With the development of new activities planned to be carried out on celestial bodies, a new trend is emerging. The emergence of space mining may boost the space economy and subsequently, the systems may become ideal targets to disrupt another State's or company's activity.
- Positioning, Navigation, and Timing (PNT) satellites aim to provide accurate positioning and timing information. These space-based assets are essential for the performance of everyday life since they are used for precision targeting, tracking, and provision of precise timing that is also vital for the function of economic and banking networks.[49]

With the increasing number of satellites launched in different orbits, and the creation of new constellations, the number of entry points via which attackers may enter has increased. Security-related space infrastructure has suffered a decline of attention over the years, leaving it vulnerable to hostile cyber operations.[50]

The different space applications may lead to different long-term consequences related to hostile cyber operations. When a hostile cyber operation occurs, the targeted victim faces numerous consequences including the appropriation of sensitive information. Earth Observation satellites operated by civilians may possess classified information that should not be disclosed and needs to be protected.

Any kind of interruption of a space activity may cause disastrous outcomes due to the ultra-hazardous environment. The disruption, however, can be partial and non-damaging to any system of the satellite. In this case, the system would be momentarily compromised and would not lead to any major consequences. However, if the system is permanently compromised the launching State would face numerous consequences. This could result in a monetary loss due to the fact that systems need to be replaced. Subsequently, the whole mission could be threatened because it needs to redevelop new technologies to prevent the repetition of such outcomes.

Disruption of a single system can threaten an entire mission and its activities. The interruption of communication during a mission may lead to the loss

49 Antonio Carlo, Lacroix & Zarkan, "The Challenge of Protecting Space-based Assets Against Cyber Threats," International Astronautical Congress 2020: Cyberspace Edition (2020).

50 Alex Mathew, "Cyber Security – How Vulnerable are Satellites to Cyberattacks" *International Journal for Research in Applied Science & Engineering Technology*, v. 7/III (2019): 2427–2430, http://doi.org/10.22214/ijraset.2019.3443.

of control of the space segment and lead to the collision of satellites. The intent of an attack could be to cause a collision between satellites turning the satellite itself into a weapon – also known as an anti-satellite weapon (ASAT).[51] The destruction of a space object would result in the creation of a large amount of space debris making utilisation of the orbit impossible due to the danger that those objects would pose. Collisions of debris larger than 10 cm may result in catastrophes, releasing hazardous debris clouds which can lead to an escalatory chain reaction and potentially make some orbital zones unusable.[52]

4.2 *Reconstructing and Incident Response*

As technology continues to evolve, so do the opportunities and challenges it poses. In particular, the ever-increasing dependence on technologies exposes stakeholders to a whole set of risks associated with cyberattacks. Hostile cyber actors are continuously trying to break into close and highly secure systems while the cyber threat landscape continues to expand and evolve rapidly.[53] To counter these issues, security and defence of the space systems need to be updated and secured. Many governments, companies, and institutions have created *ad hoc* Computer Emergency Response Teams (CERTs) and Computer Security Incident Response Teams (CSIRTs) coordinated by Security Operational Centres (SOCs) in order to pre-empt possible cyber events. However, when these entities do not manage to stop an attack there are different ways to deal with the reconstruction of infrastructure. Attacked entities have to face not only the damage of the attack itself, but also its consequences such as the loss of trust and reputation. The reconstruction of a stronger system should be done by private-public partnerships (PPPs), technical personnel, and lawyers in parallel.

Strong national and international cooperation could lead to the sharing of best practices and unique know-how to prevent, strengthen, and reconstruct a system after a cyber event. Information Sharing and Analysis Centres (ISACs) were created in order to answer this need, to make cyber threat data and best practices more accessible internationally. ISACs also provide a central resource

51 John Pike, "The Military Uses of Outer Space" *SIPRI Yearbook 2002: Armaments, Disarmaments and International Security* (2003): 613–655.

52 Antonio Carlo & Giannakou, "Active Debris Removal: The Legal Challenges and the Way Forward," *Proceedings of the AIDAA XXV Congress of Aeronautics and Astronautics* (2019): 1261–1273.

53 Center for Strategic and International Studies, *Significant Cyber Incidents since 2006* (2020) https://csis-website-prod.s3.amazonaws.com/s3fs-public/201218_Significant_Cyber_Events.pdf.

for gathering information on cyber threats and events to critical infrastructure. Further, constant monitoring of the activities and risk assessment may lead to the reduction of such events. For instance, Estonia entrusted terabytes of information on its citizens to Luxembourg after assessing that this option could prevent cyberattacks directed at gathering this information.[54] Such sharing of data led to so-called cyber diplomacy between two allied countries within the European Union.

Cyber diplomacy drives International Organizations to establish strong cooperation.[55] Such as, in 2003, when the European Union (EU) and the North Atlantic Treaty Organization (NATO) signed the "Berlin Plus" agreement, which established the milestone principle of allowing the European Union the possibility to use NATO forces when necessary. This cooperation was successfully implemented in Macedonia and Bosnia. In 2016 the European Union and NATO signed a Technical Arrangement to facilitate technical info-sharing between CERT-EU and NATO Computer Incident Response Capability (NCIRC) leading to an international cooperation in information sharing.[56] In particular, the NATO Cooperative Cyber Defence Centre of Excellence (NATO CCDCOE) is now liaising with the European Defence Agency (EDA) by exchanging information on common topics of concern. To construct a strong and resilient system, public and private cooperation and cyber diplomacy are essential together with the establishment of CERTs and SOCs that monitor and organize the cyber operations.

Section 4.1 has outlined the methodologically process of defining and reacting to a cyber risk, including responses from international cooperation ranking from *ad hoc* response teams to international cooperation in EU and NATO. The following part will focus on the internal organisational responses processes in the shape of ICT Governance Strategies.

54 Yuliya Talmazan, "Data Security Meets Diplomacy: Why Estonia is Storing its Data in Luxembourg," *NBC News* (2019) https://www.nbcnews.com/news/world/data-security-meets-diplomacy-why-estonia-storing-its-data-luxembourg-n1018171.

55 Attila Mesterhazy, *NATO-EU Cooperation after Warsaw*, NATO Parliamentary Assembly, Defence and Security Committee Report (2017) https://www.nato-pa.int/download-file?filename=/sites/default/files/2017-11/2017%20-%20163%20DSCTC%2017%20E%20rev%201%20fin%20-%20EU%20AND%20NATO%20COOPERATION%20-%20MESTERHAZY%20REPORT.pdf.

56 NATO, "NATO and the European Union Enhance Cyber Defence Cooperation" (10 February 2016) https://www.nato.int/cps/en/natohq/news_127836.htm.

4.3 *ICT Governance Strategies*

The promotion of an Information and Communications Technology (ICT) governance framework for space-based assets represents a vital step toward improving cyber resilience, reducing the incidence of catastrophic cyber incidents, and conducive to the maintenance of peace and stability across the final frontier. Consequently, existing ICT governance frameworks across the information security and technology profession provides opportunities for individual space enterprises to pick and devise frameworks suited to their individual circumstances.

The application of ICT governance is pertinent in protecting space-based assets against cyber threats from an organizational perspective. This section addresses the preemptive, proactive, and remedial processes in promoting a best-practice approach to cyber-threat intelligence, determining the taxonomy of threats, and in advancing measures conducive to estimating cyber-insurance covers for space assets. Improving ICT governance mechanisms concerning space-related technologies are a vital part in encouraging positive behaviors, improving top-level decision making, reducing the possibility and effects of catastrophic incidents, and enabling better strategic planning vis-a-vis cybersecurity matters.

The significant risk posed by potential cyberattacks against space assets warrant the need for a cybersecurity framework and control structure. ICT governance frameworks help organizations assess and manage the cyber risks across an expanded attack surface.

Specific challenges arise in the application of terrestrial ICT governance framework to space-based technologies and systems. Some of these challenges include: compliance with international treaties, national space laws, the difficulties associated with access to space, the harsh outer space environment, and the difficulty of affecting physical repairs to space-based infrastructure. This is complemented by traditional information security risks posed to ICT infrastructure – including data breaches, cyberattacks, supply chain cybersecurity, and insider threats. Within this context, the tailored application of relevant governance frameworks and standards assumes a vital role in creating a safe and sustainable outer space environment.

4.3.1 Context

ICT governance exists as a subset of corporate governance, which represents a system of directing and controlling the action of the governing organization. ICT governance also ensures that businesses have the proper decision-making processes and controls in place to balance the interests of all stakeholders.[57] Furthermore, the concept of management can be distinguished from that of governance in several aspects. Management involves the planning, building, and running of activities in alignment with the directions set by the governance body to achieve the enterprise objectives. They are usually established by executives at the highest management level (C-level) and cover all functions and processes to govern and manage the organization at large.

Consequently, the objective of ICT governance seeks to facilitate the means of specifying the decision, rights, and accountability framework tied to an organization's use of technology. The process encourages desirable behaviors in the use of technology and technical systems across both public and private sector organizations.

A codified governance framework takes stakeholders' interests into account, as well as the needs of staff and the processes they follow. Governance ensures that stakeholder needs, conditions and options are evaluated to determine balanced, agreed-upon enterprise objectives to be achieved; setting direction through prioritization and decision making; and monitoring performance and compliance against agreed-on directions and objects.

The need for an ICT governance framework for space is driven by several realities.[58] First, the notion of continuous expansion, which is when an innovative space sector is contingent upon increased competitive offerings across a variety of space companies. This accounts for the needs and requirements of various stakeholders. This results in customers wanting more secure products and services, investors requesting increased returns, and regulators seeking increased accountability and responsibility.

Second, the realization of size and complexity as traits inherent to the space industry and environment. Noting predictions of future trillion-dollar space-based enterprises, the rise of mega corporations in the outer space domain necessitates the need for standards and guidance. The reason for standards and guidance is to empower executives and managers to implement effective whole-of-organization ICT governance measures.[59]

---

57 "What is IT Governance?" *IT Governance* (2020) https://www.itgovernance.co.uk/it_governance.

58 Deloitte, *Developing an Effective Governance Operating Model – A Guide for Financial Services Boards and Management Teams* (Deloitte, 2013): 2.

59 Deepak Sethi, "The First Trillionaire Will Be Made in Space Mining," *Medium* (11 December 2020) https://medium.com/datadriveninvestor/the-first-trillionaire-will-be-made-in-space-mining-cea665c1b00d.

Third, the emergence of new legislative instruments and regulations concerning outer space applications. Noting the possibility of space companies such as Swarm Technologies conducting activities outside government authorization,[60] both regulatory changes and lapses in governance are likely to continue. This highlights the potential need for executives and managers to extend governance processes deeper into their organizations.

The implementation of an ICT Governance Framework is predicated upon several major elements. First, structure and policy define the decision process, which includes outlining the policies and individual responsibilities to be created.[61] Second, procedure and process specify how decisions are made and what processes exist to propose and approve investments. Third, communication involving the mechanisms involved in communicating ICT investment decisions to the board of directors, employees, and shareholders.

These elements span the formation of a strategic vision for an organization, and coordination between different pieces of ICT-related work and infrastructure. Proper application of an ICT governance framework can result directly in increases to productivity, higher quality product offerings, and improved financial performance. Conversely, poor governance can result in programmatic waste, needless and confusing bureaucracy, diminished overall financial performance governance, and ultimately the demise of an organization.[62]

4.3.2 ICT Governance Frameworks

The notion of a "framework" represents a conceptual structure, defined by the governance of an organization to set out policies, principles, and a model demonstrating ICT governance tasks and activities within the organization.[63] Frameworks embody a top-down approach, identifying the main stakeholders first, along with their needs and appetite for risk. This is followed by identifying the stakeholders who will manage policies on a day-to-day basis. As opposed to a "guideline," frameworks provide for clear controls and policies that need to

60 Loren Gush, "Company that Launched Satellites without Permission Gets New License to Launch More Probes," *The Verge* (4 October 2018) https://www.theverge.com/2018/10/4/17928452/swarm-technologies-spacebees-satellites-spacex-falcon-9-fcc-license.

61 "IT Governance Framework," *CIO Wiki* (2020) https://cio-wiki.org/wiki/IT_Governance_Framework.

62 Australian Public Service Commission, "Building Better Governance' on Australian Government" (12 June 2018) https://www.apsc.gov.au/building-better-governance.

63 "Understanding Guidelines, Frameworks and Standards from a Governance Standpoint," *Spector* (12 September 2019) https://www.spector.ie/blog/understanding-guidelines-frameworks-and-standards-from-a-governance-standpoint/.

be in place to adhere to. Presently, within the cybersecurity industry there exist several ICT governance frameworks of note.

The IT Infrastructure Library (ITIL),[64] developed by the UK Cabinet Office as a library of best-practice processes for IT service management, has been widely adopted around the world. ITIL represents a framework that focuses on and enables ICT services to be managed across their lifecycle. The framework is supported by ISO/IEC 20000:2011, against which independent certification can be achieved, and structured across several areas – including service strategy, service design, service transition, service operation, and continuous service improvement.

COBIT19,[65] an internationally recognized ICT governance control framework that aims to connect business goals to technical goals, assigns objectives and duties to both business and ICT leaders. The framework helps organizations meet contemporary business challenges across regulatory compliance, risk management, in aligning their technology strategy with organizational goals. The underlying rationale of COBIT19 is highlighted within its six core principles, representing a design philosophy: 1) providing stakeholder value; 2) enabling a holistic approach; 3) dynamic governance system; 4) governance distinct from management; 5) tailored to enterprise needs; and 6) covering the enterprise end-to-end.

Val IT[66] is a governance framework utilized to create business value from IT investments. Developed by Information Systems Audit and Control Association (ISACA), the framework is a comprehensive and pragmatic organizing framework that enables the creation of business value from ICT-enabled investments. Val IT integrates a set of practical and proven governance principles, processes, practices and supporting guidelines that help boards and enterprise leaders optimize the realization of value from ICT investments. The framework's main processes encompass value governance, portfolio management, and investment management.

In summary, it must be emphasized that none of the ICT frameworks covered represent a single definitive solution to improving an organizations' cyber resilience. The creation of an ICT framework does not specifically need to derive from one source. Organizations can elect to adopt a tailored approach

64 Stephen Watts, "COBIT vs ITIL: IT Governance Frameworks," *BMC blogs* (15 May 2017) https://www.bmc.com/blogs/cobit-vs-itil-understanding-governance-frameworks/.

65 Kim Lindros, "What Is IT Governance? A Formal Way to Align IT & Business Strategy," *CIO* (1 August 2017) https://www.cio.com/article/2438931/governanceit-governance-definition-and-solutions.html.

66 "VAL IT Framework," *CIO Wiki* (2020) https://cio-wiki.org/wiki/Val_IT_Framework.

in drawing from several frameworks, and their underlying standards to develop their own structure, as suited to the unique requirements and capabilities of each organization.

4.3.3 US Approach to IT Governance in Space

The US government has adopted an interagency process for governance and policy coordination on outer space affairs.[67] This encompasses the Federal Communications Commission (FCC), the Federal Aviation Administration (FAA), the Department of Commerce, NASA, and the Department of Defense. The Executive Branch of the US government has continuously updated and reviewed its authorization and oversight framework for private sector space activities. Consequently, a sectoral approach to information security and cybersecurity matters across each government body would prove to be overly bureaucratic, slow, and unsustainable.

Since 2014, the US federal governance structure for general ICT-based cybersecurity has made strides with the maturation of the National Institute of Standards and Technology (NIST) Risk Management Framework and Cybersecurity Framework. NIST cybersecurity maturity standards and guidelines are best-suited in covering ground-based space infrastructure and assets by assisting organizations in improving their cybersecurity measures and best practices. However, these are not directly applicable to the space domain. While efforts have been made to mold these frameworks for space systems (per the Committee on National Security Systems Instruction – 1253F), uniformity is deficient and updated standards for spacecraft and their associated IoT systems are necessary.

However, overarching governance and policies lack the necessary integration between cybersecurity and the space domain. Governance efforts in the space and cyber domains remain highly siloed, which may limit meaningful progress. Strategy documents covering the improvement of cybersecurity in the space domain include the 2017 National Security Strategy, 2018 National Cyber Strategy, Space Policy Directive-3, and Space Policy Directive-5 (SPD-5).[68] The most relevant is SPD-5, issued by the Trump administration in September 2020, representing a government framework incorporating cybersecurity into

67 Daniel L. Oltrogge & Ian A. Christensen, "Space Governance in the Newspace Era", *Journal of Space Safety Engineering* v. 7, 436 (2020).

68 Presidential Memoranda, "Memorandum on Space Policy Directive-5—Cybersecurity Principles for Space Systems" (4 September 2020) https://trumpwhitehouse.archives.gov/presidential-actions/memorandum-space-policy-directive-5-cybersecurity-principles-space-systems/.

all phases of space system development. The intent behind SPD-5 is to develop a culture of prevention, active defense, risk management, and the sharing of best practices.[69] This includes security by design, cybersecurity hygiene practices, supply chain cybersecurity, and the leveraging of widely adopted best practices. However, while SPD-5 serves as a high-level policy direction, it should not be interpreted as a substantive ICT governance framework or standards.

A broader literature analysis highlighting research from Chatham House describes the deficiencies on a global scale in relation to NATO. While the majority of documents addressing cybersecurity issues in space outline policy and governance challenges, few are solution-oriented in reducing cyber risk to space systems concerning human spaceflight vehicles.

In lieu of the development of a structured ICT governance framework by the US government, a threat-based principles approach to managing cybersecurity risks to spacecraft provides an alternate means of addressing this concern. This is predicated upon the application of defense-in-depth (DiD) principles to reduce the risk of cyberattack on a spacecraft. These principles should provide decision-makers, acquisition professionals, program managers, and system designers alike with considerations while acquiring and designing cyber-resilient spacecraft.

4.3.4 Benefits of ICT Governance for Space

The adoption of ICT governance framework covering space-based assets is conducive to boosting organizational cyber resilience. From a general perspective, the clear instructions and established best practice information technology standards advanced play a significant role in improving performance and promoting adaptability and responsiveness to changes in the cyber-threat environment.[70] These organizational and business improvements flow from the potential of ICT governance to address several key information security challenges affecting cybersecurity for outer space assets.

First, a tailored ICT governance framework addresses the unique environmental, technical, and policy challenges associated with outer space, elevating the protection of space-based assets against cyber threats. A framework helps both ordinary employees and senior management understand and

69 Jonathan Blair, "Space Policy Directive-5 Establishes Comprehensive Cybersecurity Policy for Space Systems," LMI Advisors (4 September 2020) https://www.lmiadvisors.com/space-policy-directive-5-establishes-comprehensive-cybersecurity-policy-for-space-systems/.

70 "6 Benefits of Good IT Governance," *O'Reilly* (2021) https://www.oreilly.com/library/view/governance-of-it/9781780171548/19_ch06.xhtml.

communicate about the business risk and threat landscape within which the business operates. This feeds into Business Continuity Management (BCM) in the creation of interdependent contingency planning and response operations documents. These measures help preserve competitive advantages, keep business functions, and enable ICT operations in the event of a cyberattack upon both space-based assets and their ground-based infrastructure.[71]

Second, an adaptable ICT governance framework promotes novel approaches to the identification of cyber threats to satellites. The integration of cyber risk identification standards under a tailored ICT governance framework helps identify, assess, and drive the management of residual risk.[72] Within the outer space context, it is established that malicious actors can be sorted into various categories (Figure 3.1) and summarised into four main groups – including Nation State Actors, Private Economic Actors, Hacktivists/ Natural Persons, and International Entities. The integration of ISO/IEC 385000 standards herein is beneficial in recognising the specific interests and scope of activities of each of these actors within the outer space context, and illustrating the different levels of sophistication within their offensive cyber capabilities targeting space-based and ground-based ICT networks for satellites.[73]

4.4 *Technical Strategies*

After having identified governance strategies to cyber threats above, Section 4.4 presents an overview of the technical strategies to be adopted in space systems to mitigate risks related to cyberattacks. A system's security policy combines a series of intended and performed operations with respect to security. Different areas of actions concur to operate and integrate inside a space system maintaining the requested level of security. They are explored in the following paragraphs.

4.4.1 Software Assurance Methods

Software assurance risks are due to accidental design or implementation errors that can provoke failures or worse hazards and accidents. In a space system the exploitations of software vulnerabilities can cause undesirable events or

71 Brahum Herbane et al., "Business Continuity Management: Time for a Strategic Role?" *Long Range Planning,* v. 37/5 (2004): 435.

72 "Cyber Risk Identification," *Cyberwatching.eu* (2021) https://www.cyberwatching.eu/cyber-risk-identification.

73 Australian Cyber Security Centre, "Using a Risk Management Framework" (2021) http://cyber.gov.au/acsc/view-all-content/guidance/applying-risk-based-approach-cyber-security.

system damage that can result in the loss of spacecraft's control, data or even of the mission[25]. Software safety best practices and methodologies compliant with Safety Standards[74] should be performed during the entire software lifecycle. The security by design approach is defined by six phases: 1) identification of requirements; 2) design; 3) implementation; 4) testing and verification; 5) release; and 6) maintenance.

In the first phase, clear security requirements are defined, also with respect to requested levels of security of developed software. System security architecture and design guidelines are specified in the design phase. The attacker's point of view is considered, and threat modelling and mitigation planning is required. In the implementation phase, secure programming practices[75] should be taken into account. The use of a combination of manual and automated tools for code generation, analysis, and testing minimize possible human errors and detect relevant bugs that can lead to vulnerabilities. In the testing and verification phase, diversified vulnerability scanning tools give the overall detection and analysis of vulnerabilities. Penetration testing of the system, manual or automated, should be performed by independent and expert teams and they could be both internal and external (external are suggested). Automated tools give a range of services for identifying and exploiting security weaknesses.[76] Regarding the release and maintenance of software, space missions should be designed to support on-going upgrades of all systems including the space segment in order to prevent attacks based on already known and exploited vulnerabilities.

4.4.2 Software and Firmware Integrity Protections

The integrity of a platform's firmware and software is crucial to ensure the programmed behaviour of a system without malware in the space domain. Attacks on the firmware could affect the device's operations injecting malicious functionality that compromises interoperability within the platform. As suggested by Bailey and his fellow authors, only authenticated updates and proper configuration management must be implemented for all software and firmware residing in any system.[77] The Root of Trust guarantees the security

74 Bryan O'Connor, *"NASA Software Safety Guidebook,"* NASA Technical Standard NASA-GB-8719.13 (2004).

75 Owasp.org, *OWASP Secure Coding Practices-Quick Reference Guide* (2021) https://owasp.org/www-project-secure-coding-practices-quick-reference-guide.

76 Gilberto Najera-Gutierrez et al., *"Web Penetration Testing with Kali Linux: Explore the Methods and Tools of Ethical Hacking with Kali Linux"* (Packt Publishing Ltd, 2018).

77 B. Bailey et al., *Defending Spacecraft in the Cyber Domain* (The Aerospace Corporation 2019).

mechanism of detection, protection, and recovery of firmware code and critical data. A Root of Trust is a source that provides security functions and it is typically the first element in a Chain of Trust. Only authenticated and authorized firmware update mechanisms must be allowed. An updated image is considered authentic if the source and integrity can be successfully verified.[78] The authentication is provided by means of cryptographic signature verification, through a Root of Trust for Update. The authorization is reached by mechanisms that legitimize the update of firmware (that is by the user, managed updates, manual recovery, *etc.*). The spacecraft and the other critical space systems, such as the ground station, should be provided with automatic recovery in such a way that they are able to detect a possible corruption of a firmware image. After detecting the modification, the systems should be able to recover from a backup firmware stored in a secure location.[55]

4.4.3 SIEMs for Logging Onboard Events and Identification and Prevention Systems

In a typical security incident and event management system (SIEM), the event sources are differentiated and cover possible risk interfaces (that is network device, application server, authentication device, *etc.*). The events (for example, logging data) are then normalized and sent to the security management platform, which analyzes them in a window and triggers security alerts to the terminal. The events are also sent to the archival forensic analysis database that maintains the events for a longer period.[25] Both the spacecraft and the ground station should maintain an independent trace of the occurring events. Commands received may be stored and sent to the ground through telemetry and then automatically checked to verify consistency between commands sent and commands received.[54] Experimenting with the creation or adoption of a security information and event management tool for space vehicles is suggested in "Defending Spacecraft in the Cyber Domain."[54] However, not having enough logging data is a limitation in characterizing and attributing cyberattacks. Log management includes guaranteeing the confidentiality, integrity, and availability of logs. To ensure that changes to archived logs are detected (that is, integrity), an option could be integrity checking, which consists of calculating a message digest for each file and storing the message digest securely.[79]

78 Andrew Regenscheid, "Platform Firmware Resiliency Guidelines," NIST Special Publication (SP) 800–193 (Draft) (2017).

79 Karen Kent & Murugiah Souppaya, "Guide to Computer Security Log Management," NIST SP 92 (2006): 1–72.

Analysis of the audit log periodically could be useful to review and report logs for urgent errors and warnings.

Currently, there exist several challenges in collecting, storing and analyzing events in a scalable and smart manner. A challenge to face is that the system should be able to learn from previous incidents, automating the correlations between alerts. Machine learning-based intrusion detection and prevention systems can block the detected anomalies and cyberattacks.

As suggested by Bailey and his fellow authors, intrusion detection systems should implement both signatures (derived from known cyber information and weakness of the system) and machine-learning-based anomaly detection techniques.[51] These systems can rely on different machine learning techniques such as Bayesian Network and Naive Bayes, Decision Tree and Decision Table, Random Forest and Random Tree, and Artificial Neural Network.[80] These algorithms should be trained on datasets that include available and standard space operations. As a result, a new research frontier is applying deep learning techniques to solve the current problems and challenges derived from applying classical machine learning algorithms (for instance diverse nature of datasets, growth in the number of unclassified new malwares, network traffic diversity *etc.*).[81]

4.4.4 Cryptographic Solutions and Crypto-agility

Cryptography is a method of protecting information through the use of algorithms and transformations – allowing for communication even in the presence of adversaries, given proper supporting protocols and management. The correct design and implementation of cryptographic solutions can offer confidentiality, data integrity, and authenticity for mission system data. Information security services, with cryptographic safeguards of sufficient security strength and reliable key management, should be implemented inside mission environments. The decreasing cost for hardware and the increasing interconnection of ground networks are two examples of reduction in attack costs, easing the process of gathering information unless sound cryptographic safeguards are in place. As a result, attackers can potentially create passive or actively malicious

80 Hamed Alqahtani et al., "Cyber Intrusion Detection Using Machine Learning Classification Techniques," *International Conference on Computing Science, Communication and Security* (Springer 2020): 121–131.

81 A.M. Aleesa et al., "Review of Intrusion Detection Systems Based on Deep Learning Techniques: Coherent Taxonomy, Challenges, Motivations, Recommendations, Substantial Analysis and Future Directions," *Neural Computing and Applications,* v. 32/14 (2020): 9827–9858.

ground stations that target mission information and communications. The Consultative Committee for Space Data Systems (CCSDS) also suggests that cryptographic algorithms and protocols can be utilized by civilian space missions to avoid loss of data or total mission loss, providing their systems and operations with the required communications protections.[82] In cryptography, however, the discovery of algorithm weaknesses, and the retirement of algorithms or other constructions, is inevitable. Other technical priorities, such as performance, are also considerations. Moreover, the phenomenon of quantum computation casts traditional or "classical" cryptographic algorithms in a new light, with some cryptosystems widely considered vulnerable[83] to sufficiently powerful quantum computers. For all these reasons, "crypto-agility" is emerging as an important requirement and valuable process inside any organization responsible for maintaining a system (or part of one) that relies on cryptography to protect missions. It is also worth noting that crypto-agility represents an important and challenging consideration for long missions, where security methods may have to remain robust for extended periods. Companies should plan and design capacity that allows them to quickly update cryptographic methods without significant change to information systems, to retain regulatory compliance, reduce the likelihood of errors in new implementations, and mitigate security risks.[84]

Section 4 has focused on the identification of risk for space systems and its responses. As has been illustrated, an all-around response is necessary in order to be protected against hostile cyber operations. These responses range from the creation of incident response teams, international cooperation, internal IT governance policies, and technology strategies that can be adopted into a space system in order to mitigate hostile cyber operations.

5 Application and Enforcement of the Law

The following sections of the chapter focus on the legal aftermath of a cyber operation. Section 5 deals with the public international law perspectives from an already established set of treaties and principles. It will therefore focus on

82 Consultative Committee for Space Data Systems, *CCSDS Cryptographic Algorithms. Recommendation for Space Data System Practices* (2019).

83 Vasileios Mavroeidis et al., "The Impact of Quantum Computing on Present Cryptography," arXiv preprint arXiv:1804.00200 (2018).

84 Lily Chen et al., "Report on Post-quantum Cryptography," v. 12 (US Department of Commerce, National Institute of Standards and Technology 2016).

State-to-State hostile cyber operations. Section 5.1 starts by outlining the main challenges of applying principles of international law to the novel threat that hostile cyber operations pose to States. This is followed by an investigation of the source of a cyber attack and the challenges relating to legal attribution under Section 5.2, from locating the source of the attack to the political willingness of States to publicly acknowledge State attribution of a hostile cyber operation. Whereas part A and B outline the challenges to the application of public international law to cyber operations, part C provides a practical example of how the rules under *jus ad bello* and *jus in bello* regarding collateral damages can be applied to cyber operations against space systems.

5.1 *The Context of Hostile Cyber Operations in International Law*

The intricate dematerialized domain of cyber operations poses challenges to the application of international law. After decades of world-wide development of cyber capabilities and the completion of countless hostile operations at the trans-national level, the international community is still struggling to create a proper regulatory framework for these types of activities. The reason behind this impasse is two-fold. First, the cyber domain's technical aspects hinder the conventional understanding and application of international law. Secondly, there is a certain reluctance – *rectius*, a lack of political will – by States with strong cyber capabilities to develop an international framework against hostile cyber operations.

5.1.1 Legal Responses to Cyber Issues

From a technical perspective, it is possible to identify two elements that are particularly problematic for the application of international law to cyber operations: 1) the constant evolution of technological capabilities, which poses a serious risk of obsolescence to any codification attempt; and 2) the issue of identifying the original source of cyber activities which can represent an obstacle to the application of the attributability principle.[85]

Due to the increased complexity when applied to the cyber world, attribution needs some further insights. Simply put, the issue of attribution from a legal perspective can be described in the following terms. Every system of law is based on a basic principle: whoever breaches a legal obligation is responsible for the consequences caused by that breach. However, in order to hold the wrongdoer responsible, the breach needs to be attributed to the wrongdoer

85 For an analysis of the issue of attribution from a non-legal perspective see below at Section 5.2.

through sufficient evidence that identifies that party as the cause of such breach.

Transposed in the realm of international cyber operations, this basic legal principle entails that any time a party conducts a hostile cyber operation against a foreign party, the latter cannot respond unless it is able to identify with evidence the source of the operation. This is true irrespective of the target's nature, whether it is private assets or public infrastructure. For civilian law enforcement authorities and governmental entities, attribution is an essential and necessary condition to further legal action.

From a practical perspective, attributing a cross-border cyber offense to a specific foreign party poses certain difficulties. The first layer of challenges comes from the specifics of cyber operations, which, as described in Section 5.2 can be performed from remote locations while concealing the operator's identity and remaining undetected for an extended period. The collection of digital evidence in foreign jurisdictions is an additional layer of challenges as it requires a transnational investigation.[86] In such cases, access to evidence entails the collaboration of the State where the source of the attack is located.[87]

Such collaboration is usually achieved by signing Mutual Legal Assistance Treaties (MLATs). MLATs are agreements between two or more countries to provide assistance on criminal legal matters.[88] However, even assuming that MLATs cover all States involved in a transnational cyber investigation, enforcing such treaties requires expertise and resources that are not accessible to all States. Developing nations may lack the capacity to adequately investigate and prosecute cybercrimes or assist in cross-border investigations, even if they have the willingness to comply.[89]

86 There are different actors that provide assistance in cross-border cybercrime investigations with the aim of facilitating collaborative efforts among international parties. Such actors are national criminal justice agencies, regional agencies, such as the European Union Agency for Law Enforcement Cooperation (Europol) promoting law enforcement cooperation in the European Union, and Eurojust promoting judicial cooperation in the European Union, and international agencies, such as INTERPOL (i.e., International Criminal Police Organization). For more information on the role and function of these actors see UNODC, "Who Conducts Cybercrime Investigation?" (n.d.) https://www.unodc.org/e4j/en/cybercrime/module-5/key-issues/who-conducts-cybercrime-investigations.html.

87 Dorothy Denning et al., *Internet Besieged: Countering Cyberspace Scofflaws* (ACM Press, 1998).

88 A good example of how MLATs work is provided by the EU, whose Member States collaborate under Council Act 2000/C 197/01 of 29 May 2000 and who also has signed MLATs with the US and Japan.

89 Alexandra Perloff-Giles, "Transnational Cyber Offenses: Overcoming Jurisdictional Challenges," *The Yale Journal of International Law*, v. 43/191 (2018): 207. See also: Jan

Moreover, collecting evidence is not enough. Legislative and adjudicative jurisdiction are established when the perpetrator is identified and a judgment is entered against the defendant. However, there is still the problem of extradition of foreign citizens. This issue requires either a treaty signed between the two States involved or a diplomatic agreement to extradite the wrongdoer. As a result, cyber operators conduct their activities in a domain dominated by little real threat of international legal liability.[90]

A possible solution to this situation could be a broadly ratified international agreement, harmonizing domestic regulations on cyber activities and providing a tool for facilitated cooperation among States. The first step in that direction was taken with the adoption of the Convention on Cybercrime, or the Budapest Convention, under the Council of Europe's auspices.[91] The Convention entered into force on 1 July 2004 and is open for signature by the member States and the non-member States that have participated in its elaboration and accession by other non-member States. The purpose of the Convention is to create a common policy aimed at protecting society against cybercrime, *inter alia*, by adopting appropriate legislation and fostering international cooperation. To this end, it contains different provisions on facilitating the detection, investigation, and prosecution of hostile cyber operations at both domestic and international levels. Furthermore, the Convention provides arrangements for fast and reliable international cooperation.[92]

Despite the positive result achieved with the Budapest Convention[93] and its considerable number of ratifications (65 as of January 2021),[94] the Convention is not beyond reproach. There is a reservation mechanism embedded in the Convention that allows different States to opt-out of some of its provisions. Moreover, missing definitions of key terms or using vague ones has lessened the efficacy of its provisions. Finally, the absence of enforcement mechanisms opens the door to inconsistencies in its implementation.[95]

Kleijssen et al., "Cybercrime, Evidence and Territoriality: Issues and Options," *Netherlands Yearbook of International Law 2016* (2016): 147 *et seq.*

90 Perloff-Giles, *Transnational Cyber Offenses*, 208.

91 Council of Europe, *Budapest Convention on Cybercrime*, ETS No. 185 (adopted in Budapest on 23 November 2001).

92 *Id.*, especially Art. 11 *et seq.*, but also Arts. 29 and 30.

93 For a recent account on the impact of this instrument see Council of Europe, *The Budapest Convention on Cybercrime: Benefits and Impact in Practice*, T-CY(2020)16 (13 July 2020).

94 See the list provided by the official website of the Budapest Convention, available at https://www.coe.int/en/web/conventions/full-list/-/conventions/treaty/185/signatures?p_auth=CokA8O8d.

95 For more on the skepticism over the Budapest Convention see Allison Peters et al., "Countering the Cyber Enforcement Gap: Strengthening Global Capacity on Cybercrime,"

In parallel to the Budapest Convention, which is mainly the expression of like-minded Western States, there have also been other regional efforts to promote international agreements on hostile cyber activities. Examples are the 2002 *Asia-Pacific Economic Cooperation* (APEC) *Cybersecurity Strategy* and the subsequent 2005 APEC *Strategy to Ensure a Trusted, Secure and Sustainable Online Environment*, which aim at promoting information and network security, harmonising frameworks for securing transactions and communications, and combating cybercrime. The 2005 *Economic Community of West African States* (ECOWAS) *Directive on Fighting Cybercrime* is another example, which provides an interesting legal framework with substantive and procedural norms against cybercrimes, as well as the 2014 *African Union Convention on Cybersecurity and Personal Data Protection*, whose aim is to address the need for harmonized legislation in the area of cybersecurity.

5.1.2 Legal and Political Responses in State-to-State Cyber Relations

The practical dynamics related to the application of the attribution principle, in terms of investigation and collection of evidence, apply in equal terms when the transnational cyber offense is undertaken by private individuals or by national governments. As US Deputy Secretary of Defense William Lynn stated in 2010, "Whereas a missile comes with a return address, a computer virus generally does not."[96] Thus, attributing a malicious activity to a State can be a politically sensitive matter. Public statements of attribution have been met with suspicion, confusion, and a request for greater transparency about the investigation and its evidential basis.[97] A possible solution can be the creation of an international independent investigation authority. A joint attribution mechanism overseen by an international authority would greatly improve States' individual and collective ability to decide who is responsible for an attack and decide how to respond. This would go a long way towards solving the problem of monitoring and enforcement.[98]

Journal of National Law and Security, v.10/3 (2020); and Perloff-Giles, *Transnational Cyber Offenses*, 217.

96 William J. Lynn, "Defending a New Domain – The Pentagon's Cyberstrategy" (2010) https://archive.defense.gov/home/features/2010/0410_cybersec/lynn-article1.aspx.

97 John Davis II et al., *Stateless Attribution – Toward International Accountability in Cyber Space* (RAND 2017): v. Moreover, it is necessary to demonstrate that the hacker was acting as an organ of the state in order to consider the cyber-attack as an act of the state under international law. *See* International Law Committee, *Responsibility of States for Internationally Wrongful Acts*, annex to General Assembly resolution 56/83 of 12 December 2001, and corrected by document A/56/49(Vol. I)/Corr.4, Arts. 4, 5 and 8.

98 Mette Eilstrup-Sangiovanni, "Why the World Needs an International Cyberwar Convention," *Philosophy & Technology*, v. 31/3 (2018): 400.

Once a hostile cyber operation is legitimately attributed to a State actor, the victim State has the possibility to put in place a legal response. However, such possibility revolves around the question: can a State-sponsored malicious cyber act constitute a breach of an international obligation?

The reason why this question is so important is that exercising the so-called "right to respond" entails an underlying breach of international law and it is only based on such breach that it is possible to determine the legal reaction available to the victim-State. When it comes to cyber operations the precise nature of a breach often remains unclear.[99] The main reason for this uncertainty lies in the absence of a proper international cyber law framework setting precise obligations on States' operations in the cyber domain. Therefore, it is often hard to determine which obligations have been breached. In this context, a possible solution is to resort to the general principles of international law, such as the prohibition to violate the sovereignty of another State, the duty of due diligence, and the obligation of causing no-harm (or, in case of telecommunication activities, no harmful interference).[100] They are all relevant concepts that can be used by a State to claim that a malicious cyber act of another State violated an international obligation. As a matter of fact, the link between these concepts and cyber operations has been at the centre of the work of the International Group of Experts that prepared the Tallinn Manual 2.0,[101] the most relevant non-governmental guide (sponsored by the NATO CCD COE) on how existing international law applies to cyber activities. Assuming that a State-sponsored malicious cyber act constituted a violation of a general principle of international law, how can the victim State legally respond?

According to the literature on the matter, even if a hostile cyber operation was legitimately attributed to a State and it was demonstrated that such conduct breached an international obligation, the crucial factor to consider is the impact of such an operation on the victim State.[102] The legal response

---

99 See the examples and analysis of this aspect carried by Harriet Moynihan, "The Application of International Law to State Cyberattacks Sovereignty and Non-intervention" (Chatham House Research Paper, Dec. 2019): 4.

100 On the intersection between cyber operations and telecommunication activities *see* Ingo Baumann, "GNSS Cybersecurity Threats: An International Law Perspective," *Inside GNSS* (3 June 2019) https://insidegnss.com/gnss-cybersecurity-threats-an-international-law-perspective/.

101 Michael Schmitt, ed., *Tallinn Manual 2.0 on the International Law Applicable to Cyber Operations* (Cambridge University Press, 2017).

102 *See*, in particular, Eric Talbot Jensen, "The Tallinn Manual 2.0: Highlights and Insights," *Georgetown Journal of International Law*, v. 48 (2017): 735 *et seq. See also* W. Stahl, "The Uncharted Waters of Cyberspace: Applying the Principles of International Maritime Law to the Problem of Cybersecurity," *Georgia Journal of International and Comparative Law*,

available to the latter depends on the harm it suffered. Obviously, it is not easy to determine how large was the scale of a hostile cyber operation after it hit the targeted State, but the response, in any case, has to be necessary and proportional. In other terms, the scale and effects of such operations define how the victim State can legally respond, from simple diplomatic measures to retaliation or counter-attacks. As a matter of fact, the choice of the most adequate reaction from the victim State is connected to the long-standing debate surrounding the definitional threshold of an armed attack according to international humanitarian law.[103] In general, it can be said that a hostile cyber operation must amount to a "use of force" under Article 2(4) of the UN Charter for the victim State to resolve to respond with the use of (defensive) force.

In the end, legal responses to hostile cyber operations in State-to-State relations are still a grey area of law. Considering the accelerating use of the cyber domain for malicious activities, there is pressure to find a solution at the international level. The current geopolitical climate, however, is slowing this process. In particular, technologically advanced States are generally skeptical of the idea of constraining their cyber activities with tight rules, as these rules can be ineffective against States that do not share the same commitment to the "rule of law." Viewing international law as asymmetrically disadvantageous, these States prefer to rely on self-help such as offensive tools and credible warnings, rather than international law, to safeguard their cyberspace.[104]

The result is that hostile cyber operations can still be conducted today in a "favorable" legal context. Both technical and political elements play a role in rendering the situation legally unsustainable. Vagueness and uncertainty leave more freedom to all actors, but also create the basis for tensions and conflicts, which render the cyber domain more "unstable" for all involved. Without certainty of the penalty, any system of law is inefficient, as its function is to dissuade and deter individuals from committing rogue actions. For this reason, building confidence among States on the measures necessary to repress vicious uses of the cyber world can bring great benefits to all, both in terms of

v. 40 (2011): 247 *et seq*. For a diverging opinion, stating that hostile cyber activities "may be undertaken, just as espionage is, without sanction from the international community," see G. Brown et al., "The Customary International Law of Cyberspace," *Strategic Studies Quarterly*, v. 6/3 (2012): 138.

103 Michael Schmitt, "'Attack' as a Term of Art in International Law: The Cyber Operations Context," *Proceedings of the 4th International Conference on Cyber Conflict* (2012): 283.

104 Yuwal Shany et al., "An International Attribution Mechanism for Hostile Cyber Operations," *International Law Studies*, v. 96 (2020): 217.

international security and in terms of safety of operations, especially the ones highly dependent on cyber technologies, like outer space activities.

The first step in that direction is a well-functioning attribution mechanism which, as underlined above, represents the basic and main problem when dealing with hostile cyber operations.[105] Thus, the next section goes on to look at the problems surrounding the detection of a hostile cyber operation's source.

5.2 *Source of Hostile Cyber Operations*

The lack of recognized standards of proof for attributing cyber activities in international law increases the uncertainty about the actor's identity.[106] Hence, the victim of a hostile cyber operation faces a double jeopardy, namely the breach itself and the legal system's gaps to make the situation stop, to execute self-defense operations, and to obtain reparation.[107]

Detecting a hostile cyber operation is the first step of attribution. When we consider the source of a cyber operation, it is meaningful to map the system architecture including the infrastructure and networks. In the realm of cyberspace, interconnected systems increase the impact of hostile cyber operations. As described in Section 2.1.1, pieces of hardware, software, and memory interact with other components. They can be vectors of a hostile operation through the two-way radio links connecting the ground and space segment or through the chips embedded in space systems. The configuration of such a hostile operation is continually evolving. As stated by Joseph Nye: "It is far safer to send electrons than agents through customs and immigration controls."[108] Therefore, knowing where data and lines of codes are, is extensively challenging as they can be duplicated, transferred, and stored in multiple locations.

5.2.1 Techniques of Attribution: Localization and Identification

After detecting an attack against a space object, identifying its source in cyberspace is difficult, but attributing the operation to one or several actors is even more challenging.[109] Identifying the perpetrators of a malicious cyber operation requires certain key indicators to localize the direct source of the

105 Beyza Unal, "Responsible Behaviour in Outer Space Protects Everyone," Chatham House (5 March 2021).

106 Nicholas Tsagourias, "Cyber attacks, Self-defence and the Problem of Attribution," *Journal of Conflict & Security Law* (2012): 235.

107 Erik M. Mudrinich, "Cyber 3.0: The Department of Defense Strategy for Operating in Cyberspace and the Attribution Problem," *Air Force Law Review*, v. 68 (2012): 172.

108 Joseph S. Nye, Jr, *Cyber Power* (Harvard Kennedy School 2010): 12.

109 Carlo, Lacroix & Zarkan, "The Challenge of Protecting Space-based Assets against Cyber Threats," 5.

activity, whether it is a machine or a human operator. While the perpetrator of an operation is necessarily located within a State's jurisdiction, relying on a geographical origin is not sufficient to attribute an operation in cyberspace. The reason for this is the fact that attacks can be delayed or be performed through a big amount of multiple networks, routers, or servers and through many jurisdictions.

Despite being faced with many challenges in cyberspace, States are starting to discuss individual solutions to address cyber issues with the risk of fragmenting the international normative and legal framework.[110] Such a strategy will soon reach its limit. In *Information Warfare and International Law*, the authors rightfully describe that "electrons may flow through networks freely across international borders, but the authority of agents of national governments does not."[111] International cooperation and the development of a global governance system for cyber activities are keys to increasing cyber awareness and being able to prosecute cybercriminals.

There is a very small possibility that a cyber hostile operation can be attributed just after an incident occurred.[112] Prudence requires the avoidance of political tensions and misinterpretations, which makes the willingness to want to prove attribution difficult. The ground segment uses integrated computer networks scattered across the world to send and receive data from satellites, control them, and monitor their parameters. Hence the ground segment is an ideal and vulnerable target to hostile cyber operations.

Satellites do not only use the air as a communication medium over the surface of the Earth. At any time, satellites are in radio visibility of a multitude of States and potential malicious orbiting spacecraft used as cyber-threat vectors. When located in MEO or in LEO, satellites are not constantly communicating with their mission's ground segment, which increases the risk of undetected interactions with a threat actor. The difficulty of detecting and attributing a malicious act increases when its source is located in outer space, especially if the radiofrequency medium is used as a point of entry. Therefore, the

110 Kerstin Vignard, "Launch Event: Joint Initiative on the Digitalization of Conflict," Academy of International Humanitarian Law and Human Rights (October 29, 2020) https://www.youtube.com/watch?v=KbKU5FRnYv8.

111 Lawrence T. Greenberg, Seymour E. Goodman, & Kevin J. Soo Hoo, *Information Warfare and International Law*, (National Defense University Press 1998): 23.

112 Duncan B. Hollis, "Why States Need an International Law for Information Operations," *Lewis & Clark Law Review*, v. 11 (2007): 1031–1032; and Duncan B. Hollis, "An e-SOS for Cyberspace," *Harvard International Law Journal*, Vol. 52 (2011): 392.

perpetrators of an attack may not only mask their positioning on the ground or spoof their IP address, but also be located anywhere on Earth.[113]

Besides geography, other elements can also be used to determine the source of an operation, such as the type of operation and its estimated cost, how disruptive it is, the type of target and collateral damages, as well as the time of the attack. Some authors have used methodical analysis of an operation premise to trace back threat agentsand sources by considering the ecosystem of hostile cyber operations to include on the one hand adversarial actors and on the other hand insider actors.[114] Other authors do not only consider the identity of the threat agents, but also the type of services affected and the impact of the operation.[115] Determining the motivations and objectives of the threat agent, as well as the methods and techniques they used is essential to trace the malicious operation back to its source.[116] Additionally, establishing the causes of the breach, the services affected, and the impact of the event is important for assessing the objectives and motivations of the perpetrators. Altogether, these elements are evidence for a State to trace back who could be behind the operation committed within its territory, jurisdiction, or against one or several of its nationals.

Actors' unwillingness to reveal they have suffered from a breach in their system, makes it both difficult to understand what is responsible State behavior when using digital technologies[117] and which cyber operations, if any, qualify as use of force under the Charter of the United Nations.[118] As a result, a persistent and disruptive operation in cyberspace that threatens international peace, security, and harms an actor's interests may never be acknowledged in order to prevent the creation of a precedent.

Even though in most cases, when committing hostile cyber operations, groups such as terrorists or hacktivists will claim responsibility for it,[119] the

113 David Wheeler & Gregory Larsen, *Techniques for Cyber Attack Attribution* (Institute for Defense Analyses 2003): 43.

114 Sébastien Bonnart et al., "The Mission as a Tree: A Novel Approach to Identifying Cyber Threats to Satellites."

115 Keith Harrison, & Gregory White, "A Taxonomy of Cyber Events Affecting Communities" *44th Hawaii International Conference System Sciences* (2011).

116 Herbert Lin, "Attribution of Malicious Cyber Incidents," Aegis Paper Series No. 1607 (Hoover Institution 2016): 2.

117 Lora Saalman, ed., *Integrating Cybersecurity and Critical Infrastructure: National, Regional and International Approaches* SIPRI (2018): 2 https://www.sipri.org/sites/default/files/2018-04/integrating_cybersecurity_0.pdf.

118 Charter of the United Nations, Art. 2(4) (1945).

119 Lee Jarvis, Stuart MacDonald, & Thomas M. Chen, *Terrorism Online: Politics, Law and Technology* (Routledge, 2016): 175.

author of a hostile operation does not always claim credit for it as "cyber conflict remains in the grey area between war and peace."[120] Tracking a hostile cyber operation is tough as the author of an hostile operation can conceal its identity or steal another user's identity.[121] Cyber weapons are easily accessible to non-governmental actors and the more open and spread an infrastructure is, the more vulnerable it becomes. Therefore, localization is more challenging as the characteristics of the operations change. For instance, time is shortened so distances do not count as much in outer space as it is the case for operations on the ground, sea, or air space.[122]

However, identifying the category and the State of origin of the threat agent is the first step to attribute a malicious cyber operation to a specific public or private actor. Not all cyber-attacks threaten national security. As identified in *The Challenge of Protecting Space-based Assets against Cyber Threats*, agents can be private entities acting against their competitors or more generally, natural persons perpetrating "an attack with a political aim or wanting to demonstrate an ability to make such a manoeuvre."[123] When identified, agents must be held responsible so the activities they carry out in cyberspace are compliant with their legal obligations.

5.2.2 Responsibility of State Actors and Non-state Actors: The Question of the Positive Obligations

In *The Mission as a Tree*, Bonnart and his fellow authors make a distinction between adversarial and insider agents and sources.[124] Among them are terrorists and criminals, foreign states, subversive or political activists, computer hackers, commercial competitors, dishonest personal, or inadvertent actions of staff members.

Three categories of perpetrators can be identified depending on the nature of the actors: natural persons, private economic actors, and Nation State actors. In *Cyberconflicts and National Security*, Schneier suggests that a common feature of hostile cyber operations is the use of "the same weaponry" and the

120 David E. Sanger, *The Perfect Weapon: War, Sabotage, and Fear in the Cyber Age* (Scribe Publications Pty Ltd, 2018): XI.

121 Martin Motte, *La mesure de la force* (Tallandier, 2018): 350.

122 Brett Williams, "Forward Defence Postures in Developing Cybersecurity Capabilities| #CSGlobal20 | s06e35," *CYBERSEC Forum*, (12 October 2020) https://www.youtube.com/watch?v=TOToVVRAWDY.

123 Carlo, Lacroix & Zarkan, "The Challenge of Protecting Space-based Assets against Cyber Threats," 5.

124 Bonnart et al., "The Mission as a Tree," 4.

exploitation of "the same vulnerabilities," whoever the perpetrator may be.[125] In other words, not all attacks are an act of war executed by another State or military force. Natural persons, acting either as a part of a group or operating on their own, can be motivated by criminal intent[126] and use cyberspace to commit espionage, subversion, fraud, and sabotage,[127] as well as personal data breaches.[128]

The reason for an attack could also be political. Often called 'hacktivism,' the most common types of operations are "virtual sit-ins and blockades, automated email bombs, web hacks and computer break-ins, and computer viruses and worms."[129] These operations can qualify as offensive. They are often executed with the aim of getting the attention of the media for their cause or disrupting normal operations of actors or activities they frown upon. Another way of "hackting" would be to collect a target's documents, policy statements, and discussions about the activities or actors they are willing to act against. It appears that some individuals are also committing hostile cyber operations on behalf of a bigger entity such as a company, to take down a competitor, a group, or a State.[130]

Also, private economic actors, including in the space sector, are less likely to disclose cybersecurity incidents and data breaches they suffered from, as they might subsequently suffer from a negative impact both economically and in reputationally. To some extent, the devastating effects of hostile cyber operations involving private economic actors have an impact on national security. The recent SolarWinds case is the perfect example of how a hostile cyber operation carried out against Fortune 500 and smaller companies can become a

125 Bruce Schneier, "Cyberconflicts and National Security," *UN Chronicle* (n.d.) https://www.un.org/en/chronicle/article/cyberconflicts-and-national-security.

126 "Deloitte Puts the Spotlight on the Cost of Cyber-Crime Operations in New Threat Study", Deloitte (2018) https://www2.deloitte.com/us/en/pages/about-deloitte/articles/press-releases/deloitte-announces-new-cyber-threat-study-on-criminal-operational-cost.html.

127 Olivier Kempf, "Cybersécurité et Résilience : Les Grandes Oubliées des Territoires," Fondation pour la Recherche Stratégique, Note de la FRS n°39/2020 (2020) https://www.frstrategie.org/publications/notes/cybersecurite-resilience-grandes-oubliees-territoires-2020.

128 Bob Gibbs, "Potential PII Compromise of NASA Servers, Internal Memo," NASA HQ (2018) http://spaceref.com/news/viewsr.html?pid=52074.

129 Dorothy E. Denning, "Activism, Hacktivism, and Cyberterrorism: The Internet as a Tool for Influencing Foreign Policy," in *Networks and Netwars: The Future of Terror, Crime, and Militancy*, ed. John Arquilla & David Ronfeldt (RAND Corporation (2001)): 263.

130 Carlo, Lacroix, & Zarkan, "The Challenge of Protecting Space-based Assets against Cyber Threats," 5.

national issue.[131] However, private economic actors cannot be responsible for protecting the national security interests of their State.

In *The Spectrum of National Responsibility for Cyberattacks*, Healey points out that finding who is responsible for a hostile cyber operation is more important than the technical attribution. Healey suggests a political approach involving nations' responsibility "for major attacks from their national territory or citizens,"[132] including when said nation ignored or prohibited the operation.[133] The author considers that nations "unable to stop or investigate attacks coming from its cyberterritory" or "having an insecure national information infrastructure" contribute to the lack of security of their national cyberspace, even in a passive way.[134]

Strictly speaking, network infrastructure and devices are located within the boundaries of a nation's sovereign territory. Hence the country is responsible for building a cooperative and robust framework to address hostile cyber operations within their sovereign territory, especially if they travel through multiple jurisdictions. In *Internet Besieged: Countering Cyberspace Scofflaws*, the authors state that tracing the source of an operation requires "the cooperation of every system administrator, and network service provider on the path."[135]

When addressing the question of attribution of conduct to Nation-State actors, it has been suggested that "the activity of a State is nothing but the activity of individuals that the law imputes to the State."[136] Hence, operations led or supervised by State organs and entities subordinated to a State are

131 Christopher Bing & Joseph Menn, "After Big Hack of US Government, Biden Enlists 'World Class' Cybersecurity Team," *Reuters* (January 2021), https://www.reuters.com/article/us-usa-biden-cyber-idUSKBN29R18I; Brad Smith, "A Moment of Reckoning: The Need for a Strong and Global Cybersecurity Response," *Microsoft Blog* (December 2020), https://blogs.microsoft.com/on-the-issues/2020/12/17/cyberattacks-cybersecurity-solarwinds-fireeye/; Lily Hay Newman, "The SolarWinds Hackers Used Tactics Other Groups Will Copy," *Wired* (January 2021), https://www.wired.com/story/solarwinds-hacker-methods-copycats/; and Martin Untersinger, "L'affaire SolarWinds, une des opérations de cyber-espionnage « les plus sophistiquées de la décennie »" *Pixels, Le Monde*, (January 2021), https://www.lemonde.fr/pixels/article/2021/01/27/la-compromission-de-solarwinds-une-des-affaires-de-cyberespionnage-les-plus-longues-et-les-plus-sophistiquees-de-la-decennie_6067777_4408996.html.

132 Jason Healey, "The Spectrum of National Responsibility for Cyberattacks," *The Brown Journal of World Affairs*, v. 18, no. 1 (2011): 57.

133 *Id.* at 59–60.

134 *Id.* at 62–63.

135 Denning et al., "Internet Besieged," 35.

136 Dionosio Anzilotti, *Cours de droit international* (Panthéon Assas, 1929–1999): 469.

attributable to this State.[137] In the context of a hostile cyber operation, the victim has to prove that the operation meets all the criteria under international law that permit attribution of behaviour to a State, one of them being the control over the operation, whether it is an "effective control"[138] or an "overall control" approach.[139] Not every cyber operation coming from computing systems located within a State's territory may be considered as having been launched from this State. However, sovereignty over cyberspace is at the core of the attribution issue. States should not allow their territory to be used for malicious activities against space systems.[140] "If such activities are carried out anyway, the control exercised by a State over its territory [does not mean] that [a] State necessarily knew, or ought to have known, of any unlawful act perpetrated therein, nor yet that it necessarily knew, or should have known, the authors."[141] However, a State could be expected to act as a reasonable and prudent actor by being aware of the cyber and space infrastructure developed within their jurisdiction by their nationals and therefore, should work on national strategies to address vulnerabilities.

Generally speaking, even though some States developed special legal provisions and a policy strategy addressing cyber threats,[142] the attribution challenge requires strong global cyber policies to trace the trail of a malicious operation. In *Unpacking the International Law on Cybersecurity Due Diligence: Lessons from the Public and Private Sectors*, Shackleford and his fellow authors argue that transit States whose territory is used for the transit of cyber operations, have due diligence obligations when the State's infrastructure was not initially set up for malicious purposes.[143] Due diligence is a principle of international law requiring states to prevent their territory from being used to harm other

---

137 Djamchid Momtaz, "Part III. The Sources of International Responsibility, Ch.19.1 Attribution of Conduct to the State: State Organs and Entities Empowered to Exercise Elements of Governmental Authority," in *The Law of International Responsibility*, ed. James Crawford, Alain Pellet et al., (2010): 238.

138 *Nicaragua v. United States of America*, I.C.J. 1984, para. 99.

139 *The Prosecutor v. Dusko Tadić*, IT-94-1-AR72, ICTY Appeals Chamber, Decision, 2 October 1995, para. 120 and Scott J. Shackelford & Richard B. Andres, "State Responsibility for Cyber Attacks: Competing Standards for a Growing Problem," *Georgetown Journal of International Law*, v. 42 (2011): 971–1017.

140 *Case of the Corfu Channel (United Kingdom of Great Britain and Northern Ireland v. Albania)*, 1949 I.C.J. Reports 1949, p. 244.

141 *Id.*

142 UNIDIR, Cyber Policy Portal (n.d.) https://unidir.org/cpp/en/.

143 Scott J. Shackelford, Scott Russell, & Andreas Kuehn, "Unpacking the International Law on Cybersecurity Due Diligence: Lessons from the Public and Private Sectors," *Chicago Journal of International Law*, v.17 (2016): 1.

States, following the Latin maxim: *sic utere tuo ut alienum non laedas* ('Use your own property in such a way that you do not injure other people's').[144] In the Case of the S.S. Lotus before the Permanent Court of International Justice in 1927, Justice Moore declared: "[i]t is well settled that a State is bound to use due diligence to prevent the commission within its dominions of criminal acts against another nation or its people."[145]

The International Group of Experts working on the Tallinn Manual 2.0 also discussed the issue. They observed that transit States must comply with due diligence requirements when they are aware of a hostile cyber operation that would reach the "requisite threshold of harm" if they are able to take measures to make it cease.[146] The latter condition makes sense regarding the existing technological differences between developed and less-developed States. The former condition however seems to weaken the whole global infrastructure as States can argue that they did not know such an operation was being carried out or considered the operation did not reach the threshold.

However, hostile cyber operations can be very complex, the lines of code sent from a system to another are not always recognizable, and only become intelligible and operational when reaching their target. For instance, Stuxnet was activated only on the Iranian systems it targeted.[147] In this case, identifying the transit of a hostile cyber operation becomes almost impossible for less technology-advanced States. In the *Tallinn Manual 2.0*, a transit State's due diligence obligation is reduced to prevent any disproportionate burdens on these less technology-advanced States.[148]

The Public International Law regime may apply to hostile cyber operations against satellites if States take measures to hold other parties accountable and deepen their collaboration to encourage responsible behavior in both outer space and cyberspace. By acknowledging the existing security issues and identifying the potential threats to space systems and ground segments, States could bridge the legal gaps and provide more clarity to prevent disastrous situations that would more likely involve collateral victims.

---

144 "Sic utere tuo ut alienum non laedas," *Oxford Reference* (n.d.) https://www.oxfordreference.com/view/10.1093/oi/authority.20110803100504563.

145 *Case of the S.S. Lotus (France v. Turkey)*, 1927 PCIJ Series A, No. 10. Justice Moore at 88, referencing the US Supreme Court case of United States v. Arjona, 120 US 479 (1887).

146 Schmitt, ed., *Tallinn Manual 2.0*, 33–34.

147 Kim Zetter, *Countdown to Zero Day: Stuxnet and the Launch of the World's First Digital Weapon* (New York: Crown Publishers, 2014).

148 Schmitt, ed., *Tallinn Manual 2.0*, 33–34.

5.3 *Collateral Victims*

Section 5.3 will examine the legal boundaries that exist for target precision for a hostile cyber operation when it comes to collateral victims. It will provide an overview of what collateral damages could be in a cyber operation against a space system, and then apply the rules under *jus ad bellum* followed by *jus in bello*. In this regard, it is noted that the application of international law, including *jus ad bellum* and *jus in bello*, to a hostile cyber activity is a legal grey area as outlined in Section 5.1.2. Without state practice or opinion, this section is instead largely guided by the international experts of the *Tallinn Manual 2.0*, noting that this a non-binding document.

Collateral damage can cause both direct and indirect effects.[149] Direct effects are 'the immediate, first order consequences (of a cyber attack), unaltered by intervening events or mechanisms.' Indirect effects are those that are 'delayed and/or displaced second-, third-, and higher-order consequences of action, created through intermediate events or mechanisms.'[150]

As outlined in Section 4.1 above, the space domain supports much of the world's critical infrastructure. Many of these systems are interlinked and serve several purposes. This is why hacking a weather satellite can have widespread effects ranging from blocking signals that disaster relief relies on to causing implications for our financial services. The existence of interlinked systems creates an increased threat consequence for collateral damage when satellites are used as a vector for an attack. The *Tallinn Manual 2.0* exemplifies collateral damage in scenarios where a cyber operation targets a military object through civilian communication cables, satellite, or other infrastructure causing harm to the infrastructure through different forms: both due to the transit and also because of the cyberattack itself.[151]

The question regarding collateral victims in peacetime, is whether a cyber operation may fall under *jus ad bellum*. These are the rules found in the UN Charter primarily under Article 2(4) regarding the prohibition of the use of force and Article 51 regarding the right to self-defense in response to an armed attack. In a cyber context, the question is, whether a hostile cyber operation can be qualified as an 'use of force' or 'armed attack.' Several States consider that it is possible for a cyber operation to meet this threshold, however, there is not an agreement about when that threshold is passed as it will depend on the

149 *Id.* at 472.
150 *Id. quoting* Joint Chiefs of Staff, Joint publication 3–60 and Joint Targeting 1–10 (2007).
151 Schmitt, *Tallinn Manual 2.0*, 471.

specific circumstances of the case and its consequences.[152] Without an agreed threshold there is no clarity, leaving any evaluation uncertain. This makes it difficult to evaluate whether a victim that is a direct or indirect target of a hostile cyber operation can claim that this operation broke the prohibition on the use of force. Furthermore, it also makes it difficult to determine whether the effects are severe enough for it to justify self-defense. Where most States do not address the specific circumstances, the Dutch Minister of Defence, Ank Bijleveld gave an example of a hostile cyber operation that could reach the use of force threshold through an attack that targets the entire Dutch financial system.[153] To make this scenario more concrete, a hostile state may be interested in attacking another state's GNSS for the purpose of impeding their transportation system. If this also affected financial services that rely on this signal, the Dutch may, according to their Minister of Defence's previous statement, support the application of international law. However, in general States have not given very clear statements. The *Tallinn Manual 2.0* highlights factors that should be included when assessing whether a non-destructive cyber operation reaches the use of force threshold, including severity, directness, immediacy, invasiveness, measurability of effects, military character of the operation, degree of State involvement, presumptive legality, prevailing political environment, identity of the attacker, and nature of the target.[154]

For wartime operations, *jus in bello* or International Humanitarian Law are the rules of the law of armed conflict. Collateral damage refers to the incidental loss of civilian life, injury to civilians, or damage to civilian objects.[155] In itself, collateral damage is not unlawful under *jus in bello,* but there are certain restrictions. These restrictions include, among others, the principle of distinction, which ensures that attacks are directed at legitimate military objectives, and minimize the collateral damage.[156] The restrictions also include the principle of proportionality, which insists that the military advantage to be gained from attacking a target outweighs the anticipated incidental civilian loss of life

152 Micheal Schmitt, "France's Major Statement on International Law and Cyber: An Assessment" *Just Security* (September 2019) https://www.justsecurity.org/66194/frances-major-statement-on-international-law-and-cyber-an-assessment/.

153 Ank Bijkeveld, "Keynote Address by the Minister of Defence, Ms. Ank Bijleveld, Marking the First Anniversary of the Tallinn Manual 2.0 on the 20th of June 2018" (2018) https://english.defensie.nl/downloads/speeches/2018/06/21/keynote-address-by-the-minister-of-defence-ms.-ank-bijleveld-marking-the-first-anniversary-of-the-tallinn-manual-2.0-on-the-20th-of-june-2018.

154 Schmitt, *Tallinn Manual 2.0,* 331–337.

155 *Id.* at 472.

156 Articles 48 and 52(2) of the Additional Protocol I (1977) to the Geneva Conventions (1949).

and property.[157] The dual nature of information and communications infrastructure means that the implementation of *jus in bello* rules is challenging in cyberspace, and France, Germany and the United States have stated that a careful individual assessment should be applied in determining whether for example a civilian computer can be considered a military objective.[158]

Compliance with efforts to reduce the spread of malicious code can be used to determine how a cyber- attack conforms to the law of armed conflict. Collateral damage can be more difficult to estimate in cyber than regular warfare because of the interconnectedness of the systems. The spread of malicious code can be constrained by limiting the targets to the geography of the target's physical location, limiting the code to attack a certain function in a bigger system, be it a business, government, or other groups.[159]

Malware control examples include a "kill switch," as used for the Wannacry ransomware, that was able to be shut down through registration of an URL that the code was set to search.[160] Stoned and Morris Worm checked to see whether the target was already infected and if it was, the code would not re-infect it.[161] The code can also be limited to deliver the payload on a specific date, for example the Jerusalem virus that was triggered on any Friday 13th or the Michelangelo virus that deleted important data on March 6th.[162] The Stuxnet code was one of the most tightly controlled malware codes. The code limitations were achieved by developing a code that only targeted the control system used by the Iranian nuclear refinement centrifuges. In addition, the code deleted itself from infected USB drives after three infections and deleted itself after 21 days off of non-targeted systems.[163] However, these control

157 Article 51(5)(b) of the Additional Protocol I (1977) to the Geneva Conventions (1949).

158 "Military Objectives – International Cyber Law: Interactive Toolkit" (2021) *Cyberlaw. Ccdcoe.Org*. https://cyberlaw.ccdcoe.org/wiki/Military_objectives#cite_note-14. French Ministry of Armed Forces (Ministère de la Défense). "International Law Applied to Operations in Cyberspace," Délégation à l'information et à la communication de la défense. (2019).

159 Robert Fanelli & Gregory Conti, "A Methodology for Cyber Operations Targeting and Control of Collateral Damage in the Context oof Lawful Armed Conflict," *4th International Conference on Cyber Conflict* (Tallinn: NATO CCD COE 2012): 6.

160 Lily Newman, "How An Accidental 'Kill Switch' Slowed Friday's Massive Ransomware Attack", *Wired* (2017) https://www.wired.com/2017/05/accidental-kill-switch-slowed-fridays-massive-ransomware-attack/.

161 David Raymond et al., "A Control Measure Framework to Limit Collateral Damage and Propagation of Cyber Weapons," *5th International Conference on Cyber Conflict* (Tallinn: NATO CCD COE 2013): 5.

162 *Id* at 7.

163 *Id* at 8.

mechanisms were not completely functional. Stuxnet ended up infecting computer systems in Azerbaijan, Indonesia, India, Pakistan, and the United States. It has been claimed that Stuxnet created collateral damage to an Indian INSAT-4B Satellite although this has not been proven.[164]

The ability to control malware is only as good as the intelligence informing its development. Just as kinetic weapons should not be used without sufficient intelligence regarding the target, cyber weapons should not be used unless intelligence is available to adequately limit potential damage to non-target systems.

6 Private International Law Aftermath of the Hostile Cyber Operation

Section 6 will examine and analyze the private international aspects of a hostile cyber operation, which covers hostile cyber operations incidents where the perpetrators and victims are non-state actors. For example, a cyber operation could be covered by the contractual provisions or excluded by cross-waivers, which will be explored in Section 6.1. Disputes relating to a breach can be solved either through private arbitration or in Court. The former will be explored in Section 6.2, and the latter in Section 6.3 that will address the challenges relating to establishing jurisdiction in cases relating to unlawful cyber operations. Finally, Section 6.4 explores how private actors can protect themselves through insurance. An examination of the field of space and cyber insurance will be conducted, with a particular focus on its ability to help shape minimum requirements for risk mitigations.

6.1 *Contract Terms and Cross Waivers*

While dealing with the aftermath of hostile cyber operations is usually a reactive endeavor, there are legal mechanisms set in place from a proactive approach. The benefit of approaching the aftermath of hostile cyber operations from a proactive approach is that, in the context of space and cyber law, it provides the benefit of clarifying each party's responsibility and liability for certain events. Waivers of liability are a legal mechanism used in lieu of satellite contract arbitration when there is a satellite loss due to a launch failure or defective

164 Jeffrey Carr, "Did the Stuxnet Worm Kill India's INSAT-4B Satellite?" *Forbes* (2010) https://www.forbes.com/sites/firewall/2010/09/29/did-the-stuxnet-worm-kill-indias-insat-4b-satellite/?sh=3f0db2a7127d.

satellite in orbit.[165] When it comes to commercial satellite contracts there is no shortage of reciprocal waivers, also known as cross-waivers. Reciprocal waivers are customary in launch services, satellite purchase contracts, and related sub-contracts. For instance, both the United States and France have a comprehensive liability waiver regime in place to cover launches. The purpose of the reciprocal waiver of claims is twofold. First, reciprocal waivers limit the number of possible claims from the launch.[166] Second, these waivers eliminate the need for the parties to obtain property and casualty insurance to protect themselves against such claims. Moreover, cross-waivers are an efficient way to enable and promote private space companies to engage in high investment and high-risk scenarios.[167]

The most famous example of a cross-waiver is the liability arrangement applicable to inter-party damage aboard the International Space Station (ISS). Through this arrangement, except for gross negligence or willful misconduct, international activities on the ISS can function free from legal disputes that may arise from third parties. While the ISS is an exceptional case because of the intergovernmental agreements, it presents a promising sign that when issues of third-party liability rise it may be possible to adapt cross-waivers to the private enterprise side of the space industry.[168] This section continues by examining cross waivers in specific organizations, NASA and ESA, respectively.

In the United States provisions for cross-waivers are embedded in the Commercial Space Launch Act of 1984 (CSLA).[169] As a prerequisite to the launch license, the CSLA requires a US licensed launch provider to execute a waiver of liability when launching US government payloads. As a result, each party waives claims against and releases from liability the other party, its contractor, and subcontractors involved in the launch.[170] Moreover, each party assumes the risk and financial responsibility for loss or damage to the satellite. This is similar to what is embedded in the National Aeronautics and Space Act of 1958 that created NASA (which was later modified by the Commercial Space Launch Act of 1984 to allow civilian use of NASA systems in launching space vehicles).[171] As stated in the US Code of Federal Regulations, each Party agrees

165 Pamela L. Meredith and Marshall M Lammers, *Commercial Satellite Contract Arbitration: Special Legal Considerations* (2013): 423.

166 Commercial Space Launch Act Amendments of 1988, 100 Pub. L. 657 (1988).

167 Ingo Baumann and Lesley Jane Smith, *Contracting for Space: An Overview Of Contract Practice in The European Space Sector* (Ashgate Publishing Group 2011): 63.

168 *Id.*

169 Commercial Space Launch Act Amendments of 1984, 98 Pub. L. 575 (1984).

170 Meredith and Lammers, *Commercial Satellite Contract Arbitration*, 423.

171 National Aeronautics and Space Act, 85 Pub.L. 568 (1958).

to a cross-waiver of liability pursuant to which each Party waives all claims against any damage arising out of Protected Space Operations.[172] "Protected Space Operations" meaning all launch or transfer vehicle activities and payload activities on Earth, in outer space, or transit between Earth and outer space in implementation of an agreement for launch services. Due to how integrated cybersecurity operations are with space operations, it can be argued that even though cybersecurity provisions are not explicitly stated here, this section of the code does cover damages from cyberattacks.

Similar to NASA, ESA has embedded provisions regarding cross-waiver liability within their General Clauses and Conditions (GCC). One main difference is that with ESA the GCC only relates to damages of goods or to the staff. Moreover, similar to NASA, cybersecurity provisions are not explicitly mentioned in the GCC. However, while ESA is not subject to national or EU laws, there are provisions regarding personal data protection. ESA has adopted a Personal Data Protection Policy in line with the EU's General Data Protection Regulation.[173] This Personal Data Protection Policy, adopted by the ESA Council in 2017, established governance and operations necessary for the effective personal data protection. Unfortunately, as a result, it is unlikely that contracts between NASA or ESA with private companies will include provisions for claims for the type of cyberattacks the previous sections have outlined. Moreover, even with legal mechanisms in place, the space industry is still vulnerable to damages in the form of hostile cyber operations and cybersecurity breaches. The next section looks at how space companies and the legal system handles damages in the cyber context.

6.2 *International Commercial Arbitration*

International commercial arbitration involves contracts between sophisticated business parties in different countries. Companies doing business across borders regularly turn to international arbitration to resolve their disputes and aerospace companies are no exception. As stated in *Houston, We Have an Arbitration,* arbitration is well suited for aerospace companies because the "results that are quick, less intrusive, can be decided by people with expert-level knowledge of the subject matter, and can be resolved outside of the

172 14 C.F.R. § 1266.104 (2021).

173 Marco Ferrazzani and Ilaria Ziliolo, "ESA Facing Cybersecurity Issues," Presentation, University of Genoa (2018). https://www.eu-space.eu/images/2018/document/Slides/Slides-Ferrazzani-Zilioli.pdf. The EU's General Data Protect Regulation not only places obligations within the EU, but it can impose obligations onto organizations located anywhere if they collect data related to people in the EU.

public eye."[174] These characteristics are particularly relevant for an aerospace company because arbitration can provide added protection for its intellectual property and reputation. The reason for this is because arbitration provides confidentiality. From a civil procedural perspective, discovery is more limited than in the courts, which protects companies from inadvertently disclosing other sensitive intellectual property not related to the dispute at hand. As a result, the closed system of arbitration provides substantially more protection than public litigation in a national court.

6.3 *Prescriptive Jurisdiction vs Long-Arm Jurisdiction*

Cybercrime jurisdiction is established by factors such as the nationality of the offender, the nationality of the victim, and the impacts of the cybercrime on the interests and security of the state as long as there exists "a 'sufficient connection' or 'genuine link' between the hostile cyber operation and the state exercising jurisdiction."[175] This section offers a brief overview of the types of jurisdictional matters in the cybersecurity context, as well as the nuances that come into play from the inherent nature of cyberattacks.

The use of prescriptive jurisdiction under international law is largely inadequate for governing the modern challenge of cyberterrorism.[176] This is unsurprising given that these jurisdictional theories were formulated long before the creation of the Internet. Moreover, the Internet's borderless nature and the techniques used by cyberterrorists make it pointless to apply traditional notions of jurisdiction such as territoriality to hostile cyber operations. However, out of the classical theories of prescriptive jurisdiction under international law – territoriality, nationality, passive personality, protection, and universality – the protective principle is best suited to reduce the number of conflicting jurisdictional claims and mitigate international discord found in hostile cyber operations.[177] One reason why the protective principle works well in the case of hostile cyber operations is that applying the principle provides nations with the stronger capacity to prosecute cyber criminals outside their

174 W. Carson Bennett, "Houston, We Have an Arbitration: International Arbitration's Role In Resolving Commercial Aerospace Disputes," *Pepperdine Dispute Resolution Law Journal* v.19/1 (2019).

175 UNODC, "Cybercrime Module 7 Key Issues: Sovereignty and Jurisdiction" (2019) https://www.unodc.org/e4j/en/cybercrime/module-7/key-issues/sovereignty-and-jurisdiction.html.

176 Paul N. Stockton & Michele Golabek-Goldman, "Prosecuting Cyberterrorists: Applying Traditional Jurisdictional Frameworks to a Modern Threat," *Stanford Law and Policy Review*, v. 25 (2021): 230.

177 *Id.*

jurisdiction when the attacks occur. In addition, there is a judicial precedent that provides strong support for applying the protective principle to hostile cyber operations that will be addressed later in this section.

Articles 7 and 8 of the 1935 Harvard Draft Convention on Jurisdiction with Respect to Crime described the principle as conferring jurisdiction on a nation "with respect to any crime committed outside [the nation's] territory by an alien against the security, territorial integrity or political independence of that State."[178] The protective principle is grounded on the axiom that every nation is entitled to defend itself from hostile attacks.[179] As a result, in the context of hostile cyber operations, the application of the protective principle can provide nations with the authority to preventively prosecute and apprehend individuals outside the sovereign State's jurisdiction when hostile cyber operations take place. Under international law, this unique technique makes the protective doctrine the only jurisdictional basis that authorizes extraterritorial jurisdiction over potentially dangerous crimes that threaten a state's security.

The *United States v. Yousef*[180] is an example that depicts judicial precedents providing strong support for extending the protective principle. In this manner, it can also be used to prosecute cyberterrorists. In what has been described as one of the most "seminal cases involving terrorism," the court held that it did not exceed the US government's authority to exercise jurisdiction over a terrorist whose conduct occurred outside the United States.[181] In a similar case, the *United States v. Reumayr*,[182] the court exercised extraterritorial jurisdiction over Canadian defendants who attempted to detonate the TransAlaska Oil Pipeline based on the protective principle. Both these cases illustrate how hostile cyber operations may fall under the purview of protective jurisdiction.

While the protective principle is arguably the best legal mechanism to prosecute those who engage in hostile cyber operations, it is not all-encompassing to address some of the jurisdictional nuance present when dealing with hostile cyber operations. For instance, if a cyberattack is planned to happen in more than one country simultaneously, then a problem arises when trying to

178 "Draft Convention on Jurisdiction with Respect to Crime," *American Journal of International Law*, v29(S1) (1935): 439–442.
179 Stockton & Golabek-Goldman, "Prosecuting Cyberterrorists," 230.
180 927 F. Supp. 673 (S.D.N.Y. 1996).
181 Stockton & Golabek-Goldman, "Prosecuting Cyberterrorists," 254.
182 530 F. Supp. 2d 1210 (2008).

determine which country can exercise the protective principle. With the number of hostile cyber operations increasing globally, it is imperative that the legal community takes proactive steps in the form of treaties or guidelines to address this inevitable issue.[183]

Moreover, multinational companies traditionally faced challenges when attempting to enforce cybersecurity claims against employees due to the employees being located in foreign jurisdictions. Traditionally, a Court is able to exercise personal jurisdiction over an out-of-state defendant based on the connection the defendant has with the state where the act was committed.[184] This is referred to as long-arm jurisdiction. However, establishing what "connection" the out-of-state defendant has with the state where the crime has been committed has been difficult in terms of cybercrimes. The case of *MacDermid, Inc. v. Deiter*[185] made it possible for the Court to establish long-arm jurisdiction in cases of cybercrime occurring outside US borders.[186] MacDermid, a company located in Connecticut, sued an employee named Deiter who worked remotely in Canada for the misuse of a computer and misappropriation of trade secrets. Based on Connecticut's long-arm statute, the Court held that they could exercise jurisdiction over Deiter, because she knew MacDermid's computer servers were located in Connecticut when she knowingly accessed the files. The Connecticut long-arm statute permitted the exercise of jurisdiction over anyone who uses a computer or a computer network located within the state.

However, as previously stated, a hostile cyber operation on space operations or data storage across multiple sovereignties and jurisdictions adds another level of complexity to a complex subject. This daunting reality along with the evolving techniques and technology used to initiate a hostile cyber operation is why, in the context of cybersecurity, there needs to be a proactive approach similar to the protective principle instead of reactive when dealing with the legal ramifications of cyberattacks.

---

183 Rob Sobers, "134 Cybersecurity Statistics and Trends For 2021," *Varonis* (2021) https://www.varonis.com/blog/cybersecurity-statistics/.

184 "Long-Arm Statute," *LII / Legal Information Institute* (accessed 20 January 2021) https://www.law.cornell.edu/wex/long-arm_statute.

185 2012 WL 6684580 (2nd Cir. 2012).

186 Shawn Tuma, "What is the Proper Jurisdiction for an International Computer Fraud Lawsuit?" *Business Cyber Risk* (2013) https://shawnetuma.com/2013/01/12/what-is-the-proper-jurisdiction-for-an-international-computer-fraud-lawsuit/.

6.4 *Space and Cyber Insurance*

6.4.1 Liability Convention and Insurance

The next section provides a brief yet detailed overview of the global cybersecurity insurance within the space industry. The insurance market related to space activities represents a critical factor in the exploration and utilization of outer space. Specifically, the insurance market provides coverage of the risks to which a spacecraft is exposed during its lifecycle.[187] The need for space insurance is due, in part, to the obligations set upon spacefaring Nations by the international space treaties. These obligations involve aspects of national liability for public and private activities beyond the atmosphere. The general framework developed at the international level frames the issue of liability by means, principally, of Article VII of the Outer Space Treaty (1967) and the Liability Convention (1972). For both treaties the issue is focused on what is the basis of fault and who would be liable to pay damages caused by space objects. However, the treaties are silent with regards to the extent insurance might (have to) cover a potential liability compensation. Instead, this aspect is left to national regulations to determine the appropriate insurance required from the private operator.[188] Moreover, the problem lies in the fact that liability is triggered by damage being caused by another space object as opposed to a non-physical cyberattack.

The four main insurance products related to the space market are: pre-launch insurance, launch insurance, orbital insurance, and third-party liability insurance. Space assets like satellites are most vulnerable to cyber-attacks during their operational phase. However, cyber-attacks are rarely included in orbital insurance policies.[189] The exclusion of cyber-attacks represents a growing concern for stakeholders because it represents a crucial gap for the space insurance market. This is unfortunate because the United States and Europe have the most advanced cybersecurity markets in the world. In 2016 the US and Europe accounted for $3 billion and $300 million, respectively, of $3.5 billion in global cyber-insurance premium.[190] In the satellite context, a 2019 report issued by the insurance company AXA XL stated that 43% of GEO satellites

187 M. Zajac, "Overview of Space Insurance," *Risques*, v. III/1 (2017): 42–46.

188 Armel Kerrest de Rozavel and Frans G. von der Dunk, "Liability and Insurance in the Context of National Authorization," in *National Space Legislation in Europe: Issues of Authorisation of Private Space Activities in the Light of Developments in European Space Cooperation*, ed. Frans G. von der Dunk (Martinus Nijhoff, 2011): 125–61.

189 For more on this see Andrea Capurso & McLee Kerolle, "How to Estimate Insurance Coverage for Cybersecurity Protection for Satellites: A Case Study," International Astronautical Congress 2020: Cyberspace Edition (2020).

190 Nir Kshetri, "The Economics of Cyber-Insurance," *IT Professional* v.20/6(2018): 9–14.

are insured on orbit and 25% of GEO operators buy little or no in-orbit insurance beyond their first year in space.[191] As for LEO, only 6% of satellites have orbital insurance. Overall, the market is looking at 86% of the active satellites being uninsured while operating in outer space.[192] For insurers that do provide cybersecurity insurance, it is for first-party insurance and third-party insurance. First-party cybersecurity insurance focuses on compensating or mitigating the costs of the policyholder.[193] While third-party insurance covers the business and people that are found to be "responsible" for a breach.

Unfortunately, cybersecurity insurance cannot be analyzed in a straightforward manner due to the lack of standardization of the cybersecurity insurance market and the high uncertainty in pricing cybersecurity risks. According to a survey by Marsh & McLennan, 49% of policyholders said that they had "insufficient knowledge" about their cyber risk exposures to assess the type and coverage of insurances they need.[194] This insufficient knowledge highlights the lack of standardization of the cybersecurity insurance market. If there was standardization then policyholders would have a clear understanding of their cyber risk exposures, as well as the amount of coverage based on the situation, to determine the type of coverage required.

Due to the sensitivity of classified data regarding satellite coverage, it is difficult to estimate the costs of cyberattacks. Satellite coverage data is not only scarce to the public, but to the insurers as well. As a result, it also becomes difficult for companies to measure the nature and extent of cyber-related exposure in order to make decisions as to what coverages for how much to purchase. Insurers tend to be conservative and overcharge for cyber risk coverage because of the uncertainty in pricing cyber risk coverage.

As stated above, in order to increase the number of insured satellites in orbit, a crucial role must be played by national legislation which can impose insurance requirements on private operators in order to obtain and maintain the necessary licenses. Many spacefaring nations have put in place such mechanisms. However, the focus has been traditionally brought on third-party liability insurance, leaving product insurance often overlooked.

---

191 AXA XL, "Space Insurance Update" (2019) https://iuai.org/IUAI/Study_Groups/Space_Risks/Public/Study_Groups/Space_Risk.aspx.

192 *Id.*

193 "What is Cybersecurity Insurance," *Cyberinsureone* (2021) https://cyberinsureone.com/faq/what-is-cyber-security-insurance/.

194 Kshetri, "The Economics of Cyber-Insurance."

6.4.2 Minimum Requirements for Risk Mitigations (the Notion of Prudent and Reasonable Actor): Insurance Aspects

Cyber insurance works as a redistribution of risk. Insurance companies can incentivize their clients to implement *ex-ante* actions creating a more secure system, as well as offer *ex-post* remedial support. The former, which is the focus of this section, asks what role insurance companies can have in influencing cybersecurity governance. Some scholars believe that insurance has the potential to spread minimum requirements for cyber risk mitigation, thereby creating a common reference point for prudent and reasonable cybersecure behavior.[195] This idea is tied to a liberal theory of governance that de-emphasizes state responsibility.[196]

The idea is that insurance companies can influence cybersecurity practice by, for instance, including compliance to security standards as a requirement for coverage.[197] As mentioned in Section 4.3 there are different standards that companies can rely on to mitigate their exposure to cyber threats. However, there is no consensus of what constitutes minimum standards for cybersecurity. Because the cyber insurance market is not a widespread and standardized market it cannot currently create a widespread cybersecurity implementation. With no standardized form, content or vocabulary for cyber insurance policies, they are "the wild west of insurance policies."[198]

In order to perform the risk calculations, insurance companies will have to boost their technical capabilities. This can be done by either hiring experts or partnering with companies that have those capabilities. In addition, as the market grows, the information from the claims will contribute to the generation of information about the nature and extent of cyberattacks in general. Insurance companies can also gather information about breaches when assessing premiums. If the companies are not forthcoming, providers can deny coverage.[199] Creating an obligation to disclose can create transparency and make it easier

195 Bruce Schneier, "Insurance and the Computer Industry," *Communications of the ACM*, v. 44/3 (2001): 114; and Scott J. Shackelford, "Should Your Firm Invest in Cyber Risk Insurance?" *Business Horizons*, v. 55/4 (2012): 349–356.

196 Daniel Woods & Tyler Moore, "Does Insurance Have a Future in Governing Cybersecurity?" *IEEE Security & Privacy*, v. 18/1 (2020): 21.

197 Shauhin A. Talesh, "Data Breach, Privacy, and Cyber Insurance: How Insurance Companies Act as 'Compliance Managers' for Businesses," *Law & Social Inquiry*, v. 43/2 (2018): 13.

198 Ericka Chickowski, "10 Things IT Probably Doesn't Know About Cyber Insurance," *Dark Reading* (2021) https://www.darkreading.com/operations/10-things-it-probably-doesnt-know-about-cyber-insurance/d/d-id/1316862.

199 Scott J. Shackelford, "Should Your Firm Invest in Cyber Risk Insurance?", 353.

for insurers to calculate premiums in the future. Such obligations may not only stem from insurers, but also from governments.

These are potential opportunities that the market may leverage, but in their research Woods and Moore show there is little evidence that insurance companies are currently providing a strong form of governance.[200] The little research that exists on the topic indicates that in practice, insurance companies are not performing the assumed health checks of the companies before extending coverage.[201] Instead, insurers are relying more on *ex-post* remedies such as incident response after a breach. Such products are popular because the insurers lessen the cost of a claim they would otherwise have to cover. Moreover, the benefits of risk mitigation are more difficult to observe, although it could prevent the breach from happening at all.[202] It is also exactly these technological complexities that might bar insurance companies from having the same effect on markets, such as safety measures for property insurance. It is more difficult to measure a software product's effectiveness at reducing losses than, for instance, a manufacturer of fire doors. In addition, underwriters find it difficult to analyze the risks because they lack data about cyber operations. Only a few breaches are reported and those that are quickly become outdated because of the rapid technological development.[203] Unknown vulnerabilities will have an effect on the policy coverage and premiums.[204]

Another way of influencing cybersecurity best practice is by adding surcharges to companies for using old operating systems and providing monetary incentives to reduce premiums for secure cyber behavior – similar to safe driving discounts. Currently, there is no widely accepted discount for cybersecurity reduction fees and insurance companies tend to prefer a holistic risk assessment.[205] Insurers are focusing more on organizational procedures than technical controls, meaning that they rarely include basic security procedures in the contract.

200 Woods & Moore, "Does Insurance Have a Future in Governing Cybersecurity?", 23.

201 Sasha Romanosky et al. "Content Analysis of Cyber Insurance Policies: How Do Carriers Write Policies and Price Cyber Risk?", *Journal of Cybersecurity,* v. 5/1 (2019): 10–11 and Daniel Woods et al., "Mapping the Coverage of Security Controls in Cyber Insurance Proposal Forms," *Journal of Internet Services and Applications,* v. 8 /1 (2017): 9.

202 Woods & Moore, "Does Insurance Have a Future in Governing Cybersecurity?", 24.

203 Nicole Perlroth & Elizabeth A. Harris, "Cyberattack Insurance: A Challenge for Business", *New York Times* (8 June 2014) https://www.nytimes.com/2014/06/09/business/cyberattack-insurance-a-challenge-for-business.html.

204 Meland, Tondel & Solhaug, "Mitigating Risk with Cyberinsurance", 39.

205 Woods & Moore, "Does Insurance Have a Future in Governing Cybersecurity?", 24.

Even if insurance companies succeed in creating a standardized risk approach, companies will still need to pay attention to their security. The risk of relying too heavily on insurance to provide all the tools necessary to stay cyber secure is that they neglect other cybersecurity investments. To only adapt to the insurance company's risk indicators might not sufficiently protect the insured from breaches. As threats are constantly evolving, it is important that both insurers and companies innovate in their response to the dynamics of cybercrime. A secure solution will balance prevention, detection and recovery.[206]

Most standards will not have to be space-specific, meaning that the space industry can benefit from more broad cybersecurity standards. Cybersecurity insurance in itself is a relatively new market, but cybersecurity coverage for satellite systems is not a widely spread product and in fact favored to be excluded by insurers.[207] Insurance companies are taking to include cyber war risk exclusions in their policies, but the lack of rules on international attribution for States engaging in cyber conflicts makes it uncertain how such exclusions would hold up in court.[208] In order for this industry to take off, it will require a willingness from insurance companies to accept the risks involved. If cybersecurity is included in the insurance coverage, it could either see a market forming that is stand-alone or as part of a broader product. A stand-alone product will ensure technical expertise. Moreover, it will ensure that attention is kept on cybersecurity awareness and the generation of knowledge. The challenge for the market to take off is that there is a trend for space companies not to insure their satellites. In order for cybersecurity insurance to be attractive, it requires a balance between the assessment of the threat and the price of premiums. This balance can be achieved by gathering more actuarial data that will enable better risk assessment. Providing *ex-ante* services, such as support from security professionals after a cyber operation, will enable the insurers to understand the risks better. In addition, more data could be collected during the claims processes if the insurers request a forensic investigation.[209] A market with a specialized insurance product that gathers actuarial data has the

206 Mark Camillo, "Cyber Risk and the Changing Role of Insurance", *Journal of Cyber Policy,* v.2/1 (2017): 55.

207 Kerolle and Capurso, "How to Estimate Insurance Coverage for Cybersecurity Protection for Satellites", 4.

208 Daniel Woods & Jessica Weinkle, "Insruance definitions of Cyber War", *The Geneva Papers on Risk Insurance – Issues and Practice,* 45 (2020): 653.

209 Daniel Woods & Andrew Simpson, "Policy Measures and Cyber Insurance: A Framework", *Journal of Cyber Policy,* v. 2/2 (2017): 211.

potential to support the establishment of minimum requirements for cyber risk management in the future. Due to the economic self-interest of insurance companies in setting standards and deciding whether they are met, regulators should also play a role in the development of minimum standards whilst insurers can provide additional guidance and promotion of their adherence.[210] In such a scenario cyber insurance would not only function as risk transfer but would also support avoidance and mitigation elements.[211]

7 Conclusion

This chapter has provided an overview of cyber threats against space systems from the attack to the aftermath. It has done so by using the diverse background of the authors to provide an all-around tour: from the technical structure of satellite systems, the entry points and characterization of threats to responses at entity level through IT governance, technical strategies, contractual clauses and insurance to the challenges of international responses in a public international law fora. The chapter reflects the complexity of mitigating threats from both a technical and legal perspective. showing that keeping a satellite system cyber secure is a task for all types of stakeholders, from both the public and the private sector, to continually work on as the threats evolve.

210 Jan Martin Lemnitzer, "Why Cybersecurity Insurance Should be Regulated and Compulsory", *Journal of Cyber Policy* (2021): 8–9.

211 Ulrik Franke, "The Cyber Insurance Market in Sweden", *Computers & Security,* v. 68 (2017): 130.

CHAPTER 4

Space Technology and Cybersecurity: Challenges and Technical Approaches for the Regulation of Large Constellations

Rada Popova

1 Introductory Remarks[1]

Cybersecurity issues related to space assets are not significantly distinctive from the cyber-related risks for other technologies. Nevertheless, the complex character of the space infrastructure coupled with the reliance upon space assets magnifies the challenges to be met. Paradoxically, despite the growing awareness about space-related cyber threats and the advances in space technology, the sophistication of the cybersecurity of space assets is lagging behind. One particularly pertinent issue is the cybersecurity of small satellites and large constellations, which, as one of the moving forces behind the modern space industry, offer a significant vulnerability surface.

This chapter will analyse the issues stemming from cyber dependency and the cyber vulnerability of large constellations of small satellites. In doing so, it will discuss the existing technical approaches for cyber threat detection, management, and prevention as they can serve as the basis for establishing specific legal requirements for the cybersecurity of space assets.

As the applicability of the general international law and space law on cyber activities pertaining to outer space has been the subject of detailed analyses[2]

1 All parts of this chapter, except of the last section, which was updated in 2021, have been completed in 2020 on the basis of the author's presentation at the 2019 SES Legal Workshop "Space Law in a Networked World." The references have been updated as of January 2021.

2 Martha Mejia-Kaiser, "Space Law and Unauthorized Cyber Activities," in *Peacetime Regime for State Activities in Cyberspace*, ed. Katharina Tsiolkovsky (NATO Cooperative Cyber Defence Centre of Excellence, 2013); Rada Popova, "Cyber Law and Outer Space (Activities): Legal and Regulatory Challenges," in *Proceedings of the 61st Colloquium of the International Institute of Space Law* (Utrecht: Eleven, 2019): 659–670; *See* also the chapter "Space (Law) and Cybersecurity," in Federico Bergamasco, Roberto Cassar, Rada Popova, and Benjamyn I. Scott *Cybersecurity: Key Legal Considerations for the Aviation and Space Sectors*, (Kluwer, 2020): 103–127. For an overview of the legal problems relating to satellite constellations, *see* Damian Bielicki, "Legal Aspects of Satellite Constellations," *Air & Space Law* 45, no. 3 (2020): 245–263. For detailed accounts on single aspects, *see,* for example, Frans von der Dunk, "Liability for

 | DOI:10.1163/9789004527270_005

and can be affirmed, this chapter will not dwell further into this topic. Here, it suffices to highlight that the existing approaches to cybersecurity in international law, as well as in some regional legal instruments, have not evolved into a specific normative body to address the cybersecurity of space technology.[3]

In order to assess the significant relevance of cybersecurity for space activities and space applications, and to establish the role of regulation for its implementation in practice, first it must be understood what role cybersecurity plays for space technology in general. Second, the specific features of small satellites and large constellations will be outlined as an important factor for the change of paradigm in the space industry to a highly commercialised sector that is indispensable for numerous other spheres. To this end, this chapter will focus on the various risks stemming from cyber-related threats for small satellites specifically, before an overview on the technical, management, and regulatory measures that can bolster the management of cyber risks is given.

2 Growing Dependency on and Vulnerability of Outer Space Technology: Two Sides of the Same Coin

During the past decade, the space industry has experienced unparalleled growth – both in terms of the number of new space actors, as well as in the diversity of space activities. The three main, "classical" types of space applications – Earth observation, navigation, and telecommunications, have been diversified and supported by numerous activities, which can be characterised

Damages Caused by Small Satellites – A Non-Issue?," in *Small Satellites: Regulatory Challenges and Chances*, ed. Irmgard Marboe (Leiden: Brill, 2016): 154–173; Cordula Steinkogler, "Small Satellites and Debris Mitigation," in *Small Satellites: Regulatory Challenges and Chances*, ed. Irmgard Marboe (Leiden: Brill, 2016): 211–236; and Cecile Gaubert, "Do Small Satellites Need Insurance?," in *Small Satellites: Regulatory Challenges and Chances*, ed. Irmgard Marboe. (Leiden: Brill, 2016): 369–383.

3 Due to a remarkable lack of established cybersecurity terminology, both in academic writings and in emerging policy documents and regulatory attempts, any research work in the field of cybersecurity regulation is inevitably challenged by the diverging uses of relevant cyber-related notions. As there is no universally accepted definition of what constitutes a "cyber attack" (a term that is very widely used), there is also no legally binding definition of the term 'cybersecurity.' Taking into consideration existing definition attempts from the governmental and commercial sectors, however, it can be stated that the term 'cybersecurity' is mostly used as an overarching notion concerning the measures undertaken to prevent or to manage the risk from cyber activities with harmful potential and cyber-related vulnerabilities in various fields of activities. Cybersecurity relates both to the safety as well as to the security aspects of space activities, *see* Bergamasco et al., *Cybersecurity*, 19–21.

as "NewSpace," especially through the development of the global small satellite industry and affordable, increasingly privately initiated launch solutions. In addition to the growth of the global space industry as a major branch of economy, also the global dependency on satellite technology for the management of critical infrastructure,[4] navigation services, Earth observation, telecommunications, disaster management, science, agriculture, and a large spectrum of commercial uses is growing.

An increasing number of industry sectors rely on the availability of satellite data and on the stability of space systems. This reliance, along with the exposure of space systems to cyber threats, underlines the enormous relevance of cybersecurity of space-based assets. Employing a cyber vulnerability of a space system may result in far-reaching, wide-spread consequences in numerous spheres of life and economy and lead to considerable, possibly catastrophic losses at any location on the globe. Accordingly, the continuous expansion of the commercial space sector within almost all technology-based activities on Earth makes satellites an attractive target for malicious actors and a concern for policymakers, space industry stakeholders, and end-users. In sum, the reliance on the use of satellite-based services and applications is proportionate to the cyber vulnerability stemming therefrom and results in an undividable dyad between the growing dependency on space systems and the need to efficiently protect them from cyber intrusions.

Although the taking over of physical control over a satellite through cyber means seems to be a theoretical rather than a realistic scenario in the short-term, acts aiming at breaching satellite functionality or at compromising satellite-transmitted data streams may cause global effects.[5] That such scenarios are not

4 There is probably no critical infrastructure nowadays that does not depend on space technology. Absent a universal definition, this term can be understood to mean the "totality of assets and networks essential to the functioning of the economy and the society," in key sectors such as energy, financial services, transportation, emergency services, governmental facilities, *see* Bergamasco et al., *Cybersecurity*, 37 *et seq.* While the cybersecurity of critical infrastructure seems to be the subject of considerable efforts, the cybersecurity of space systems upon which this infrastructure depends still needs to be implemented effectively. For example, recent dedicated research on the cybersecurity of domestic critical infrastructure in the USA that depends on ground and satellite-based online systems, including the water and energy sectors, are so exposed to cyber vulnerabilities, that their systems "could be accessed by anyone." *See* Edvardas Mikalauskas, "Critical US Infrastructure can be Hacked by Anyone," cybernews.com (July 17, 2020) https://cybernews.com/security/critical-us-infrastructure-can-be-hacked-by-anyone/.

5 For example, critical infrastructure providing electricity supplies and enabling global transportation relies on the data provided by Global Positioning System (GPS) satellites. Loss or disruption in this data and in real-time signals may cause considerable failure and irreparable consequences. Additionally, worldwide communications systems function on

of a merely theoretical nature has already been demonstrated in practice. Not even the most prominent space object – the International Space Station (ISS) – and governmental agencies are completely secure from cyber intrusions. For example, in 2011, algorithms used by NASA for command and control of the ISS were lost following the theft of an unencrypted NASA notebook.[6] Prior to that, in 2010, as reported by the NASA Inspector General, thousands of computer security weaknesses were made use of to install malicious software on NASA systems. These "hacks" originated from various intruders, including individuals to organised criminal enterprises and caused "significant disruption to mission operations, and resulted in the theft of export-controlled and otherwise sensitive data."[7] The cost to NASA was estimated at more than $7 million USD.[8]

2.1 *The Role of Digitalisation in the Space Industry*

The main reason behind the growing relevance of cybersecurity in the space industry is digitalisation. Technological systems on Earth, including critical infrastructure, become increasingly digitalised through and even completely dependent on cyber-based data transmission. In the today's reality of the Internet of Things (IoT),[9] the number of interconnected devices is exponentially growing and so is the need for accessibility to broadband Internet and technology in general.

This is increasingly the case also for space infrastructure.[10] Originally, space systems used to consist of analogue devices. Until recently, Internet access in outer space was an exception. Only in 2010, the ISS crew accessed the world

the basis of telecommunications satellite infrastructure, thus any considerable intrusion may disrupt businesses and the word economy altogether.

6 Matt Liebowitz, "Stolen NASA Laptop Had Space Station Control Codes," Space.com (March 1, 2012) https://www.space.com/14750-stolen-nasa-laptop.html.

7 Paul K. Martin, "NASA Cybersecurity: An Examination of the Agency's Information Security," Testimony before the Subcommittee on Investigations and Oversight, House Committee on Science, Space, and Technology, NASA, (February 29, 2012): 1, https://oig.nasa.gov/docs/FINAL_written_statement_for_%20IT_%20hearing_February_26_edit_v2.pdf.

8 Martin, "NASA Cybersecurity," 2.

9 The Cambridge Dictionary defines IoT as: "objects with computing devices in them that are able to connect to each other and exchange data using the internet." IoT is characterized by "the ever-increasing networking capabilities of machines and everyday devices used in the home, office equipment, mobile and wearable technologies, vehicles, entire factories and supply chains, and even urban infrastructure," EY, *Cybersecurity and the Internet of Things* (March, 2015) https://www.ey.com/Publication/vwLUAssets/EY-cybersecurity-and-the-internet-of-things/%24FILE/EY-cybersecurity-and-the-internet-of-things.pdf.

10 On the digitalisation of the space industry, *see* Organisation for Economic Co-operation and Development, *The Space Economy in Figures: How Space Contributes to the Global Economy* (July 5, 2019): 13, https://www.oecd-ilibrary.org/docserver/c5996201-en.pdf.

wide web using a NASA-provided satellite link service "to connect to a computer in Houston in remote desktop mode, and get online from there."[11] Nowadays, the use of cyber-based network technology (thus, technology which does not rely only on radio, or on infrared wireless communication) for space missions has become a standard. Almost all new satellites are equipped with an on-board computer and a router and are able to provide wireless links for various types of data flows.[12]

Along with the process of growing digitalization of outer space, satellites have become devices that, in their reliance on cyber technology, are not much different from any other device in the global IoT.[13] In the course of this technological development, outer space and cyberspace have merged into a co-dependent ecosystem.[14]

2.2 *Dependence on Internet Accessibility in Outer Space and on Earth*

Digitalization and the use of the Internet in outer space have multiple applications. For example, space objects do not only depend on Internet connectivity – they may also enable it. Soon, via space-based data transmission services, high-speed Internet with nearly continuous coverage[15] will be provided from space across the globe.[16] A booming market[17] for such services is created by the

---

11 Igor Kuksov, "Internet in Space: Is There Net on Mars?," Kaspersky Daily (September 13, 2019) https://www.kaspersky.com/blog/internet-in-space/28267/.

12 Such as, for example, voice, telemetry, video, and other EVA data flows, Consultative Committee for Space Data Systems, *Wireless Network Communications Overview for Space Mission Operations*, CCSDS 880.0-G-3, (May 2017): 3–14.

13 For an account on satellites as "things on the IoT," *see* P.J. Blount, "Satellites are Just Things on the Internet of Things," *Journal of Air and Space Law* 42, no. 3 (2017): 273–294.

14 Paul Kyle Kallender, "Waking Up to a New Threat: Cyber Threats and Space," *Trans. JSASS Aerospace Tech. Japan* 12, no. 29 (2014): Tv_8.

15 Lake A. Singh et al., "Low Cost Satellite Constellations for Nearly Continuous Global Coverage," *Nature Communications* 52 (2020).

16 Less than a decade ago, smartphones were not yet a common standard. Today, a smartphone is an everyday commodity which, in many functions, has replaced our desktop computers in covering telephony, text communication, e-mail, radio, television, and data transfer services. It is expected that in 2021, there will be an estimated 3.8 billion smartphone users worldwide, which will equal 48% of the world population, considering that it is expected to reach approximately 7,874 billion by then. *See* Statista, "Number of smartphone users from 2016 to 2021" (August 20, 2020) https://www.statista.com/statistics/330695/number-of-smartphone-users-worldwide/ and the statistical data provided by the World Bank (n.d.) https://data.worldbank.org/indicator/SP.POP.TOTL?end=2021&start=2021&view=bar. *See* also Worldometer, World Population Projections (n.d.) https://www.worldometers.info/world-population/world-population-projections/.

17 According to Morgan Stanley, the revenue generated by the global space industry may increase to more than $1 trillion by 2040, "Space: Investing in the Final Frontier," Morgan

need to supply almost half of the world's population that still has no Internet access with broadband connectivity.[18]

The global crisis that started in 2020 following the SARS-CoV-2 (COVID-19) pandemic is the most recent flagship example of how important the access to broadband Internet has become for the worldwide economy, for businesses, and for social lives. The periods of lockdown, followed by a gradual, but only partial and very modest return to "normal" have illustrated clearer than ever before how much humankind relies and effectively depends on connectivity and access to cyberspace. Even before the pandemic, as of 2019, over 74,500 GB of data were sent every single second on average.[19] Because of COVID-19, work processes, banking, international negotiations, conferences, education, and even medical care[20] have been relocated, at least partially, to cyberspace. Virtual communication and collaboration have replaced the "classical" communication in person.

This tendency of a constantly growing demand for bandwidth for the functioning of the economy is expected to last and become the "new normal" in most spheres of life.[21] These processes have accelerated the process of global digitalisation and will continue to shape the needs of modern society in an

---

Stanley (July 24, 2020) https://www.morganstanley.com/ideas/investing-in-space. *See* further, Josephine Milward, "What Role Will Satellites Play in the Booming IoT Market?," Seraphim Capital (February 10, 2020) https://seraphimcapital.passle.net/post/102fyh3/what-role-will-satellites-play-in-the-booming-iot-market; and "Space Market Booming, Investors Exploring Top Stocks" (July, 21 2020) https://www.marketwatch.com/press-release/space-market-booming-investors-exploring-top-stocks-2020-07-21?mod=mw_quote_news.

18 It has been estimated that approx. 49% of the world's population has no access to broadband Internet, thus opening a huge market for such services. *See* "The State of Broadband: Broadband as a Foundation for Sustainable Development," ITU (September 2019) https://www.itu.int/dms_pub/itu-s/opb/pol/S-POL-BROADBAND.20-2019-PDF-E.pdf.

19 *Id.* at IX.

20 Reed Abelson, "Doctors and Patients Turn to Telemedicine in the Coronavirus Outbreak," *The New York Times* (March 11, 2020) https://www.nytimes.com/2020/03/11/health/telemedicine-coronavirus.html.

21 For an assessment on the societal and economic impact of COVID-19, *see*, for example, KPMG, "The New Normal" (2020) https://home.kpmg/de/en/home/insights/2020/03/the-new-normal.html and Olaf Acker, Clément Mengue, and Neil Siri, "A Digital Technology Agenda Driving an Accelerated Transition to the New Normal," Strategy & PwC (June 15, 2020) https://www.strategyand.pwc.com/de/de/implications-of-covid-19/digital-technology-agenda.html. On safety aspects, *see* Europol, "Safety Guide for the 'New Normal' after COVID-19," https://www.europol.europa.eu/activities-services/public-awareness-and-prevention-guides/safety-guide-for-new-normal-after-covid-19.

increasingly cyber-based and technology-dependent world in which up to 100 % of businesses relied on the Internet for their business operations.[22] This is where large constellations[23] will play a crucial role as networks consisting of hundreds and thousands of small satellites may enable not only high-speed, low-latency services[24] with broad geographical coverage, but also fast connection for high data transfer rates in real time.[25]

2.3 *Overview of the Cyber-Related Vulnerabilities of Satellite Systems*

Although satellites are exposed to threats as any other technology accessing cyberspace, their cyber vulnerability is amplified by the numerous attack vectors in the complex satellite infrastructure.[26]

Satellite systems consist of multiple segments (a ground segment, a space segment, the communication links that connect them, and additionally, the user segment)[27] and can thus be impugned via any of them,[28] suffering various

---

22 It has been estimated than only a decade ago, this number was less than 25%. *See Ninth Annual Cost of Cybercrime Study* Accenture (March 6, 2019): 8, https://www.accenture.com/_acnmedia/PDF-96/Accenture-2019-Cost-of-Cybercrime-Study-Final.pdf#zoom=50.

23 For more information on SpaceX's Starlink, *see* https://www.starlink.com/; on the Airbus and OneWeb partnership, *see* Airbus, "OneWeb Satellites Constellation" (n.d.) https://www.airbus.com/space/telecommunications-satellites/oneweb-satellites-connection-for-people-all-over-the-globe.html; on Amazon's Project Kuiper, see Amazon, "Projekt Kuiper" (July 31, 2020) https://blog.aboutamazon.com/company-news/amazon-receives-fcc-approval-for-project-kuiper-satellite-constellation. For an overview of further plans for large constellations, their activities and investment schemes, *see* SSI, "Space Security Index 2019" (2019): 82–84, http://spacesecurityindex.org/ssi_editions/space-security-2019/.

24 Data transmission speed from Low Earth Orbit (LEO) may be comparable to fibre-optic. For example, it is expected that the Starlink constellation that will consist of 42,000 satellites, will provide internet speed of up to 40–50 Mbps. This is considerably faster than DSL Internet and in the range of broadband Internet, *see* Federal Communications Commission, "FCC Broadband Speed Guide" (n.d.) https://www.fcc.gov/consumers/guides/broadband-speed-guide.

25 "OneWeb's Satellites Deliver Real-Time HD Streaming from Space," OneWeb (July 16, 2019) https://www.oneweb.world/media-center/onewebs-satellites-deliver-real-time-hd-streaming-from-space; SpaceX, "High Speed Internet Access Across the Globe" (n.d.) https://www.starlink.com.

26 The term "cyber attack" must be used with caution. It is widely used as a synonym for cyber activities that may produce negative effects and which must not necessarily involve or rise to the level of use of force. For an overview and analysis of the notion of "cyber attack" as used in the commercial and military context, *see* Bergamasco et al., *Cybersecurity*, 23–24 and 52.

27 *Id.* at 110 et seq.

28 For example, the ground segment encompasses the ground infrastructure, including the hardware and software on the ground station or in a network of ground systems and

levels of harmful impact.[29] As a matter of fact, physical access is not needed to gain access to a satellite system, as almost any satellite with an onboard computer can be attacked through cyber means.[30]

Today, the satellite infrastructure increasingly relies on live Internet transmission between the ground and the space segment, and both the control and the data streams of space systems[31] are possible inlets to gain access to the infrastructure itself and to its data streams through malicious cyber activities.[32]

Such activities fall in the category of non-kinetic threats.[33] They can be aimed at degrading, damaging, or destroying software, hardware, and data transmitted by or stored on satellites and space-based networks. The intrusions can be effectuated, for example, through electronic and physical attacks on ground stations, as well as through the exploitation of vulnerabilities of communication links through manipulation of the radio spectrum[34] (so-called jamming[35] and spoofing).[36] Such activities can result in the disruption of the

---

the space segment includes the space object itself along with the computer system and installed software on board the satellite, as well as other interconnected space objects.

29 Brandon Bailey et al., "Defending Spacecraft in the Cyber Domain," Aerospace Corp. (November 6, 2019): 4, https://aerospace.org/sites/default/files/2019-11/Bailey_Defending Spacecraft_11052019.pdf.

30 Already more than 20 years ago, several cases became known in which cyber attackers had penetrated satellite command and control systems and were able to issue commands to the space object, *see* Christopher J. Alberts et al., "Operationally Critical Threat and Vulnerability Evaluation Framework, Technical Report," Carnegie Mellon University (September 1999) https://resources.sei.cmu.edu/asset_files/TechnicalReport/1999_005_001_16769.pdf.

31 Including ground control networks, SDR transceivers, and co-orbital assets.

32 Although the ground segment used to be a favoured target, nowadays, the space segment, through data transmission links, is increasingly susceptible to cyber risks, *see* M. Manulis et al., "Cyber Security in New Space: Analysis of Threats, Key Enabling Technologies and Challenges," *International Journal of Information Security*, (May 12, 2020): 1; Ly Vessels, Kenneth Heffner, and Daniel Johnson, "Cybersecurity Risk Assessment for Space Systems," 2019 IEEE Space Computing Conference (SCC) (July 30, 2019): 12.

33 Todd Harrison, Kaitlyn Johnson, and Thomas G. Roberts, "Space Threat Assessment 2018," CSIS (April 12, 2018): 4–5, https://www.csis.org/analysis/space-threat-assessment-2018. *See* also Rajeswari Pillai Rajagopalan, *Electronic and Cyber Warfare in Outer Space*, UNIDIR (May 5, 2020) https://www.unidir.org/files/publications/pdfs/electronic-and-cyber-warfare-in-outer-space-en-784.pdf.

34 Radio spectrum is the part of the electromagnetic spectrum used by radiocommunications.

35 Jamming is a reversible electromagnetic type of interference employed to overpower the signals being sent to or from a satellite by using a signal at the same frequency and at a higher power. The receiver, therefore, is no longer able to accurately recover the legitimate signal.

36 Spoofing is a type of electromagnetic interference, which, similarly to jamming, uses the radio spectrum. It is aimed at interfering with the satellite's regular transmissions so as

command and control systems both of the ground station and of the satellite and result in the partial or complete loss of operational availability, in the loss of confidentiality or disruption of data[37] and, although less probable, even in the physical harm or destruction of the space object.[38]

As the equipment and the techniques needed to exploit the vulnerabilities of satellites and related infrastructure are inexpensive, malicious cyber activities are considerably cheaper than a kinetic attack and offer a financially affordable option of penetration.[39] Consequently, cyber intrusions can be employed not only by States, terrorists and non-state groups, but also by single persons rather easily.[40] With this, both the practical and the financial means needed to carry out a cyberattack are out of proportion to the damage they can incur.[41] Overall, the advantages of cyber intrusions, including automated attacks, magnified by the low barriers for access caused by deficient cybersecurity,[42] are excessively asymmetrical in relation to the harmful outcome, and in particular, to the difficulty in detection and recovery therefrom.[43]

---

not to corrupt, but to "trick" the true signal, by mimicking it with a false one. In this way, false or corrupted information can be introduced into the communication system. *See* Bergamasco et al., *Cybersecurity*, 37 and Harrison et al., "Space Threat Assessment 2018," 4.

37 "Report Concerning Space Data System Standards: Security Threats Against Space Missions," CCSDS (December 2015): 2–1, https://public.ccsds.org/Pubs/350x1g2.pdf.

38 Bergamasco et al., *Cybersecurity*, 113.

39 "IO Active Reveals Major Satellite Communication and Operating System Vulnerabilities at Black Hat USA 2018 & DEF CON 26," CISION (August 10, 2018) https://www.prnewswire.com/news-releases/ioactive-reveals-major-satellite-communication-and-operating-system-vulnerabilities-at-black-hat-usa-2018--def-con-26-300695401.html.

40 Dan Swinhoe, "How Much Does it Cost to Launch a Cyberattack?," CSO (May 1, 2020) https://www.csoonline.com/article/3340049/how-much-does-it-cost-to-launch-a-cyberattack.html and Accenture, "Ninth Annual Cost of Cybercrime Study," (March 6, 2019): 17, https://www.accenture.com/_acnmedia/PDF-96/Accenture-2019-Cost-of-Cybercrime-Study-Final.pdf#zoom=50.

41 Information theft is the most expensive and fastest rising consequence of cybercrime and attacks on data integrity – or preventing data toxicity – is the next frontier. *Id.*

42 Bailey et al., "Defending Spacecraft in the Cyber Domain," 6.

43 The cost of malicious cyber activities to the US economy was estimated at between $57 billion and $109 billion in 2016, *see* "The Council of Economic Advisers, The Cost of Malicious Cyber Activity to the U.S." (February 2018): 1, https://www.whitehouse.gov/wp-content/uploads/2018/03/The-Cost-of-Malicious-Cyber-Activity-to-the-U.S.-Economy.pdf. According to Accenture's Report, the average cost of cybercrime for an organization increased US$1.4 million to US$13.0 million while the total value at risk will reach 5.2 trillion US Dollars globally over the next five years. *See* Accenture, "Ninth Annual Cost of Cybercrime Study," 17.

3 Cybersecurity of Small Satellites: A Case for Special Treatment or Business as Usual?

3.1 *The Small Satellite Industry and the Big Picture*

Nowadays, space applications are not the result predominantly of costly governmental missions. The share of satellite services in the space industry is constantly growing, having reached 45% of the overall global revenues in the satellite industry and 33% of the global space industry by 2020.[44] The commercialisation (often referred to as the "new space race") of outer space has gained unprecedented momentum, and the number of space objects launched for commercial purposes is constantly growing.[45] A considerable part of so-called NewSpace activities[46] is dedicated to the launching and the operation of small satellites[47] predominantly in Low-Earth Orbit (LEO),[48] with launch numbers having nearly doubled between 2012 and 2019.[49]

After initially having been used mostly for demonstration purposes and educational outreach,[50] during the past decade small satellites have quickly become a game changer in the space industry. Through the use of miniaturized

44 According to the Bryce Space and Technology *2020 State of the Satellite Industry Report*, the global space economy amounted to 366 billion USD in 2019.

45 World Economic Forum, "Who Owns the Orbit: Just How Many Satellites are there in Space?" weforum.org (October 23, 2020).

46 With a launch rate growing by 66% annually over the 5-year period between 2012 and 2017, *see* NASA, "The Emerging Commercial Marketplace in Low-Earth Orbit," NASA (February 27, 2020) https://www.nasa.gov/mission_pages/station/research/news/b4h-3rd/ev-emerging-commercial-market-in-leo.

47 There is no universally accepted definition of a small satellite, *see* "Providing Maximum Launchability – A Guide to Defined SmallSat Classification," The Aerospace Corporation (May 22, 2018) https://aerospace.org/sites/default/files/2018-08/DefinedSmallSat_STE052218.pdf and Bhavya Lal et al., "Global Trends in Small Satellites," IDA (July 2017) III, https://www.ida.org/-/media/feature/publications/g/gl/global-trends-in-small-satellites/p-8638.ashx. According to the majority of classification attempts, within the class of small satellites, minisatellites have a mass of approx. 100–500 kg; microsatellites – 10–100 kg; nanosatellites – 1–10 kg; picosatellites – 0,1–1 kg. For a prudent literature review of small satellites nomenclature, *see* Sreeja Nag, Jacqueline LeMolgue, and Olivier de Weck, "Cost and Risk Analysis of Small Satellite Constellations for Earth Observation," Sreeja Nag (2014) http://sreejanag.com/Documents/IEEE2014_Cost_SN.pdf.

48 The advantage provided by satellites in low earth orbit include a quicker orbital speed and lower latency, which help faster communication with the ground segment.

49 Data provided by Bryce Space and Technology, "Smallsats by the Numbers" (2020). According to the report, 45% of the total number of launches in 2019 included small satellites.

50 D. Selva and D. Krejci, "A Survey and Assessment of the Capabilities of Cubesats for Earth Observation," *Acta Astronauica* 74 (2012): 50–68. The share of commercial services in the

electronics, they have advanced the use of standardized components, reduced launch costs in commercial launch services, and have become a competitive alternative to conventional satellite missions for numerous space activities.[51]

Small satellites offer a number of considerable advantages – both in terms of costs, as well as in terms of versatility. First, they are characterized by shorter development and production times and can thus greatly reduce the time needed to obtain science and technology results.[52] Second, due to their compact size and low mass,[53] small satellites incur affordable, generally foreseeable launching and deployment costs. Moreover, their effectiveness has considerably increased through the considerable leverage in their upmass potential when compared to the onset of the small satellite industry.[54] Nowadays, apart from new applications such as providng global broadband connectivity, small satellites increasingly enable services which earlier fully depended on the use of medium and large satellites, including remote sensing[55] and earth observation.[56]

Due to all these advantages, small satellites and their deployment in large constellations have disrupted and democratised the global satellite industry.

3.2 *Current Trends in the Small Satellite Industry*

So far, more than half of the small satellites are being developed by the private sector[57] and provide commercial services ranging from high resolution

---

small satellites sector is constantly growing, reaching 62% in 2019, as compared to 6% in 2012; *see* the estimates in Bryce Space and Technology, "Smallsats by the Numbers," 9.

51 Such as remote sensing, technology development, communications, scientific applications, and experiments.

52 Daniel N. Baker and S. Pete Worden, "The Large Benefits of Small-Satellite Missions, Eos, Transactions," *American Geophysical Union* 89, no. 33 (2008). The authors contend that "in many cases, 80% (or more) of program goals can be achieved for 20% of the cost by using small-spacecraft solutions." *Id.* at 301–302.

53 Nevertheless, it must be noted that the average mass of small satellites is not decreasing, as the share of mini satellites as the largest class of small satellites (generally ranging from 100/200 kg to 500 kg) has been growing. *See* Bryce Space and Technology, "Smallsats by the Numbers," 6–7. This can be explained with the growing share of small satellites offering commercial services requiring more complex system architecture as opposed to the capabilities of pico- or nanosatellites that are mainly used for scientific or test missions.

54 The report of Bryce Space and Technology, "Smallsats by the Numbers" accounts an 11x increase in proportion of upmass over 7 years (2012–2019).

55 Bhavya Lal et al., "Global Trends in Small Satellites," 2–7 *et seq.*

56 *Id.* at 3–5.

57 Micheal Johnson, "The Emerging Commercial Marketplace in Low-Earth Orbit," NASA (February 27, 2020) https://www.nasa.gov/mission_pages/station/research/news/b4h-3rd/ev-emerging-commercial-market-in-leo.

imagery,[58] global Internet, testing of new technology, precision agriculture, AI-enabled applications, including analytics and monitoring services,[59] to defence and security.[60]

The ability to operate small satellites as autonomous swarms allows an increase in the amount of transmitted data as well as in its processing/analysing within shorter periods of time – all at a lower cost.[61] Considering that data (including the collection, transmission, access to and the storage of data)[62] is the commodity of the future, such optimization is a promising growth factor for the small satellite business.[63] At the same time, data is an attractive target for intruders as it may, first, offer sensitive information and second, be turned into financial profit. Thus, from a cybersecurity perspective, due to the growing demand for small satellite services, the value of data stored and transmitted as well as because of the vulnerability of the satellite infrastructure in general, small satellites open the door for considerable threats.[64]

3.3 *Cyber-Related Vulnerabilities of Small Satellites and Large Constellations*

3.3.1 Vulnerabilities of Small Satellites in General

The reasons for the exposure of small satellites to cyber risks are complex and concern their design, composition, functionality and operational capabilities.

58 *See*, for example, Planet (https://www.planet.com), which is reported to own/operate more than half of the remote sensing small satellites, and Bryce Space and Technology, "Smallsats by the Numbers," 8.

59 Black Sky (https://blacksky.com) provide on-demand global monitoring services; HawkEye360 (https://www.he360.com/about/) offer mapping of radio frequency emissions. *See* also Debra Werner, "Small Satellites, Big Weaknesses," *Aerospace America* 57, no. 8 (2019): 12.

60 David Livingston and Patricia Lewis, *Space, the Final Frontier for Cybersecurity?*, Chatham House (September 22, 2016): 21, https://www.chathamhouse.org/sites/default/files/publications/research/2016-09-22-space-final-frontier-cybersecurity-livingstone-lewis.pdf.

61 Anusuya Datta, "The NewSpace Revolution: The Emerging Commercial Space Industry and New Technologies," *Geospatial World* (January 8, 2017) https://www.geospatialworld.net/article/emerging-commercial-space-industry-new-technologies/.

62 As far as data in space is concerned, it must be noted that in the past, data had to be transmitted back to Earth for processing because the computational capabilities and limited electrical power available to satellites prevented edge computing. With advances in onboard processing and power capabilities, data processing in space is now possible. Dan Matthews, "Data Storage in Space? It's Already in the Works," SmartData Collective (April 2, 2018) https://www.smartdatacollective.com/data-storage-space-works/ and Bernard Marr, "Why Space Data is the New Big Data," *Forbes* (October 19, 2017) https://www.forbes.com/sites/bernardmarr/2017/10/19/why-space-data-is-the-new-big-data/#50eb9c5869a1.

63 Marr, "Why Space Data is the New Big Data."

64 Livingston and Lewis, *Space, the Final Frontier for Cybersecurity?*, 21.

As a general rule, the likelihood and success rate of a malicious cyber activity against satellites do not depend on the capability of the attacker in the first place,[65] but on the security level of the attacked object and of the ground control networks via which it is controlled.[66] At the same time, the level of security is predefined by the components and the software on the object, which may be a flaw particularly for small, low-cost satellites.

First, small satellite equipment must be economically viable. In order to strike a balance between the functionality, the mass and the size of a given space object, manufacturers and investors strive at an affordable design process and at producing the lightest, thus the least complex configurations. Moreover, often further trade-offs are made at the cost of encryption,[67] because the costs and the time needed to implement effective means of encryption may sometimes be considered to outweigh the potential risks of intrusion.[68] It must be emphasized that while encryption is one of the most effective cybersecurity measures, to be effective, it must be implemented not only for the hardware equipment, but also for software, data traffic, and signals.[69]

Second, the various elements of satellite systems normally originate from various manufacturers in a complex supply chain.[70] In most cases, purchasers

65 Persons or organisations interested in "attacking" satellite systems may vary from private individuals who test their capabilities to state-backed organisations and generally, can rarely be identified due to the considerable challenges in establishing attribution in cyberspace. *See, for example*, Bergamasco et al., *Cybersecurity*, 113.

66 Generally, the protection of ground control networks is possible. However, as radios can be used to contact and interfere with the space object outside the ground control system, ground protection is not a sufficient means to prevent cyber intrusions. For all attacks outside the ground control networks, the security of the satellite depends on the technical security controls on board the satellites. *See* Vessels et al., "Cybersecurity Risk Assessment for Space Systems," 12.

67 Shaun Waterman, "Space is Cybersecurity's New Frontier," AFCEA (May 1, 2020) https://www.afcea.org/content/space-cybersecuritys-new-frontier.

68 Andrew Kurzrok, Manuel Diaz Ramos, and Flora S. Mechentel, "Evaluating the Risk Posed by Propulsive Small-satellites with Unencrypted Communications Channels to High-Value Orbital Regimes," 32nd Annual AIAA/USU Conference on Small Satellites (2018): 4.

69 This was demonstrated during a 2019 Hack-a-Sat competition organized by the US Air Force and the Defense Digital Service when a team managed to intercept sensitive satellite-transmitted data with equipment worth 300 USD and free software. *See* Vilius Petkauskas, "Satellites are not Safe Enough. This is What Should Worry you," cybernews.com (January 21, 2021) https://cybernews.com/editorial/satellites-are-not-safe-enough-heres-why-that-should-worry-you/.

70 Generally, the supply chain that ensures the functionality of satellite infrastructure includes many components that are external in relation to the satellite system itself, including ground network staff, providers, user terminals, end-user devices, maintenance

have no or very little control over the code for a given component and the contractors who manage the infrastructure are not the actors that own the assets. The problem is aggravated by so-called off the shelf components (COTS). Unlike large governmental actors that are normally supplied by carefully vetted contractors, small satellite developers often buy COTS which might have varying or even deficient security levels.[71] Accordingly, appliances with poor security design or insufficient security management, bought with the primary aim to spare costs and time, may increase the vulnerability of the whole network.[72]

A third group of vulnerabilities result from the difficulties in keeping the software and particularly the hardware of satellites up to date. Considering that the time elapsing between the design, the production and the operation in outer space of a given element may be considerable, some components may have outdated cybersecurity features even before the launch. Moreover, once launched, no direct access for physical upgrading is possible.[73] The advancement in on-orbit satellite servicing which can be used as a gateway for malicious actors to interfere with satellite communications will most probably intensify the problem.

3.3.2 Vulnerabilities of Large Constellations

Large constellations consisting of hundreds or even of thousands of small satellites magnify the problems sketched above and considerably expand the threat landscape. For cost-related reasons, they are typically composed of commercially accessible space software-driven objects equipped only with the most-needed apparatus and are not well protected against malicious cyber activities.[74]

---

and systems personnel, satellite operators, subcontractors, staff devices. Gregory Falco, "Cybersecurity Principles for Space Systems," *Journal of Aerospace Information Systems* (December 2018): 2.

71 Bailey et al., "Defending Spacecraft in the Cyber Domain," 12 and Werner, "Small Satellites, Big Weaknesses," 32.

72 Werner, "Small Satellites, Big Weaknesses," 32.

73 J. M. Porup, "It's Surprisingly Simple to Hack a Satellite," *Vice* (August 21, 2015) https://www.vice.com/en_us/article/bmjq5a/its-surprisingly-simple-to-hack-a-satellite.

74 Gregory Falco, *Job for Space Force: Space Asses Cybersecurity*, Harvard Kennedy School Belfer Center for Science and International Affairs (July 12, 2018): 8, https://www.belfercenter.org/sites/default/files/files/publication/CSP%20Falco%20Space%20Asset%20-%20FINAL.pdf; Harisson Caudill, "Big Risks in Small Satellites," (April 29, 2019): 1; and Brian Weeden/Victoria Samson (eds.), *Global Counterspace Capabilities: An Open Source Assessment*, Secure World Foundation (April 2019): xii, https://swfound.org/media/206957/swf_global_counterspace_april2020_es.pdf.

Objects within a constellation are, furthermore, completely networked and normally share the same design.[75] Consequently, a cyber vulnerability to one node may affect the whole constellation.[76] This makes it almost impossible to combat a cyber threat in an isolated way, without compromising other parts of the satellite ecosystem. Moreover, as satellites enabling communications or bandwidth services are linked via ground stations to millions of users around the globe, once access has been gained, external networks and systems connected to the constellation can be easily intruded.[77] Specifically with regard to constellations for broadband Internet, additional layers of vulnerabilities may be added at an organizational level. During the operational phase of the constellation, the use of bandwidth on the satellite may be leased. As a result, access to sensitive information may be provided to numerous employees of multiple leasees which may aggravate vulnerabilities and create multiple, additional pathways for intrusion.

3.4 *The Relevance of Cybersecurity in the Small Satellite Industry*

The technical characteristics and vulnerabilities of small satellites and of large constellations as discussed above allow for a few conclusions with regard to the relevance of cybersecurity of small satellites to be drawn.

First, the access to interconnected space objects is characterised by the low barriers for potential attacks and by a significant disproportion between the accessibility of intrusion and the outcome. Not in the last place, this problem is scaled up due to the feasibility of automated cyber attacks.[78]

Second, not only is the vulnerability threshold low and the risk of harm considerable. In addition, this disproportion is aggravated by the high probability of irreversible, non-reparable effects.

Third, due to the criticality and the value of data transmitted by small satellites, these space objects along with all related networks represent an attractive target for malicious cyber actors.[79]

---

75 Werner, "Fine Resolution from Small Satellites," 29.

76 Bailey et al., "Defending Spacecraft in the Cyber Domain," 8.

77 As other contemporary industrial control systems, also large constellations use networks (e.g., corporate networks and the Internet) to enable business processes. In effect, this leads to larger exposure of all links within these networks.

78 Automated cyber attacks can be directed through self-directed tools and processes, and thus though their multiplication factor exploit vulnerabilities more effectively than humans.

79 Additional factors, which will not be looked into more details here, but must be kept in mind, concern the increasing role of commercial small satellites in the military sector. As the underlying cyberinfrastructure is predominantly in the hands of private companies

Consequently, the complexity and the scale of cyber-related risks for space systems in general are particularly magnified with regard to small satellites and large constellations.

4 Means to Counteract Cyber-Related Vulnerabilities of Small Satellites and Large Constellations

Without doubt, along with the growth in the number of small space objects,[80] cyber risks and their large-scale impacts will constantly expand, thus encouraging malicious actors to exploit the high vulnerability surface.[81]

All these factors trigger the question whether prevention is a feasible means to protect space objects from cyber intrusions and to build cyber resilience. The answer is straightforward: as defensive options are limited,[82] risks cannot be fully prevented but only reduced. Therefore, the primary objective of cybersecurity measures should not be to avert, but rather to minimize and to manage the risks for space assets. Moreover, cybersecurity efforts should be focused at maintaining the availability of the satellite even after an attack, even if this may result in the temporary loss of the functional availability of the space object. Accordingly, the feasible cybersecurity solutions must be centered primarily around concepts for risk reduction and risk management.[83]

The available means in this respect can be classified in three categories: technical measures, management measures, and legal and regulatory measures, which will be briefly outlined in the following.

---

and specific national laws ensuring sufficient cyber risk prevention and management are lacking, governmental controls are restricted on more than one plane. *See* Livingston and Lewis, *Space, the Final Frontier for Cybersecurity?*, 21.

80 For a regularly updated, comprehensive set of data on space objects orbiting the Earth, *see* the online Satellite Database of the Union of Concerned Scientists available at https://www.ucsusa.org/resources/satellite-database.

81 The types of malicious actors can range from private persons (criminals, hackers, commercial competitors) to states with their intelligence services, Bergamasco et al., *Cybersecurity*, 113.

82 Carolin Baylon, *Challenges at the Intersection of Cyber Security and Space Security: Country and International Perspectives*, Chatham House (December 29, 2014): 38, https://www.chathamhouse.org/publication/challenges-intersection-cyber-security-and-space-security-country-and-international.

83 *Id.* at 36 and Bergamasco et al., *Cybersecurity*, 127.

4.1 *Technical Measures*

Technical cybersecurity measures concern the design, the scrutinizing, and the encryption of hardware and software in satellite infrastructure.[84]

Generally, risk management on the technical level must be based on the assessment of vulnerabilities and of the robustness to be attained in order to ensure resilience.[85] In a first step, a so-called "security architecture," that is the establishment of security controls and assets, must be created. The next step is to define system-related security risk elements and to assign risk metrics hereto. In this way, threat levels can be measured, and targeted prevention measures can be developed. Moreover, security models can be created to determine the specific paths of a cyber attack and to identify threat scenarios. Along with the calculation of the threat probability, these steps may allow the anticipation of vulnerabilities and the sources of the attack, and on this basis, to produce a combination of security measures that can block a cyber attack, even after it has been deployed, from exploiting the vulnerabilities of the system. Additionally, ensuring an abundance of systems can ensure that the failure of one single system or component does not compromise the activities of the overall system.[86]

In terms of the single segments of the space systems, the ground segment is particularly vulnerable[87] and must be protected accordingly. This includes the monitoring of control centres and antennas,[88] securing processors and other hardware components through encryption,[89] strengthening the capabilities of internal networks and servers and routinely monitoring communications traffic so that anomalies can be detected.

As far as the communication links between the ground and the space segment are concerned, helpful measures that are feasible already now[90] include

---

84 Werner, "Small Satellites, Big Weaknesses," 31.

85 The term 'resilience' in cybersecurity is mostly used to describe the ability of an information system to support the functions necessary for successful operation even in cases or periods of reduced capability and across a wider range of scenarios, conditions, and threats, in spite of hostile action or adverse conditions. *See*, Bergamasco et al., *Cybersecurity*, 39–40.

86 *See*, generally, Harrison Caudill and Chris Wake, eds., *Commercial Space System Security Guidelines, rev. 1.0.1*, Orbital Security Alliance (February 1, 2020).

87 Werner, "Small Satellites, Big Weaknesses," 31.

88 European Space Agency, "Cybersecurity in Orbit: Safeguarding Space Infrastructure," (n.d.) https://www.esa.int/Safety_Security/ESA_practices_cybersecurity.

89 Gregory Falco, "Cybersecurity Principles for Space Systems," 3.

90 Caudill and Wake, *Commercial Space System Security Guidelines*, 7–8, refers to a parallel to the SWIFT customer security controls framework requiring a) environment security, b) limit of access, c) detection and response.

the securing of the telemetry, the tracking and command (TT&C) system integrity in order to ensure the cybersecurity of telemetry links,[91] and the interoperability of protocols.

With regard to the space segment, prevention measures principally conform with those applicable to the ground segment, except for the impossibility of physical updating of satellite components. Encryption is one of the most relevant methods of protection. However, as it requires processing power and can slow communications traffic, it may create difficulties in implementation for small satellites.[92]

In addition to preventive measures, the ability to monitor and to respond to attacks could allow the detection of an attack can even before it renders the satellite unresponsive. Therefore, design measures, including onboard intrusion detection, as well as the use of stringent protocols and logs of traffic can be used to enable the detection of fraudulent and suspicious activity.[93] Most satellite operators already encrypt telemetry, tracking, and command messages to prevent the interception of communications. However, without mandatory requirements,[94] uniform adherence cannot be presumed. Especially in the case of small companies, encryption, and other technical efforts may be secondary due to cost-related reasons.

4.2 *Management Measures*

As pointed out above, risk from cyber intrusions cannot be completely eliminated. Nevertheless, risk can be managed, provided that cybersecurity threats can be anticipated and understood across all phases of a satellite project – from design, through operation, and until end-of-life.[95]

---

91 *Id.* at 13.

92 Max Eddy, "Want to Hack a Satellite? It Might be Easier Than you Think," *PC Mag UK* (March 7, 2019) https://uk.pcmag.com/news/119996/want-to-hack-a-satellite-it-might-be-easier-than-you-think.

93 For example, the security controls on satellites can be equipped with the ability to monitor attacks, *see* Vessels et al., "Cybersecurity Risk Assessment for Space Systems," 12 and Caudill and Wake, *Commercial Space System Security Guidelines*, 35.

94 Section 25.271 of the FCC rules, relating to control of transmitting stations, for example, specifies some measures for security of earth stations authorized under Part 25, but does not include any provisions regarding encryption of communications. *See* 47 CFR § 25.271(c) (securing transmitting stations operating by remote control), 25.271(d) (securing transmitting earth station facilities against unauthorized access or use whenever an operator is not present at the transmitter).

95 While the duration of a satellite lifecycle depends on the specific mission, the sequence of creating and implementing it includes a few phases. For more details on the phases of a satellite project and the participating actors, *see*, for example, S. Hobe, R. Popova, H. El

For every mission, a prioritisation must be undertaken in order to define which systems are indispensable so as to secure their components to the maximum extent possible and ensure abundance. Because not every malicious cyber activity leaves identifiable traces, the detection of occurrences is difficult. Thus, on the management level it is important, furthermore, to create and check logs records in order to track occurrences and filter the dangerous ones. To support these operations, threat intelligence can be used. Threat intelligence methods and platforms help to adopt suitable methodologies on the basis of specific data characterization and allow to differentiate between alarming and not relevant activities.[96]

Additionally, on the management level, the following steps are recommended for improving cybersecurity of space assets:[97]

- Improvement of the policies on access control;
- Funding allocation, combined with allocation of management force and of security specialists;
- Tailor-made security tools and solutions for any specific system;
- Cyber risk assessment procedures in order to adapt mitigation techniques for specific missions;
- Cyber threat information exchange between stakeholders in the satellite industry;
- And, as the main source of attacks are enabled by human error, the training of cyber and IT specialists.[98]

4.3 *Legal and Regulatory Measures*

Although clarity exists with regard to the available and advisable cybersecurity technical measures, on the legal and regulatory level, cybersecurity standards for commercial satellites are either very low, vary widely, or do not exist.[99] At present, no international framework exists for the regulation of cyber activities in general, or for space cybersecurity in particular.[100] Additionally, regulatory

---

Bajatti, and J. Scheu, "The Protection of Satellite Telecommunication Activities under BITs," *Journal of World Investment and Trade,* 6 no. 5 (2018): 1024–1058.

96 Caudill and Wake, *Commercial Space System Security Guidelines*, 23.

97 *Id.*

98 European Space Agency, "Cybersecurity in Orbit: Safeguarding Space Infrastructure."

99 Shaun Waterman, "DOD Looks to Increase Cybersecurity from Commercial Satellite Providers," *Air Force Magazine* (November 14, 2019) https://www.airforcemag.com/DOD-Looks-to-Increase-Cybersecurity-from-Commercial-Satellite-Providers/ and Bailey et al., "Defending Spacecraft in the Cyber Domain," 12.

100 The only binding instrument related to obligations of States in cyberspace is the Convention on Cybercrime, ETS 185 (opened for signature 23 November 2001, entered into force 1 July 2004) (Budapest Convention). It regulates "criminal offences through the

oversight is lacking. And while specific international instruments addressing cyberattacks are yet to be elaborated, various initiatives and policies addressing cybersecurity have been initiated.

For example, under the auspices of NATO,[101] Member States have been working on baseline requirements for space security.[102] Furthermore, the Consultative Committee for Space Data Systems (CCSDS),[103] in a joint effort of eleven space agencies, has been elaborating cybersecurity standards for space data systems and space mission operations.[104]

On the national level, the existing frameworks mainly address the regulation of content and data privacy,[105] but may, over time, advance to impose requirements with regard to cybersecurity in various sectors.[106] In general, however, standards specifically tailored to the cybersecurity of space systems are yet to evolve.

In the private sector, even though international and national regulation is absent, some companies do implement certain cybersecurity measures.

---

use of computer networks and/or electronic information," (*see* Recital 5) and "action[s] directed against the confidentiality, integrity and availability of computer systems, networks and computer data as well as the misuse of such systems, networks and data" (*see* Recital 8).

101 As the missions of the largest peacetime military alliance in the world – NATO – rely on space-based communications, a focus on the cybersecurity of satellite infrastructure has been put in the work of NATO. These include *NATO Cyber Defence* (February 2019) https://www.nato.int/nato_static_fl2014/assets/pdf/pdf_2019_02/20190208_1902-factsheet-cyber-defence-en.pdf. *See also* "NATO Industry Cyber Partnership Seeking Cooperation with the Private Industry," (n.d.) https://www.ncia.nato.int/business/partnerships/nato-industry-cyber-partnership.html.

102 Beyza Unal, *Cybersecurity of NATO's Space-based Strategic Assets*, Chatham House Research Paper (July 2019) https://www.chathamhouse.org/publication/cybersecurity-nato-s-space-based-strategic-assets/2019-06-27-Space-Cybersecurity-2.pdf.

103 The CCSDS is a multi-national forum for the development of communications and data systems standards for spaceflight in with currently 11 Member Space Agencies, *see* https://public.ccsds.org/participation/member_agencies.aspx.

104 *See* The Consultative Committee for Space Data Systems, *Security Guide for Mission Planners, Informational Report*, CCSDS 350.7-G-1 (October 2011); Consultative Committee for Space Data Systems, *Report Concerning Space Data System Standards: Security Threats Against Space Missions*, CCSDS 350.1.-G-2 (December 2015); and The Consultative Committee for Space Data Systems, *Wireless Network Communications Overview for Space Mission Operations*, CCSDS 880.0-G-3 (May 2017).

105 Stephan Hobe and Rada Popova, "Law in Cyberspace?," *German Journal for Air and Space Law* 67, no. 2 (2018): 268.

106 *See, for instance*, French Military Programming Act of 18 December 2013 (Articles L, 1332-6-1 to L, 1332-6-6 of the French Defence Code). For an overview of some national laws and policies, *see* Bergamasco et al., *Cybersecurity*, 222–226.

However, this is true mostly for big companies who have to protect their assets and their reputation and, more importantly, possess sufficient financial, technical, and manpower means to do so. Smaller companies, however, may not have the possibilities to invest (enough) in cybersecurity and in this regard, regulation can play a decisive role in the dissemination and implementation of cybersecurity in practice.

Therefore, the establishment of effective cybersecurity must be based upon technology-based measures, coupled with a complex of policy, regulatory, and strategy-based approaches towards cybersecurity risk mitigation, prevention, and management. Some patterns and know-how can be transferred to the space sector from other industries.

For example, for TT&C systems of small satellites and large constellations, an analogy can be made with the Society for Worldwide Interbank Financial Telecommunications (SWIFT) network. Therefore, it has been suggested to apply the cybersecurity measures recommended for users of the international SWIFT computerized banking payments system.[107]

Moreover, to secure supply chains, the standards employed by the nuclear power industry have been put forth as a model for the space industry. Thereby, it has been argued that although "the physical security standards from the nuclear power industry would actually be overkill [for the space industry]," the supply chain standards "would be about right."[108]

Due to the global implications of cyber vulnerabilities, these and other approaches for cybersecurity of space assets need to be undertaken on a national, regional, and international level, in close interaction between the governmental, non-governmental, and commercial sectors.

4.4 *Recent Regulatory Efforts in the United States*

On 4 September 2020, a new national space cybersecurity regulatory initiative became public when the United States White House released the Space Policy Directive "Cybersecurity Principles for Space Systems" (SPD-5).[109] Chronologically, SPD-5 follows four other space policy directives that have been issued by the Trump administration between 2017 and 2019 with regard

107 Physical tokens and standalone dedicated PCs that are not web-enabled are used for multifactor authentication, Shaun Waterman, "Space is Cybersecurity's New Frontier," The Cyber Edge (May 1, 2020) https://www.afcea.org/content/space-cybersecuritys-new-frontier.

108 *Id.*

109 The White House, Space Policy Directive – 5: Cybersecurity Principles for Space Systems, (September 4, 2020) https://www.whitehouse.gov/presidential-actions/memorandum-space-policy-directive-5-cybersecurity-principles-space-systems/.

to the US National Space Council.[110] SPD-5 is a set of cybersecurity principles intended to address and improve the cybersecurity of United States space systems and is the so far first comprehensive United States government policy addressing the cybersecurity of satellites and related systems.

The Directive underlines the key importance of space systems for critical infrastructure and global communications, thereby referring to the relevance of protection from malicious cyber activities[111] and their potential outcome.[112] While pointing out that cybersecurity principles and practices applying to terrestrial systems are applicable also to space systems, the Directive emphasizes the importance of cybersecurity of the space segment.[113] The integration into the design of space infrastructure and software of the ability to perform updates and to remotely respond to incidents,[114] along with the incorporation of cybersecurity measures within the full lifecycle of the satellite system are considered as critical cybersecurity measures.[115] Moreover, according to the Directive, "effective cybersecurity practices" must be built upon four pivotal aspects: prevention, active defence, risk management, and sharing of best practices. Thereby, the ability to "continuously monitor, anticipate, and adapt to mitigate evolving malicious cyber activities" is crucial for achieving the resilience and survival ability of the space system.[116]

Moreover, the Directive imposes requirements on the owners and operators of space systems to incorporate cybersecurity plans and capabilities in their space systems, so that the control of space vehicles can be retained or

110 The White House, "SPD-1, Presidential Memorandum on Reinvigorating America's Human Space Exploration Program," (11 December 2017); The White House, Space Policy Directive – 2, Streamlining Regulations on Commercial Use of Space (24 May 2018); The White House, Space Policy Directive – 3, National Space Traffic Management Policy (18 June 2018); The White House, Space Policy Directive – 4, Establishment of the United States Space Force, (19 February 2019).

111 SPD-5, Section 1: "Examples of malicious cyber activities harmful to space operations include spoofing sensor data; corrupting sensor systems; jamming or sending unauthorized commands for guidance and control; injecting malicious code; and conducting denial-of-service attacks."

112 SPD-5, Section 1: "Consequences of such activities could include loss of mission data; decreased lifespan or capability of space systems or constellations; or the loss of positive control of space vehicles, potentially resulting in collisions that can impair systems or generate harmful orbital debris."

113 SPD-5, Section 3.

114 Design must be based upon risk-based, cybersecurity-informed engineering, SPD-5, Section 4.

115 SPD-5, Section 3.

116 SPD-5, Section 4, Principle (a).

recovered even in cases of attacks. For this purpose, a minimum of measures are recommended, such as: protection against unauthorized access to critical functions; physical protection of command, control, and telemetry receiver systems; signal strength monitoring; authentication; encryption; adoption of best practices; intrusion detection; and physical security for automated information systems.[117]

Furthermore, for the protection of ground systems, information processing systems and operational technology, a reference is made to cybersecurity best practices, in particular to the ones formulated by the National Institute of Standards and Technology (NIST) within the NIST Cyber Security Framework.[118] With regard to the supply chain, risks should be minimized through tracking of manufactured products and sourcing requirements.[119]

As the set of guidelines in the Directive are non-binding and do not impose firm or regulatory requirements, it is recommended to implement them through rules, regulations, and guidance and of cybersecurity best practices and norms of behaviour.[120]

So far it seems that there is no intent to transform or transfer these principles into legally binding requirements,[121] but it is hoped that this will happen. In any case, they are an important impetus towards the formulation and adoption of technical and regulatory standards for cybersecurity for space systems.

4.5 *"Honeypots": A Solution for Large Constellations?*

While it is clear that an effective cybersecurity framework for space activities still has to evolve, some technical models for risk prevention that are applied already could serve the cybersecurity of large constellations. For example, professionals specialized in information systems resort to so-called "honeypots" (servers that are identical to the Internet or intranet company servers, except that they are laced with spyware) to track the behaviour of hackers.[122] Satellite honeypots can be used to create attack logs and to identify vulnerabilities. Thereby, with the help of the information gained, they can serve to develop defenses. With regard to the small satellite industry, and in particular to large

117 SPD-5, Section 4, Principle (b).

118 SPD-5, Section 4, Principle (b), (IV). National Institute of Standards and Technology, *Framework for Improving Critical Infrastructure Cybersecurity, Version 1.1* (16 April 2018).

119 SPD-5, Section 4, Principle (b), (VI).

120 SPD-5, Section 4, Principle (c).

121 Jeff Foust, "White House Issues Cybersecurity Space Policy," spacenews.com (September 4, 2020) https://spacenews.com/white-house-issues-cybersecurity-space-policy/.

122 Werner, "Small Satellites, Big Weaknesses," 33.

constellations, this can be a helpful strategy to optimize and bolster the cybersecurity in the constellation.[123]

Additionally, the cybersecurity of small satellite constellations can be improved through the deployment of commercial and open-source solutions such as, for example, software for predictive analytics.[124]

5 The Way Forward

Against the backdrop of growing cyber threats, the probability of which cannot be eliminated, but only minimized, cybersecurity of space infrastructure must be built upon a few premises, including:

- creating a robust, resilient infrastructure with well-protected components that can resort to abundance;
- applying highest security standards both in the design and encryption of assets, as well as with regard to components and manpower in the supply chain;
- employment of risk assessment and risk management procedures; and
- monitoring and threat detection in the operations sector[125] with the aim to ensure adaptability.

To these ends, human initiated measures must be backed also with methods based on artificial intelligence and machine learning. However, it must be underlined that there are no standard or one-size-fits-all solutions and each specific mission requires tailored risk management approach.

Without doubt, the awareness of the risks outlined above is a relevant step, but only the first of many necessary ones towards implementing measures to develop techniques and strategies enhancing cybersecurity for small satellites and large constellations.

Presently, the commercial space segment is unregulated in terms of cybersecurity, and efforts in this direction are in a nascent state. This is no coincidence, considering that there is no straightforward "go to" answer to the

123 *Id.* at 33.

124 Bailey et. al., "Defending Spacecraft in the Cyber Domain," 12.

125 These include the continuous monitoring of telemetry, command sequences, command receiver status, shared bus traffic, and flight software configuration and operating states. From a telemetry monitoring perspective, several parameters exist that have the highest likelihood of indicating a cyberattack against a spacecraft and should be actively monitored on the ground and looking into the future onboard the spacecraft with the IDS. *See* Jon Martin, "Satellite Telemetry Indicators for Identifying Potential Cyber Attacks, Aerospace," TOR-2019–02178, Aerospace Corporation (August 16, 2019).

question on how the law can in itself help to enhance cybersecurity. There is no established field of 'cyber' or 'cybersecurity' law; rather, the inherently technical cyber-related aspects of various, and ever-increasing fields of activity thread through the respective legal fields. The space sector is no exception.

Any practicable solution towards cybersecurity for space cannot be invented through the law and must inevitably stem from the IT sector. The law can help to document, streamline, and introduce standards and requirements for operators, but it is, in fact, an auxiliary instrument that acts as a facilitator of the very core of the solution which is technological. The main task for any regulation in the field of cybersecurity will thus be to "transpose" and translate technical solutions into normative language. Accordingly, the yet-to-be established legal structure on national, international, or customary level towards space assets cybersecurity must inevitably go hand in hand with technical solutions and the necessary logistical and financial resources necessary for their implementation.

Two examples from the recent practice illustrate that the regulatory initiative can be shifted from the governmental top-down level towards the industry, placing trust on commercial players to come up with ideas and proposals.

The United States – which is notoriously a pioneer in regulating cybersecurity – has recently adopted an approach that focuses less on mandating regulatory changes but rather recommends and anticipates action from commercial operators towards securing their satellites from intrusions.[126] In September 2021, it was announced that the Department of Defense has been tasked with updating rules for the cybersecurity of large constellations,[127] while allowing the industry to assess its own cybersecurity needs and create solutions.

In Europe, a coordinated supranational approach is still missing. For example, only in 2021 the space community gathered purposely to discuss all relevant aspects of cybersecurity when the first conference on European space

126 SPD-5, Section 4, Principle (b), (v) recommends operators to adopt "appropriate cybersecurity hygiene practices, physical security for automated information systems, and intrusion detection methodologies for system elements such as information systems, antennas, terminals, receivers, routers, associated local and wide area networks, and power supplies."

127 Theresa Hitchens, "DoD to Update Satellite Cyber Rules for Megaconstellations," *Breaking Defense* (9 September 2021) https://breakingdefense.com/2021/09/dod-to-update-satellite-cyber-rules-for-megaconstellations/. The DoD, via its Commercial Satellite Communications Office (CSCO), will check that suppliers have met the relevant cybersecurity standards set by the National Institute of Standards and Technology (NIST). See Matthew Scholl, *Draft NISTR 8270, Introduction to Commercial Satellite Operations* (June 2021) https://nvlpubs.nist.gov/nistpubs/ir/2021/NIST.IR.8270-draft.pdf.

cybersecurity (CYSAT) took place.[128] The event demonstrated the pressing necessity of interaction between governments and industry, but also between the IT and the space sector. Currently, private companies are hired by the European Space Agency (ESA) to protect governmental data exchanged via commercial satellites.[129] Moreover, ESA cooperates with the private sector to organise a demo hacking event, Hack OPS-SAT.[130] During the event, ethical hackers are invited to hack an orbiting satellite and challenge its cybersecurity, with the main aim to demonstrate that satellite hacking is an increasingly realistic scenario and to raise awareness on the urgency of cybersecurity in the space sector.

What is obvious is that any efforts to create the needed normative framework for cybersecurity – both nationally and internationally, are inherently dependent on the thorough understanding of what is technically required but also, what is technically feasible. Governments, commercial operators and end-users all have an interest in an adequate protection of the privacy and security of satellite-transmitted data. Therefore, the way forward must be premised on symbiotic, cooperative, interdisciplinary action ensuring that regulation is flexible and far-sighted enough to adapt and to react to the most effective and most up-to-date technical solutions available.

For the time being, the normative framework provides neither a satisfying solution to the challenges resulting from the cyber vulnerability[131] of space architecture in general, nor of large constellations in particular. The relevant, so far adopted practices focus mostly on the ground segment.[132] Absent binding regulations on the international and national level, their sophistication

---

128 The first edition of CYSAT took place online, from 17–19 March 2021, in Davos, Switzerland, https://conf.cysat.eu/.

129 European Space Agency, "ESA Acts to Protect Governmental Data," (11 November 2021) https://www.esa.int/Applications/Telecommunications_Integrated_Applications/ESA_acts_to_protect_governmental_data.

130 OPS-SAT is a cubesat launched by the European Space Agency on December 18th, 2019. It is operated from ESOC in Darmstadt, Germany and orbits at an altitude of 515 km and serves as a "flying laboratory" for testing and validating new techniques in mission control and on-board satellite systems. Over 100 companies and institutions from 17 European countries have registered experimental proposals to fly on OPS-SAT. The satellite and communicates with mission control via a network of ground stations spread worldwide, *see* https://hackopssat.cysat.eu/.

131 Vulnerability in the context of cybersecurity depicts the weakness in an information system, or of those components that could be exploited to violate system security policy.

132 Bailey et al, "Defending Spacecraft in the Cyber Domain," 2–3. Such practices have been adopted with the National Institute of Standards and Technology (NIST) Risk Management Framework and Cybersecurity Framework, Committee on National Security Systems [CNSS] Instruction [CNSSI] 1253F, and others.

and effectiveness depends completely on voluntary and fragmented implementation which, on its part, is contingent on the individual technical and financial capabilities, and on the motivation of space actors. Increasingly, also insurers will introduce requirements for cybersecurity as the health of the whole ecosystem will depend on providing adequate cybersecurity concepts. As a result, the lack of cybersecurity, apart from aggravating the risk of considerable, large-scale damage and financial losses, may inhibit the development and the growth of the small satellite industry altogether.

To achieve adequate, efficient, and encompassing cybersecurity compliance, future strategies must focus on a thorough protection of all segments of space infrastructure, including the TT&C links and, in particular, encompass the supply chain that increases the vulnerability surface,[133] and must transpose the technical measures and standards into specific, preferably binding, regulatory measures.

The two examples from the United States and Europe show that although until now, technical, financial, and logistical hurdles may have halted the development of cybersecurity for the space segment, the governmental sector is very much open to input from the industry,

Recommendations stemming from the industry that are based on voluntary adherence must be solidified by incentives, audits or enforcement measures, which lie within the discretionary powers of the State. Hence, apart from efforts that can be undertaken on the international level (but will, arguably, take more time to achieve tangible results), States can play the key role in imposing standards and requirements on their national space operators – for new missions, already on the level of licensing/authorization/certification requirements and, thus, contribute to enhancing cybersecurity for the space sector in general and for small satellites in particular as large constellations are moving from concept to practice.

---

133 In this regard, supply chain risk management programs and secure software development processes are key measures. *See* Bailey et al., "Defending Spacecraft in the Cyber Domain," 10. On coding rules for making the analysis of critical software more reliable, *see* Gerard J. Holzmann, "The Power of Ten – Rules for Developing Safety-Critical Code," NASA/JPL Laboratory for Reliable Software (June 2006).

SECTION II

Connectivity and Accessiblity

CHAPTER 5

Disruptions of Satellite Communication: Comparing Cyber Attacks and Harmful Interference for the Purposes of Legal Regulation

Simona Spassova

1 Introduction[1]

Every-day life on Earth is inextricably connected to and reliant upon multitudes and multitudes of capabilities provided by space systems. Thousands of satellites in outer space provide for our navigation systems, communications technologies, weather monitoring, Earth observation, and other applications. The uses of the information, assembled and transmitted from and through outer space, are countless: from telephony and TV to banking, agriculture, and military services. As a result of these ubiquitous applications, there is a continuous and dramatic increase over the past decades in the quantity and sophistication of satellite systems in the Earth's orbit. Naturally, what follows is also an increase in the threats to these systems and in the possible manners of compromising communications –which raises new legal questions on how to approach such dangers.

Although satellite technologies continue to evolve rapidly, the basic resources needed for their functioning are still: 1) an artificial satellite orbiting the Earth; 2) a terrestrial segment receiving or transmitting information and 3) an interference-free electromagnetic spectrum carrying radio waves, that is electromagnetic radiation at certain frequencies. The disruption of satellite communication can be affected either by destroying the physical components of the system (in space or on Earth) or by overwhelming or interfering with the medium via which these radio waves travel. There is also a third option – to disrupt the functioning of the system through the data stream itself.[2]

---

1 This article is based on a presentation, delivered jointly with Federico Bergamasco from the University of Luxembourg. Due credit should be given for all his constructive ideas and meticulous research, which have found their way into this article. Concurrently, any and all deficiencies of the current contribution are the responsibility of the author alone.

2 Duncan Hollis, "Why States Need an International Law for Information Operations," *Lewis & Clark Law Review* v. 11 (2007): 1023.

 | DOI:10.1163/9789004527270_006

The purpose of this contribution is twofold. Firstly, it aims to clarify the notion of a 'cyber attack against a satellite system' in order to distinguish it from 'harmful interference against a satellite system.' These concepts have often been used interchangeably – wrongly so. There is only a very limited, extremely unlikely scenario of a potential overlap. Hence, it will be crucial to define the concepts and understand the underlying technology to be able to suggest, apply, and implement an appropriate governing legal regime. Second, this chapter will elaborate on the legal framework of the ITU in relation to these two concepts in order to examine the current and potential future role of the organization in the formation of legally binding international rules/standards on cybersecurity. The ITU is worth examining in this context for it is the main UN agency responsible for information technologies. The organization has long been at the forefront of global efforts to coordinate and regulate telecommunications, and most notably, it is predominantly a 'technical' organization, of engineers, who understand the operational side of communications.

2 The Problem of Definitions and Understanding the Definitions

A general lack of clear definitions and understanding of concepts has often led to confusion as to which legal framework *can* and *should* be applicable to the situation at hand. This situation is further exacerbated by the fact that there is no international regulatory instrument that provides a globally accepted definition of 'cyber attack.' Even the term itself – 'cyber attack' is not totally uncontroversial, as different terms such as 'cyber operation,' 'information operation,' 'malicious cyber activity,' or 'cyber crime' have all been utilised depending on the context. To make things worse, even when a definition is put forward, it is not always well understood as its constitutive elements are themselves "too technical". It has been suggested, for example, that the ITU rules on harmful interference could be applied to instances of cyber attacks. Such suggestions have pointed out to the definition of harmful interference "as that which 'endangers … *safety services,* or seriously degrades, obstructs or repeatedly interrupts a radio communication service.'"[3] Then they elaborate "that safety services include technologies 'used permanently or temporarily for the safeguarding of human life and property', which may refer to public services such as health, police, and public transport, along with critical infrastructure

3 *Quoted in* Scott J. Shackelford, "The Law of Cyber Peace," *Chicago Journal of International Law* v.18(1) (2017): 37.

more generally, all of which are vulnerable to cyber attacks."[4] The critique is then directed towards the lack of enforcement mechanisms of the ITU and the political resistance against empowering it. However, the crucial element of defining and understanding the 'interference' itself, as per the ITU legal documents has been skipped, leading to the erroneous suggestion that these rules could apply to instances of cyber attacks.

Clearly, a uniform understanding of the constitutive elements of a definition is key for avoiding ambiguity in interpretation, and for warranting the application of a law to a specific case. The more technologically complex the case at hand, the greater is the need for definitions.

Lately, especially, this need is even more pronounced. Particularly because States are attempting to legislate in relation to the cybersecurity of space systems. Just recently, on 4 September 2020, the US President signed a Space Policy Directive-5 on space cybersecurity. The goal of this SPD-5 is to establish a set of principles to protect the country's space assets from cyber threats. Notably, the background to this Policy states the following: "As the space domain is contested, it is necessary for developers, manufacturers, owners, and operators of space systems to design, build, operate, and manage them so that they are resilient to cyber incidents and radio-frequency spectrum interference."[5] 'Cyber incidents' and 'spectrum interference' are both and separately mentioned in this policy because they may lead to the same consequences – for instance, loss of mission data, decreased capability of space systems or constellations, loss of positive control of space vehicles, potentially resulting in collisions that can impair systems or generate harmful orbital debris.[6] However, these are different types of activities. That is not to say that they may not be regulated concurrently, but rather that a differentiation is needed. On an international level, there is a clear and general consensus about what constitutes 'spectrum interference.' There is also a universally accepted international legal document, which instructs States to refrain from it.[7] There is much less unanimity on preventing 'cyber incidents.'

4 *Id.* at 37–38.

5 White House, Space Policy Directive-5: Cybersecurity Principles for Space Systems (2020).

6 *Id.*

7 ITU Constitution, Art. 45. It stipulates that "all stations, whatever their purpose, must be established and operated in such a manner as *not to cause harmful interference* to the radio services or communications of other member states or of recognized operating agencies, or of other duly authorized operating agencies which carry on a radio service, and which operate in accordance with the provisions of the Radio Regulations."

Hence, the following two sections first look at the notion of 'harmful interference,' an established and well-defined concept, in order to build upon it and differentiate from the rather more elusive term 'cyber attack.'

3 Harmful Interference

Linguistically speaking, the words 'attack' and 'interference' are more synonymous than one would expect. The origin of the verb 'interfere' is linked to the Latin verb 'ferire', which means "to strike or to hurt."[8] Concurrently, the verb 'attack' means "to set upon or work against forcefully" or "to assail with unfriendly or bitter words."[9] The expected harm to be caused is somehow implied within the words themselves. Nowadays, however, there is an implied recognition that not all interference can be harmful. This is true also in the realm of satellite communication, relevant to this analysis. For example, the International Telecommunication Union identifies three types of interference: permissible, accepted, and harmful.[10] Interference only becomes harmful once it meets certain criteria as to the effects it has produced.

In the realm of space communication specifically and telecommunication in general, interference alone is defined as "the effect of unwanted *energy* due to one or a combination of *emissions, radiations, or inductions* upon reception in a radiocommunication system, manifested by any performance degradation, misinterpretation, or loss of information which could be extracted in the absence of such unwanted energy."[11] Notably, this interference only becomes harmful once it "*endangers* the functioning of a radionavigation service or other safety services or seriously degrades, obstructs or repeatedly interrupts a radiocommunication service operating in accordance with Radio Regulations."[12] A technical definition, indeed, and *it does not* differentiate on the basis of the *element of intent*. Rather, the emphasis here is on the effect that is produced. In addition, for any 'energy effect' to be recognized as harmful, it needs to impact upon a radiocommunication service, which operates

8 "Interfere." Merriam-Webster.com Dictionary (accessed 31 December 2020) https://www.merriam-webster.com/dictionary/interfere.

9 "Attack." Merriam-Webster.com Dictionary (accessed 31 December 2020) https://www.merriam-webster.com/dictionary/attack.

10 ITU, Radio Regulations, Art 1.166.

11 *Id.*

12 *Id.*

in accordance with the Radio Regulations. Hence, this radiocommunication service must have met certain universally agreed criteria beforehand.

The uniform consensus on this definition and its constitutive elements is confirmed not only by the fact that the almost all countries on the Earth have acceded to the Radio Regulations, but also because this definition has been 'internalized' within the national jurisdictions of many countries, as well as made its way to other legal and regulatory instruments. It was verbatim incorporated into European Union legislation,[13] as well as in many national legislations.[14]

4 Cyber Attacks

In contrast to the exhaustive technical definition of harmful interference, the term 'cyber attack' still lacks a universal, unambiguous definition. There is a plethora of different proposals, elaborated by international organizations, standardization bodies, and national administrations with scarce or no coordination among themselves. For instance, according to the US Department of Defense, "cyberspace attacks" are "actions taken in cyberspace that create noticeable denial effects (i.e., degradation, disruption, or destruction) in cyberspace or manipulation that leads to denial that appears in a physical domain, and is considered a form of fires."[15] The US Department of Defense makes use also of the different and wider concept of "cyber operation," defining it as "the employment of cyberspace capabilities where the primary purpose is to achieve objectives in or through cyberspace."[16] The previously mentioned SPD-5 further elaborates on the examples of 'malicious cyber activities,' which can be 'harmful' to space operations. These include "spoofing sensor data; corrupting sensor systems; jamming or sending unauthorized commands for

13 For example, in the 2009 amendment of the Framework Directive 2002/21/EC.

14 Gerry Oberst, "European Law as an Instrument for Avoiding Harmful Interference," in Mahulena Hofmann, ed., *Harmful Interference in Regulatory Perspective* (Baden Baden: Nomos 2015): 125.

15 Joint Chiefs of Staff, *Cyber Space Operations* (2018) https://www.jcs.mil/Portals/36/Documents/Doctrine/pubs/jp3_12.pdf. In this context and terminology, cyberspace attack capabilities create *fires* in and through cyberspace and are often employed with little or no associated physical destruction. However, modification or destruction of computers that control physical processes can lead to cascading effects (including collateral effects) in the physical domain.

16 *Id.*

guidance and control; injecting malicious code; and conducting denial-of service attacks."[17]

The European Union, on the other hand, has its own terms and definitions. According to the European Union Agency for Cybersecurity (commonly known as ENISA) glossary, a cyber attack "covers all cyber incidents triggered by *malicious intent* where damages, disruptions or dysfunctionalities are caused," whereas a cyber incident is "any occurrence that has impact on any of the components of the cyber space or on the functioning of the cyber space, independent if it's natural or human made; malicious or non-malicious intent; deliberate, accidental or due to incompetence; due to development or due to operational interactions," and could also be caused by "any incident generated by any of cyber space components even if the damage/disruption, dysfunctionality is caused outside the cyber space."[18]

For the purposes of the current contribution, it would be proper to use and present the definition provided by the ITU. The ITU does not define a 'cyber attack' *per se*, but it clarifies that a cyber attack occurs when a threat breaches security controls around a physical or an information asset.[19] Cyber attacks are further categorized as active or passive and inside or outside. An "active" attack aims to alter system resources or affect their operation. Conversely, a "passive" attack seeks to use information from a system but does not affect system resources of that system. As expected, an 'inside attack' is initiated by an entity inside the security perimeter (an "insider"). In contrast, unauthorised or illegitimate users initiate "outside" attacks outside the security perimeter.[20]

In addition, ITU defines 'cybersecurity' as "the collection of tools, policies, security concepts, security safeguards, guidelines, risk management approaches, actions, training, best practices, assurance and technologies that can be used to protect the cyber environment and organization and user's assets. Organization and user's assets include connected computing devices, personnel, infrastructure, applications, services, telecommunications systems, and the totality of transmitted and/or stored information in the cyber environment. Cybersecurity strives to ensure the attainment and maintenance of the security properties of the organization and user's assets against relevant

17 Space Policy Directive – 5.

18 ENISA, *ENISA overview of cybersecurity and related terminology* (2017) https://www.enisa.europa.eu/publications/enisa-position-papers-and-opinions/enisa-overview-of-cybersecurity-and-related-terminology.

19 ITU, *ITU National Cybersecurity Strategy Guide* (2011) http://www.itu.int/ITU-D/cyb/cybersecurity/docs/itu-national-cybersecurity-guide.pdf.

20 *Id.*

security risks in the cyber environment."[21] Concurrently, 'cyberspace' is the environment in which communication over computer networks occurs, even though this is not a particularly precise definition.

From all the above definitions, it can be inferred that a cyber attack, in order to be qualified as such, has to be a *hostile voluntary action* that involves, to some extent, the so-called "cyberspace," either as medium or target of the attack. Notably, all such definitions are neutral with regard to the nature of the perpetrator and to the motivation behind the action. They are technical definitions, that focus on the involvement of the cyberspace element, and from a legal point of view they can be relevant both to "cybercrime" – which generally involves national criminal laws – and to State-to-State cyber operations within a public international law dimension.

Unfortunately, the problem seems circular, as no globally accepted definition of cyberspace exists either. ISO provides in its Guidelines on Cybersecurity a definition of it as "the complex environment resulting from the interaction of people, software and services on the internet by means of technology devices and networks connected to it, which does not exist in any physical form."[22] ENISA defines it as "the time-dependent set of tangible and intangible assets, which store and/or transfer electronic information."[23]

Therefore, the question, particularly relevant for the aim of this contribution, is whether cyberspace refers only to the virtual world created by the interaction of code, or if it refers in general to the storage and exchange of information in a given system or system of systems by any means – including radio transmissions.

In order to understand the difference, for mere explanatory purposes it is possible to make reference to the US Department of Defense doctrine on cyber electromagnetic activities. Here a clear distinction is drafted between the cyberspace environment and the electromagnetic spectrum. The first domain has peculiar characteristics: it has a non-physical dimension, and it is ruled by human-made laws, that is computer code. The second one, instead, consists of the range of frequencies of electromagnetic radiation from zero to infinity. It exists in nature and is ruled by the law of physics.

While the electromagnetic spectrum has an undisputed physical dimension though non-tangible, cyberspace can be conceived in two ways: in its

21 ITU, "Definition of Cybersecurity" (n.d.) https://www.itu.int/en/ITU-T/studygroups/com17/Pages/cybersecurity.aspx.

22 ISO/IEC 27032:2015, Information Technology – Security Techniques – Guidelines for Cybersecurity, First Edition (July 2012).

23 ENISA, *ENISA Overview of Cybersecurity and Related Terminology*.

narrow definition it is a non-physical space, or, in other terms, it is a virtual space, made of and ruled by computer code. In its broad definition it includes a physical layer, consisting of all the physical equipment associated with links (wired, wireless, and optical) that support the transfer of code and data on the networks and nodes. For example, physical networks components may include wires, cables, radio frequencies, routers, servers, computers, radars, weapons systems, telecommunications systems, personal digital assistants, and other networked devices where data is created, manipulated, processed, and stored.

5 Is Electromagnetic Interference a Cyber Attack?

Intentional electromagnetic interference would by definition affect the electromagnetic spectrum environment, and therefore, according to the US Department of Defense terminology, be qualified as an electronic attack. It may also fall within the ITU regulatory framework, although the latter makes no difference between intentional and unintentional electromagnetic interference. Would it also be qualified as a cyberspace attack?

The answer seems to depend on the definition of cyberspace that we decide to employ. If we adopt the narrow approach, a jamming or spoofing operation has no effect on the virtual environment, that is on the non-physical world governed by computer code. A cyberattack, in this perspective, is qualified as such because it makes use of cyberspace-borne tools – so-called "malware," – such as viruses, worms, Trojans and botnets or of cyber-borne techniques, such as denial of service, infiltration, social engineering, probing, sniffing, and mapping. If we adopt a broad definition, inclusive of the physical networks that support cyberspace in its narrow concept, radio frequencies would be encompassed.

Consequently, it seems that electromagnetic interference on these radio frequencies – in the form of jamming or spoofing – could be qualified as a cyberattack, but not necessarily. On an equal foot, also kinetic attacks would be qualified as such, as long as their consequence affects the cyberspace as the primary target. For instance, the physical destruction of a server would fall under this category. Still, however, the involvement of cyberspace in the narrow sense of the term seems to be necessary. A jamming or spoofing attack would therefore need to impact the satellite software – for instance by infecting it with a malware – or to use the satellite to reroute a malware on a computer system on the ground to be qualified as cyberattack. An intentional electromagnetic interference that does not involve cyberspace in any form, for instance the jamming of a TV channel, would not be qualified as a cyberattack in this respect, given the total absence of the "cyber" element.

Lastly, reminding ourselves of the definition of interference and harmful interference, as per the Radio Regulations of the ITU, the "effect of unwanted energy" has to be "due to one or a combination of emissions, radiations, or inductions upon reception in a radiocommunication system, manifested by any performance degradation, misinterpretation, or loss of information which could be extracted in the absence of such unwanted energy."[24] For that effect to be harmful, it would have to endanger the functioning of a radionavigation service or of other safety services or seriously degrade, obstruct, or repeatedly interrupt a radiocommunication service operating in accordance with Radio Regulations.[25] To put it simply, the ITU definition of harmful interference does not really cover cyber attacks, hence the legally binding Radio Regulations would not be applicable to such events.

For the sake of exhaustiveness and purely theoretically speaking, there exists an unlikely scenario of a possible overlap. This means that an attempt would be made to upload malware into the satellite on-board computer via a radio signal. Would that constitute a cyberattack? Yes, since it would make use of cyber capabilities. Would it constitute harmful interference? Going back to the definition in the preceding paragraph – it depends. Theoretically this is possible, but unlikely, since the interference with the legitimate signal would raise suspicions and since, practically speaking, it is easier to target the ground computer network that controls the satellite rather than the satellite in space. In other words, the applicability of the Radio Regulations to cyber attacks is unlikely and would be purely coincidental.

6 The ITU, Harmful Interference and Cybersecurity

It was pointed out that when the issue of harmful interference comes up, the starting research point ought to be the International Telecommunications Union and its legally binding Constitution and Radio Regulations. The ITU is an international organization, made up of sovereign member States and is the sole global agency through which electrical communications, whether wireless or wired, are regulated on the basis of bilateral and multilateral agreements. Even if the procedural and structural base of this organizations have

24 ITU Radio Regulations, 1.166.

25 ITU Radio Regulations, 166 & 169.

evolved through time, the original purpose of the institution remains its 'bedrock'[26] which has remained relevant even in light of the radical technological changes – from the time of the telegraph through the internet. After all, the notion of the Internet began in the 19th century with the telegraph system. Like the Internet, the telegraph system relied on the concept of submitting data between two devices.

The issue of harmful interference is recognized as a very significant topic within the ITU Constitution. The Constitution contains a specific Article 45, entitled "Harmful Interference." In a constitutive legal document of an international organization, this explicit attention to harmful interference denotes the central position of the topic for member States.

What about cyber attacks? One of the frequent caveats when talking about cyber attacks and the ITU in the legal arena is an inherent misunderstanding as to precisely which documents of the Union would be relevant and why. An erroneous suggestion was outlined earlier, hinting that the ITU rules on harmful interference could be applied to cyber attacks because they can "conceivably refer to public services such as health, police and public transport, along with critical infrastructure more generally, all of which are vulnerable to cyber attacks."[27] While the Radio Regulations may not be the most adequate legal instrument on that front, one should not forget that the mission of the ITU is to promote the development of telecommunication networks and access to telecommunication services by fostering cooperation.[28] And when it comes to cybersecurity, the ITU is equipped with a strong mandate. In particular, following its endorsement at the World Summit on the Information Society, the ITU launched in 2007 the Global Cybersecurity Agenda, a framework for international cooperation aimed at enhancing confidence and security in the information society. This initiative includes a specific working area focused on the elaboration of legislative responses to address evolving legal issues in cybersecurity. The organization is mandated to "focus resources and programmes on those national, regional and international areas of cybersecurity within its core mandate and expertise, notably the technical and development spheres, and not including areas related to member States' application of legal or policy

26 Francis Lyall, *International Telecommunications: The International Telecommunications Union and The Universal. Postal Union* (Surrey: Ashgate 2011): 127.

27 Shackelford, "The Law of Cyber Peace," 37–38.

28 For instance, the ITU Global Cybersecurity Agenda was launched in 2007, as a framework for international cooperation aimed at enhancing confidence and security in the information society. ITU, "Global Cybersecurity Agenda" (n.d.) https://www.itu.int/en/action/cybersecurity/Pages/gca.aspx.

principles related to national defence, national security, content and cybercrime, which are within their sovereign rights, although this does not exclude ITU from carrying out its mandate to develop technical recommendations designed to reduce vulnerabilities in the ICT infrastructure."[29]

An integral component of any national cybersecurity strategy is the adoption of appropriate legislation against the misuse of ICTs for criminal purposes – which is harmonized with regional and international policy and practices. To help ensure a safe, secure and equitable Internet – and combat cybercrime – the ITU is assisting member States in implementing appropriate cybersecurity legislation and harmonizing the legal and policy framework.[30] Other current ITU cybersecurity-related activities are the Global Cybersecurity Index, a project to measure the cybersecurity capabilities of nation States by ranking their level of 'cybersecurity development', and the CIRTs, a capacity building programme to assist countries in establishing their National Computer Incident Response Team (CIRT). Additionally, the ITU assists least-developed countries with the production of guidelines on cybersecurity legislations and regulations.

Hence, in its function as a coordinator and a technical regulatory organization, the ITU is more concerned with ensuring cybersecurity, rather than imposing any measures of consequences. Its activities in the field are mandated, but do not go as far as to impose obligations or sanctions. Given that harmful interference and cyber attacks are clearly distinct from each other, the Radio Regulations should not be applied to cyber attacks, but that is not to say that the Union should not have a role to play when it comes to the regulatory norms regarding such operations.

7 Conclusion

Both cyberattacks and harmful interference against a satellite in space have the potential to impact international relationships, businesses, economics, political situations, or at least cause huge financial losses. Intentional disruptions of communications have often been classified as attacks against a state, terrorism, or even acts of war. For example, this is the case with the now infamous

29 ITU Resolution 130 (Rev. Dubai, 2018), Strengthening the Role of ITU in Building Confidence and Security in the Use of Information and Communication Technologies (2018) https://www.itu.int/en/action/cybersecurity/PublishingImages/Lists/resolutions/AllItems/Res%20130.pdf.

30 ITU, Legislation (n.d.) https://www.itu.int/en/ITU-D/Cybersecurity/Pages/legislation.aspx.

Internet attack against Estonian websites in 2007, when the country's Minister of Defense declared that such actions constituted "an attack against the state."[31] Similar notions have been put forward when it comes to the suggested use of jamming technology on the territory of the Ukraine.[32]

On the international level, cybersecurity is concerned with the application of international law to the realities of network and computer technologies. Generally speaking, there are two main challenges with the creation of international legal norms concerning cybercrime and cybersecurity: the problems of jurisdiction and attribution of behaviour. These issues remain relevant and are even exacerbated when the subject matter concerns telecommunication systems based in outer space. In recent years especially, cyberspace is growingly inclusive of and dependent upon satellite communication. In the complex and fragmented landscape of international efforts to regulate this subject matter, the International Telecommunication Union is the UN entity that has accumulated the greatest technical expertise in both fields, even though the organization and its activities, standards, and regulations are often overlooked in the relevant academic discourse. Upon analyzing the regulatory work of the International Telecommunication Union, we need to be mindful that the international norms that it has set on the subject of harmful interference cannot be simply transposed and interpreted as if applying to cyber attacks. Rather, we should shift our focus to the capacity-building and the advisory role the ITU has played when it comes to cybersecurity, and look for guidance there.

31 In April of 2007, the Government of Estonia relocated a memorial from the Soviet era from the center of its capital city, a move opposed by the Russian Government. Following this, the country experienced a series of major cyber-attacks which in some cases lasted for weeks. Online services of Estonian banks, media outlets and government bodies were taken down by unprecedented levels of internet traffic. The attacks have been described as a retaliatory move against the decision to move the statue. *See* Hollis, "Why States Need an International Law for Information Operations," 1023.

32 Niall Firth, "How to Fight a War in Space (and Get away with It)," *MIT Technology Review* (2019) https://www.technologyreview.com/2019/06/26/725/satellite-space-wars/.

CHAPTER 6

Non-Geostationary Satellite Systems: New Rules of Bringing Them into Use and Phasing Their Deployment

Elina Morozova

1 Introduction

Lately, interest has been generally growing for the use of non-geostationary orbits (non-GSOs) for various types of satellite services. Compared to the traditional geostationary orbit (GSO) – which is located about 36,000 km from the Earth's equator – low, medium, and high Earth orbits pass at lower altitudes. Relatively low altitudes enable non-GSO satellites to transmit data at a high speed and with low latency all over the world, including the most remote and rural areas as well as strategically important locations like the Arctic, while new technologies make it possible to process extremely large amounts of information, which only contributes to the rapid growth of non-GSOs' popularity.

Unlike GSO satellites which appear motionless to any fixed geographical point, non-GSO satellites are in constant motion relative to Earth observers. Hence, in order to continuously cover the entire globe and provide satellite services, non-GSO operators deploy not one but several or even a multitude of satellites in various orbital planes, usually called non-GSO multi-satellite systems or, in everyday speech, constellations. Both GSO and non-GSO satellites use the radio frequency spectrum and satellite orbits which are limited natural resources of outer space. The responsibilities related to the management of such resources are assigned to the International Telecommunication Union (ITU) headquartered in Geneva, Switzerland, which is the United Nations specialized agency for information and communication technologies.[1]

The obligation of the ITU, as it is stipulated in its Constitution,[2] to ensure the rational, equitable, efficient, and economical use of the radio frequency

1 The ITU was founded in Paris in 1865 as the International Telegraph Union. It took its present name in 1934 and became a specialized agency of the United Nations in 1947. ITU's global membership includes 193 member States as well as some 900 companies, universities, and international and regional organizations.

2 Constitution and Convention of the International Telecommunication Union (1992): Nos. 78, 196.

 DOI:10.1163/9789004527270_007

spectrum and associated orbits in accordance with the ITU Radio Regulations (RR),[3] is equally applicable to both the GSO and non-GSOs. Yet, for non-GSO satellite systems, some important provisions are missing from the RR. This is due to the fact that the use of the orbit and spectrum resource of the GSO, where the largest number of communication and broadcasting satellites have traditionally been located, has a rich history and a well developed regulatory framework elaborated in detail over the years, while the regulation of non-GSOs has only recently acquired high relevance. In particular, these missing provisions are the requirements to bring into use (BIU) and bring back into use (BBIU) frequency assignments[4] in non-GSOs.

2 The BIU and BBIU Procedures

BIU is an important stage in every satellite project that marks its transition from paper into real life. Its implementation begins with the submission to the ITU of a general description of a future satellite network or system which is made publicly available. Then, coordination with operators of 'neighbouring' satellite networks and systems takes place to ensure safe and trouble-free simultaneous operations. The results of such coordination are taken into account when designing a frequency plan of a spacecraft and when making an entry in the Master International Frequency Register (Master Register). After being recorded in the Master Register, the frequency assignment receives the right to international recognition. Practically, this right means that other operators must avoid causing harmful interference to such recorded frequency assignments.

However, such recognition is granted to the recorded frequencies on a provisional basis and must be followed by their utilization. This is the practical meaning of BIU; it confirms that the orbit/spectrum resource provided to the operator at its request is actually used and prevents such resource from

3 Radio Regulations are an international treaty for governing the use of the radio-frequency spectrum and satellite orbits for wireless communications and ensure interference-free operations of radiocommunication systems. The previous edition, edition of 2016, was in force until 31 December 2020; the edition of 2020, as amended by the 2019 World Radiocommunication Conference, entered into force on 1 January 2021.

4 The term 'frequency assignments' means an authorization to use certain radio frequencies under specific conditions. *See* Radio Regulations, No. 1.18. One of such conditions is the timely bringing frequencies into use and, if the use of frequencies has been suspended (for instance, because of a satellite's malfunction and its further replacement by a new one), the timely bringing them back into use.

standing idle. If BIU is not completed in a timely manner, frequency assignments may be cancelled, and the relevant frequencies again become available to any other operator.

The regulatory deadline for BIU is provided for in the Radio Regulations: it must be carried out within seven years[5] from the date of receipt by the ITU Radiocommunication Bureau (BR, Bureau) of advance publication information or a request for coordination related to a new satellite network or system. The Radio Regulations also set the regulatory deadline for the so-called bringing back into use (BBIU), which must be performed within three years[6] after the suspension of the use of the relevant network or system. A suspension may be required if, for example, after the start of using the satellite network or system, an accident occurs on the satellite and its replacement with another one is required. The suspension is granted to the operator if requested, but only for a certain period. At the end of this period, the operation of the satellite network or system must be resumed in order to continue the actual use of frequencies. The consequences of a non-compliance with the BBIU regulatory deadline are similar to those of a non-compliance with the BIU regulatory deadline, that is if the regulatory deadlines are not met, frequency assignments may be cancelled. Such cancellation may eventually undermine the whole satellite project.

Such harsh measures are justified by the task that the ITU fulfills – it ensures the rational, equitable, efficient, and economical use of limited natural resources of outer space, which, as proclaimed by the ITU documents, are radio frequencies and associated orbits.[7]

3 Requirements for BIU and BBIU

For the GSO satellite networks, the requirements for the BIU and BBIU of the frequency assignments are clarified in the RR. A frequency assignment in the geostationary-satellite orbit is considered as having been brought into use when a space station[8] with the capability of transmitting or receiving on

5 Radio Regulations, No. 11.44.

6 Radio Regulations, No. 11.49. The three-year period may be proportionately reduced if the six-month suspension notification period established by the Radio Regulations is not complied with.

7 Radio Regulations, No. 0.3; Constitution of the ITU, No. 196.

8 The term 'space station' is used in the Radio Regulations and means "a station located on an object which is beyond, is intended to go beyond, or has been beyond, the major

that frequency assignment has been deployed and maintained at the notified orbital position for a continuous period of ninety days.[9] The commencement of the ninety-day period is deemed to be the date when the frequency assignment is brought into use.[10] The bringing back into use of a frequency assignment to a space station in the GSO is carried out in the same manner.[11]

In the absence of any specific regulation concerning non-GSOs, the ITU Radiocommunication Bureau applied the requirements created and adopted for the GSOs to them. This means that in accordance with the established practice,[12] the BIU of the frequency assignment to a non-GSO system was considered successful when at least one satellite capable of transmitting or receiving that frequency assignment was deployed and held for ninety days on one of the notified orbital planes regardless of the total number of satellites and orbital planes in the constellation concerned. Such BIU by a single satellite made it possible to complete the recording of the frequency assignment to the entire non-GSO system.

Some technical explanation should be given for the approach chosen by the BR. Each satellite, whether GSO or non-GSO, requires telemetry, tracking, and control (TT&C). Thus, TT&C capability must be available to all satellites in a constellation. It means that some of the frequency assignments associated with the constellation are already in use after the launch of the first satellite which must be managed in the context of other satellites in a particular constellation regardless of its structure.[13] However, for the BIU purposes, the Bureau did not separate specific frequencies used for TT&C, rather it recorded the relevant frequency assignment in the Master Register as a whole.

This practice of the Bureau has been applied for many years and has not caused problems until recently, given the relatively small number of the existing non-GSO systems. However, one needs to consider the growing demand

---

portion of the Earth's atmosphere." *See* Radio Regulations, No. 1.64. Such objects include satellites and other spacecraft.

9 Radio Regulations, No. 11.44B.

10 Radio Regulations, No. 11.44.2.

11 Radio Regulations, No. 11.49.1.

12 For non-GSO systems in fixed satellite service (FSS) and mobile satellite service (MSS), this practice of the Radiocommunication Bureau was reflected in the Rules of Procedure for the RR, No. 11.44. The Rules of Procedure are not, however, an international treaty binding upon ITU member States, rather they are mandatory for the BR.

13 Annex 22 to Working Party 4A Chairman's Report, Document 4A/63-E (Annex 22 "Working document toward preliminary draft CPM text for WRC-19 agenda item 7, Issue A: Factors related to the bringing into use of frequency assignments of non-GSO systems subject to coordination") (13 May 2016): No. 3.2.

for the use of low and medium orbits which may soon significantly increase the number of such systems. In addition, the total number of satellites in the non-GSO systems is also increasing. For example, in recent years, the BR has received requests concerning frequency assignments to large and complex non-GSO systems consisting of several hundred to tens of thousands (from 70,000 to more than 230,000) of satellites in more than 1,000 orbital planes.[14] Some ambitious projects of this scale have already begun to be implemented.

In these circumstances, it becomes obvious that one has to make sure that the radio frequency spectrum and the associated satellite orbits are properly used by all kinds of satellite services. The application of the same rules of BIU and BBIU frequency assignments to both geostationary satellites and non-geostationary multi-satellite systems cannot solve the situation because it suffers several disadvantages.

4 Core of the Problem

The practice of the ITU Radiocommunication Bureau considering a non-GSO system to be brought into use by a single satellite regardless of the complexity and size of orbital parameters of the system, can hardly ensure a rational, equitable, efficient, and economical use of radio frequencies and satellite orbits.

Each frequency filing after whose processing an operator gets an authorization to use the frequencies – a frequency assignment – contains information about the planned number of frequencies to be used. The larger the system is and the more satellites requiring communications with the Earth and with each other, the more frequencies are needed for its operation. When filing a large system, the operator is expected to use the entire spectrum necessary for its operation. The same is true for BIU and BBIU. These formal procedures must confirm that the operator actually uses the entire filed number of the orbit/frequency resources. Therefore, it does matter how many satellites are actually deployed in the non-GSO system. If the entire system can be brought (or brought back) into use by a single satellite, any further control over the use of the spectrum is lost, though obviously needed.

First, when deploying a multi-satellite non-GSO system, its operator may change the plans and, for example, launch significantly fewer satellites than specified in the filing. At the same time, after the launch of the first and possibly

14 Progress report recommending possible revision to Decision 482 concerning complex/large non-GSO satellite filings and exceptionally complex GSO satellite filings, Document C19/36-R (Revision 1) (7 June 2019): Section 2 "Background."

the only spacecraft, the whole frequency assignment originally intended for the operation of a large satellite constellation will be considered brought into use. Consequently, the part of the radio frequency spectrum that is not actually used by such system will become unavailable to other operators which may lead to spectrum warehousing. Secondly, there is a risk of submitting filings of a speculative nature – those which do not cover the actual operation of a spacecraft but are merely aimed at blocking the spectrum, thus remaining for many years as ink on paper. This could lead to the revival of so-called 'paper satellites.'

The simplest solution, at first glance, leading to the proper use of the non-GSO orbit/spectrum resource, would be to require that all satellites in a constellation are deployed no later than before the expiry of the seven-year deadline for the BIU. In this case, the frequency assignment would be considered to be brought into use if the condition for a full deployment of the non-GSO system was met, whichwould apparently prevent any abuse related to the use of radio frequencies and satellite orbits by the system operator.

However, for design considerations, such as the need for production facilities and launch vehicles, it would be unrealistic to expect that multiple satellites would bedeployed within this seven-year regulatory period. Some exceptionally large non-GSO constellations require additional months or even years to deploy all spacecraft andputting such systems into full operation can significantly exceed the BIU deadline. When discussing the bringing into use non-GSO systems, it should be taken into account that non-GSO operators, unlike those of GSO, need to ensure the in-orbit delivery of not one but several or even multiple satellites. In such circumstances, non-GSO operators should not be subjected to excessive time constraints connected to the deployment of their systems.

5 Historical Background

For the first time, the issue of bringing into use the frequency assignments to non-geostationary satellite systems was raised before the World Radiocommunication Conference (WRC, Conference)[15] in 2015.[16] In the report

15 World Radiocommunication Conferences are the highest body of the ITU Radiocommunication Sector (ITU-R), which are held every three to four years to review and, if necessary, revise the ITU Radio Regulations and address any radiocommunication matter of worldwide character. *See* Constitution of the ITU, Ch. II, Art. 13, and Convention of the ITU, Sect. 5, Art. 7.

16 Geneva, Switzerland, 2–27 November 2015.

that summarized the experience of the Radiocommunication Bureau in the application of radio regulatory procedures and other related matters,[17] the Director of the BR pointed out the importance of this issue and suggested a possible solution to the Conference. In the opinion of BR, this might be a division of the procedure for the BIU of frequency assignments to non-GSO systems into several phases demarcated by so called "milestones".

The first phase of this procedure would be defined by the end of the seven-year regulatory period; in this phase, one satellite or a certain percentage of the total number of the envisaged satellites, must be deployed in order to bring a frequency assignment into use. The deployment of the entire constellation must be completed later, within a reasonable time after the frequency assignment has been brought into use, in either one or two steps – for example, within three years from the date of the BIU (phase two) and within six years from the date of the BIU (phase three). It was assumed that failure to meet one of these milestones could lead to the cancellation of the frequency assignments at the end of the seven-year period (if the milestone for the first phase is not met), or to the adjustment of the notification information of the non-GSO system based on the actual number of satellites in operation at the end of the three- or six-year deployment period (if the milestones for the second or third phase are not met).

This phased approach could help to balance out the interests of different parties. If the milestones were met in all three phases in a timely manner, the frequency assignment that was brought into use by the first spacecraft would continue to be considered as brought into use according to the relevant filing. However, if the requirements of any of the phases were violated, the frequency assignment would not be brought into use at all or would be considered to have been brought into use only for the part of the radio frequency spectrum that was actually used by the active satellites. In this way, those radio frequencies that were filed but not used would not be blocked but become available to any interested users after the expiry of the relevant time period. At the same time, due to the inability to deploy the notified non-GSO constellation on a full scale, its operator would not have lost the entire notified orbit/spectrum resource, but would have kept the system, even if not in full, but within the part of the resource actually used.

17 Report of the Director of the Radiocommunication Sector on the activities of the Radiocommunication Sector, Document 4(Add.2)-E (Revision 1) (29 September 2015): Part 2 "Experience in the application of radio regulatory procedures and other related matters" and No. 3.2.2.4.4.

6 ITU Recognizes the Problem

WRC-15 discussed the Bureau's experience in the application of the radio regulatory procedures with respect to the BIU of frequency assignments for non-GSO systems, and recognized a lack of specific provisions dealing with this question in the Radio Regulations.[18] Still, the Conference was unable to adopt any particular conclusion on the issue. Instead, it invited the ITU Radiocommunication Sector (ITU-R) to consider drafting regulatory provisions requiring additional milestones to those which currently existed under the RR.[19]

Preparatory studies of the technical, operational, and procedural matters to be considered by World Radiocommunication Conferences are carried out by radiocommunication study groups.[20] More than 5,000 specialists from administrations, the telecommunication industry as a whole, and academic organizations throughout the world participate in their work. Since the Study Group 4 (SG4) on Satellite Services is in charge of analysing the efficiency of the management and use of the orbit/spectrum resource, its Working Party A (WP 4A) was assigned to carry out the preparatory work on the issue ofnon-GSOs.[21] At its first meeting after the WRC-15, WP 4A began discussing possible changes to the RR for non-GSO satellite systems, and presented a preliminary analysis containing the factors to be taken into account in the future study.[22] The whole study process took a full four-year cycle – from WRC-15 to WRC-19.

The ITU-R studied both the bringing into use of frequency assignments to non-geostationary satellite systems, and the possibility of adopting a milestone-based approach for the deployment of non-GSO multi-satellite constellations. Taking into account the inputs from the ITU-R working bodies and contributions from the membership of the ITU, the Conference Preparatory

---

18 Minutes of the seventh Plenary Meeting, WRC-15, Document 504-E (20 November 2015): No. 3.21.

19 Specifically, Nos. 11.25 and 11.44 of the Radio Regulations which are, respectively, the deadline for submitting requests for coordination to the BR no earlier than three years before the frequency assignments are brought into use and the seven-year deadline for the frequency assignments to be brought into use.

20 Constitution of the ITU, Nos. 80, 84 and Convention of the ITU, Nos. 148–160.

21 The task was assigned by the 2019 Conference Preparatory Meeting (CPM-19) at its first session held in Geneva, Switzerland, from 30 November to 1 December 2015, in order to organize and coordinate the conference preparatory studies for WRC-19.

22 Annex 22 to Working Party 4A Chairman's Report, Document 4A/63-E (Annex 22 "Working document toward preliminary draft CPM text for WRC-19 agenda item 7, Issue A: Factors related to the bringing into use of frequency assignments of non-GSO systems subject to coordination") (13 May 2016): No. 3.2.

Meeting (CPM) drafted and approved a consolidated report on technical, operational, and regulatory/procedural matters to be considered by the 2019 World Radiocommunication Conference.[23]

7 Preliminary Conclusions and Proposals

Based on the ITU-R studies, two general conclusions were drawn as reflected in the CPM Report,[24] one of which related to the concept of the BIU, and the other related to the milestone-based approach to the deployment of non-GSO systems, each with multiple options for implementation.

The first general conclusion of these debates was that bringing into use of frequency assignments to non-GSO systems should continue on the basis of the deployment of one satellite into one of the notified orbital planes within seven years of the date of receipt of the advance publication information or request for coordination, depending on the situation. This conclusion is applicable to the frequency assignments to all non-GSO systems in all frequency bands and services. Related to this conclusion, four options were proposed with respect to the minimum period during which a satellite must be maintained on a notified orbital plane spanning from a ninety day period or less to no fixed period at all.

The second general conclusion was that a new WRC Resolution should be adopted to implement a milestone-based approach to the deployment of non-GSO systems in specific, highly sought-after, frequency bands and services. This milestone-based approach would provide an additional term, beyond the seven-year regulatory period, for the deployment of a number of satellites, as notified in the filing or recorded in the Master Register. Several options of possible implementation of this approach were proposed with respect to the milestone periods, the required percentage of satellites deployed to satisfy each milestone, and the consequences of a failing to meet a milestone. It was also suggested that appropriate transitional measures should be provided to fairly and equitably address both future non-GSO systems and those that are already

23 The second (and the last) session of CPM-19 was held in Geneva, Switzerland, on 18–28 February 2019.

24 Report of the CPM on technical, operational and regulatory/procedural matters to be considered by the World Radiocommunication Conference 2019 (2019): Chapter 3 – Satellite services, 3/7/1 Issue A – Bringing into use of frequency assignments to all non-GSO systems, and consideration of a milestone-based approach for the deployment of non-GSO systems in specific frequency bands and services.

recorded and operational (or would be registered and operational before the end of the time limit as specified by WRC-19).

The CPM Report was, no doubt, meant to merely assist the ITU members and contained no more than suggestions, leaving the final decision to the WRC.

8 New Regulation Adopted by the WRC-19

Bringing into use of frequency assignments to non-GSO satellite networks and systems and a milestone-based approach to the deployment of non-GSO systems in specific frequency bands and services were considered by the WRC-19 as agenda item 7(A). It is important to note that the two procedures – BIU (and BBIU) and deployment – remain separate though interrelated.

8.1 *BIU (BBIU) a Frequency Assignment to Non-GSO Systems*

WRC-19 clarified the rules for the bringing into use and bringing back into use of frequency assignments to non-GSO satellite networks and systems, which vary for different satellite services. These rules are reflected in the new version of the Radio Regulations which entered into force on 1 January 2021. It is important to underline that the regulatory periods for bringing into use and bringing back into use of frequency assignments are kept common for both GSO and non-GSOs. For the BIU, this period is seven years[25] from the date when the ITU receives the advance publication information or a request for coordination.[26] For the BBIU, this period is three years from the date of suspension of the use of the frequency assignment to a network or system, taking into account the possible proportionate reduction of this three-year period if the six-month suspension notification period established by the RR is not complied with.[27]

The procedure for BIU frequency assignments of non-GSOs used for a fixed satellite service (FSS), mobile satellite service (MSS), and broadcasting satellite service (BSS)[28] is similar to the existing procedure for BIU frequency assignments to a space station in the GSO:[29] a frequency assignment is considered to be brought into use when a space station with the capability of transmitting or receiving on that frequency assignment has been deployed and maintained on

25 The eight-year period for BIU of planned frequencies can only be applied to the GSO, since there is no plan for the frequencies of non-GSO networks and systems.

26 Radio Regulations, No. 11.44.

27 Radio Regulations, No. 11.49.

28 Radio Regulations, No. 11.44C.

29 Radio Regulations, No. 11.44B.

one of the notified orbital plane(s) of the FSS, MSS, or BSS non-GSO network or system for a continuous period of ninety days. The BIU is considered to have taken place regardless of the notified number of orbital planes and satellites in the orbital plane in a non-GSO constellation. After a suspension, the BBIU of the frequency assignment to a non-GSO network or system is to be performed using the same procedure,[30] which also repeats the current procedure for GSO networks.[31]

The frequency assignments to non-GSO satellite networks or systems operating in Earth orbits providing other satellite services (those that are not FSS, MSS, and BSS and, hence, are less commercially attractive and demanded) are brought into use by deploying a space station that can transmit or receive within these frequency assignments in one of the notified orbital planes of the relevant network or system irrespective of the notified number of orbital planes and satellites per orbital plane.[32] This procedure is characterized by the absence of any requirements for the maintenance of a space station on orbit, including the absence of the minimum duration of the period of maintenance. For those satellite services that are not FSS, MSS, and BSS, a single deployment of a spacecraft is sufficient for the BIU. The BBIU of the frequency assignments to such non-GSO networks or systems is to be carried out in the same manner.[33]

The difference between the rules for bringing into use frequency assignments to various satellite services can be explained by the desire of States to impose stricter requirements for non-GSO networks and systems that are mainly focused on profit-making (these are FSS, MSS, and BSS), while for networks and systems that solve socially significant and other global tasks States have agreed to less stringent requirements. The latter include, for example, radionavigation satellite services (RNSS) such as BeiDou, Galileo, GLONASS, GPS, and satellite search and rescue systems – such as the Cospas-Sarsat, the space segment of which, in addition to GSO satellites, includes satellites in low and medium Earth orbits.

8.2 *Implementation of Non-GSO Systems*

Since the bringing into use of frequency assignments to space stations in non-GSOs and their recording in the Master Register by the end of the seven-year regulatory period do not require confirmation of the deployment of all satellites associated with these frequency assignments, the WRC-19 adopted a new

30 Radio Regulations, No. 11.49.2.
31 Radio Regulations, No. 11.49.1.
32 Radio Regulations, No. 11.44D.
33 Radio Regulations, No. 11.49.3.

milestone-based approach for the implementation of non-GSO systems in specific frequency bands and services. This approach is reflected in a separate resolution of the WRC-19 which was made mandatory by adding a new section to Article 11 of the ITU RR, namely Section III "Maintenance of the recording of frequency assignments to non-geostationary-satellite systems in the Master Register (WRC-19)". Its only paragraph[34] establishes that the new Resolution 35 (WRC-19) must apply to frequency assignments to some non-GSO systems in specific bands and services. The frequency bands and space radiocommunication services to which the milestone-based approach is applied are different for the three ITU Regions[35] and are listed in the Resolution.

It is important to note that the entry into force of the new edition of the ITU Radio Regulations on 1 January 2021 does not mean that non-GSO systems that were notified or put into operation before this date will 'slip through the net' under the old rules. The new Resolution, which provides for the obligation to deploy systems in three phases and implies negative consequences if the requirements for each of them are not met, applies to all non-GSO systems, but with some differences depending on whether the system is operational or just planned.

Thus, operators of non-GSO systems, for which the seven-year regulatory period ended before 1 January 2021, were required to inform the Radiocommunication Bureau no later than 1 February 2021 of any space stations that had already been deployed. Operators of non-GSO systems, for which the deadline expired on or after 1 January 2021, needed to present this information to the BR within thirty days of the end of the seven-year regulatory period or the end of the ninety-day satellite's on-orbit stationing that is required for BIU, whichever came later.

The list of information to be submitted on the deployed space stations is set out in Annex 1 to the Resolution and is divided into three blocks. The first one includes the satellite system information: the name of the system; the name of the notifying administration;[36] the country symbol; the reference to advance publication information or request for coordination, or notification

34 Radio Regulations, No. 11.51.

35 For the allocation of frequencies, the world has been divided by the ITU RR into three Regions. *See* Radio Regulations, Nos. 5.2–5.9.

36 Notifying administration means any national governmental department or service of the ITU member State responsible for discharging obligations under the ITU Constitution, Convention, and Administrative Regulations (the latter includes the Radio Regulations), which has made the relevant filing. *See* Radio Regulations, No. 1.2. All communications with the ITU are carried out by the administrations that can act also in the interests of the private space sector.

information, if available; the total number of space stations deployed into each notified orbital plane of the satellite system with the capability of transmitting or receiving the frequency assignments; and the orbital plane number into which each space station is deployed. The second block contains the launch information to be provided for each deployed space station, specifically: the name of the launch vehicle provider; the name of the launch vehicle; the name and location of the launch facility; and the launch date. The last (third) block is the characteristics of each deployed space station, including its name, orbital characteristics, and frequency bands which are listed in the notification information and in which the space station can transmit or receive.

Upon receipt of the required deployment information, the BR publishes it and, if the number of deployed satellites is smaller than the initial number of satellites notified for the entire non-GSO system, adds a remark to the corresponding Master Register entry or to the latest notification information on the system stating that the frequency assignments are subject to the application of Resolution 35 (WRC-19) on a milestone-based approach to the implementation of the frequency assignments and, accordingly, that a phased deployment of the system is required.

When comparing the number of notified and actually deployed space stations, a discrepancy of one satellite is allowed regardless of the scale of the system. In other words, the deployment will be recognized as 100% complete if, for example, four out of five satellites are in orbit, but it will not be recognized as 100% complete if 998 out of a thousand satellites are deployed in orbit. Such a seemingly illogical approach setting this acceptable deviation not in percentage but in absolute figures, regardless of the total number of satellites in the system, can be explained by the desire of States to protect small regional satellite systems consisting of several satellites for which a failed launch of one satellite would not require resubmitting the filing, without giving excessive flexibility to large and complex global multi-satellite systems consisting of hundreds and thousands of spacecraft.

8.3 *Three Phases of Deploying Non-GSO Systems*

As indicated above, the phased deployment applies to both operating and prospective non-GSO systems. The number and duration of the phases are the same for all systems: there are three phases, which are completed in two, five, and seven years. The starting point for each of the three phases differs depending on the moment of expiry of the regulatory deadline for bringing the relevant system into use: before 1 January 2021, which is the date of the ITU RR new edition's entry into force, or later.

Operators of non-GSO systems, for which the seven-year regulatory period expired before 1 January 2021, will deploy their systems by 1 January 2023, 1 January 2026, and 1 January 2028 (which corresponds to two, five, and seven years added to the zero-time set by the WRC-19 – that is 1 January 2021). Operators of non-GSO systems for which the regulatory deadline came due on or after 1 January 2021, deploy their systems at the end of the two-, five-, and seven-year period from the expiration of the seven-year regulatory deadline. Suspending the use of frequency assignments to non-GSO systems with the possibility of their subsequent bringing back into use, does not change the procedure for a phased deployment – the above mentioned deadlines and the requirements set out below for each of the phases remain strict.

Within thirty days of the end of each of the three phased periods, the notifying administrations must provide the Radiocommunication Bureau with information on the space stations deployed – the information that is specified in thethree blocks in Annex 1 to the Resolution and described above.

The BR publishes the information received and compares the number of satellites actually deployed with the minimum number of satellites to be deployed by the end of each of the three phased periods, as this number is established by Resolution 35 (WRC-19). The minimum number is 10% of the total number of satellites in a notified or registered system by the end of the first phase; the second phase involves the deployment of at least half of the satellites, and the last (third) phase requires the full deployment of the system (for calculating the full deployment of a system, the same acceptable deviation applies: either the actual 100% or 100% minus one satellite is recognized as 100%).

As soon as an operator deploys 100% of its system, the BR removes the remark of applying the new Resolution on a milestone-based approach to the implementation of frequency assignments in a fully deployed system.

8.4 *Modifications to the Characteristics of a Frequency Assignment as Penalty for Failure to Meet the Requirements for the Phased Deployment*

If a check-up by the BR reveals a discrepancy (that is, if an operator should have deployed more stations than it actually did), the adverse consequences stipulated in the new Resolution will follow. This means modifications to the characteristics of the notified or recorded frequency assignments relating to the scale of the non-GSO system which must be made by the relevant administration no later than ninety days after the end of the milestone period. This is a period when the number of deployed satellites does not correspond to the established minimum number.

If the characteristics are modified at the end of the first milestone period, when the operator was able to deploy less than 10% of the total number of satellites, the modified total number of satellites in the system should not exceed ten times the number of satellites actually deployed. For example, if a non-GSO system was declared to consist of 700 space stations and forty-five satellites were actually deployed instead of seventy (10%) at the end of the first milestone period, the modified number of satellites in such a system may be 450 or less. If the modified total number of satellites is calculated at the end of the second milestone period, when the operator failed to deploy half of the system, the modified total number of satellites should not be greater than two times the number of satellites actually deployed. In our example, where 700 satellites were declared to compose the non-GSO system, 350 satellites, which make up the required 50%, are to be deployed at the end of the second milestone period. If the operator of this system succeeds in only deploying 300 spacecraft, then, according to the modified characteristics, there should be no more than 600 satellites in the system. If the requirement for a full 100% deployment of the system is not met at the end of the last (third) milestone period, the modified total number of satellites in the system becomes equal to the number of satellites actually deployed. Recurring to the example of a non-GSO system consisting of 700 satellites, its actual deployment with 700 or 699 satellites will be considered to have taken place 100%, as required, and no changes to the 700-satellite system will be needed, whereas the deployment of, for example, 685 satellites will reduce the total number of satellites in such system to 685 or fewer.

If a notifying administration modifies the recorded frequency assignments of a non-GSO system by only reducing the total number of satellites and orbital planes,[37] and guarantees that the modified characteristics will not cause more interference or require more protection than the original characteristics, and the BR, in turn, makes a favourable finding, the original date of recording frequency assignments in the Master Register is retained.

This date is of key importance to each operator, since from this exact date the operator's priority over 'neighbouring' networks and systems is counted. Frequency assignments that are filed later must take into account the satellite networks and systems that were filed earlier and may already be operating. New entrants must plan their work in such a way as not to cause interference

37 Some other minor modifications are also allowed, such as modifications to the right ascension of the ascending node of each plane, the longitude of the ascending node and its date and time associated with the remaining orbital planes, the initial phase angle of the space stations within planes. *See* Resolution 35 (WRC-19), paragraph 14 (c) (ii).

to the 'oldies.' Hence, the change of the original date of recording the frequency assignments to a later one may lead to the loss of priority over some networks and systems that were submitted between these two dates (the original date and the new one) and were not initially taken into account when the non-GSO system was constructed. However, now, being at the bottom of the list, the operator must adjust to the operation of all networks and systems that are higher on the list. The entire satellite project may require significant revision or even cease to be feasible.

8.5 *Exception to the General Rule on the Modifications to the Characteristics for Failure to Meet the Requirements for a Phased Deployment*

This exception may only be granted to those frequency assignments to non-GSO systems for which the seven-year regulatory period for bringing into use ends before 28 November 2022, subject to a number of conditions.

First, an exception may be given if the minimum number of satellites is not deployed at the end of the first milestone period – if the operator has deployed less than 10% of the total number of satellites. There is no exception for a failure to deploy half and 100% of the total number of satellites at the end of the second and third milestone periods, respectively. This condition can be explained by the need for smooth adaptation of satellite operators to the new regulation which affects satellite networks and systems filed under the previous edition of the ITU RR that did not require a phased deployment. It was thus decided to make allowances in case of a non-fulfillment of the first milestone, whereas by the time of the second and third milestones, all operators must adjust to the new regulation.

Secondly, by 1 March 2023, the notifying administration must submit a complete information listed in Annex 2 to Resolution 35 (WRC-19) to the Radiocommunication Bureau. This information includes, among other things, a description of the current status of the deployment, operation, and coordination of the non-GSO system. The notifying administration must also provide the BR with a clear evidence of a binding manufacturing or procurement agreement, as well as a binding agreement to launch a sufficient number of satellites to meet the requirements of the next milestone period.[38] The relevant

38 As specified in the note to Annex 2 to Resolution 35 (WRC-19), the manufacturing or procurement agreement should identify the contract milestones leading to the completion of the manufacture or procurement of satellites required, and the launch agreement should identify the launch window, launch site and launch service provider. The information required under Annex 2 must be submitted in the form of a written commitment by

administration is responsible for the authenticity of information confirming the existence of the contracts. If possible, the notifying administration should also provide evidence of guaranteed funding arrangements for the project. This condition can be explained by the readiness to make an exception only for those systems that are really close to the start of operation in the filed configuration, and not to make exceptions for systems that are likely to remain only on paper.

Thirdly, an exception is possible with a favourable determination by the ITU Radio Regulations Board (RRB)[39] or WRC. Issues of granting exceptions are planned to be considered no later than at the second meeting of the RRB in 2023, when the Board will have the opportunity to make positive conclusions about granting exceptions. Cases in which, in the opinion of the RRB, there is no possibility to grant exceptions, along with the RRB's conclusions and recommendations, should be included in its report to the WRC-23.

8.6 *Satellite Hopping Is Still out of Favour*

As a rule, a satellite project implies that a new spacecraft (or a number of spacecraft, if a non-GSO system is concerned), will be designed, built, and launched for its implementation. This is due to the fact that each such project is to some extent unique: it selects its own set of frequencies in different bands and polarisations, which are included in the frequency plan of the satellite. In practice, this means that not every satellite can operate in any network or system, although partial coincidence of frequency plans on different satellites may occur. If an accident happens on a satellite or its operational lifetime ends, a new spacecraft usually comes to replace it. At the same time, there are situations when a satellite operator relocates an existing satellite in orbit, the frequency plan of which is similar to the frequency plan of the satellite being replaced. This can be done, for example, in order to resume suspended operations as quickly as possible in an orbital location that is fundamentally important to the operator, the location from which critical services are provided or a large number of users are serviced.

Since any on-orbit manoeuvre implies expenditure of valuable fuel which is utilized for satellites' station keeping and, consequently, directly impacts their operational lifetimes, it is possible that a satellite would be moved for

the responsible administration, including the manufacturer's or launch provider's letters or declarations.

39 The ITU Radio Regulations Board is a collegiate body of the ITU-R that consists of twelve skilled experts thoroughly qualified in the field of radiocommunication, possessing practical experience in the assignment and utilization of frequencies. *See* Constitution of the ITU, Nos. 63, 82, 93–101.

operational reasons once or twice, while it is highly unlikely that a satellite will be frequently relocated back and forth in space, hopping on and off orbital slots and shells.

The latter occurs in practice for the only reason: when the regulatory deadline is nearing and the operator is not yet ready for BIU or BBIU but desperately wants to protect its frequency rights and prevent its frequency assignment from being cancelled. Then it buys the (B)BIU service from another operator that has a similar satellite in orbit, called a "gapfiller". The gapfiller gets into an orbital position or shell and formally fulfills the requirements of the ITU RR with regard to BIU or BBIU. However, such a temporary satellite does not use the frequencies for their intended purpose, that is it does not provide any useful services originally planned under the satellite project. It only buys time for the operator at the beginning of the implementation of its project. This is called a commercial (B)BIU, which does not formally violate the provisions of the RR, but obviously does not contribute to the rational, equitable, efficient, and economical use of radio frequencies and associated orbits.

Although this so-called 'satellite hopping' is not prohibited by the Radio Regulations or other ITU documents, the Bureau monitors cases when a single satellite brings into use multiple frequency assignments. This trend is also reflected in the new Resolution on a milestone-based approach to the implementation of frequency assignments to space stations in non-GSO satellite systems.

For example, if any satellites counted as of the expiry of the relevant milestone period were previously used to satisfy the milestone obligations associated with other non-GSO satellite systems subject to the new Resolution, the notifying administration must inform the Bureau, indicating the number of satellites and other satellite systems in question. The obligation to inform the Bureau is assigned to both parties participating in the 'hopping': if the number of satellites in a non-GSO system has decreased after meeting the requirements of any of the three milestone periods, the notifying administration must explain the circumstances that led to this reduction.

If anysatellites are being used or are planned to be used to meet the requirements for the phased deployment of other non-GSO systems, the administration should also inform the Bureau, indicating the number of satellites and the name of the systems using them to meet the requirements of the new Resolution on a milestone-based approach to the implementation of frequency assignments. If the notifying administration that 'gave away' its satellites properly informs the Bureau, the Bureau will continue to take into account the total number of satellites deployed during the milestone period, as reported by the notifying administration.

In other words, the mere transfer of satellites between non-GSO systems does not have negative consequences since it is not prohibited under ITU regulations. Still, the obligation to duly inform the BR must be observed.

9 Conclusion

Until recently, the use of non-GSO networks and systems whose regime was not elaborated in detail in the ITU documents did not raise serious questions and did not have a significant impact on the effectiveness of the use of orbit/spectrum resource. However, given the growing number of filings and requests for coordination with respect to non-GSOs, in 2015, the World Radiocommunication Conference recognized certain gaps in the ITU Radio Regulations and instructed the Radiocommunication Sector to work on filling them, which was implemented by WRC-19.

The 2019 Conference not only clarified the procedures for bringing into use and bringing back into use non-GSO networks and systems, which differ depending on the type of space radiocommunication service, but also adopted a new Resolution regulating the milestone-based implementation of frequency assignments to non-GSO systems in specific frequency bands and satellite services. According to the ITU Radiocommunication Sector studies, this will help to ensure that the Master Register – the desk companion of every satellite operator – reasonably reflects the actual deployment of such non-GSO systems.

Despite the fact that the issues of operation of non-GSO constellations proved to be as controversial as possible, WRC-19 was able to establish the right balance between preventing the inefficient use of the spectrum and its possible abuse, on the one hand, and the proper functioning of the ITU mechanisms for managing frequency assignments to non-GSO systems without creating an unnecessary burden on their operators, on the other hand. This balance, according to the Conference, is the step-by-step approach to the implementation of frequency assignments to non-GSO systems established by Resolution 35 (WRC-19).

Since in its new Resolution, the WRC instructed the Radiocommunication Bureau to continue to identify specific frequency bands in specific services that may have a problem similar to the one that led to the creation of the Resolution and report them no later than before the second session of the CPM to WRC-23, satellite operators should be prepared that the scope of the milestone-based approach to the deployment of non-GSO systems may be expanded in the near future.

CHAPTER 7

Software Certification as a Limit on Liability: The Case of CubeSat Operations

*Marco Crepaldi, Ross Horne, and Sjouke Mauw**

1 Introduction[1]

This interdisciplinary chapter adopts perspectives from both space lawand software engineering. To see how these remote disciplines impact each other, it is necessary to begin by explaining our argument in such a way that legal experts can understand why they should be aware of software engineering professional standards. Correspondingly, basic legal notions are introduced to provide software engineers with the legal context required to confirm our reasoning. Such interactions are essential for strengthening the transnational interdisciplinary networks of governments and professional bodies that influence space policy.[2] Moreover, this work appeals to space program managers, policy makers, and regulators due to its implications.

Under international space law, launching States are liable for damages caused by space activities – both public and private. Therefore, the oversight of space missions falls under States' responsibility and liability (per Article VI of the Outer Space Treaty, and Articles II and III of the Liability Convention).

While traditionally space missions used highly dependable software, the recent surge in smaller and cheaper missions changes this perspective. More precisely, a recent class of space objects, CubeSats,[3] use software that is not highly dependable. If the increasing rate of deployment of CubeSats does not slow down – as seems to be the case – then the quality of the software on board becomes an important issue to address …

* Computer Science Department, University of Luxembourg.

1 The authors would like to thank Stanislav Dashevskyi for his contributions to this chapter.

2 Andrea Hamann and Hélène Ruiz Fabri, "Transnational Networks and Constitutionalism," *International Journal of Constitutional Law* 6.3–4 (2008): 481–508.

3 James Cutler, Greg Hutchins, and Robert Twiggs, "OPAL: Smaller, Simpler, and Just Plain Luckier," *Proceedings of the 14th AIAA/USU Conference on Small Satellites, Logan UT, August 21–24. SSC-VII-4* (2000) url: http://www.space.aau.dk/cubesat/documents/pdf-docs-from-net/SmallSat2000-Opal.pdf.

 | DOI:10.1163/9789004527270_008

... or does it? From the perspective of the satellite operators, if costs are low, then launching large constellations of satellites of which a significant percentage is expected to fail is rational. However, this argument is unlikely to hold from the perspective of launching States that are liable for space activities on the basis outlined above. This is the case if States might be considered at fault when licensing spacecraft running software that is not highly dependable, which could make them liable for subsequent damages in outer space to persons or property of another operator.

In recent years, risks associated with space missions have increased significantly due to the surge in the number of launches. Among such risks one finds orbital conjunctions, the increase in space debris, and the degradation of the space environment. Successful strategies for managing risks in the medium to long-term, assuming the trend continues as projected, require functional spacecrafts to actively cooperate with tracking and to implement manoeuvres for both collision avoidance and responsible decommissioning. Indeed, the ISO standard for Cube satellites requires (in Clause 5.6.1)[4] that CubeSat mission design and hardware shall be in accordance with the ISO standard for limiting orbital debris.[5] However, granted that standards are not mandatory, we argue that it is possible to interpret current international space law to argue that a duty to ensure a certain degree of dependability of critical software systems already exists.

The fundamental problem when resolving disputes concerning liability in the event of conjunctions in orbit is that the precise cause of collisions is unlikely to be uncovered. There will be little data to witness the event and physical evidence is prohibitively expensive to obtain. However, we expect, as with the historical collision between Iridium-33 and Kosmos-2251 in 2009, that collisions are likely to occur in scenarios where one of the satellites was already in an inactive state prior to the collision. In the aforementioned collision, Kosmos-2251 was a decommissioned Soviet satellite that had been left in orbit. Consequently, more questions were asked concerning the responsibility of Russia, a successor of the launching state of Kosmos-2251, than of the United States, the launching state of the Iridium spacecraft.[6]

---

4 ISO, *Space systems – Cube satellites*, Tech. rep. 19990 (2017).

5 ISO, *Space systems – Space debris mitigation requirements*, Tech. rep. 24113 (2019).

6 Ram S. Jakhu. "Iridium-Cosmos Collision and Its Implications for Space Operations," in Kai-Uwe Schrogl et al., eds., *Yearbook on Space Policy 2008/2009: Setting New Trends* (Springer, 2010): 254–275 and Alexander F Cohen, "Cosmos 954 and the International Law of Satellite Accidents," *Yale J. Int'l L.* 10 (1984): 78.

An inactive satellite cannot engage in decommissioning, collision avoidance manoeuvres, and cannot actively cooperate with tracking, thereby it poses a hazard to other spacecrafts. To avoid inactivity due to failure, launching States should set baseline engineering requirements for a critical core of the system, sufficient to operate a communication channel (which involves critical components managing power, stabilisation, and communication). This critical core consists of hardware and software. In this work, we focus on the most crucial software component which is typically a real-time operating system (RTOS) which manages both the hardware resources and software processes of critical components.

While there exist ISO standards which can guide the use of hardware in CubeSats,[7] baseline standards for software have not yet been emphasised. This paper addressed this gap by analysing RTOS projects commonly used today in CubeSats and demonstrating that even a lightweight empirical evaluation of these projects indicates that commonly deployed RTOS software – most notably Amazon's FreeRTOS – cannot be considered to be sufficiently dependable. The precise degree of dependability varies according to the risks and stakes of each space mission, and it falls under the competence of the launching States. It is clear that demanding compliance with full avionics standards that typically apply to spacecraft would be undesirable, since it would result in a surge in the costs for CubeSat operators. Nonetheless, improvements on current practices can be made. In the next pages we show that at least one open RTOS project – namely seL4[8] – follows dependability principles in software engineering.

On this basis, we conclude that launching States should consider including in their registration processes measures to ensure that the critical software deployed on CubeSats does not excessively increase the risk associated with the operations of these space objects.

The above argument for launching States to manage risks associated with software in CubeSats is developed and substantiated as follows. Section 2 starts by considering the recent surge in small satellite projects, by providing a primer on the liability for space activities under international space law and explaining the relevance of the role of real-time operating systems on board CubeSats. Then, Section 3 provides the results of our empirical analysis on

---

7 ISO, *Space systems – Design qualification and acceptance tests of small spacecraft and units*, Tech. rep. 19683 (2017): 85.

8 Gerwin Klein et al., "SeL4: Formal Verification of an OS Kernel," *Proceedings of the ACM SIGOPS 22nd Symposium on Operating Systems Principles. SOSP '09. Big Sky, Montana, USA* (Association for Computing Machinery, 2009): 207–220.

three open-source real-time operating systems, namely, FreeRTOS, Kubos, and eCos currently deployed on CubeSats. Our results are compared to the seL4 system, which has a formally verified, hence highly dependable core. Section 4, consequently, considers the implications of poor software engineering practices from the perspective of CubeSats' operations and on the attribution of the fault in the case of damage caused by CubeSats. Later, Section 5 suggests possible mitigation strategies.

2 Background: Connecting Software Engineering with Fault and Collision Liability

The following sections introduce the relevant background notions for the current argument, expanding on our introductory remarks. Accordingly, in Section 2.1, we provide evidence of the increasing exposure of States to liability stemming from in-orbit conjunctions by observing trends of space missions and the challenges associated with the increase in the number of small satellites. In Section 2.2, a primer on the legal framework regulating the liability for space activities is offered, drawing attention to the relevant norms in the Outer Space Treaty and Liability Convention. In particular, we connect the liability of launching States for in-orbit conjunctions with the notion of fault. In Section 2.3, we emphasise that the quality of engineering practices can impact the likely cause of fault, and emphasise that perhaps the most critical software component not currently covered by engineering recommendations is the real-time operating system (RTOS), thereby arguing that the reliability of the RTOS should be brought into consideration.

2.1 *Current Trends: Increase Risk of Conjunctions*

This section highlights the current trend in the increase of small satellite missions and provides essential information on a specific class of nanosatellites, that is, CubeSats. It aims to show that the trend in CubeSat missions is unlikely to slow down and, consequently, concerns related to the number or space objects in crowded orbits – such as LEO – will increase in the medium and long-term.

A new era for small satellites has begun. While it is true that the first missions were small – for instance, Sputnik 1 of 1957 was about the size of a beach ball (58 cm in diameter) and weighed only 83.6 kg – the rapid increase in the number of smaller-than-usual space objects is a recent phenomenon. Small satellites (below 500 kg) are divided into several categories according to their mass, for example, microsatellites are considered to be 10–100 kg while a

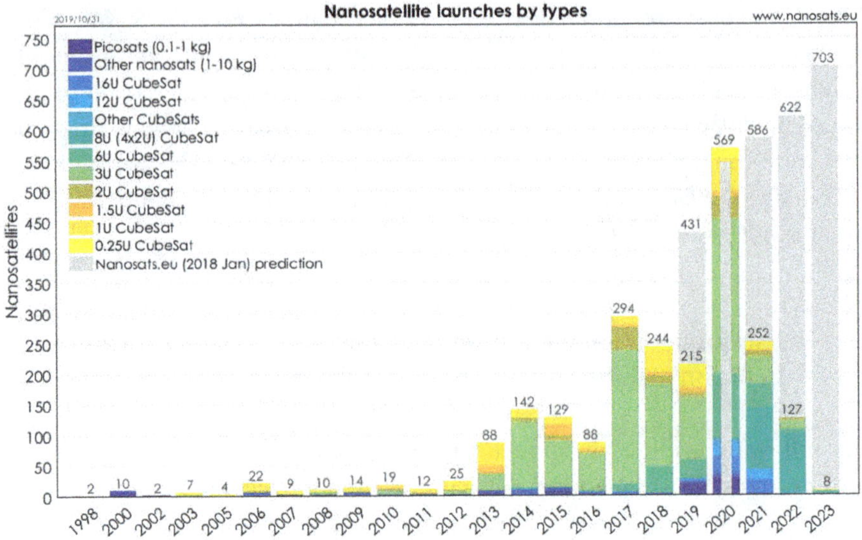

FIGURE 7.1 Nanosatellites launches with forecast, and Cubesats types
SOURCE: DATA RETRIEVED FROM HTTPS://WWW.NANOSATS.EU/DATABASE

femtosatellite's mass is 10–100 g. The explanation for the recent surge in small satellite missions is manifold. Primarily, these spacecraft tend to be cheaper and, therefore, expendable. The small size also allows small satellites to be secondary or even tertiary payloads on launch missions, thereby decreasing costs. Analogously, recent technological advances allow for reducing size while preserving complex functionalities.

This work focuses on a specific type of small satellites, namely CubeSats. As the name suggests, the core version, known as 1U, of a CubeSat measures 10 x 10 x 10 cm. Multiple configuration are possible ranging between 1 and 40 kg according to the CubeSat standard.[9] The standardization allows for smaller and larger satellites made of fraction or multiple of the base unit U, for example, 1.5U, 3U, and 6U CubeSats have been deployed, and may be in the range of 0.25U to 27U.[10] While CubeSats were initially developed for educational purposes, scientific, commercial, and military deployment of these satellites has also occurred. Standardization is also responsible for the lower costs of deployments; for example, a CubeSat mission can cost as little as 50.000 USD.[11]

9 A. Mehrparvar, "CubeSat Design Specification," *The CubeSat Program, Cal Poly SLO* (2014).

10 Entry of the Nanosats Database: https://www.nanosats.eu/cubesat.

11 Kiran Krishan Nair, *Small Satellites and Sustainable Development: Solutions in International Space Law* (Springer, 2019).

Lower costs and standardization enable broader access to outer space (mainly LEO orbit), which is a welcome development. For example, it enables developing countries to launch their first space objects. Figure 7.1 illustrates the increasing trend in the launch of nanosatellites with a focus on CubeSat missions.[12]

The growth in the number of small satellites raises several challenges. Most of these challenges are common to all small satellites. Among these challenges one finds, the increase of space debris in crowded LEO, the lack of legal sources that deal with small satellites along with qualification issues, and the dubious status of the future mega-constellations comprising thousands of small satellites.[13] Think, for example, of the Starlink constellation for which SpaceX in 2019 filed for approval of 30,000 more units in addition to the already approved 12,000.[14]

Of course, issues connected to space debris are common to all space activities.[15] That said, our attention is placed on an issue that is specific to CubeSats, which are designed and deployed quickly on a small budget, hence have reliability issues, such as the dependability of the real-time operating systems used for their control software. Our argument is that, under international space law, launching States have a duty to oversee space missions so that failure to provide adequate guarantees for critical components such as the RTOS on board spacecraft is relevant for the regime of the liability for space activities. Therefore, launching States might be considered liable (explored further in Section 4) for the damages caused by CubeSats in LEO. On this basis, it is necessary to digress and describe, albeit briefly, the current international legal framework governing the liability for space activities.

2.2 *The Liability for Space Activities: A Primer*

This subsection provides a primer on the provisions governing the liability for space activities.[16] It is uncontroversial that CubeSats are to be regarded as space

12 Robyn M Millan et al., "Small Satellites for Space Science," *Advances in Space Research* (2019).

13 Mark Matney, Andrew Vavrin, and Alyssa Manis, *Effects of CubeSat Deployments in Low-Earth Orbit* (2017) and Alan Shaw and Peter Rosher, "Micro Satellites: The Smaller the Satellites, the Bigger the Challenges?" *Air and Space Law* 41.4 (2016): 311–328.

14 Caleb Henry, "SpaceX Submits Paperwork for 30,000 More Starlink Satellites," SpaceNews (October 15, 2019) https://spacenews.com/spacex-submits-paperwork-for-30000-more-starlink-satellites/.

15 Francis Lyall and Paul B Larsen, *Space Law: A Treatise* (Ashgate, 2009).

16 George Anthony Long, "Small Satellites and Liability Associated with Space Traffic Situational Awareness," Space Traffic Management Conference (2014).

objects and that, consequently, the relevant sources of international law apply. There are two treaties relevant to our subject, namely, the Treaty on Principles Governing the Activities of States in the Exploration and Use of Outer Space, including the Moon and Other Celestial Bodies of 1967 (henceforth the Outer Space Treaty) and the Convention on International Liability for Damage Caused by Space Objects of 1972 (henceforth the Liability Convention). The relevant norms are Articles VI and VII of the Outer Space Treaty and Article III of the Liability Convention. We examine each one in turn.

The Outer Space Treaty. Article VI of the Outer Space Treaty establishes a general responsibility of the Parties to the Treaty with regard to space activities. More precisely, Article VI states the following:

> State Parties to the Treaty shall bear international responsibility for national activities in outer space, including the Moon and other celestial bodies, whether such activities are carried on by governmental agencies or by non-governmental entities, and for assuring that national activities are carried out in conformity with the provision set forth in the present Treaty.

This disposition establishes international responsibility of States for the activities carried out in space both by governmental agencies and non-governmental entities, including, private entities and universities.

Article VII of the Outer Space Treaty deals with the liability of States for damage caused by their space objects; however, it has been noted that the linguistic distinction between responsibility and liability is only found in the official English version of the treaty.[17] This norm clarifies that liability for space activities falls jointly on several States involved in space activities:

> Each State Party to the Treaty that launches or procures the launching of an object into outer space, including the Moon and other celestial bodies, and each State Party from whose territory or facility an object is launched, is internationally liable for damage to another State Party to the Treaty or to its natural or juridical persons by such object or its component parts on the Earth, in air space or in outer space, including the Moon and other celestial bodies.

17 Ram S. Jakhu and Joseph N. Pelton, *Small Satellites and their Regulation,* vol. 3 (Springer, 2014). However, also i.e German uses different terms for responsibility (Verantwortlichkeit), and liability (Haftung).

Several interpretative issues need not concern us, such as what constitutes damage, what precisely constitutes a space object and the standard of proof required to establish causation.[18] It is also important to stress that the principle of state responsibility and liability for space activities is considered as a customary norm in international space law, somewhat of a higher level than the norms found in the treaties.[19]

The Liability Convention. The second relevant source of law regarding matters of liability is the Liability Convention. It is important to note that, as of the 1 April 2019, the Outer Space Treaty has broader application than the Liability Convention because it has been ratified by 109 countries versus the 96 that ratified the Liability Convention.[20] The Liability Convention covers only the issue of liability so that it can be considered as *lex specialis* in relation to the Outer Space Treaty. However, States parties to both instruments might determine which one to invoke when they seek compensation. The relevant disposition for our purposes is Article III.

Note that Article II is not taken into consideration because it establishes a strict liability regime for damage caused by space objects on the surface of the Earth, for example, upon a failed re-entry causing damage to property before the start of outer space wherever that might be. The notion of strict liability entails that launching states are absolutely liable for damages caused by spacecraft even if they took all possible measures to avoid the event in which such damage was inflicted. Therefore, while better reliability engineering would reduce the risk of damage caused by failed launches and re-entries, it would not affect the liability regime of the launching States in such events. Therefore, it need not concern us, for the ongoing argument hinges on the presence of the fault when operating a spacecraft for which sound software engineering practices are violated.

On the contrary to Article II, we observe that Article III does establish a fault-based liability regime for damage caused in outer space.[21] It dictates:

> In the event of damage being caused elsewhere than on the surface of the Earth to a space object of one launching State or to persons or property

---

18 Stephan Hobe, Bernhard Schmidt-Tedd, and K Schrogl, *Cologne Commentary on Space Law. Vol. 1: Outer Space Treaty* (2009).

19 R Venkata Rao, V Gopalakrishnan, and Kumar Abhijeet, *Recent Developments in Space Law: Opportunities and Challenges* (Springer, 2017).

20 *Status of International Agreements Relating to Activities in Outer Space as of 1 January 2021.* United Nations Office for Outer Space Affairs. A/AC.105/C.2/2021/CRP.10 (2021) http://www.unoosa.org/oosa/en/ourwork/spacelaw/treaties/status/index.html.

21 Stephan Hobe et al., *Cologne Commentary on Space Law: Rescue Agreement, Liability Convention, Registration Convention, Moon Agreement* (2013).

> on board such a space object by a space object of another launching State, the latter shall be liable only if the damage is due to its fault or the fault of persons for whom it is responsible.

Under international law, fault occurs if States fail to adhere to or breach an obligation imposed by law. Moreover, the presupposition of fault should be excluded if guidelines and standards have been complied with. Note that this is the case even if standards and guidelines are non-binding; the claim that software engineering practices are relevant for establishing the fault is defended further in Section 4. For now, it is important to stress that, in general, the body of space law is agnostic to size.[22] In other words, size does not matter concerning the liability of space objects, so that the same rules apply to space objects of varying sizes, ranging from big satellites as the forthcoming James Webb telescope to small satellites of only a few kilograms in mass.[23]

To sum up, liability for space activities – regardless of the size of the space object – is imposed upon States that (a) launch or procure the launch of a space object, (b) launch a space object from their territory or their facility, (c) if damage is caused by a space object to the property of another State or of persons, natural or juridical, of another State or to property of intergovernmental organizations. The aforementioned liability regime varies on the basis of where damages occur. On the one hand, if damages are caused on the surface of the Earth or to aircraft in flight, States are absolutely liable, that is, strict liability is imposed for space activities that cause damages not in outer space. On the other hand, if damages are caused in outer space, the liability regime is based on fault. It is relevant to stress that States are responsible for the space activities carried out by their nationals. This contribution deals with the latter scenario and examines the effects of software engineering practices related to CubeSats.

---

22 Frans von der Dunk, "Liability for Damage Caused by Small Satellites – A Non-Issue?" in Irmgard Marboe, ed., *Small Satellites: Regulatory Challenges and Chances* (Leiden: Brill, 2016).

23 Jakhu and Pelton, *Small Satellites and their Regulation*; Irmgard Marboe, "Small Is Beautiful? Legal Challenges of Small Satellites," in Patricia Margaret Sterns and Leslie I. Tennen, eds., *Private Law, Public Law, Metalaw and Public Policy in Space: A Liber Amicorum in Honor of Ernst Fasan* (Springer, 2016): 1–16; and Nair, *Small Satellites and Sustainable Development*.

2.3 *On the Relationship between Fault, RTOS, and Software Certification*

In the previous two subsections, we established that, first, in-orbit conjunctions are increasingly likely, and, second, that the conditions for a launching State being held liable for an in-orbit conjunction depends on fault. We now connect the notion of fault with spacecraft engineering practices, drawing attention in particular to the case of CubeSats and their most critical software components.

For space systems in general there is an ISO standard[24] stipulating safety requirements that makes recommendations concerning software, not only hardware. ISO 14620–1: Space systems – Safety requirements, highlights that "software that supports a safety critical function" should undergo a "formal software safety program consisting of software hazard analysis, software design requirements analysis, test, and verification and validation." The clauses of the standard most relevant to this study are 6.4.4.1 and 6.4.4.4, which respectively concern software that implements or controls safety critical functions and software verification.

However, this work focuses specifically on CubeSats, rather than space systems in general. For small spacecraft, such as CubeSats, there is a dedicated recommendation,[25] which addresses the following problem:

> Applying the same test requirements as those applied to traditional large/medium satellites, however, will nullify the low-cost and fast-delivery advantages possessed by small spacecraft.

Notably, the above-mentioned ISO standard for CubeSats makes allowances for the use of non-space-qualified commercial-off-the-shelf units (COTS) and does not explicitly cover software testing. Following this ISO standard, almost no software safety standards are set for CubeSats. There are however hardware testing requirements defined in the standard ensuring that non-space-qualified hardware is in fact adequate for purpose.

From the above evidence, we see that there is a significant gap between the standards for CubeSats and those for other spacecraft – the absence or presence, respectively, of the requirement to verify safety-critical software. For this reason, we focus on what we argue is one of the most critical pieces of software – the Real-Time Operating System (RTOS). An RTOS is a dedicated

24 ISO, *Space systems – Safety requirements*, Tech. rep. 14620–1 (2018).

25 ISO, *Space systems – Design qualification and acceptance tests of small spacecraft and units*, Tech. rep. ISO 19683:2017 (2017).

operating system that is installed on embedded systems in general, including, for example, aircraft, smart vehicles, IoT devices, or industrial appliances. They are particularly relevant for such applications, due to the requirement to precisely coordinate the timing of reading of various input sensors and response actions. Operating systems, in general, provide a layer that sits between the hardware and software of a system, exposing interfaces between its components. For example, the RTOS enables a software application, which responds to telecommands for manoeuvring a satellite, to talk with the hardware that receives communications via antennae another piece of hardware that deploys thrust to implement a manoeuvre. Another example of a critical operation managed via the RTOS is battery management, ensuring that a payload, which typically consumes more power than is available, when fully operational, does not result in the failure of critical components. Notice that failure to properly manage either of these processes may result in the loss the telecommunications channel, possibly permanently. A telecommunications channel is a component indispensable for operational purposes; hence its failure turns the satellite into a dangerous object in orbit.

Indeed, a study spanning launches from 2009 to 2018 has indicated that almost half of satellite failures can be attributed to the failure of the communications system or power system,[26] both of which are managed via an RTOS.

While failures of critical operations managing the communication channel may be caused by failures of hardware – for instance, the antennae, circuitry, or battery – failures caused by software should not be ruled out. Possible reasons for software to fail could be inadequate functional requirements, software bugs, or even cyberattacks exploiting vulnerabilities.[27] In Figure 7.2, we provide a simplified fault tree which is a method safety engineers employ to communicate and measure causes of faults. By using fault trees and historic failure data for related hardware components and software, it may be possible for an engineer to measure the likelihood of the cause of a fault being due to a failure in the RTOS, relative to other types of component failure. Note the hardware branch of the fault tree in Figure 7.2 can grow large as more detail is added by refining components into sub-components. Such a fault tree analysis is explicitly recommended to be conducted for spacecraft in ISO standard

26 Kara O'Donnell and Gregory Richardson, "Small Satellite Trending & Reliability 2009–2018," Small Satellite Conference (2020) https://digitalcommons.usu.edu/smallsat/2020/all2020/185/.

27 P. J. Blount. "Satellites Are Just Things on the Internet of Things," *Air and Space Law* 42 (2017).

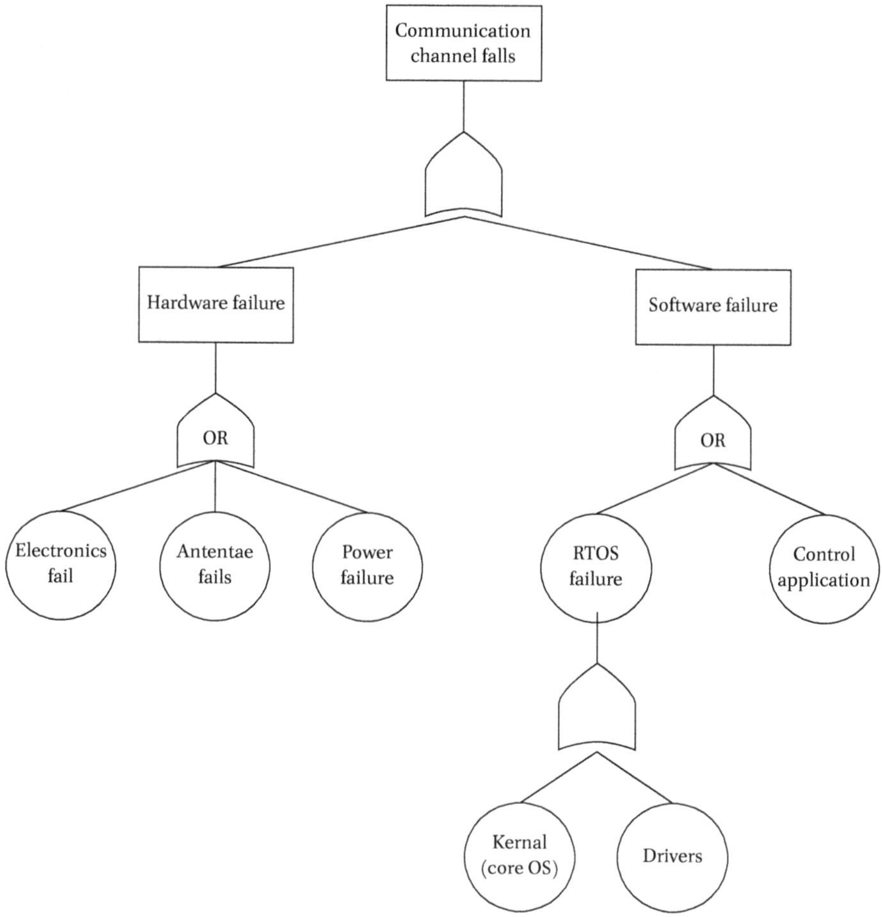

FIGURE 7.2 Sample of a fault tree suggesting possible causes for a telecommunications channel to be lost, indicating the RTOS Kernel

14620–1,[28] hence adding a branch for critical software failures should not be overly demanding for engineers.

The point of concern is that, for CubeSats, it is commonplace to make use of an RTOS which was designed by the open-source community for non-space-going purpose, hence did not follow practices for software verification. For example, Amazon Free RTOS was designed for IoT sensor networks, for example, for gathering data in smart cities. Other RTOS projects used in CubeSats

28 ISO, *Space systems – Safety requirements*, Tech. rep. 14620–1 (2018).

include eCos and Kubos. In the next section, we provide empirical evidence for our claim that some of these projects are likely unreliable even for CubeSat projects, whereas others appear to be better designed. Thus, even if obtaining an RTOS that meets the avionics standard for RTOS software (ARINC 653)[29] would unreasonably restrict the low-cost and fast-delivery advantages of CubeSat, it can be still reasonable to recommend that a RTOS with a good level of reliability is used in CubeSat projects. Similarly, demanding the highest level of software certification, such as EAL7 – a level of certification which almost no software has attained – would stifle innovation in orbit, by making outer space inaccessible to all but the largest multinationals and national agencies. Thus, it is important to measure what is a realistic level of certification to recommend, as we investigate in the next section.

While the failure of critical software may lead to channel failure, notice that if the software managing a payload, for instance, a camera and other remote sensing apparatus, fails, then it is easier to reinstate or even patch that software via the critical core of the CubeSat that manages the communication channel and its interface with the payload. Thus, requiring all software deployed on a CubeSat to meet high standards of dependability would impede innovation concerning the payload. For this reason, we restrict our focus to the RTOS. While it might also have been reasonable to take into account some critical applications that run inside an RTOS, it would not make sense to consider analysing the dependability of all software deployed on a CubeSat.

3 Empirical Evaluation of the Quality of CubeSat Real-Time Operating Systems

This section concerns the technical evaluation of the quality of RTOS software deployed in CubeSats, which in previous sections we argued is the key possible cause of mission failure resulting in the creation of a dangerous object in orbit, which is not yet covered by CubeSat recommendations. Confirming whether or not a software project meets certification standards can take hundreds of person-years. For this reason, we adopt an empirical approach to back up and substantiate our claim that improvements should be made in the quality of

29 P.J. Prisaznuk, "ARINC 653 role in Integrated Modular Avionics (IMA)," 2008 IEEE/AIAA 27th Digital Avionics Systems Conference (2008): 1.E.5–1–1.E.5–10; *Avionics application software standard interface part 3A: Conformity Test Specifications for ARINC 653 Required Services*. Tech. rep. ARINC Industry Activities (2019): 1–471.

critical software typically deployed in CubeSats. In empirical software engineering, we use metrics which are indicators of the coding style used in the project. Good coding style can indicate diligence in managing the complexity of a software project and hence can increase confidence that fewer vulnerabilities have been introduced via poor coding practice.

For this study, we considered four open-source real-time operating systems (operating systems appropriate for control systems). Three – FreeRTOS, Kubos and eCos – are deployed in CubeSats. The fourth – seL4 – has been deployed on military-grade helicopters.[30] Note real-time operating systems meeting exceptionally high certification standards are deployed on aircraft (VxWare, LynxOS, Deos DO-178, INTEGRITY-178B, and suchlike). For example, the INTEGRITY-178B RTOS meets the second highest Evaluation Assurance Level set by the Common Criteria (EAL6)[31] – a software engineering standard. However, since, firstly, the source code of such RTOS projects is not in public domain, and, secondly, such software is likely out of budget for CubeSat operators, we take seL4 as our ground truth representing a verified RTOS. Interestingly, although seL4 is formally verified, it is not certified as being formally verified, since it used modern verification methods not yet acknowledged by the Common Criteria as being a replacement for traditional testing methods.[32]

In what follows we present some key metrics and suggest why the score for seL4 differs significantly from other projects. We note that in each project we consider only C code, which forms the most of the code in all projects, except Kubos where 60% of the code is in the Rust language and 30% is in C. The Rust language has been designed to improve memory safety compared to C, which means that, for code written in Rust, the chances of software failures and vulnerabilities should be reduced. We used a tool by Spinellis et al.[33] to collect these metrics. In particular, we considered software complexity metrics and generic coding practices. We discuss them below.

30 D. Cofer et al., "A Formal Approach to Constructing Secure Air Vehicle Software," *Computer* 51.11 (2018): 14–23.

31 ISO, *Common Criteria for Information Technology Security Evaluation. Part 3: Security assurance components*, Tech. rep. 15408, ver. 3.1, rev. 5 (2017) https://www.commoncriteriaportal.org/files/ccfiles/CCPART3V3.1R5.pdf.

32 Gerwin Klein et al., "Formally Verified Software in the Real World," *Communications of the ACM* 61.10 (2018): 68–77.

33 Diomidis Spinellis, Panos Louridas, and Maria Kechagia, "The Evolution of C Programming Practices: A Study of the Unix Operating System 1973–2015," *2016 IEEE/ACM 38th International Conference on Software Engineering (ICSE). IEEE* (2016): 748–759.

3.1 *Size of the Codebase*

The size of the codebase (SLoC), that is the number of lines of code, is often used as a coarse-grained, yet relatively "cheap" metric that can serve as a proxy for reasoning about the complexity of a software project.[34] There are several studies in the software engineering community that explore the relation between the size of a code base and its maintainability, as well as software defect density.[35]

Consider first the seL4 project, with 45,781 SLoC. Verifying functional correctness of a project of this size is still beyond the means of most companies. However, the most critical 8700 SLoC within the project have already been verified taking around 18 person-years using current state-of-the-art verification technology.[36]

Now contrast the above to FreeRTOS, which features over 2.1 million SLoC. Assuming a linear relationship between SLoC and verification time (which is optimistic), verification effort for the entire project could exceed 4000 person-years. Even the effort for verifying a critical core of the system would likely be in the order of hundreds of person-years, which is beyond the budget of the biggest players in the space industry. Thus, SLoC is already a clear indicator that critical vulnerabilities are likely to be present in the FreeRTOS code base.

The eCos project also features a large code base just short of 1 million SLoC remaining well outside the realm of verifiable software. The Kubos code base fares better with around 60 thousand SLoC, hence it may be possible to identify a critical core of the project to which verification techniques may be applied. Note that, although Kubos has not been formally verified like seL4, it does employ the Rust language which offers some lightweight guarantees.[37]

3.2 *Halstead and Cyclomatic Complexity*

There is a relationship between the code that has a high degree of complexity and the number of potential bugs/vulnerabilities.[38] The Halstead complexity

34 Sheng Yu and Shijie Zhou, "A Survey on Metric of Software Complexity," *IEEE International Conference on Information Management and Engineering* (IEEE, 2010): 352–356.

35 A. Gunes Koru et al., "An Investigation into the Functional Form of the Size-defect Relationship for Software Modules," *Transactions on Software Engineering* 35.2 (2009): 293–304 and Andrea Capiluppi, "Models for the Evolution of OS Projects," *Proceedings of International Conference on Software Maintenance. Los Alamitos, CA, USA* (2003): 65–74.

36 Klein et al., "Formally Verified Software in the Real World," 68–77.

37 Nicholas D. Matsakis and Felix S. Klock II, "The Rust Language," *Ada Lett* 34.3 (2014): 103–104.

38 Yonghee Shin and Laurie Williams, "An Empirical Model to Predict Security Vulnerabilities Using Code Complexity Metrics," *Proceedings of International Symposium on Empirical*

metric calculates the data stream complexity and ignores control flow complexity (branches); it is language-independent and can be used as a predictor for the potential defect density. On the other hand, cyclomatic complexity captures control flow complexity, but ignores data flow complexity (thus, can be used to complement Halstead). See[39] for a comparison between Halstead and cyclomatic complexity measures and the "good" and "bad" values.

Complexity metrics can be a better indicator of the cost of certifying code than SLoC, since "system growth is not necessarily associated with structural complexity increases."[40] In other words, large software (SLoCs, files, and suchlike) does not have to be overly complex. However, these metrics do not have any absolute meaning – for instance, the fact that eCos has twice as high a Halstead complexity compared to seL4 does not necessarily mean that eCos is twice as expensive to verify as seL4. Therefore, we do not present the values on the y-axis of Figure 7.3, since the values are only approximate and relative indicators of complexity.

Cyclomatic complexity considers the depth of structure of code which can be used to indicate whether more expertise for an implementation is needed to be correct. The mean cyclomatic complexity of seL4 is around 2.6 which is slightly lower than 3.2 for FreeRTOS and 5.2 for eCos, indicating that it is generally easier to verify the control flow of code in seL4. A stronger difference can be seen by looking at files with the high cyclomatic complexity. If we look at files with high cyclomatic complexity above 12, seL4 features just one file with registering a cyclomatic complexity of 23, whereas FreeRTOS and eCos feature respectively 71 and 81 such files, peaking with a cyclomatic complexity of 131 and 194. Almost all complex files in the FreeRTOS project are in libraries and vendor specific drivers, suggesting complexity is imported from 3rd-party components.

The Halstead metric which indicates the complexity of the data processed independently confirms the above story. The mean Halstead complexity of seL4 is 270 whereas FreeRTOS and eCos register at 440 and 600 respectively. As with cyclomatic complexity, the gap between FreeRTOS and seL4 widens

---

Software Engineering and Measurement (2008); Yonghee Shin et al. "Evaluating Complexity, Code Churn, and Developer Activity Metrics as Indicators of Software Vulnerabilities," *Transactions on Software Engineering* 37.6 (2011): 772–787.

39 Yu and Zhou, "A Survey on Metric of Software Complexity."

40 Spinellis, Louridas, and Kechagia, "The Evolution of C Programming Practices"; Antonio Terceiro et al., "Understanding Structural Complexity Evolution: A Quantitative Analysis," *2012 16th European Conference on Software Maintenance and Reengineering* (IEEE, 2012): 85–94.

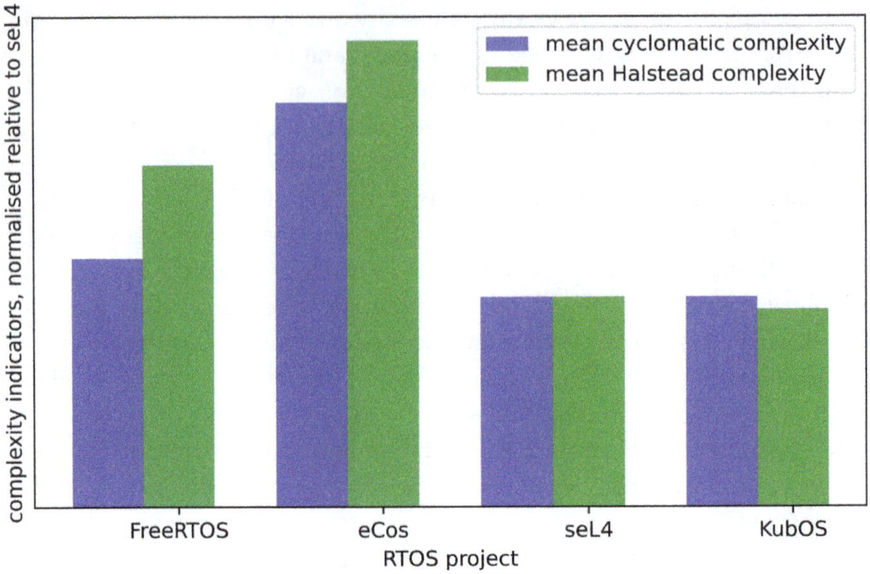

FIGURE 7.3 Normalised mean halstead and cyclomatic complexity

when considering the files with highest Halstead complexity (for instance, the 92 most complex files in FreeRTOS exceed the complexity of all but the most complex file in seL4). Having significantly more complex files may demand more advanced verification techniques, hence more human effort and expertise in order for the software to meet some level of certification.

The complexity scores for Kubos are comparable to seL4. However, recall, some of the more complex functionality may be written in the Rust language, whereas we considered only the C code in this evaluation.

3.3 *Keywords: Goto, Inline, etc.*

The extraneous use of the goto statement, a low-level keyword in the C language whose effect can almost always be captured by higher-level loops can lead to the *spaghetti code* anti-pattern and significantly complicate program understanding.[41] This, in turn, leads to low maintainability of the code and a higher number of potential software defects.

41 Edsger W. Dijkstra. "Goto Statement Considered Harmful," *Communications of the ACM* 11.3 (1968): 147–148.

FIGURE 7.4 Scatter chart showing the density of goto statements in files in the FreeRTOS, eCos and KubOS projects with at least one goto statement

The project seL4 has zero goto statements, whereas the FreeRTOS and eCos projects contain 3922 and 2480 goto statements each. Since this is amongst the clearest indicators separating seL4 from other projects, we interpret below our observation for each project. A visualisation of the distribution of goto statements are illustrated in the scatter chart in Figure 7.4. This helps identify outliers where the number of goto statements are not linearly correlated with SLoC.

In FreeRTOS, all these goto statements are in imported libraries and vendor specific drivers. The number of statements grows approximately linearly with the size of the file, with the notable exceptions being in a driver for the wifi vendor Espressif which features the files with the most goto statements (between 67 and 114 statements). The above observations suggest that FreeRTOS may have vulnerabilities due to the libraries and drivers used, and, in particular, the components that could be considered risky to use in a CubeSat running FreeRTOS can be singled out, such as those developed by the wifi vendor Espressif.

The main outlier in the eCos project is the network packet implementation for IPv6 (ICMP), with 128 goto statements in a file of 3614 SLoC (indicated by the single isolated blue dot towards the top left of Figure 7.4). The eCos project consistently employs a high density of goto statements throughout the project, with a large proportion of files with at least 10 goto statements concerning networking. Since networking is an important function, this could be an alarming weakness of FreeRTOS worthy of further inspection before FreeRTOS is deployed in a CubeSat project where dependability is a requirement.

The 26 goto statements in Kubos are mainly contained in a JSON library. JSON is used for structuring messages and system configuration files; hence, we recommend that this library should be tested or verified.

Other keywords can indicate the quality of code. The presence of inline and register keywords in C code were introduced in the earlier versions of the language to alleviate the deficiencies that the compilers had with allocating registers and inline functions. Since the compilers are getting better, extraneous use of such keywords should indicate that the codebase (or at least the part thereof) is quite old and has not been modified/refactored since a long time ago.[42]

The significant presence of inline and register keywords suggests the presence of legacy code in FreeRTOS and eCos. While the seL4 project uses only 4 register keywords, FreeRTOS uses 175, and eCos uses 2113. The seL4 project uses 95 inline keywords, is still eclipsed by the 693 inline in the FreeRTOS project and 376 in the eCos project. Kubos fares better since it contains zero legacy keywords.

4 Legal Implications for Launching States

The goal of this section is to defend the interpretation that a launching State could be liable for damage caused by a space object in outer space if it authorizes CubeSats missions that do not meet certain software reliability requirements. In particular, we emphasise that the RTOS is a critical software component given its role in managing the software and hardware that manages critical

42 Spinellis, Louridas, and Kechagia, "The Evolution of C Programming Practices"; Gregory J Chaitin, "Register Allocation & Spilling via Graph Coloring," *ACM Sigplan Notices* 17.6 (ACM, 1982) 98–105.

functionality, notably the communication channel that enables a CubeSat to be controlled remotely. This would create an incentive for policy makers to introduce mitigation strategies at the national level, which would improve the current state of the art.

Our task in this section is to answer whether the licensing a CubeSat mission with a poor RTOS violates a duty established by law. Under current international space law, the response appears positive. There are two interpretative paths to establish the fault of States that license a mission with an RTOS that does not meet specific software reliability standards.

The first interpretation is based on considering that Article VI of the Outer Space Treaty – the norm that establishes the responsibility of States for activities in outer space – includes a specific standard of diligence which would be violated if States were to license space missions with inadequate critical software on-board. This argument is corroborated by Article IX of the Outer Space Treaty which establishes that States Parties shall conduct their space activities with due regard to the corresponding interests of all other space Parties. While the standard of conduct contained in Article IX is not precisely defined, it seems possible to conclude that "due regard" requires launching States to not authorize activities that pose a significant risk for space operations of other States Parties (including their nationals). In this case, States would be held liable on the basis of international responsibility and liability established by Articles VI, VII, and IX of the Outer Space Treaty.[43]

A second, but more tenuous, interpretative way relies on a creative interpretation of the Article IV of the Outer Space Treaty and may not be corroborated by expert opinion. In more detail, it could be possible to argue that licensing a CubeSat mission with a poor RTOS may constitute a breach to Article IV as it could hamper the peaceful use of outer space. This is because failures that may be caused by a faulty RTOS increase the risk of in-orbit conjunctions and can contribute to environmental degradation of outer space, thereby preventing other parties from conducting affairs in space 'peaceably.'[44] The launching State should be held liable if a CubeSat causes damage in outer space because of malfunctioning under Article III of the Liability Convention. It is important to stress that, in this case,fault is presupposed as a consequence of poor software engineering practices, so thatthe launching State would be able to exonerate itself if it proves that something else caused the damage – such as

43 James Crawford, "Articles on Responsibility of States for Internationally Wrongful Acts," *United Nations Audiovisual Library of International Law* (2012) http://legal.un.org/avl/ha/rsiwa/rsiwa.htm.

44 Nair, *Small Satellites and Sustainable Development*.

an anomaly in space weather. The practical effect of this interpretation would be a reversal of the burden of proof. Put simply, it will be on the entity which caused the damage to prove that another event was the cause of the damage instead of its conduct. Conversely, it is usually the party who suffered the damage that has to prove that the conduct of the other party caused the damaging event.

Of course, due to the nature of this contribution, some essential elements necessary to establish liability for damages caused by space activities have not been discussed – for example the kind of damages, the procedural aspects, as well as the empirical difficulty of reconstructing the event that caused the damage in outer space. Nonetheless, our aim is to demonstrate that the successful management of the new wave of small satellites such as CubeSats, logically presupposes that these satellites run adequately dependable critical software. That is, CubeSat software ought to adhere to a set of standards to ensure that the risk of malfunction is mitigated. According to the interpretations presented above, the matter becomes urgent because launching States might have to bear the risks associated with poor critical software components. Alongside ethical and engineering reasons to impose requirements on RTOS, there are legal ones as well. More importantly, we argued that an obligation to require a certain degree of software dependability is already enshrined in international space law. On this basis, the next section examines threepossibilities to address the issue at hand. Each solution will be discussed before arguing in favour of heightened requirements for the authorization of space missions.

5 Strategies for Mitigating Liability

This section explores possible strategies to mitigate the liability of launching States for CubeSats missions without a dependable RTOS. It examines two options and concludes that it would be desirable for States to require more stringent controls on the quality of RTOS in the authorization process of space missions.

There are two possibilities to manage the risks of damages caused by CubeSats with non-dependable software on board. Balance is needed between robust certification procedures – for instance, Avionics standards, such as ARINC 653 – and a laissez-faire approach to software engineering practices. The peaceful use of space, along with environmental concerns, ought to be guarded by States in the licensing phase. On the one hand, strong software requirements are likely to require new procedures and extensive scrutiny by authorities on space missions, thereby leading to an increase in mission costs.

On the other hand, the principle of freedom of access to outer space requires that licensing procedures do not excessively restrict the recent trend toward the 'democratization' of space. The problem here is ofbalancing values. In the previous pages, we have demonstrated that some practices should be discouraged because they increase the concerns associated with the surge in CubeSats missions. Additionally, we argued that a laissez-faire attitude on software engineering practices could make launching States liable for damages caused in outer space. Therefore, a higher degree of scrutiny for RTOS is desirable, the issue then becomeshow to achieve it without overregulating. For example, the standards developed for avionics appear to be too much to ask in this case. This is because the decrease in the costs associated with the access to space is a desirable aim, which should be guarded. With this aim in mind, this section examines two strategies to address the issues at hand.

The first option is to intervene at the level of the authorization of space missions. The duty of States to authorize and supervise space missions is established by Article VI of the Outer Space Treaty. The Convention on Registration of Objects Launched into Outer Space (henceforth the Registration Convention) specifies the duty of registration on launching States connected with the authorization process. Neither the Outer Space Treaty nor the Registration Convention indicate the requirements for the authorization of space missions, which, consequently, vary significantly. States could require that the software deployed on CubeSats meets specific requirements. We should note that States could require all space missions to deploy highly dependable software, however, we focus our attention on CubeSats because other missions generally have a higher success rate. There are many options in this case, ranging from formal verification to testing. States should evaluate different solutions according to the objective of the mission under authorization. What is important here is that States could – to mitigate the risks explained above – intervene at the level of the authorization of space missions by mandating space operators to use critical software that meet certain criteria.

The second option does not require intervention on the authorization processes. Instead, it entails modifying or introducing specific insurance requirements for CubeSats missions. Many States already require insurance for space missions. Therefore, a possibility is to introduce stronger insurance requirements for missions that do not provide guarantees concerning critical software components. A similar solution that considers unmanageable objects has already been discussed.[45] In this case, by mandating higher insurance

45 Ting Wang, "A Liability and Insurance Regime for Space Debris Mitigation," *Science Global Security* 24.1 (2016): 22–36.

requirements, an incentive to develop guarantees for the software would be created. Of course, this might have the negative effect of restricting access to space for missions with lower budgets. However, States could consider exceptions for some space missions such as the ones carried out for educational purposes. Yet, this might not be necessary as the software examined above – seL4 – is highly dependable and open source.

From the two options, the first one appears more desirable. It would allow States to comply with the objectives and the spirit of international space law while protecting the space environment and alleviating the problem of space debris which would increase with the number of uncontrollable space objects. Also, States could influence the degree of control by requiring different standards of certification. So that, for example, a private mission that deploys CubeSats with an open OS might be mandated to formally verify the software while educational missions – like the ones operated by universities – might only be required to perform software testing.

Regardless of the solution adopted, critical software components ought to be highly dependable. For these reasons, and because – as shown in Section 4 – poor software engineering practices might lead to the liability of launching States, it is desirable to implement measures to ensure the dependability of critical software systems deployed on CubeSats sooner rather than later.

6 Conclusion

CubeSats are here to stay, so is the current international legal framework regulating space activities. In light of the increase in the risks of operating spacecrafts due to the surge in launches of small satellites, this contribution argues for the imposition of stricter requirements for critical software components of CubeSats in the authorization phase. We have put forward both legal and technical reasons to support this conclusion. On the one hand, it has been argued that current space law already contains a duty for launching States to demand certain standards for the software deployed on board spacecrafts. This duty arises from obligations already enshrined in the international legal framework governing space activities. Its relevance has been shown in the context of the liability for damages caused by malfunctioning CubeSats in the event of orbital-conjunctions. Simply put, if launching States aim to avoid the liability risk, stricter requirements for critical software components should be imposed. On the other hand, this conclusion has been empirically supported by evaluating different RTOS deployed on CubeSats to show that better dependability is possible and in reach of space operators. More importantly, we have shown that better solutions are available without imposing excessive additional costs on CubeSats operators. On this basis, we provided two mitigation strategies. We concluded that including software requirements in the authorization phase of space missions at the national level is more desirable when compared to the other option, a mandatory insurance schema. It is only at the authorization phase that environmental and ethical concerns can be addressed effectively.

SECTION III

Data Processing

CHAPTER 8

Law and Policy of Data from Space: Satellite Navigation and Remote Sensing

Leopold Mantl

1 Introduction[1]

Imagine an autonomous robot tasked to transport a package from building A to building B. To do so, the robot will or would require access to geo-referenced data, including from space. The robot will or would also need precise positioning information, using global navigation satellite systems (GNSS) or other means of navigation. Finally, the robot may have to communicate with other devices linked to the internet. To perform its tasks, the robot would have to depend on an integration of space technologies that were, in the past, separate.

1.1 *Future of Space Technologies: Integration and Fusion*

Geographical (or geographic) information systems (GIS) are a case in point for the integration and fusion of space technologies. GIS include "a spatial database, a graphic user interface, and a set of tools to manipulate spatial data."[2] Spatial data relates to a specific location or geographical area.[3] A substantial part of the data stored in spatial databases comes from remote sensing, namely "the sensing of the Earth's surface from space by making use of the properties of electromagnetic waves emitted, reflected or diffracted by the sensed objects, for the purpose of improving natural resources management, land use and the protection of the environment."[4]

1 The article is based on a presentation given at the Workshop "Space Law in a Networked World" and reflects exclusively the personal views of the author.

2 Jesus A. Gonzalez, "Geographic Information Systems and Geomatics," *Handbook of Satellite Applications (2nd edition)*, ed. Joseph N. Pelton, Scott Madry, and Sergio Camacho-Lara (Cham: Springer International Publishing Switzerland, 2017), 1119.

3 See also the definition of the term in point 2) of Article 3 of Directive 2007/2/EC of the European Parliament and of the Council of 14 March 2007 establishing an Infrastructure for Spatial Information in the European Community (INSPIRE), *OJ L 108, 25.4.2007, p. 1* (the "INSPIRE Directive").

4 See the Principles relating to Remote Sensing of the Earth from Space adopted by the General Assembly in Resolution 41/65 of 3 December 1986 (the "Remote Sensing Principles"), point (a) of Principle I.

 | DOI:10.1163/9789004527270_009

Remote sensing activities were initially carried out *in situ* or from planes. Such activities now also depend on satellites which produce a large variety of data: "very high spatial resolution optical data such as WorldView, Ikonos, GeoEye, and Quickbird (commercial sensors operated by Digital Globe) to Aster, Landsat, SPOT toward medium resolution MODIS and coarse-scale NOAA AVHRR data; furthermore, a broad variety of satellite-borne SAR data from sensors like ALOS, RADARSAT, TerraSAR-X, or Sentinel-1 are available."[5] These space systems produce exponentially growing amounts of data to meet worldwide information needs.[6] In 2019, users downloaded more than 70 petabytes of Copernicus Sentinel data alone.[7] The advent of mega-constellations, comprising a very high number of individual satellites,[8] will further accelerate generation of space remote sensing data.

In addition to an ever-growing amount of raw data, which could be referred to as "space big data," users can today make use of large data storage space, including through cloud computing, and advanced computing capabilities. In particular, machine learning algorithms can be deployed for automated data analysis.[9] Big data is "a radical shift rather than an incremental change for most of the existing digital infrastructures."[10] Hence the importance of user interfaces and data analysis tools in GIS.

5 Natascha Oppelt, Rolf Scheiber, Peter Gege, Martin Wegmann, Hannes Taubenboeck, and Michael Berger, "Fundamentals of Remote Sensing for Terrestrial Applications: Evolution, Current State of the Art, and Future Possibilities," in *Remotely Sensed Data Characterization, Classification, and Accuracies*, ed. Prasad S. Thenkabail (Boca Raton: Taylor & Francis Group, 2015), 63, 68.

6 Dimitra Stefoudi, "Space Big Data, Small Earth Laws: Overcoming the Regulatory Barriers to the Use of Space Big Data," in *Proceedings of the 2017 Conference on Big Data from Space: BIDS' 2017*, ed. Pierre Soille and Pier Giorgio Marchetti (Luxembourg: Publications Office of the European Union, 2017), 86.

7 See the Copernicus Sentinel Data Access Annual Report 2019, https://scihub.copernicus.eu/twiki/pub/SciHubWebPortal/AnnualReport2019/COPE-SERCO-RP-20-0570_-_Sentinel_Data_Access_Annual_Report_Y2019_v1.0.pdf, 2.

8 Matteo Cappella, "The Principle of Equitable Access in the Age of Mega-Constellations," in *Legal Aspects Around Satellite Constellations*, ed. Annette Froehlich (Cham: Springer Nature Switzerland AG, 2019), 17.

9 Cristiana Santos and Lucien Rapp, "Satellite Imagery, Very High-Resolution and Processing-Intensive Image Analysis: Potential Risks under the GDPR," *Air & Space Law* v. 44, no. 3 (2019): 275, 277.

10 Stefano Nativi, Joost van Bemmelen, Mattia Santoro, and Guido Colangeli, "Big Data Challenges in GEOSS," in *Proceedings of the 2017 Conference on Big Data from Space. BIDS' 2017*, ed. Pierre Soille and Pier Giorgio Marchetti (Luxembourg: Publications Office of the European Union, 2017), 98.

In many cases, GIS also include information from positioning systems, including GNSS. This is the case for mass-market car navigation devices and services, whereby GNSS signals are used to update the position of vehicles. Depending on this position, the user can optimize the route planning or can receive useful information such as the addresses of gas stations, or restaurants. In this context, many GIS operate in a web environment.[11] In such an environment, even "cell phones are no longer simple portable devices for making voice calls. Your phone likely serves as your map, your newspaper, your books, your email, your TV – and cable company, your watch, your video game system, and even your marketplace."[12]

The convergence of big data from space, GNSS, and web-based services allows the provision of a plethora of downstream applications, also beyond the mass market.[13] Firstly, augmented and virtual reality, and GIS can be combined to create innovative applications, mainly "to simulate how the real world would look like if we added artificial objects to it." Such applications exist in the area of gaming, landscape visualisation and underground infrastructure visualisation.[14] In the transport sector, electronic chart display and information systems (ECDIS), generally connected to a GNSS, radar, and other sensors, allow "drawing the path that the vessel should follow in the navigation chart." GIS based applications are also used to support all four phases of disaster management (mitigation, preparedness, response, or recovery), including for both man-made and natural disasters.[15] Distress signals, processed by the Galileo Search and Rescue Service, also need to be linked to geographic information in order to establish the appropriate rescue coordination centre.[16] Finally, the

11 Gonzalez, "Geographic Information Systems and Geomatics," 1119, 1129.

12 P.J. Blount, "Satellites Are Just Things on the Internet of Things," *Air & Space Law* v. 42, no. 3 (2017): 276.

13 From the perspective of GNSS, more than 93% of worldwide revenues are generated in the road sector (In-Vehicle Systems, Advanced Driver Assistance Systems and Fleet Management) and through consumer solutions (mainly data revenues of smartphones and tablets using location-based services), see in particular the 6th edition of the GNSS Market Report 2019, https://www.gsa.europa.eu/system/files/reports/market_report_issue_6_v2.pdf, 11.

14 Gonzalez, "Geographic Information Systems and Geomatics," 1133.

15 Gonzalez, "Geographic Information Systems and Geomatics," 1131–1132. For the Copernicus emergency services, see "OBSERVER: The Copernicus Emergency Management Service: a global, versatile and operational tool for emergency managers and disaster risk reduction stakeholders," Copernicus, https://www.copernicus.eu/en/news/news/observer-copernicus-emergency-management-service-global-versatile-and-operational-tool.

16 For more detailed information, see "Search and Rescue (SAR)/ Galileo Service," EUSPA https://www.gsa.europa.eu/european-gnss/galileo/services/search-and-rescue-sar-galileo-service.

combination of *"satellite navigation, increased processing capacities, sensory technology and connectivity,"* is also powering the development of automated self-driving systems.[17] These are examples of the integration not only of different space based data, but also positioning and geographic information from other sources.

1.2 *From Technological Trends to Legal Definitions*

Before analysing the horizontal legal challenges posed by the integration of different space technologies, it is useful to make some preliminary remarks. Firstly, many of the terms in the previous section describe technological trends and developments. They do not always have a separate and specific legal meaning, or at least are not used as such in currently applicable legislation. For example, even the term GIS itself is not used in key pieces of Union legislation, such as the INSPIRE Directive, Directive (EU) 2019/1024 (the "Open Data Directive"),[18] Regulation (EU) No 377/2014 (the "Copernicus Regulation"),[19] Commission Delegated Regulation (EU) No 1159/2013,[20] and the General Data Protection Regulation (EU) 2016/679 (GDPR).[21] Despite all the complexities of data processing and analysis, big data from space does not necessarily have to be dealt with differently from a legal perspective than small amounts of data. Mega-constellations risk producing bigger quantities of space debris, which could necessitate a more detailed binding framework for space debris removal

---

17 Lorenz Brunner and Gudrun Waniek, "Technological and Legal Aspects of Self-driving Vehicles," in *Satellite-Based Earth Observation: Trends and Challenges for Economy and Society*, ed. Christian Brünner, Georg Königsberger, Hannes Mayer, and Anita Rinner (Cham: Springer Nature Switzerland AG, 2018), 133.

18 Directive (EU) 2019/1024 of the European Parliament and of the Council of 20 June 2019 on open data and the re-use of public sector information, OJ L 172, 26.6.2019, p. 56 (the "Open Data Directive"). This Directive replaces Directive 2003/98/EC of the European Parliament and of the Council of 17 November 2003 on the re-use of public sector information, OJ L 345, 31.12.2003, p. 90 (the "PSI Directive").

19 Regulation (EU) No 377/2014 of the European Parliament and of the Council of 3 April 2014 establishing the Copernicus Programme and repealing Regulation (EU) No 911/2010, OJ L 122, 24.4.2014, p. 44.

20 Commission Delegated Regulation (EU) No 1159/2013 of 12 July 2013 supplementing Regulation (EU) No 911/2010 of the European Parliament and of the Council on the European Earth monitoring programme (GMES) by establishing registration and licensing conditions for GMES users and defining criteria for restricting access to GMES dedicated data and GMES service information, OJ L 309, 19.11.2013, p. 1.

21 Regulation (EU) 2016/679 of the European Parliament and of the Council of 27 April 2016 on the protection of natural persons with regard to the processing of personal data and on the free movement of such data, and repealing Directive 95/46/EC (General Data Protection Regulation), OJ L 119, 4.5.2016, p. 1.

in the future. However, mega-constellations are not automatically different under currently applicable rules from a small constellation, apart perhaps regarding frequency management.[22]

This "definition conundrum" applies in particular to the terms "downstream" sector, applications or services, as opposed to the "upstream" space segment, consisting of launch services, and satellite and ground segment development and operation. The integration of location data generated using GNSS signals and remote sensing in GIS takes place largely at the downstream level. However, the exact boundaries between the upstream and downstream level are not clear. Additionally, it can be assumed that a "big tech" company providing a mapping service would not consider itself a downstream space service provider, but simply a service provider.[23] The OECD Space Forum proposed a market segmentation based on three components, namely the upstream space sector (scientific research, R&D, manufacturing, production), downstream space sector (space enabled activities which would not exist or function without space data), and space related or derived activities in other sectors, which are derived from space technology, but do not depend on it to function.[24]

This is a useful approach, but it is not reflected in current legislation, at least not in the European Union. For example, the Copernicus Regulation contains the terms "downstream sector" (in recital 36 and Article 23(1)(b)), "downstream users" (in recitals 41 and 47, and the second subparagraph of Article 32(1)), "downstream services" (in Article 4(3)(b)), and "downstream applications" (in Article 5(3)(b)(II)) but proffers no definition of these terms. Regulation (EU) No 1285/2013 (the "GNSS Regulation")[25] uses the generic term "downstream

---

22 Even in this area, the ITU does not appear to have the intention to establish an entirely new system of regulations for very large constellations in low earth orbit, comparable to the distinct regime for the geostationary orbit established in the 1970s, see Alice Rivière, "The Rise of the LEO: Is There a Need to Create a Distinct Legal Regime for Constellations of Satellites?" in *Legal Aspects Around Satellite Constellations*, ed. Annette Froehlich (Cham: Springer Nature Switzerland AG, 2019), 51.

23 Murielle Lafaye, "Benefit Assessment of the Application of Satellite Earth Observation for Society and Policy: Assessing the Socioeconomic Impacts of the Development of Downstream Space-Based Earth Observation Applications," in *Satellite Earth Observations and Their Impact on Society and Policy*, ed. Masami Onoda and Oran R. Young (Singapore: Springer Nature, 2018), 97–98. This book is licensed under the terms of the Creative Commons Attribution 4.0 International License (http://creativecommons.org/licenses/by/4.0/).

24 OECD, *Space and Innovation*, OECD Publishing, Paris, https://doi.org/10.1787/9789264264014-en (2016), 28.

25 Regulation (EU) No 1285/2013 of the European Parliament and of the Council of 11 December 2013 on the implementation and exploitation of European satellite

markets" (in recital 14 and of Article 14(1)(c)) but refers generally to applications and services based on the GNSS systems (see for example the second subparagraph of Article 2(1)). Regulation (EU) 2021/696 (the "Space Programme Regulation"),[26] which provides the legal basis for the space activities of the European Union after 2020, contains references to downstream applications (for example in Article 29 (2)(c)), but likewise no definition of the term.

Similar considerations apply to terms such as "cyberspace," "cyber law" and "cyber security." Technically, space is "strongly linked to cyberspace."[27] In the upstream space sector, satellites function both as an internet transmission infrastructure and as an end device, where internet protocol-based technologies are used to "better facilitate not only the uplink and downlink communications between a satellite and ground stations, but also the performance of a multitude of scientific and commercial services in space."[28] The internet is also a means to provide web-based services in the downstream sector. This means that data generated in outer space, outside the jurisdiction of states, is injected into cyberspace, where determining jurisdiction becomes more and more difficult, due also to "artificial intelligence because it can move effortlessly across physical boundaries and as a new development act autonomously from humans in a distant forum."[29] To understand the legal impact of these developments, it is useful to analyse the architecture of the Internet. This architecture can be described as a four-layered model, including a physical layer, a logical layer, an application layer, and a content layer. Other models exist. Satellites and ground infrastructure are part of the physical layer of the Internet.[30] The logical layer uses standardised protocols[31] to establish "a standardized system

navigation systems and repealing Council Regulation (EC) No 876/2002 and Regulation (EC) No 683/2008 of the European Parliament and of the Council, OJ L 347, 20.12.2013, p. 1.

26 Regulation (EU) 2021/696 of the European Parliament and of the Council of 28 April 2021 establishing the Union Space Programme and the European Union Agency for the Space Programme and repealing Regulations (EU) No 912/2010, (EU) No 1285/2013 and (EU) No 377/2014 and Decision No 541/2014/EU, OJ L 170, 12.5.2021, p. 69.

27 Blount, "Satellites Are Just Things on the Internet of Things," 278.

28 Stephan Hobe, "The IISL Assumes Responsibility for Questions of Cyber Law," *ZLW* v. 66, no. 4 (2017): 654–655.

29 Woodrow Barfield, "Towards a Law of Artificial Intelligence," in *Research Handbook on the Law of Artificial Intelligence*, ed. Woodrow Barfield and Ugo Pagallo (Cheltenham: Edward Elgar Publishing Limited, 2018), 31.

30 See also Article 2(1) of Directive (EU) 2018/1972 of the European Parliament and of the Council of 11 December 2018 establishing the European Electronic Communications Code (Recast), OJ L 321, 17.12.2018, p. 36, which lists satellite networks as part of electronic communication networks.

31 In particular the Transfer Control Protocol and the Internet Protocol (TCP/IP).

for transferring information from digital machine to digital machine." The application layer consists of the programmes and applications installed on end-user devices to provide all types of content (content layer).[32]

Many, if not most, of the legal challenges of the integration of GIS and GNSS concern the application and content layer. However, international space law mainly concerns "infrastructure regulation," apart from the general principles laid down in the Outer Space Treaty.[33] These include the "space freedoms" enshrined in Article I of the Outer Space Treaty (freedom of exploration and use, the freedom of scientific investigation and the freedom of access to celestial bodies) and the obligation of States under Article VI of the Outer Space Treaty to authorise and continuously supervise outer space activities of non-governmental entities.[34] The focus on space objects, rather than space data or space-based services, is evident already from the title of the Convention on Registration of Objects Launched into Outer Space.[35] The same applies to the Convention on International Liability for Damage Caused by Space Objects[36]. The general interpretation of this Convention is that it covers only direct damage caused by physical impact, but not non-physical damage such as radio interference or indirect damage caused for example by an erroneous GNSS signal.[37]

At the international level, the space data integrated in GIS at application and content level is mainly covered by "soft law,"[38] and in particular by the Remote Sensing Principles. Although the Remote Sensing Principles are now (fully or at least partly) part of customary international law according to most scholars,[39] they do not provide answers to many of the legal questions arising from the integration of space technologies and data, for two main and interdependent reasons. Firstly, the potential – and risks – of digitalisation, very

32 Stephan Hobe, "The IISL Assumes Responsibility for Questions of Cyber Law," 651–653.

33 Treaty on Principles Governing the Activities of States in the Exploration and Use of Outer Space, including the Moon and other Celestial Bodies, 610 U.N.T.S. 205 (1967).

34 Lesley Jane Smith and Gina Petrovici, "Legal Aspects of Satellite Based Earth Observation – An Introduction," in *Satellite-Based Earth Observation: Trends and Challenges for Economy and Society*, ed. Christian Brünner, Georg Königsberger, Hannes Mayer, and Anita Rinner (Cham: Springer Nature Switzerland AG, 2018), 175.

35 1023 U.N.T.S. 15.

36 961 U.N.T.S. 187.

37 Frans G. von der Dunk, "Space Law and GNSS – A Look at the Legal Frameworks for 'Outer Space'," *Inside GNSS* 12:3 (May/June 2017): 39.

38 The concept is analysed in detail in Irmgard Marboe, *Soft Law in Outer Space: The Function of Non-binding Norms in International Space Law* (Wien: Böhlau Verlag, 2012).

39 See for example Diego Zannoni, *Disaster Management and International Space Law* (Leiden: BRILL, 2019), 155.

high-resolution imaging and the integration of space technologies and data were foreseeable in 1986 only to a very limited extent. The Remote Sensing Principles are therefore silent on one fundamental aspect exacerbated by these developments, namely the protection of personal data. Additionally, even the core Principle XII concerning in particular data access on a non-discriminatory basis may be less relevant in an environment where mass-market GIS and mapping services using remote sensing data are made available free of charge to any user worldwide, including officials of a sensed State. The "price" to be paid is a more or less large quantity of personal data mined by the service providers for advertising purposes.

Finally, the trend to substitute legal-norm making at international level by non-legally binding instruments to extend the *corpus iuris spatialis* often means that national or, in the case of the European Union, supranational rules are needed, although this "can lead to diverging 'rules of the road' for inherently global space activities."[40] However, the alternative of new international space law treaties covering specifically space data and services or liability issues is not realistic for the moment, although many of the challenges at hand, in particular in the area of environmental monitoring, would require an international response and transboundary cooperation.[41] The challenges of integrated downstream and space related services and applications will therefore be analysed from the perspective of the public sector, and existing rules mainly at national and supranational level.

2 Legal Challenges for the Public Sector

For the public sector, including international organisations, the supranational European Union, and national, regional and local authorities, the integration of GIS and GNSS is of relevance in particular in four different areas. Firstly, the public sector is a user of integrated related services and applications. In addition, the public sector operates many remote sensing missions and all of the existing GNSS constellations. The public sector also, third, takes actions to support market uptake of integrated space data and, fourth, is responsible

40 Jenni Tapio and Alexander Soucek, "National Implementation of Non-Legally Binding Instruments: Managing Uncertainty in Space Law?" *Air & Space Law* v. 44, no. 6 (2019): 570–571, 577.

41 Oran R. Young and Masami Onoda, "Satellite Earth Observations in Environmental Problem-Solving," in *Satellite Earth Observations and Their Impact on Society and Policy*, ed. Masami Onoda and Oran R. Young (Singapore: Springer Nature, 2018), 3.

for putting into place a stable legal framework. These four areas are different mainly in terms of the purpose and scope of activities, but not necessarily in terms of the tools used. For example, legislative action may provide a legal basis both for the operation of space systems and support to market uptake.

2.1 *The Public Sector as a User*

The public sector uses services and applications integrating GIS and GNSS for policy making, for example in the areas of transport, agriculture, security, disaster management, urban and regional planning, climate change mitigation and adaption, and environmental protection.[42] In this context, the public sector is the main user of the flagship European space programme (component) Copernicus.[43] Integrated services and applications are also means to monitor the implementation of these policies. For example, remote sensing is used for evaluating the impact of the Common Agricultural Policy (CAP) of the European Union on the environment, though the Land Use/Cover Area frame Survey (LUCAS).[44] The use of remote sensing for compliance monitoring by the public sector may require a tailor-made legal framework to ensure legal certainty. Specific rules, for instance, were adopted in the European Union through Commission Implementing Regulation (EU) 2018/746.[45] Its recital 2 states that "... New technologies such as Unmanned Aircraft Systems, geo-tagged photographs, GNSS-receivers combined with EGNOS and Galileo, data captured by the Copernicus Sentinels satellites and others, provide relevant data on activities carried out on agricultural areas. With a view to reducing the burden of controls for the competent authorities and beneficiaries, particularly the number of physical inspections in the field, and boosting the use of new technologies in the integrated administration and control system, it is appropriate to allow relevant evidence collected by using such technologies as well as any other relevant documentary evidence to be used for checking

---

42 See for example the Communication from the Commission to the European Parliament, the Council, the European Economic and Social Committee and the Committee of the Regions, European Space Strategy, COM(2016) 705 final of 26.10.2016 (the "European Space Strategy"), 3.

43 Josef Aschbacher, "ESA's Earth Observation Strategy and Copernicus," in *Satellite Earth Observations and Their Impact on Society and Policy*, ed. Masami Onoda and Oran R. Young (Singapore: Springer Nature, 2018), 82.

44 See "Land cover / use statistics – Overview," Eurostat, https://ec.europa.eu/eurostat/web/lucas.

45 Commission Implementing Regulation (EU) 2018/746 of 18 May 2018 amending Implementing Regulation (EU) No 809/2014 as regards modification of single applications and payment claims and checks, C/2018/2976, OJ L 125, 22.5.2018, p. 1.

compliance with eligibility criteria, commitments or other obligations." Finally, the use of integrated space-based services and applications as evidence in Court proceedings, including by the public sector, still raises a number of important legal issues.[46]

2.2 *The Public Sector as a System Operator/Service Provider*

In the upstream space sector, the public sector operates many remote sensing space missions worldwide, in addition to all GNSS constellations, and manages system upgrades to meet evolving user needs. This is also because civil downstream users can be expected to integrate space data into their services and applications only if they can rely on the continued availability of the space data.[47] The public expenditure is justified by socioeconomic benefits,[48] or strategic interest. At the upstream level, the integration of Earth observation missions and GNSS is less relevant. The systems are based on different technologies and need to be designed, developed, and operated separately. A limited number of synergies can be envisaged, such as aggregating demand for launch services,[49] or even the installation of navigation and remote sensing payloads on the same platform, but this is less of a legal issue.

Many downstream and space related services are provided by private players. The public sector is active in the downstream space sector in certain situations.[50] In this case, many of the legal topics covered in the next sections and linked specifically to the integration of GIS and GNSS will have to be factored into service design and provision by the public sector, including data protection.

2.3 *Public Sector Support to Downstream Market Uptake*

Many horizontal public sector interventions can benefit entities in the downstream space sector, such as equipment manufacturers and providers of services integrating GIS and GNSS. Examples include financial instruments to support access to finance, in particular for small and medium-sized enterprises (SME), and the establishment of a "business- and innovation-friendly

46 For a detailed analysis of this aspect, see Ray Purdy and Denise Leung, eds., *Evidence from Earth Observation Satellites. Emerging Legal Issues* (Leiden, Boston: Martinus Nijhoff Publishers, 2013).

47 European Space Strategy, 3.

48 Josef Aschbacher, "ESA's Earth Observation Strategy and Copernicus," 83.

49 European Space Strategy, 9.

50 The Copernicus services are a case in point. While they are not considered "downstream services" within the meaning of the Copernicus Regulation, they would probably fall under the OECD definition of the downstream space sector referred to in footnote 23.

ecosystem."[51] Other interventions focus on the space sector,[52] or even more specifically the downstream space sector. They include research, awareness raising, and a data policy focused on market uptake. The European Union currently finances research activities in the downstream sector through its multi-annual framework programmes. For the period 2014–2020, the Horizon 2020 programme had the purpose, *inter alia*, of "… promoting the development of innovative products and services based on remote sensing, geo-positioning or other types of satellite enabled data."[53] Further synergies are expected to be achieved by entrusting the European Union Agency for the Space Programme with the management of all downstream applications, and not only GNSS related ones, as is currently the case.[54] The same applies to communication and awareness raising activities in the European Union,[55] which were somewhat managed separately for GNSS and remote sensing in the past. Finally, an open data and intellectual property rights policy can be an important tool to support uptake of services integrating GNSS and GIS. This will be explored in more detail in Section 3.

2.4 *Stable and Clear Legal Framework*

The fourth challenge for the public sector concerns the question how legal certainty can be ensured for players in the downstream sector in a context where many of the emerging legal issues cannot be solved exclusively by, or even primarily based on international space law. These issues include, in particular, standardisation, (cyber)security, downstream regulation in different sectors such as road transport or aviation, liability, and data protection. They will be analysed in Sections 4 to 6.

---

51 European Space Strategy, 7.

52 For example, the Business Incubation Centres established by the European Space Agency (ESA), see "ESA Business Incubation Centres," ESA http://www.esa.int/Applications/Telecommunications_Integrated_Applications/Business_Incubation/ESA_Business_Incubation_Centres12.

53 See section 1.6.1.2 of Annex I of Council Decision of 3 December 2013 establishing the specific programme implementing Horizon 2020 – the Framework Programme for Research and Innovation (2014–2020) and repealing Decisions 2006/971/EC, 2006/972/EC, 2006/973/EC, 2006/974/EC and 2006/975/EC (2013/743/EU), OJ 347/96 of 20.12.2013, p. 1 (the "Decision on the Horizon 2020 specific programme"). Its successor programme Horizon Europe will continue these efforts.

54 The Space Programme Regulation provides that the European GNSS Agency is given additional tasks (including those listed in Article 29(2)(c)). It is therefore renamed European Union Agency for the Space Programme.

55 See for example paragraphs (1)(c) and (2)(d) of Article 29 of the Space Programme Regulation.

3 Data and Intellectual Property Rights (IPR) Policy

3.1 *General Considerations and Upstream Space Sector*

In the upstream sector, the term "data policy" is used primarily, if not exclusively, for remote sensing data. Satellite navigation does not make use "of the properties of electromagnetic waves emitted, reflected or diffracted by the sensed objects."[56] Signals broadcast by GNSS satellites contain orbital data and the precise time the signal was emitted. "The receiver compares the time of broadcast encoded in the transmission with the time of reception measured by an internal clock, thereby measuring the time-of-flight to the satellite. Several such measurements can be made at the same time to different satellites, allowing a continual fix to be generated in real time."[57] Apart perhaps for scientific use, the orbital data and time references broadcast by GNSS satellites at a specific point in time is relevant only for the calculation of the position of users at that point in time. Although the policy for distributing orbital data and time references through GNSS (free of charge at least for mass-market services) could be considered a "GNSS data policy" in a broad sense, this term does not appear to be used, at least not in European Union legislation. For GNSS, a more relevant issue is the use of the IPR concerning the system itself (in particular patents) by equipment manufacturers. They need access to these IPR to produce GNSS receivers capable of receiving and processing signals from different GNSS constellations. The conditions for this access could be called "GNSS IPR policy."

Normally, the entities that generate data, or finance data generation, and/or own data, define the data policy. Whether remote sensing data can be owned is largely a matter of applicable IPR law. Apart from trade secrets, this mostly concerns copyright law. The relevant legislation generally does not refer explicitly to remote sensing.[58] In this context, the question of possible copyright

56 See the definition in point (a) of Principle I of the Remote Sensing Principles.

57 Joseph N. Pelton and Sergio Camacho-Lara, "Introduction to Satellite Navigation Systems," in *Handbook of Satellite Applications, 2nd edition,* ed. Joseph N. Pelton, Scott Madry, and Sergio Camacho-Lara (Cham, Springer International Publishing Switzerland, 2017), 727–728.

58 In the EU, see for example Directive (EU) 2019/790 of the European Parliament and of the Council of 17 April 2019 on copyright and related rights in the Digital Single Market and amending Directives 96/9/EC and 2001/29/EC, OJ L 130, 17.5.2019, p. 92, Directive 2001/29/EC of the European Parliament and of the Council of 22 May 2001 on the harmonisation of certain aspects of copyright and related rights in the information society, OJ L 167, 22.6.2001, p. 10, and Directive 96/9/EC of the European Parliament and of the Council of 11 March 1996 on the legal protection of databases, OJ L 77, 27.3.1996, p. 20 (the "Database Directive").

protection cannot be answered in an abstract manner, without analysing the specific datasets in question. Depending on the applicable law, copyright protection may not only depend on the requirement of creativity involving original expressions.[59] In some jurisdictions, including Germany, it may also be necessary that the author is a natural person.[60] Raw data generated through automated processes may not meet these criteria, unless *sui generis* protection under the Database Directive is possible.[61] This would apply also to the orbital data and timing references transmitted with GNSS signals. In practice, commercial entities distributing remote sensing data often refer to copyright protection, whereas for example the legal notice on the use of Copernicus Sentinel Data and Service Information[62] requires users to acknowledge the source of the data, without mentioning copyright.

For the public sector, the mechanisms for adopting data policies depend on the applicable institutional framework. For example, the revised ESA data policy for ERS, Envisat, and Earth Explorer missions took the form of a document, approved by the ESA Earth Observation Programme Board in May 2010.[63] The principles of the data policy for the Copernicus programme are contained in the Copernicus Regulation. Commission Delegated Regulation (EU) No 1159/2013 determines more detailed rules. Conversely, the owners of privately owned remote sensing missions define data policy on a commercial basis, within the framework of applicable law, including security rules (see Section 4.2.).

As the combination of GNSS and GIS is mainly of relevance for the downstream sector, remote sensing data policy for the upstream sector will not be analysed in detail.[64] The following three general aspects can nevertheless be highlighted, focusing on Europe.[65] Firstly, the public sector cannot define data

59 Atsuyo Ito, *Legal Aspects of Satellite Remote Sensing* (Leiden: Brill, 2011), 217.

60 Martha Meija-Kaiser, "Copyright Claims for Meteosat and Landsat Images under Court Challenge," *Journal of Space Law v. 32*, no. 2 (Winter 2006): 299–300.

61 For more details, see Martha Meija-Kaiser, "Satellite Remote Sensing Data in Databases: Copyright or Sui Generis Protection in Europe?" *Annals of Air and Space Law*, v. XXII(1) (1997): 495.

62 European Commission, "Legal notice on the use of Copernicus Sentinel Data and Service Information," https://sentinels.copernicus.eu/documents/247904/690755/Sentinel_Data_Legal_Notice.

63 ESA, "ESA Data Policy for ERS, Envisat and Earth Explorer missions," (October 2012), https://earth.esa.int/c/document_library/get_file?folderId=296006&name=DLFE-3602.pdf.

64 For a more detailed overview, see for example Lesley Jane Smith and Gina Petrovici, "Legal Aspects of Satellite Based Earth Observation," 167–183.

65 For the United States, see Masami Onoda and Molly Macauley, "Innovation in Earth Observations as a National Strategic Investment: The Experience of the U.S.," in *Satellite*

policies without due consideration of international rules and general legislation concerning access to and re-use of public sector data and information. Regarding the international level, in addition to the Remote Sensing Principles (in particular Principle XII), the Convention on Access to Information, Public Participation in Decision-Making and Access to Justice in Environmental Matters, concluded in Aarhus Denmark on 25 June 1998,[66] can be quoted as an example. At an European Union level, consistency inter alia with the INSPIRE Directive and the PSI Directive (now replaced by the Open Data Directive) was an essential factor for the decision to make Sentinel data (and Copernicus information in general) available "on a full, open and free-of-charge basis," subject to a number of limitations.[67] Section 4.2. contains a discussion of security restrictions.

Secondly, economic considerations may determine data policy also for missions financed and implemented by the public sector. When the Landsat data policy shifted to open access in 2008, its use and commercial exploitation increased substantially (by a factor of more than 100 between 2007 and 2011). A full, free, and open data policy is a tool to promote the development of downstream markets, given also that the value of raw data increased by value-added products and services.[68] In the case of missions generating data that is sufficiently valuable commercially, allowing coverage of the development and operations costs, it would also have to be asked why financial public sector involvement (beyond definition of general conditions such as security rules) would be necessary in the first place. Support to market uptake by receiver manufacturers was also a reason why the IPR owned by the European Union and needed to produce Galileo compliant receivers is made available free of charge,[69] "taking into account the need to protect and give value to the Union's intellectual property rights, the interests of all stakeholders, and the necessity of harmonious development of the markets and of new technologies."[70]

Finally, the quantity of data generated (big data or small amounts of data) does not appear decisive for defining the legal framework for data generation and distribution, apart from priority rules in case access requests exceed

---

Earth Observations and Their Impact on Society and Policy, ed. Masami Onoda and Oran R. Young (Singapore: Springer Nature, 2018), 63–72.

66 2161 U.N.T.S. 447.

67 Copernicus Regulation, Art. 23(2).

68 Josef Aschbacher, "ESA's Earth Observation Strategy and Copernicus," 83–84.

69 For more details, see the authorisation included in an Annex to the Open Service Interface Control Document available at https://galileognss.eu/wp-content/uploads/2020/08/Galileo-OS-SDD_v1.1.pdf.

70 See GNSS Regulation, Art. 6.

capacity.[71] Big data, rather, poses a technical challenge in terms of distribution and analysis. The Commission therefore launched "… several enabling platform services offering access to additional datasets and online processing capabilities in which European industry will take a leading role. These measures will open up new business opportunities for European industry, including SMEs and start-ups, and will allow research institutions, public authorities and companies to develop and benefit from space solutions."[72]

3.2 *Downstream Space Sector and Space Related Services*

Many of downstream space services and space related services depend on a combination of GNSS and remote sensing data. Looking at mapping services for mass-market use on mobile devices as an example, several aspects need to be taken into consideration. Firstly, from a remote sensing perspective, such services would often rather fall under the category of space related services in the OECD terminology,[73] rather than downstream space services. Normally, the use of (optical) satellite images is one option, and the service would also work without them. Conversely, in some cases satellite-based navigation may be indispensable for the proper functioning of mapping services, which would rather point to a classification as downstream space service from the GNSS perspective. This depends on a case-by-case analysis of the service in question. Many location-based services (LBS) also use alternative means of positioning, such as Light Detection and Ranging (LIDAR) and/or 360°cameras and computer vision technology (in particular for autonomous driving).[74]

Secondly, the information generated at this level will in many cases fall under the definition of "analysed information" within the meaning of Principle I(d) of the Remote Sensing Principles, that is "the information resulting from the interpretation of processed data, inputs of data and knowledge from other sources." In this context, in the contractual relationship between the different players in the value chain in the downstream space sector and for space related services, including service providers and end users, normally the conditions for making available data and information are not referred to as "data policy." For

71 See, for example, Commission Delegated Regulation (EU) No 1159/2013, Art. 17.

72 European Space Strategy, 4. For more information on the Copernicus Data and Information Access Services (DIAS), see "Data and Information Access Services," Copernicus, https://www.copernicus.eu/en/access-data/dias.

73 See, *supra*, footnote 23.

74 For an overview of LBS, see Gaurav Sinha, Barry J. Kronenfeld, and Jeffrey C. Brunskill, "Toward Democratization of Geographic Information: GIS, Remote Sensing, and GNSS Applications in Everyday Life," in *Remotely Sensed Data Characterization, Classification, and Accuracies*, ed. Prasad S. Thenkabail (Taylor & Francis Group, 2015), 431–433.

the Copernicus services, which are based on processing or modelling of space-based Copernicus data and other inputs in several areas (atmosphere monitoring, marine environment monitoring, land monitoring, climate change, emergency management and security), the term "information policy" was coined.[75] For commercial services, terms such as "terms of service," "conditions of use," or "license agreements" are used. These contractual terms normally differ depending on whether services are provided to end-users or intermediate service providers that use platforms run by "big tech" companies, to provide their own services. In addition to commercial considerations, such terms need to reflect applicable law in the relevant jurisdiction, including contracts law and IPR law. From the copyright perspective, the contractual framework may have to make a difference between modifications of data, including remote sensing images, which do not meet the requirements of derivative works as defined in the applicable law and adaptations decoupled from the source data that can be considered derivative works.

According to the second sentence of Principle XII of the Remote Sensing Principles, "[t]he sensed State shall also have access to the available analysed information concerning the territory under its jurisdiction in the possession of any State participating in remote sensing activities on the same basis and terms, taking particularly into account the needs and interests of the developing countries." Apart from the question of the binding nature of this Principle,[76] it is not clear how the right of access by sensed States to analysed information can be enforced in an interconnected world when information analysis takes place in multiple jurisdictions in a complex value chain. Equally importantly, for services with a business model based on advertising revenues, rather than user charges, the essential issue is not necessarily the policy for making available data and information to users (including authorities of a sensed State), but rather the rules for the making available of data and information by users. The rules for processing personal data have become one of the most complex issues concerning the combination of GIS and GNSS. This will be further analysed in Section 6.

4 Optimising the Application of the Regulatory Framework

4.1 *Interoperability – Standardisation*

The interoperability of GNSS and remote sensing depends on the use of specific common standards, beyond the internet standards that were instrumental

75 See Copernicus Regulation, Arts. 3(8), 5, and 23.

76 See, *supra*, section 1.2.

for establishing worldwide connectivity. In the upstream space sector, the United States started developing standards from the 1960s. Europe followed suit, with the European Cooperation for Space Standardization.[77] Regarding examples of standard setting of relevance for the downstream space sector, the International Organization for Standardization (ISO) has established a technical committee to work on standards for geographic information/geomatics.[78] The technical committee 287 of the European Committee for Standardization was established to develop the standards required to create an infrastructure for geospatial information in Europe – based in particular on INSPIRE rules.[79] Standardisation in the downstream sector is an important topic for EU research efforts to maximise the exploitation of space data.[80]

4.2 *(Cyber)security*

Cyberspace can "be both a tool for and a theatre of war and a medium for criminal activity."[81] Beyond cyberspace, continuity of space services can also be jeopardized by physical attacks on ground and space infrastructure. In the upstream space sector, tailor-made rules have been adopted to avoid security threats. Considering remote sensing data from space, States have adopted different types of provision to prevent the unauthorized acquisition and distribution of security relevant, and hence normally very high resolution, satellite data. This is generally referred to as "shutter control."[82] The German Satellite Data Security Act (Satellitendatensicherheitsgesetz) of 2007[83] can be cited as an example in Europe. For the protection of GNSS signals, specific rules apply,

77 Marcello Spagnulo, Rick Fleeter, Mauro Balduccini, and Federico Nasini, *Space Program Management. Methods and Tools* (New York: Springer-Verlag: 2013), 60. See also European Cooperation for Space Standardization, https://ecss.nl/.

78 "ISO/TC 211: Geographic information/Geomatics," ISO, https://www.iso.org/committee/54904.html.

79 Leszek Litwin and Maciej Rossa, *Geoinformation Metadata in INSPIRE and SDI: Understanding. Editing. Publishing* (Berlin, Heidelberg: Springer-Verlag: 2011), 44–45.

80 See section 1.6.3 of Annex I of the Decision on the Horizon 2020 specific programme.

81 Edward Burger and Giulia Bordacchini, "Security in Outer Space: Rising Stakes for Civilian Space Programmes," in *Yearbook on Space Policy 2017.* (Cham: Springer Nature Switzerland AG, 2019), 9, with examples of cyber-attacks in 2017.

82 Ulrike Bohlmann and Alexander Soucek, "From 'Shutter Control' to 'Big Data': Trends in the Legal Treatment of Earth Observation Data," in *Satellite-Based Earth Observation: Trends and Challenges for Economy and Society*, ed. Christian Brünner, Georg Königsberger, Hannes Mayer, Anita Rinner (Cham: Springer Nature Switzerland AG, 2018), 189–190.

83 Act to give Protection against the Security Risk to the Federal Republic of Germany by the Dissemination of High-Grade Earth Remote Sensing Data of 23 November 2007, 2590 Federal Gazette (BGBl.) Year 2007 Part I No. 58, issued in Bonn on 28 November 2007, as amended.

such as the provisions adopted for the Public Regulated Service of Galileo.[84] Additionally, (procurement) contracts concluded for the development and operation of GNSS and remote sensing space infrastructure normally include detailed rules concerning security issues.

Additionally, horizontal cybersecurity rules may apply, taking into consideration that there is no general definition of this term in international law. It is therefore necessary to analyse national and EU law, such as Council Directive 2008/114/EC of 8 December 2008 on the identification and designation of European critical infrastructures and the assessment of the need to improve their protection.[85] It contains rules for the protection of vital infrastructure in the energy and transport sectors and is applicable to the Galileo infrastructure.[86]

Additionally, the Directive on the security of network and information systems (NIS Directive),[87] the United States Internet of Things Cybersecurity Act, and the Tallinn Manual 2.0 are of relevance.[88] Article 4(1) of the NIS Directive contains a broad definition of the term "network and information systems." It does not only include electronic communication networks (point a), but also devices used to process digital data (point b), and the "data stored, processed, retrieved or transmitted by elements covered under points (a) and (b)." This definition is so broad that in the EU networks and devices used for a combination of GNSS and GIS could well be covered, although space data is not mentioned explicitly. More specifically, based on the list of entities in Annex

84 See for example Decision No 1104/2011/EU of the European Parliament and of the Council of 25 October 2011 on the rules for access to the public regulated service provided by the global navigation satellite system established under the Galileo programme, OJ L 287, 4.11.2011, p. 1.

85 OJ L 345, 23.12.2008, p. 75. At the end of 2020, the Commission tabled a legislative proposal for a Directive of the European Parliament and of the Council on the resilience of critical entities (COM(2020) 829 final of 16.12.2020), which is expected to replace Council Directive 2008/114/EC.

86 See Annex II of Commission Staff Working Document SWD (2013) 318 final of 28.8.2013 on a new approach to the European Programme for Critical Infrastructure Protection – Making European Critical Infrastructures more secure.

87 Directive (EU) 2016/1148 of the European Parliament and of the Council of 6 July 2016 concerning measures for a high common level of security of network and information systems across the Union, OJ L 194, 19.7.2016, p. 1. At the end of 2020, the Commission tabled a legislative proposal for a Directive of the European Parliament and of the Council on measures for a high common level of cybersecurity across the Union, repealing Directive (EU) 2016/1148 (COM(2020) 823 final of 16.12.2020).

88 Dimitra Stefoudi, "The Relevance and Applicability of Cybersecurity Laws with Regard to Data Storage on Board Satellites and on the Ground," *Air & Space Law* v. 44, no. 4&5 (2019): 431–432.

II of the NIS Directive, providers of downstream and space related services combining GNSS and GIS will in many cases not be considered "operator[s] of essential services" pursuant to Articles 4(4) and 5 of the NIS Directive. However, the national strategies on the security of network and information systems referred to in Article 7 of the NIS Directive also need to cover services such as online searches and cloud computing. This could be of direct relevance for the data processing in GIS. Further, it could even have an at least indirect impact on the design of systems in the upstream space sector. This will also depend on where electronic communication networks, devices and data are located.[89]

4.3 *Downstream Regulation*

The combination of GIS and GNSS may also be subject to a plethora of sector-specific downstream regulations, in particular concerning safety-critical applications for transport and emergency management. These regulations may be of relevance either for equipment manufacturers, or service providers, or both. Examples include air traffic management rules, provisions on digital tachographs,[90] and e-calls from mobile phones.[91]

5 Liability

The issue of liability has been discussed intensively in the past, albeit mostly in the context of GNSS only,[92] and – to a lesser extent – remote sensing,[93] and

89 Stefoudi, "The Relevance and Applicability of Cybersecurity Laws with Regard to Data Storage on Board Satellites and on the Ground," 441.

90 See for example Commission Implementing Regulation (EU) 2016/799 of 18 March 2016 implementing Regulation (EU) No 165/2014 of the European Parliament and of the Council laying down the requirements for the construction, testing, installation, operation and repair of tachographs and their components, OJ L 139, 26.5.2016, p. 1. According to its Article 3(1), "Manufacturers shall ensure that smart tachographs are compatible with the positioning services provided by the Galileo and the European Geostationary Navigation Overlay Service ('EGNOS') systems."

91 See for example Commission Delegated Regulation (EU) 2019/320 of 12 December 2018 supplementing of Directive 2014/53/EU of the European Parliament and of the Council with regard to the application of the essential requirements referred to in Article 3(3)(g) of that Directive in order to ensure caller location in emergency communications from mobile devices, OJ L 55, 25.2.2019, p. 1, requiring compatibility with EGNOS and Galileo.

92 See for example Dejian Kong, *Civil Liability for Damage Caused by Global Navigation Satellite System* (Alphen aan den Rijn: Kluwer Law International, 2019).

93 See for example Atsuyo Ito, *Legal Aspects of Satellite Remote Sensing,* 244–298.

often with a focus on international space law. As set out in the previous sections, however, users will often not only rely on the precise timing information provided by GNSS signals, and the calculation of their position in terms of spatial coordinates. Normally, this timing and location information is combined with geographical information at the downstream level. The analysis of liability issues will depend on the service in question, the type of service provider and its role in the value chain and the question as to whether damage needs to be analysed in the light of the rules of contractual or non-contractual liability.

Regarding applicable law, as outlined in Section 1.2. above, answers to liability questions will often not be found in the *corpus iuris spatialis,* which predominantly comprises space objects, and not (downstream) services. This does not mean that there is a legal vacuum.[94] Liability issues will have to be dealt with according to national tort, contract, product liability and criminal law. Under most, if not all jurisdictions, it may become more complicated to establish a causal link between the damage and the malfunctioning of specific inputs in an environment where location data, based on multi-constellation GNSS signals, terrestrial sensors and remote sensing data are combined to provide downstream or space related services.

Two specific aspects concerning GNSS should be highlighted. It should be recalled that most GNSS signals are provided by the public sector, including the military. This has an impact on the ability of victims to bring lawsuits based on erroneous signals or system malfunctions.[95] Galileo is an exception insofar as the services are provided by a private Galileo Service operator under a procurement contract concluded with a civilian Union agency, the European GNSS Agency, renamed European Union Agency for the Space Programme.[96] Also, in most cases the position of a user is calculated at receiver level, using – *inter alia* – GNSS signals from different constellations. The position is not transmitted to mass-market end users via the internet, unlike remote sensing data (including satellite images and updated maps). This means that with regard to GNSS, there is normally a "more direct link to space."

94 Andreas Loukakis, *Non-contractual Liabilities from Civilian Versions of GNSS: Current Trends, Legal Challenges and Potential* (Baden-Baden: Nomos; 2017), 105.

95 For a discussion of the Federal Tort Claims Act in the US, see Frans G. von der Dunk, "Liability for Global Navigation Satellite Services: A Comparative Analysis of GPS and Galileo," *Journal of Space Law* 30, No. 1 (Spring 2004): 142–143.

96 See "GSA Signs Galileo Service Operator Contract," EUSPA, https://www.gsa.europa.eu/newsroom/news/gsa-signs-galileo-service-operator-contract.

6 Data Protection

In many cases, the protection of personal data becomes a relevant legal issue only when GNSS and remote sensing data are combined. This is for a simple technical reason: despite the push towards higher and higher (sub-meter) resolution, "[i]t is not currently possible to directly identify an individual's face using today's satellites. The resolution does not suffice to depict optical characteristics of a person's features. Satellite imaging consists of coarse resolutions that do not typically allow for recognition of individual's faces, and they tend to image structures and features that are themselves publicly viewable."[97] However, a combination with other data, including precise location data based on GNSS signals, could lead to the generation of "information relating to an identified or identifiable natural person."[98]

There is no international legal framework for the protection of personal data generated with space technologies, including in the *corpus iuris spatialis*. Data protection issues will therefore have to be assessed based on national or supranational rules, such as the GDPR in the European Union. As a first step, it therefore has to be analysed for a given downstream or space related service involving the processing of personal data which law is applicable. For example, in accordance with Article 3(1) GDPR, determining its territorial scope, it "applies to the processing of personal data in the context of the activities of an establishment of a controller or a processor in the Union, regardless of whether the processing takes place in the Union or not." In a complex service combining several inputs from different types of satellites, the determination of the applicable law in itself will not always be straightforward.

If the GDPR is applicable, the persons or entities determining the purposes and means of the processing of personal data (controllers)[99] must ensure processing according to the principles enshrined in Article 5 of the GDPR, including lawfulness, fairness, and transparency. Article 6 of the GDPR sets out in which cases data processing is lawful (for example "where the data subject has given consent to the processing of his or her personal data for one or more specific purposes").[100] There are no specific obligations concerning space-based data.

97 Santos and Rapp, "Satellite Imagery, Very High-Resolution and Processing-Intensive Image Analysis," 285.

98 See the definition of the term "personal data" in GDPR, Art. 4(1).

99 GDPR, Art. 4(7).

100 GDPR, Art. 6(1)(a).

However, amongst the obligations of controllers, Article 25 of the GDPR concerning data protection by design and by default, could be of particular relevance for the processing of space- based information relating to an identified or identifiable natural person. Paragraph 1 of this provision states that "[t]aking into account the state of the art, the cost of implementation and the nature, scope, context and purposes of processing as well as the risks of varying likelihood and severity for rights and freedoms of natural persons posed by the processing, the controller shall, both at the time of the determination of the means for processing and at the time of the processing itself, implement appropriate technical and organisational measures, such as pseudonymisation, which are designed to implement data-protection principles, such as data minimisation, in an effective manner and to integrate the necessary safeguards into the processing in order to meet the requirements of this Regulation and protect the rights of data subjects." This notes an obligation to factor in data protection issues in the design of downstream and space related services, but potentially also of space missions themselves.[101]

7 Conclusions

Like in other sectors, such as electronic communications, space activities move from an infrastructure centric to a service orientated approach. This applies also to the combination of GNSS and remote sensing, which mostly takes place at the downstream service level. As international space law mostly concerns space infrastructure, in many cases it cannot provide answers to legal issues such as liability and data protection at service level. However, there is no legal vacuum. Depending on the type of service, the role of service providers and the place of service provision, national and supranational legislation will apply. While this can lead to fragmentation, in the absence of international rules a case-by-case analysis of the relevant service is unavoidable. For the space lawyer, it is to be noted that rules applicable to downstream and space related services may have an impact on space mission design, for example to ensure implementation of data protection principles.

101 For a more general analysis of this topic, see Aurelia Tamò-Larrieux, *Designing for Privacy and its Legal Framework – Data Protection by Design and Default for the Internet of Things* (Cham: Springer Nature Switzerland AG, 2018).

CHAPTER 9

Space in Clouds and Clouds in Space – Dealing with Massive Amounts of EO Data

Ingo Baumann and Erik Pellander

1 Introduction

More and more EO data is becoming available through public missions such as the European Copernicus and through commercial systems, including some with large satellite constellations. NASA alone has accumulated about 40 petabytes (PB) of Earth science data, which is about twice as much as all of the information stored by the Library of Congress. In the next five years, NASA's data will grow up to 250 PB – more than six times larger than what NASA has now. The so-called Sentinel Data Dashboard of ESA currently shows almost 400 thousand registered users, 35 million different data products and more than 300 PB of data downloads.[1] Cumulatively, nearly 500 PB of raw EO data is expected to be downlinked over the next ten years onto cloud servers.[2]

The massive amount of data creates new challenges for mission owners and operators regarding storage, cataloguing, formatting, and long-term preservation. Users need easy access, comprehensive computing power and innovative processing and value-adding methods, increasingly including machine learning and artificial intelligence elements. All this would not be possible without the use of cloud computing.

Cloud computing facilitates large-volume storage and enables fast and easy access to multiple different sources of Earth observation data. As users do no longer need to download and store the data on their own hardware, it reduces time and costs of access. In addition, cloud computing provides the on-demand delivery of computing power for search, upload, online-analytics, processing and value adding. Advanced algorithms and software tools in the cloud, many of which are open source, greatly support the development of new Earth observation applications, services and solutions. These resources

---

1 Sentinel Data Dashboard, under https://dashboard.copernicus.eu/, visited 29 January 2021.

2 Northern Sky Research, Cloud Computing: Ratcheting the Satellite Industry Forward, 15 June 2020, under https://www.nsr.com/cloud-computing-ratcheting-the-satellite-industry-forward/, visited 29 January 2021.

 | DOI:10.1163/9789004527270_010

feed into new business models for the Earth observation and the broader geospatial markets.

2 Implementation of EO Cloud Computing Platforms

The EO community is in the middle of a paradigm shift towards digital online business. Scalable cloud-based online platforms offering Data as a Service (DaaS), Infrastructure as a Service (IaaS), Software as a Service (SaaS) or Platform as a Service (PaaS) allow the scientific communities, EO value-adding companies, service providers and other users to search, analyse and process significantly higher volumes of data, to reduce costs of production and service delivery, and to reach their customers in more effective ways.

According to the 2019 Copernicus Market Report, *"cloud platform holders, providing storage and easy access as well as cloud processing power and tools for basic image processing, are expected to play a major role in the EO data market in the coming decade"*.[3] With the help of these platforms, the EO market is moving from the traditional data product delivery to online EO information services.

The EO ecosystem can be grouped into a data generation layer, a resource tier layer, a platform service layers and the exploitation layer.

Under the traditional set-up mission ground segments make data available for download at the data generation layer, the users download the data on their own infrastructures, and then the users process the data on their own at the exploitation layer. Over the past years, numerous EO platforms have been launched in Europe, in order to close the gap between the data generation layer and the exploitation layer. Such platforms provide access to data at the resource tier layer and offer processing tools at the platform services layer by making use of cloud infrastructures.

On the public side, this includes

- the five so-called DIAS (Copernicus Data and Information Access Providers),[4] the ESA Copernicus Space Component Data Access system[5] and the Copernicus Open Access Hub,[6]

3 COPERNICUS Market report, February 2019, under https://www.copernicus.eu/sites/default/files/2019-02/PwC_Copernicus_Market_Report_2019_PDF_version.pdf, visited 29 January 2021.

4 An overview on the DIAS platforms is available under https://www.copernicus.eu/en/access-data/dias, visited 29 January 2021.

5 The Copernicus Space Component Data Access system is accessible under https://spacedata.copernicus.eu/, visited 29 January 2021.

6 The Copernicus Open Access Hub is accessible under https://scihub.copernicus.eu/, visited 29 January 2021.

- a total of currently seven ESA Thematic Exploitation Platforms (TEP),[7] as well as
- an increasing number of national platforms within EU member states created in the context of the so-called Copernicus Collaborative Ground Segment.[8]

Many of the public-driven platforms are operated by industry under contract with ESA or the relevant national public stakeholders.

On the commercial side, there is a diverse spectrum, including

- platforms operated by very large Cloud-/IT companies such as Google, Amazon, Microsoft, SAP, Deutsche Telekom or Orange,
- platforms by leading geospatial industry companies such as ESRI or Hexagon,
- platforms by operators and data providers such as Maxar and Planet, as well as
- smaller specialized platforms such as the recently launched Bathymetry Web Store by EOMAP.

In 2018, EARSC did undertake an industry survey on the use of the different EO data platforms. The survey was based on a questionnaire which was filed to users as well as to resources providers. Among other matters, it analysed awareness and use of existing EO data exploitation platforms at the time when the survey was undertaken.

As regards awareness and use of platforms

- 90% of the respondents reported that they were aware of the ESA Open Access Hub to access Copernicus data and services, whilst 73% of the respondents reported that they were actually using it;
- ESA TEPs were known by almost 92% of the respondents, whilst only 8%–15% were using one or more of them,
- only 46% of the respondents were aware of DIAS, only a few were using DIAS, and each respondent was using a unique DIAS;
- 64% of the respondents were aware of a national platform created in the context of the so-called Copernicus Collaborative Ground Segment, whilst 50% of the respondents were using such platforms;
- 92% of the respondents were aware of at least a commercial platform and 82% of the respondents were using commercial platforms, whilst awareness and use varied a lot between platforms.

7 An overview on the ESA TEPs is available under https://eo4society.esa.int/thematic-exploitation-platforms-overview/, visited 29 January 2021.

8 An overview on existing/planned collaborative ground segments is available under https://sentinel.esa.int/web/sentinel/missions/collaborative/existing-planned, visited 29 January 2021.

Overall, these numbers provide evidence on the paradigm shift towards digital online business provided by or through the EO exploitation, though awareness and use differed among different types of platforms at the time when the survey was undertaken. An updated survey is currently being undertaken; however, the results have not yet been available at the time of writing. It can be expected that both awareness and use has increased considerably since the 2018 survey.

3 Legal Issues in Relation to EO Data in Clouds

Cloud computing raises a lot of legal issues, which however are not specific to EO platforms. For the purpose of this chapter, we have selected the following aspects: security of data, privacy of data, and ownership.

3.1 *Security*

Loss of data, unauthorized access, misuse of information and other cybersecurity threats such as proliferation of malware are major concerns for both cloud providers and users. Throughout the years, concerns on security have been reported as major factors preventing users to move data to the cloud. However, security standards of cloud providers regularly go far beyond the level which users could maintain within their own IT infrastructure. Among other standards and certificates, the ISO/IEC 27000-series providing best practice recommendations on information security management is of particular relevance:

> ISO/IEC 27001 sets down general requirements on information security systems and for assessing and treating information security risks.
>
> ISO/IEC 27002 provides guidelines for organizational information security standards and information security management practices. This includes the selection, implementation and management of controls in accordance with the specific information security risk environment(s).

These general standards on information security are supplemented and specified by standards on information security in relation to cloud services:

> ISO/IEC 27017 provides implementation guidance for cloud services on relevant controls specified in ISO/IEC 27002 and establishes additional controls together with implementation guidance specifically related to

cloud services. These implementation guidance and controls are relevant for both cloud service providers and cloud service customers.

ISO/IEC 27018 provides control objectives, controls and guidelines for implementing measures on protection of personal data in accordance with privacy principles established under ISO/IEC 29100 for the public cloud computing environment. It specifies, in particular, guidelines for organizational information security standards and information security management practices under ISO/IEC 27002 with special emphasis on regulatory requirements applicable in the context of information security risk environments of a cloud service provider. This document is directed towards a cloud services provider which is processing personal data on behalf of the customer under a service contract. It does not deal with the additional obligations of the so-called controller in terms of data protection law, namely the EU General Data Protection Regulation (GDPR). Further details on these roles and responsibilities are provided in the following section.

Though these technical standards are not binding in legal terms, they may serve as a reference when determining standards of care in the areas they are addressing.

Besides the high security standards used by cloud providers, important risks remain, and they grow along the increasing adoption of cloud services and overall market expansion. According to the Sophos State of Cloud Security Report 2020, almost three-quarters of organizations hosting data or workloads in the public cloud experienced a security incident in the reporting period.[9] 70 % of organizations reported they were hit by malware, ransomware, data theft, account compromise attempts, or crypto-jacking. 96 % of organizations are concerned about their current level of cloud security. Data loss/leakage remains the number one concern.

3.2 *Privacy of Data*

Legal issues concerning the protection of personal data may arise in relation to certain data provided by the user to the cloud service provider in connection with the creation or administration of its account such as usernames, email addresses, and billing information; and EO data stored, processed and disseminated through cloud infrastructures, to the extent that they contain personal data.

9 Sophos, State of Cloud Security 2020 Report, under https://secure2.sophos.com/en-us/content/state-of-cloud-security.aspx, visited 29 January 2021.

In the above-mentioned industry survey undertaken by EARSC in 2018, 83% of the service providers and 84% of the users of EO exploitation platforms agreed on the importance to protect user registration data and other personal data in compliance with the GDPR.[10]

Personal data are defined under Art. 4 (1) of the GDPR as follows:

> 'personal data' means any information relating to an identified or identifiable natural person ('data subject'); an identifiable natural person is one who can be identified, directly or indirectly, in particular by reference to an identifier such as a name, an identification number, location data, an online identifier or to one or more factors specific to the physical, physiological, genetic, mental, economic, cultural or social identity of that natural person;

Registration and user data provided by the customer such as name, email, address, and billing information are clearly covered by this definition. It is however less clear whether and to what extent EO data stored and processed in the cloud are personal data in terms of the GDPR.

For EO raw data, data protection authorities came to the conclusion that even with Very-High-Resolution images (30 cm resolution), it is not (yet) possible to directly identify an individual person from space.[11] Accordingly, EO raw data stored, processed and disseminated through cloud infrastructures do generally not imply privacy concerns. As for processed data, most recently, European Space Imaging announced that through their partnership with Maxar they are now offering a 15 cm HD imagery to customers by increasing the number of pixels of native 30 cm data.[12] There are not yet any authoritative findings by data protection authorities whether 15 cm resolution implies that a person becomes identifiable in terms of data protection law. However, irrespective of the level of resolution, a person may become identifiable when EO data are combined with other data sets in the course of processing, for

10 REGULATION (EU) 2016/679 OF THE EUROPEAN PARLIAMENT AND OF THE COUNCIL of 27 April 2016 on the protection of natural persons with regard to the processing of personal data and on the free movement of such data, and repealing Directive 95/46/EC (General Data Protection Regulation), under https://eur-lex.europa.eu/legal-content/EN/TXT/HTML/?uri=CELEX:32016R0679&from=DE, visited 29 January 2021.

11 Rat für Sozial- und Wirtschaftsdaten, Georeferenzierung von Daten, 2012, under https://www.ratswd.de/publikationen/georeferenzierung-von-daten, visited 29 January 2021, 50.

12 European Space Imaging, 15cm HD Imagery – providing the next level of detail, under https://www.euspaceimaging.com/hd, visited 29 January 2021.

instance social data, addresses etc.[13] Such data sets may fall under the scope of the GDPR. Upload of such data by the user or the creation of such data by the user through processing tools provided in the cloud may therefore cause privacy concerns. As processing tools provided through EO cloud infrastructures are capable of combining several data sets, privacy concerns may increase through the uptake of cloud processing platforms.

In addition to the material scope of the GDPR, the territorial scope is of particular importance when assessing legal implications for EO platforms.

According to Article 3 of the GDPR, the territorial scope of the GDPR is determined on the basis of two main criteria – the establishment of the controller, as well as the target of the processing. As for the establishment, the GPPR applies to the processing of personal data in the context of the activities of an establishment of a controller[14] or a processor in the European Union regardless of whether the processing takes place in the European Union or not.[15] As for the target of the processing, the GDPR applies when goods or services are offered to data subjects in the European Union, and/or the processing is related to the monitoring of behaviour taking place in the European Union.[16]

The scope of the GDPR is accordingly not limited to cloud infrastructure (i.e., hardware) located in the European Union. In other words, the location of the cloud infrastructure is not decisive for determining the territorial scope of the GDPR.

Responsibilities of the user and the cloud service provider on the protection of these data in accordance with the GDPR vary dependent on the question who the controller is, that is the person or entity determining the purposes and means of the processing of personal data,[17] and who is the processor, that is the person or entity which processes personal data on behalf of the controller.[18]

It is the responsibility of the controller to ensure that the processing of personal data is performed in accordance with the GDPR.[19] Where processing is to be carried out on behalf of a controller, it is the responsibility of the controller

13 Weichert, T, Geodaten – datenschutzrechtliche Erfahrungen, Erwartungen und Empfehlungen, Datenschutz und Datensicherheit 33, 347–352 (2009), 348.
14 By virtue of Article 3 (3) GDPR this does also concern a controller not established in the Union, but in a place where Member State law applies by virtue of public international law.
15 Article 3 (1) GDPR.
16 Article 3 (2) GDPR.
17 Article 4 (7) GDPR.
18 Article 4 (8) GDPR.
19 Article 24 (1) GDPR.

to *"use only processors providing sufficient guarantees to implement appropriate technical and rganizational measures in such a manner that processing will meet the requirements of this Regulation and ensure the protection of the rights of the data subject".*[20]

Under Article 28 (3) of the GDPR, processing of personal data carried out on behalf of a controller shall be governed by a contract setting out at a minimum:
- subject-matter and duration of the processing;
- the nature and purpose of the processing;
- the type of personal data and categories of data subjects;
- the obligation that the processor processes personal data only on documented instructions from the controller, including transfers of personal data to a third country or an international organisation, unless required by Union or Member State law to which the processor is subject;
- the obligation of the processor to inform the controller of a legal requirement to process personal data without the instructions from the controller, unless such information is prohibited by law or on important grounds of public interest;
- the obligation of the processor to ensure that persons authorised to process personal data have committed themselves to confidentiality or are under an appropriate statutory obligation of confidentiality;
- the obligation of the processor to take measures on the security of processing required under Article 32 of the GDPR;
- the obligation of the processor not to engage another processor without prior specific or general written authorisation of the controller;
- the obligation of the processor to flow down its contractual obligations towards the controller to any other person engaged with the processing;
- the obligation of the processor to assists the controller by appropriate technical and organisational measures, insofar as this is possible, for the fulfilment of the controller's obligation to respond to requests for exercising the data subject's rights laid down in Chapter 3 of the GDPR; and
- the obligation of the processor to assist the controller in ensuring compliance with its obligations in relation to security of personal data, data protection impact assessment, and prior consultation with the supervisory authority.

It is the responsibility of both the controller and processor to ensure that any transfer of personal data to a non-EU/EEA country shall take place only if certain conditions under the GDPR are complied with.[21] Under the GDPR, the

20 Article 18 (1) GDPR.

21 Article 44 GDPR.

transfer to another country is generally permissible if the country is subject to an adequacy decision by the European Commission, meaning that data can be transferred without any further safeguards or being subject to additional conditions.[22] Without such an adequacy decision, the data exporter can transfer EO data containing personal data from the European Union to a third country by providing appropriate safeguards and on condition that enforceable rights and effective legal remedies are available for individuals.[23] In absence of an adequacy decision or appropriate safeguards, the GDPR foresees a number of specific situations which may enable the transfer of personal data to a third country such as the explicit consent of an individual after having been provided with all necessary information about the risks associated with the transfer.[24] In the light of the recent verdict of the European Court of Justice which invalidated Decision 2016/1250 on the adequacy of the protection provided by the EU-US Privacy Shield,[25] these issues are most relevant as regards the provision of cloud services by providers with infrastructures in the United States.

When the user provides certain personal data to the cloud service provider in connection with the creation or administration of its account, the cloud service provider is determining the purposes and means of the processing.

In this scenario, it is the responsibility of the cloud service provider

- to ensure that these data are processed in accordance with the GDPR;
- to ensure through the above-mentioned contractual safeguards that processing will meet the requirements of the GDPR, in case processing is carried out on behalf of the cloud service provider by any third party; and
- to ensure compliance with the requirements of the GDPR when data are transferred to a non-EU/EEC country.

When the user stores EO data containing personal data or creates EO data containing personal data by using cloud processing tools, the user is to be considered as the controller of the data determining the purposes and means of the processing, whilst the cloud service provider is to be considered as the processor which processes personal data on behalf of the user.

In this scenario, it is the responsibility of the user

- to ensure that these data are processed in accordance with the GDPR;
- to ensure through the above-mentioned contractual safeguards laid down in the service contract with the cloud service provider that processing will meet the requirements of the GDPR; and

22 Article 45 (1) GDPR.

23 Article 46 GDPR.

24 Article 49 GDPR.

25 European Court of Justice, Judgement of 16 July 2020 – C-311/18 – Facebook Ireland und Schrems.

– to ensure compliance with the requirements of the GDPR when data are transferred to a non-EU/EEA country.

It is the responsibility of the cloud service provider

– to comply with the above-mentioned contractual safeguards laid down in the service contract with the user, in order to ensure that processing will meet the requirements of the GDPR; and
– to ensure compliance with the requirements of the GDPR when data are transferred to a non-EU/EEA country.

3.3 *Ownership*

Data ownership is a complicated matter of concern with regard to cloud computing and depending on governmental regulations and service provider policies, data ownership in the cloud is not always retained. Ownership rights may come into play where: EO data are accessed by the user through the cloud, EO data are uploaded by the user to the cloud, and new data sets are created in the cloud.

In the 2018 EARSC industry survey, 94% of the service providers agreed that it is important to ensure full ownership rights to derived products and services produced on the platform. 92% of the users agreed that the provision of rights to retain full ownership to EO-data derived products is important.

As a general rule, ownership of data should remain with the originating data owner. However, issues related to ownership of data accessed through the cloud, uploaded to the cloud, or created in the cloud may still arise. In theory, a variety of ownership rights may come into play. In practice, copyright protection and the sui generis right on the protection of databases are most relevant.

As for copyright protection, accessing data through the cloud, uploading data to the cloud, or creating data in the cloud may raise complex legal issues on the determination of the applicable law. Even though many aspects of copyright laws have been standardized through the Berne Convention for the Protection of Literary and Artistic Works (Berne Convention),[26] as well as through EU Directives,[27] copyright laws vary substantially by country as regards the question what constitutes a work protected by copyright.[28] This

26 Berne Convention for the Protection of Literary and Artistic Works (as amended on September 28, 1979), WIPO Lex No. TRT/BERNE/001, under https://wipolex.wipo.int/en/treaties/textdetails/12214, visited 29 January 2021.

27 An overview on the EU's regulatory framework for copyright is available under https://ec.europa.eu/digital-single-market/en/eu-copyright-legislation, visited 29 January 2021.

28 Whilst civil law countries tend to require a minimum level of creativity, common law countries protect works where sufficient labour, skill or judgement has been used,

implies challenges for EO data owners using cloud infrastructures, especially taking into account that data stored in the cloud can be used world-wide without geographical restrictions.

Under the applicable law, it is further questionable whether and to what extent EO data are protected by copyright. National copyright laws generally require intellectual creation with a minimum level of originality.[29] Automatically generated data such as raw data from EO satellites are therefore generally not protected under national copyright laws. Processing and value adding steps are increasingly undertaken by automated software applications stored in cloud infrastructures. Whether or not such processed data and final products are copyright protected under the applicable law therefore requires individual evaluation, leaving significant uncertainties for the data owners.

EO Data *"arranged in a systematic or methodical way and individually accessible by electronic or other means"* (database) accessed through the cloud, uploaded to the cloud, or created in the cloud may, *"irrespective of the eligibility of that database for protection by copyright or by other rights"*, be subject to the sui generis right on the protection of databases as laid down in the EU Database Directive.[30] Under the sui generis right, the maker of a database is entitled *"to prevent extraction and/or re-utilization of the whole or of a substantial part, evaluated qualitatively and/or quantitatively, of the contents of that database"*.[31] These safeguards are granted through national laws in EU Member States. The scope of the sui generis right on the protection of databases is according to Article 7 of the Directive limited to databases

- whose makers or rightsholders are nationals of a Member State or who have their habitual residence in the territory of the European Union;
- to companies and firms formed in accordance with the law of a Member State and having their registered office,[32] central administration or principal place of business within the European Union;
- third countries to which the sui generis right applies by virtue of an agreement concluded by the Council acting on a proposal from the Commission; and/or

---

see: Reed, Information in the Cloud: Ownership, Control and Accountability, in: Cheung / Weber, Privacy and Legal Issues in Cloud Computing, 139–159, 141.

29 Ibid., 141 f.

30 Article 7 (4) Directive 96/9/EC of the European Parliament and of the Council of 11 March 1996 on the legal protection of databases (Database Directive).

31 Article 7 (1) Database Directive.

32 Where such a company or firm has only its registered office in the territory of the Community, its operations must be genuinely linked on an ongoing basis with the economy of a Member State.

- where such a company or firm has only its registered office in the territory of the European Union, its operations must be genuinely linked on an ongoing basis with the economy of a Member State.

This protection has uncertainties due to the divergent implementation at national level, as well as regarding protection outside of EU territory.

In the light of the uncertainties on the protection of EO data in cloud infrastructure by copyright or by the sui generis right on the protection of databases, it is required to protect ownership through appropriate contractual arrangements.

As regards data accessed through the cloud, copyright protection, or more precisely the question which level of intellectual creation is required, is governed by the law where the data have been created. If the country origin is a party to the Berne Convention, copyright subsists in all other member states of the Berne Convention.[33] If the data in question have been made publicly available, the country of origin is most probably the location of the server form which it was first made available to others.[34] However, the lack of a fixed geography of the cloud may cause difficulties in determining from where the data have been published.[35] For data which have not yet been published, the country of origin is that of which the author is a national.[36]

As mentioned above, data accessed through the cloud may be further protected under the sui generis right on the protection of databases. Determining potential infringements of this right through extraction and/or reutilization of the database might be challenging in the cloud environment, especially when either the cloud infrastructures or the persons extracting and/or reutilizing the database are located outside of EU territory.[37]

Bearing in mind the uncertainties on copyright protection and the protection under the sui generis right, owners of EO data which grant access to data through cloud infrastructures regularly protect their ownership rights by entering into a license agreement with the user. There are strong divergences among existing EO data licenses. As many public EO missions are governed by open data policies, the related license documents are often rather short and only include a limited set of conditions, namely the obligation for

33 Article 5 Berne Convention.

34 Reed, Information in the Cloud: Ownership, Control and Accountability, in: Cheung / Weber, Privacy and Legal Issues in Cloud Computing, 139–159, 146.

35 Ibid.

36 Ibid.

37 European Court of Justice, Judgement 18 October 2012 – C-173/11 – Football Dataco Ltd & Ors v Sportradar GmbH & Anor.

the user to provide appropriate credentials when distributing or modifying the data. As an example, the "Legal notice on the use of Copernicus Sentinel Data and Service Information" by the European Commission provides the following:

> Where the user communicates to the public or distributes Copernicus Sentinel Data and Service Information, he/she shall inform the recipients of the source of that Data and Information by using the following notice:
> (1) 'Copernicus Sentinel data [Year]' for Sentinel data; and/or
> (2) 'Copernicus Service information [Year]' for Copernicus Service Information.
>
> Where the Copernicus Sentinel Data and Service Information have been adapted or modified, the user shall provide the following notice:
> (1) 'Contains modified Copernicus Sentinel data [Year]' for Sentinel data; and/or
> (2) 'Contains modified Copernicus Service information [Year]' for Copernicus Service Information.[38]

Commercial owners/operators in contrast often employ highly detailed license conditions, often with several variants. As one example, Maxar provides the following information on its website:

> When you license products and services directly from a Maxar Affiliate, these Terms and Conditions will apply. These Terms and Conditions are referenced in your Order Confirmation and together with your Order Confirmation, these Terms and Conditions and the applicable End User License Terms (see below) describe how you can use our products and services.[39]

Maxar uses 9 different types of End User License Terms, including an Internal Use License, a Subscription Services License, an Evaluation License, a Display and Media License and specific licenses for US government bodies or larger corporations. The Product Terms and the Subscription Services License together comprise 18 pages of legal terms and conditions.

---

38 Legal notice on the use of Copernicus Sentinel Data and Service Information, under https://sentinel.esa.int/documents/247904/690755/Sentinel_Data_Legal_Notice, visited 29 January 2021.

39 Maxar, Legal Information, under https://www.maxar.com/legal, visited 29 January 2021.

Data licenses create several difficulties for EO exploitation platform operators and users, especially when the given EO exploitation platform provides access to data from multiple sources. The relevant issues can be summarized as follows:

- clear reference: the applicable license terms must be clearly referenced within the licensing process;
- user acceptance: no person can impose legal obligations on another person without mutual agreement which requires the consent of both parties;
- documenting user acceptance: appropriate technical measures to document and verify the user's acceptance are required to be able to demonstrate user acceptance;
- general acceptance for all future use: acceptance of data licenses, especially if provided within a registration process, should extend to all future access and use;
- need for user registration and identity checks: the licensor has to know the identity of the licensee, as otherwise he will not be able to enforce his rights under the license terms. This requires workflows, which provide for user registration and subsequent identity checks;
- legal interoperability: existence of multiple data licenses with diverging terms and conditions restricts the "legal interoperability" of the data concerned; and
- Data as a Service (DaaS): DaaS may become an issue with regard to the applicable data licenses. As online "upload" and virtual processing and value-adding are new forms of use beyond the "traditional" search, view and download functions, some – mostly public – data licenses still do not explicitly mention them.

As for EO data uploaded to the cloud by the user, placing data in the cloud will not per se change its ownership, if there is any.[40] The above-mentioned uncertainties on copyright protection and/or protection under the sui generis right on the protection of databases may also come into play in relation to EO data uploaded to the cloud by the user. As with data accessed through the cloud, appropriate contractual safeguards are required.

These safeguards are regularly implemented through cloud service terms. Cloud service terms typically provide that ownership remains with the user. Section 4.1 of the Google Earth Engine License Agreement provides, for example, that the *"Customer owns all Intellectual Property Rights in Customer*

40 Reed, Information in the Cloud: Ownership, Control and Accountability, in: Cheung / Weber, Privacy and Legal Issues in Cloud Computing, 139–159, 145.

Data, Customer Code, and Application(s)".[41] Section 8.1 of the AWS Customer Agreement stipulates that "[*e*]*xcept as provided in this Section 8, we obtain no rights under this Agreement from you (or your licensors) to Your Content*".[42]

However, most service providers obtain through their service terms permission to make certain uses of the customer's data. In order for a cloud service to work, the service provider must necessarily make some uses of the customer's data. Cloud service terms grant permission for this by requiring the user to grant a license to the cloud service provider to make certain uses of the customer's data. What kind of uses are in fact made by the cloud service provider is largely invisible for the user and usage rights of the cloud service provider are often very broad under the respective service terms. Under Section 8.1. of the AWS Customer Agreement, the user consents to use of any use of its content *"to provide the Service Offerings to you and any End Users"*. Section 4.2 of the Google Earth Engine License Agreement grants Google the right to use customer data *"to provide the Services to Customer and its End Users and to help secure and improve the Services"*.[43] By granting such broad usage rights to the cloud service provider, the user may not lose its ownership rights in relation to data uploaded to the cloud. They do rather raise concerns that the user is losing control over the uses of its data.

As for data generated in the cloud, ownership right is no different than if the information had been generated outside. The author in terms of copyright law will be the owner of copyright, to the extent that data generated have the level of creativity required under the law of the State where the data have been created. The above-mentioned uncertainties on the protection under the sui generis right are also of concern for the protection of data generated in the cloud.

4 Legal Issues in Relation to Clouds in Space

Some companies have considered to launch satellites as cloud service infrastructure, providing storage and compute capabilities in space. While still a very nascent and emerging market, high visibility cyber-attacks over recent years have spurred interest in such solutions, with potential customers will

41 Google Earth Engine License Agreement, under https://earthengine.google.com/terms/, visited 29 January 2021.

42 AWS Customer Agreement, https://aws.amazon.com/agreement/?nc1=h_ls, under 29 January 2021.

43 NSR, Space for The Cloud: Data From Orbit, 15 July 2020, under https://www.nsr.com/space-for-the-cloud-data-from-orbit/, visited 29 January 2021.

protecting/storing their data in space-based cloud services. According to market search, in-space cloud storage is forecast to present a revenue opportunity of nearly $22 million by 2029, growing at a high CAGR of 43% from now till then.[44] The company SpaceBelt is conceiving a network of 10 Low Earth Orbit (LEO) satellites for the purpose of offering space-based secure cloud data storage and global connectivity services. It promises "*a world free of insecure data and jurisdictional hazards*".[45]

Legal issues in relation to clouds in space do not substantially differ from those on Earth. The concept nevertheless raises interesting questions, such as: whether and to what extent the location of the cloud in outer space has an impact on ownership rights in the cloud infrastructure and the data stored or generated therein, and whether and to what extent the location of the cloud in outer space has an impact on the legal implications under privacy law.

4.1 *Ownership Rights in the Cloud Infrastructure*

As regards ownership rights of the cloud infrastructure, Art. VIII sentence 2 of the Outer Space Treaty[46] provides that "[*o*]*wnership of objects launched into outer space, including objects landed or constructed on a celestial body, and of their component parts, is not affected by their presence in outer space or on a celestial body or by their return to the Earth*". Article VIII of the Outer Space Treaty does not establish ownership by means of a constitutive rule. It rather clarifies that ownership of the cloud infrastructure, which is to be determined in accordance with the applicable law under the rules of international private law, is not affected by the presence of the cloud infrastructure in outer space. The applicable law governing ownership rights of the cloud infrastructure is to be determined in accordance with the lex rei sitae principle which provides that ownership rights in physical assets are governed by the law where the asset is located. As underlined by the preparatory work of the UNIDROIT Space Asset Protocol,[47] under international private law, an asset is deemed to

44 Ibid.

45 Spacebelt, About, under http://spacebelt.com/#about, visited 29 January 2021.

46 Treaty on Principles Governing the Activities of States in the Exploration and Use of Outer Space, including the Moon and Other Celestial Bodies (Outer Space Treaty), 610 UNTS 205, under https://www.unoosa.org/oosa/en/ourwork/spacelaw/treaties/outerspacetreaty.html, visited 31 January 2021.

47 Protocol to the Convention on International Interests in Mobile Equipment on Matters Specific to Space Assets, signed in Berlin on 9 March 2021, under https://www.unidroit.org/english/conventions/mobile-equipment/spaceassets-protocol-e.pdf, visited 4 October 2021. The preparatory work is available under https://www.unidroit.org/instruments/security-interests/space-protocol/preparatory-work/, visited 4 October 2021.

be located in the jurisdiction of the State of registry in terms of Article VIII of the Outer Space Treaty. Conversely, ownership of the cloud infrastructure is to be determined in accordance with the private law of the State of registry of the satellite on which the cloud infrastructure is located (or the State of registry of the cloud infrastructure, in case it is registered separately). In any case, the activities of the satellite operator require authorization and continuing supervision of the appropriate state under Article VI of the Outer Space Treaty.

4.2 *Ownership Rights in Data Stored or Generated in Clouds in Space*

The location of the cloud infrastructure in outer space raises the question as to whether it has an impact on the applicable law for copyright protection and the protection of databases and as to whether the location of the cloud in outer space affects these ownership rights.

According to Article 3 (1) (a) and 3 (2) of the Berne Convention, the Convention applies to authors who are nationals of one of the countries of the Berne Union or who have habitual residence in one of those countries. It is, thus, not the determination of jurisdiction over a space object by means of the State of registry which, in the first place, determines the status as regards protection under the Berne Convention of data stored or generated in clouds in space, but rather the author's nationality.

Determining the country of origin of EO data may as stated above depend on the place where the servers are located from which they have been made available to others. If such servers are located in outer space, the State of registry of the space object on which the servers are located is deemed to be the country of origin.

The territorial scope of the sui generis right is generally not affected by the location of the cloud infrastructure in outer space, as it depends in the first place on the question as to whether the maker or the rightsholder is a national of an EU Member State or as to whether the maker or the right holder has its habitual residence in the territory of the European Union. The location of the cloud in outer space may, however, become relevant as regards the question whether the database is located in a third country to which the sui generis right applies by virtue of an agreement concluded by the Council. This is to be determined in accordance with the registration of the space object on which the cloud infrastructure is located. It may further become relevant when determining under whose jurisdiction extraction and/or reutilization of the database takes place. When extraction and/or reutilization is undertaken through cloud infrastructures in outer space, it takes place under the jurisdiction and control of the State of registry of the space object on which the cloud infrastructure is located.

4.3 *Location of the Cloud in Terms of Data Protection Law*

As stated above, the location of the cloud infrastructure is not decisive for determining the scope of the GDPR.

However, the location of the cloud infrastructure in outer space is of particular relevance when it comes to the question whether the transfer of data from or to the cloud infrastructure in outer space is to be considered as a data transfer in terms of EU privacy law (see Table 9.1). Though outer space as such is an international common, a space object can be allocated to the State of registry exercising quasi-territorial jurisdiction and control. Bearing in mind such territorial link through the registration of a space object, the location of the data in the context of data transfer is to be determined in accordance with the registration of the space object on which the cloud infrastructure is located. The following high-level scenarios are relevant for the question whether data transfer to or from cloud infrastructure in space requires an adequacy decision by the European Commission, in order to be transferred without any further safeguards or conditions.

5 Summary and Conclusions

The use of cloud computing in the space industry is growing considerably. NSR's *Cloud Computing via Satellite* report of June 2020 forecasts a $16B cumulative revenue opportunity for cloud-based services in the satellite/space industry through the coming decade. One of the main applications of cloud computing are dedicated EO data exploitation platforms. Especially in Europe, there has been a tremendous development of such EO platforms, both public and privately financed. These platforms support the ongoing revolution of the EO market from traditional data product delivery to digital online business. Cloud computing facilitates large-volume storage and enables fast and easy access to multiple different sources of Earth observation data. As users do no longer need to download and store the data on their own hardware, it reduces time and costs of access. In addition, cloud computing provides the on-demand delivery of computing power for search, upload, online-analytics, processing and value adding. Advanced algorithms and software tools in the cloud, many of which are open source, greatly support the development of new Earth observation applications, services and solutions. These resources feed into new business models for the Earth observation and the broader geospatial markets.

However, persisting concerns over security, privacy and ownership continue to limit the potentials and further expansion of EO cloud platforms.

TABLE 9.1 Data transfer scenarios

Location of the infrastructure from which data are transferred	Location of the infrastructure to which data are transferred	Data transfer to a third country in terms of the GDPR
Non-EU/EEA country territory	Cloud in space registered with EU or EEA MS	NO
EU/EEA MS territory	Cloud in space registered with Non-EU/EEA country	YES
Cloud in space registered with Non-EU/EEA country	EU/EEA MS territory	NO
Cloud in space registered with EU/EEA MS	Non-EU/EEA country territory	YES

Data owners and providers fear data loss and provider lock-in situations. Value adding companies, mostly very small, are concerned that the algorithms and software are not safe from unauthorized access and misuse, including by the cloud provider himself. Where they process data in the cloud for creating value adding products, they are concerned about untransparent contractual terms and resulting uncertainties regarding ownership and control over such derived products. While cloud providers employ very high cyber security standards and procedures, the number of attacks and their size and impact grow along with the overall market. Contractual terms and conditions continue to be highly individualized and complex, and may oblige the customer, for the implementation of the contract, to grant to the provider a license to use the content that the customer intends to place in the cloud.

Another emerging space application of cloud computing are satellite-based cloud servers. So far, this market segment has not yet materialized, but companies are working on the establishment of satellite constellations for that purpose and are promising that their service will reduce security threats and even solve "jurisdictional issues". In view of the fact that satellites hosting cloud in space are under the jurisdiction of the State of registry and that such State (or another appropriate one) has to authorize and supervise the activities of the satellite operator, doubts regarding the alleged extra-jurisdictional impacts of such potential new systems appear justified. Such doubts are further enforced by the high-level analysis of ownership and privacy concerning the data stored, accessed or otherwise used in space-based clouds.

CHAPTER 10

EU Data Protection Considerations for the Space Sector

Laura Keogh

1 Introduction

As discussed throughout this book, since the 1960's space has played an increasing role in our society, including for telecommunication, humanitarian, commerce, and exploration purposes. "The progress of the exploration and use of outer space for peaceful purposes"[1] needs to be carried out with many considerations in mind, one of which is the focus of this chapter: privacy. The question over whether data collected about another State's territory and how it should be treated has been considered since the 1960s, with the main question being whether States should be allowed to observe or remote sense other States from space. While data about States is important, as innovation in the space sector continues, how data about individuals is treated must also be considered. The numerous planned space missions will see increasing numbers of astronauts, and thereby more data about individuals being sent through space itself; furthermore, increasing amounts of data will be transferred through and stored in space via next generation internet, data storage, and communication systems. With these current and planned developments, there is an increasing likelihood that the space sector will collect more and more data about individuals ("personal data"). As the right to privacy is a fundamental right,[2] it is important at a macro level to assess whether the space sector has reached a stage where it needs to be more aware of privacy for individuals. At a practical level, given the increasing attention to privacy rights, it is important to be aware of the applicability of privacy laws to the space sector.

1 UNGA Res. 1962(XVIII) Declaration of Legal Principles Governing the Activities of States in the Exploration and Use of Outer Space (December 13, 1963): preamb. para. 2.

2 Convention for the Protection of Human Rights and Fundamental Freedoms, 4 November 1950, 213 U.N.T.S. 221 (entered into force 3 September 1953): Art 8(1); UNGA Res 217(III)A Universal Declaration of Human Rights (1948): Art 12; and International Covenant on Civil and Political Rights (entered into force 23 March 1976): Art. 17.

© KONINKLIJKE BRILL NV, LEIDEN, 2023 | DOI:10.1163/9789004527270_011

The right to privacy is interpreted and protected differently throughout the world;[3] within the European Union the general concept of 'privacy' is essentially divided into two parts: (I) physical privacy and (II) informational privacy.[4] 'Physical privacy' is the ability to have physical solitude and to not be unduly disturbed. This is enshrined in Article 7 of the Charter of Fundamental Rights of the European Union (European Charter) as the "right to respect for private life."[5] 'Informational privacy' is the ability to control one's information. This is enshrined in Article 8 of the European Charter as the "right to personal data protection" and is regulated via data protection law.[6] This concept of 'informational privacy' within the space sector shall be the focus of this Chapter.

The European Union has a world leading approach to 'informational privacy,' which is protected through data protection law, of which the foremost law is the General Data Protection Regulation (GDPR).[7] The GDPR provides for fines reaching up to €20 million or 4% of worldwide annual turnover for non-compliance.[8] In parallel to this, the European Union's space industry is strong with the EU Space Programme,[9] national EU Member State space initiatives, and the European Space Agency (ESA, of which the majority of EU Member States are a part of). These factors make the European Union an important jurisdiction in which the applicability of 'informational privacy' laws to the space sector has to be considered.

In light of the above, this chapter shall first discuss privacy within international space law. Thereafter, this chapter shall explain the applicability of the

3 The concept of what the right to privacy means differs throughout the world, see for further discussion Whitman, "The Two Western Cultures of Privacy: Dignity Versus Liberty," 113 Yale Law Journal 1151 (2004).

4 This distinction was particularly highlighted in Information Commissioner's Office, *Conducting Privacy Impact Assessments Code of Practice, ver. 1.0* (2014): 6.

5 Charter of Fundamental Rights of the European Union, 2000 OJ (C364) and Treaty on the European Union, Official Journal of the European Union C326 (26 October 2012): Article 6(1) (TEU).

6 *Id.* and Treaty on the Functioning of the European Union, Official Journal of the European Union, C 83 (30 March 2010): Article 16 (TFEU).

7 Regulation (EU) 2016/679 of the European Parliament and of the Council of 27 April 2016 on the protection of natural persons with regard to the processing of personal data and on the free movement of such data, and repealing Directive 95/46/EC (General Data Protection Regulation) Official Journal of the European Union, Vol L119 (4 May 2016): 1–88 (hereinafter GDPR).

8 GDPR, Art. 83.

9 *See* European Commission, *Questions and Answers on the New EU Space Programme* (6 June 2018) https://ec.europa.eu/commission/presscorner/detail/en/MEMO_18_4023.

GDPR to the space sector. Third, the applicable EU data protection law to non-private entities, such as international organisations like ESA, shall be discussed. Finally, this chapter shall look at the applicable EU data protection law within the context of defence and security in the space sector. The cumulative goal of this chapter is to provide the reader with an understanding of when and how EU data protection law is applicable to entities within the space sector.

2 International Space Law and Privacy

Privacy laws have not been directly integrated into international space law. While not privacy law *per se*, figuring out how to deal with potentially sensitive data collection about another entity is a cornerstone of privacy law. The General Assembly Resolution 41/65 3 December 1986, Principles Relating to Remote Sensing of the Earth, which is not binding on UN Member States,[10] and the talks leading up to these principles signify one of the first international discussions on how to deal with the collection and use of potentially sensitive data from another entity via space technology.[11] Thus, these remote sensing discussions provide insight on how the UN Member States initially thought about the collection and use of potentially sensitive data from space. One of the topics discussed revolved around the question of, essentially, what 'data protection rights' should exist for States?[12] Remote sensing can enable States to 'spy' on other States via space surveillance satellite systems. Should it be legal for States to gather data about another State's territory from space? Four main opinions existed regarding remote sensing:[13]

1. Remote sensing is lawful;
2. Remote sensing is a violation of national territorial sovereignty;
3. Remote sensing is acceptable if the State being sensed has a right to refuse whether the remote sensing can take place, meaning that States should gain prior approval before remote sensing another State's territory; or

---

10 UN Charter, Art. 9–22.

11 UNGA Res. 41/65 Principles relating to remote sensing of the Earth from space (3 December 1986). For prior attempts to discuss remote sensing, *see* 1978 Draft Principles, UN Doc. A/AC.105/218. Annex 3 (13 April 1978): 5–8 and Convention on the Transfer and Use of Data of Remote Sensing of the Earth from Outer Space, UN Doc. A/33/162 (29 June 1978).

12 Christol, *The Modern International Law of Outer Space* (Pergamon Press, 1982): 732–746.

13 *Id.* at 732–733.

4. Remote sensing is acceptable if the State being sensed can prevent other States coming into possession of the sensed data, that is States should not be able to share remote sensing data about other States in an unfettered manner.

States were particularly concerned that data about their territory would be disseminated in an unfettered manner, and discussions arose about whether there should be a requirement to not allow dissemination of data.[14] Differing State opinions led to the topic being concluded via the adoption of Principle 12 of Resolution 41/65. This provided that if a State is being surveyed or monitored from space, that State should have the right to access the data gathered.[15] Thus, no limitations were placed on States, merely a consensus was reached that the sensed State should be able to access the data (within the parameters defined by Resolution 41/65).[16] These discussions on remote sensing draw interesting observations from a privacy perspective: (I) it represented a milestone conversation on how to deal with potentially sensitive data that could be gathered about another entity from space and showed themes that resonate closely with privacy law issues, such as the right to access, the right to object, lawfulness of data collection and data transfer, and (II) it showed the difficulty, and ultimate resolution, in obtaining international consensus on how to deal with the collection and use of potentially sensitive data from space about another entity, albeit from a State's perspective.

Ultimately, privacy laws in space are limited to the applicability of national and supra-national privacy laws. Privacy laws are applicable in space via the Outer Space Treaty, with over 100 countries party to the treaty.[17] The Outer Space Treaty codifies the fact that outer space is governed by international law and that outer space is not subject to national appropriation or claims of sovereignty (for example, a country cannot claim ownership of a certain area of the Moon).[18] Thus, no national law can govern any area of outer space.

However, objects and individuals launched into outer space may be subject to the laws of the launching State in accordance with Article VIII of the

14 Lyall and Larsen, *Space Law* (Dartmouth: Ashgate 2007): 121.

15 Draft Principles adopted by the Legal Sub-Committee, 25 ILM 1334 (13 June 1986) and Lyall and Larson, *Space Law*, 411.

16 For a full breakdown of the Principles within Resolution 41/65 see Frans von der Dunk, "United Nations Principles on Remote Sensing and the User," in Ray Harris, ed., *Earth Observation Data Policy and Europe* (Lisse: A. A. Balkema, 2002): 29–40.

17 Treaty on Principles Governing the Activities of States in the Exploration and Use of Outer Space, Including the Moon and Other Celestial Bodies, 610 U.N.T.S. 205 (entered into force 27 Jan. 1967) (Outer Space Treaty).

18 Outer Space Treaty, Arts. II & III.

Outer Space Treaty. Article VIII reads that the State which launched a space object retains "jurisdiction and control over such object, and over any personnel thereof … while in outer space …" This means that while there is no national sovereignty in space, meaning no national laws, national laws may still be applied to space objects and individuals via the launching State. For a State to be the launching State it has to either launch the space object, procure the launch, or be a State from whose territory or facility a space object is launched.[19]

The application of Article VIII of the Outer Space Treaty will become increasingly important as more permanent establishments exist in space. For example, the Artemis Accords have the goal of encouraging more civil exploration and introduces the concept of "safety zones" around landing and work sites.[20] Any space object launched into outer space, including those objects that remain in space, must abide by the laws applicable to the launching State, which can necessarily include privacy laws.[21] Therefore, the international legal landscape of privacy within the space sector leads to the national or supranational level, and, as such, the following sections shall focus specifically on the applicability of EU data protection law to the space sector.

3 The Space Sector and the GDPR

The core data protection law within the European Union is the GDPR, which has been in force since May 2018 (which replaced the previous 1995 law).[22] As a regulation, the GDPR is directly applicable on all EU Member States and does not require further implementation into national law.[23] It provides rights for

19 Convention on International Liability for Damage Caused by Space Objects, 961 U.N.T.S. 187 (entered into force 9 October 1973): Art. I(c) (Liability Convention); Convention on Registration of Objects Launched into Outer Space, 1023 U.N.T.S. 15 (entered into force 15 September 1976): Art. I (Registration Convention).

20 The Artemis Accords, announced on 15 May 2020, were released by NASA in order to establish a common set of principles to govern the civil exploration and use of outer space in general, including the Moon. Artemis Accord, Principles for a Safe, Peaceful, and Prosperous Future (2020) https://www.nasa.gov/specials/artemis-accords/index.html.

21 According to the United Nations Conference on Trade and Development, 66% of countries have legislation in place to safeguard the protection of individual's data and privacy, *see* unctad.org.

22 Directive 95/46/EC of the European Parliament and of the Council of 24 October 1995 on the protection of individuals with regard to the processing of personal data and on the free movement of such data (OJ L 281, 23.11.1995): 31.

23 TFEU, Art. 288.

individuals, whose personal data is being processed, and places obligations on entities that process personal data. There are several core EU data protection principles, many of which are referenced in Section 4; however, these can generally be distilled down into two key principles:

I. Transparency:[24] entities are required to be transparent about all aspects of personal data processing, including what personal data is collected, how personal data is used, how long it is retained, and what rights individuals have *vis a vis* their personal data.
II. Security:[25] entities are required to ensure all personal data is collected, used, processed, transferred, and stored in a secure manner (including using encryption, pseudonymisation, and regular deletion practices, if appropriate), as well as ensuring required checks, reviews, and mechanisms are in place when transferring data.

The GDPR applies whenever personal data is processed within the territorial scope of the GDPR. Processing personal data under the GDPR means carrying out any operation on personal data, including the collection, storage, and transfer of personal data.[26] Due to the large fines that can be imposed for failure to comply, it is important for entities to be aware when they may be subject to the GDPR.[27] Furthermore, breach of the GDPR can give rise to a criminal prosecution, in accordance with the national law of EU Member States.[28]

This section shall not provide the full details, obligations or requirements of the GDPR.[29] Rather, the goal of this section is to draw attention to potential personal data collection within the space sector, within the scope of the GDPR. Furthermore, Article 2 GDPR provides for the material scope of the GDPR and excludes EU institutions, national defence, and national security, among other limited situations, from the scope of the GDPR, of which discussion on some of these aspects will be covered later in the chapter. Below will explain the scope of what "personal data" is and the jurisdictional parameters of the GDPR to demonstrate how various facets of the space sector should consider whether they fall within the scope of the GDPR.

24 GDPR, Art. 5(1)(a).
25 GDPR, Art. 5(1)(f).
26 GDPR, Art. 4(2).
27 Fines can reach up to €20 million or 4% of world annual turnover. GDPR, Art. 83.
28 GDPR, Recital 149.
29 For full details please see my previous discussion of the GDPR provisions, Laura Keogh, *Data Protection Compliance* (Dublin: Clarus Press, 2019).

3.1 *Definition of Personal Data*

The definition of personal data is defined broadly in order to capture any information that can be associated with an individual. Personal data is defined as:[30]

> *any* information *relating to* an identified or identifiable natural person ('data subject'); an identifiable natural person is one who can be identified, *directly or indirectly*, in particular by reference to an identifier such as a name, an identification number, location data, an online identifier or to one or more factors specific to the physical, physiological, genetic, mental, economic, cultural or social identity of that natural person [emphasis added].

To aid in the interpretation of EU data protection law the European Union set up an independent advisory to issue non-binding advice on data protection law, known as the Article 29 Working Party (WP29).[31] Their work has now been taken over by the European Data Protection Board (EDPB);[32] however, the work of WP29 can be still used in the interpretation of the GDPR.[33] The definition of 'personal data' provides that any data that is capable of being linked or connected to an individual, even indirectly falls within the definition of personal data. As such, data that has been rendered anonymous is not personal data because it is not possible to relate it to an individual.[34] WP29 stated that useful metrics to consider include the (I) content, (II) purpose, or (III) result of the data point, and that one or more of these metrics can be used to determine whether the information can relate directly or indirectly to an individual, thereby making it personal data.[35]

3.1.1 Content

If the content of information is about an individual, then it is personal data. This includes traditional data, such as names, emails, addresses, pictures, diary inputs, timetables, as well as other identifiers, such as Internet protocol addresses, cookie identifiers, and radio frequency identification tags.[36]

---

30 GDPR, Art. 4(1).

31 Directive 95/46/EC, Art. 29.

32 GDPR, Art. 68.

33 GDPR, Art. 94.

34 This is a case-by-case determination. Data is capable of being deemed anonymous if it is no longer possible to identify an individual using reasonable (1) time, (2) cost, and (3) available technology, *see* GDPR, Recital 26.

35 Data Protection Working Party, Opinion 4/2007 on the concept of personal data, Art. 29.

36 GDPR, Recital 30.

Furthermore, even if the entity does not hold the piece of information that enables it to associate an individual with the content, it can still be personal data. This was clearly outlined in the Breyer case,[37] in which the court considered whether a dynamic IP address is personal data. Dynamic IP addresses, as opposed to static IP addresses, change each time if there is a new connection to the Internet. Generally, only the Internet service provider is able to identify an individual to which a dynamic IP address relates; however, in the case it was found that there was a legal mechanism via which an entity can request further information from the Internet service provider to identify the individual associated with the dynamic IP address.[38] Thus, the court determined that the dynamic IP address is personal data because it is capable of being indirectly identifiable. Therefore, the fact that additional data, held by a third party, is necessary to identify an individual does not prevent it from being personal data.

This 'content' metric demonstrates how certain data within the space sector is considered personal data. Space tourism and the numerous planned space missions may see increasing numbers of individuals in space, and thereby more personal data being sent through outer space; data processed about personnel and employees in space is personal data: from payroll information, to timetables, to monitoring vital signs and tracking, and researching their fitness and diet. This is also notable with the potential of more employees in space via in-orbit servicing missions, refuelling missions, or mining missions due to laws allowing for the ownership of space resources,[39] thereby making space mining a potentially profitable industry. Furthermore, plans for data transfer and storage within outer space will also mean that personal data will be processed by the space sector. In June 2020, Telesat's Phase 1 LEO satellite test demonstrated fibre-like performance,[40] proving that space will play a part in expanding 4G networks and beyond. In addition, space is and will continue to play an increasingly important role in the Internet of Things (IOT) sector. For instance, within the European Union, there is an Internet of Things Everywhere on Earth Project, which is a project that has been funded by the European Union

---

37 Patrick Breyer v Bundesrepublik Deutschland, Case C-582/14.

38 *Id.* at para. 47.

39 For example, the Luxembourg Space Resources Act of 20 July 2017 provides that "space resources are capable of being owned," see loi du 20 juillet 2017 sur l'exploration et l'utilisation des ressources de l'espace [Law of July 20 2017 on the Exploration and Use of Space Resources], Mémorial A, n° 674 (28 July 2017) Art. 1.

40 Telesat, "Performance Results" (n.d.) https://www.telesat.com/leo-satellites/performance-results/.

for satellite-enabled machine-to-machine communication that can efficiently provide IOT services from space to a wide area.[41] This demonstrates that space may not only play a role in providing people with better access to the Internet and IOT devices, but Earth may see a time when data is housed and transferred in space. Entities such as Space Belt's Cloud Constellation are already planning a cloud storage network of space-based data centres.[42]

3.1.2 Purpose

If the purpose, or likely purpose, of using the information is to review, treat differently, influence, or learn something about an individual, then it is personal data. For example, building access control systems can be used to learn when certain individuals accessed a building or certain secure areas. The access logs can be used to learn about multiple different people and are, therefore, personal data. This 'purpose' metric particularly shows how downstream space services process personal data. For instance, devices often give individuals the choice of which satellite system to use for satellite navigation and location data (whether it be GPS, GLONASS, BDS, QZSS, Galileo, et cetera) and this information, of which satellite system an individual is using, is personal data because the purpose is to provide individuals with the desired navigation service.

3.1.3 Result

If the information can have the consequence or result of learning something about an individual, or results in an individual being treated differently, this is personal data. For instance, if information about an individual is used to deny an individual entry into a building, but the information about the individual was wrong, then the data used to refuse entry is still protected as personal data. The incorrect information resulted in the person being treated differently and the definition for personal data states "any information," and does not specify whether the information needs to be correct or not. Thus, incorrect information is still protected under the GDPR if it relates to an individual.[43] In addition, information about an object can be personal data if it can be associated with an individual and this causes an individual to be treated differently. For instance, the value of a property is information relating to a house; however,

---

41 See European Commission Cordis EU Research Results, "Internet of Things Everywhere on Earth: a satellite based M2M solution" (17 February 2020) https://cordis.europa.eu/project/id/738483.

42 *See* http://spacebelt.com.

43 Article 29 Data Protection Working Party, Opinion 4/2007 on the concept of personal data, at 6.

when gathering data about individuals that are bidding to buy the house the value of the house reveals financial information about those individuals, thereby rendering it personal data. Information held may not directly reveal information about an individual, but in specific contexts it may indirectly provide information related to an individual, rendering it personal data. For example, knowing location information for a mobile phone impacts the way online advertisements, taxi apps, and other items function for an individual. Location information about a car can "become" personal data when linked to an individual, because the location of the car can reveal the location of the individuals in the car.[44]

The 'result' metric particularly shows how data collected via remote sensing could be personal data. As capabilities in remote sensing increase and the number of remote sensing satellites continues to grow, the risk that personal data may be collected as part of remote sensing and high-resolution satellite imagery will increase.[45] Remote sensing and satellite imagery is seeing increased usage for urban planning and development.

Remote sensing can be used to reveal mineral information, land use, and human settlements (house detection). Thus, if this remote sensing information is combined with a public data set of names and addresses, for example, this information can become personal data. Almost unlimited information can be learned about an individual by remote sensing; for instance, whether an individual farms their land, what type of buildings an individual owns, property features, or an individual's footfall. In addition, drones are beginning to operate in 'near space,' so it may be only a matter of time before drones cross the 'border' into outer space. All of this remote sensing data could provide information about individuals and may be used for various purposes that may impact individuals.

Remote sensing can also be used to track cargo, ships and trucks. This information can become personal data by indirectly revealing information about individuals associated with the cargo or on board a ship, such as employee location information.

Furthermore, as the resolution of satellite imagery increases, the use cases for satellite imagery will grow and the risk of gathering personal data will increase. Spatial resolution improved almost by a factor of 20 between 1980 and 2016, and sources indicate that improvements in spatial resolution are

44 *Id.* at 11.

45 C. Santos and L. Rapp, "Satellite Imagery, Very High-Resolution and Processing-Intensive Image Analysis: Potential Risks under the GDPR," *Air and Space Law* 44 (2019): 275–296.

likely to continue.[46] Again better imagery increases the risk of collecting content about individuals.

Thinking about the 'content,' 'purpose,' or 'result' demonstrates the broad definition of personal data. This enables the GDPR to have a wide scope. The fact that information can be considered personal data even by indirect means is an important consideration for the space sector. The above provided a number of examples on where there is a likelihood of personal data collection in the space sector.

3.2 *Territorial Scope of the GDPR*

The territorial scope of the GDPR is broad and seeks to ensure local entities respecting personal data rights, and that entities from anywhere in the world will likewise respect personal data rights when processing the personal data of individuals within an European Union Member State territory. Article 3 of the GDPR defines the three situations where personal data being processed will fall within the territorial scope of the GDPR:

3.2.1 Entity within the European Union

Article 3(1) of the GDPR provides that the GDPR is applicable to European Union entities that process personal data, whether or not the personal data is about individuals within the European Union. This ensures that all entities within the European Union abide by the GDPR requirements, regardless of whose personal data they are processing. For example, if a European Union satellite remote sensing operator collected data about Canadian individuals, the European Union entity must still hold this data in compliance with the GDPR.

3.2.2 Entity outside of the European Union

Article 3(2) of the GDPR provides that the GDPR is applicable to entities outside of the European Union that process personal data of individuals within the European Union if the processing involves (I) the offering of goods or services to individuals within the European Union, or (II) the monitoring of the behaviour of people within the European Union. This ensures that non-European Union entities are subject to the GDPR for processing activities that target individuals within the European Union. This section is only applicable to entities with *intent* to target the European Union.[47] For example, indicators

46 Megan M. Coffer, "Balancing Privacy Rights and the Production of High-Quality Satellite Imagery," *Environmental Science & Technology* 54/11 (2020): 6453–6455; Work of the ITU-T's Study Group 17 (n.d.) https://www.itu.int/en/ITU-T/about/groups/Pages/sg17.aspx.

47 GDPR, Recital 23.

such as relevant currency and language options provide proof of intention that an entity actually intended to offer goods and services to individuals in the European Union.[48] In addition, naturally the term "monitoring" could be very relevant for international remote sensing companies, where there may be a risk of personal data collection about individuals within the European Union. Furthermore, people are already beginning to work on an Internet system that can span the solar system and beyond[49] which could offer goods and services one day. For example, one could imagine a future where a space tourism company on Mars is targeting individuals within the European Union to take a trip to Mars, and in such a future, that Mars entity would arguably need to comply with the GDPR because they were targeting individuals within the European Union.

3.2.3 Public International Law

Article 3(3) of the GDPR provides that the GDPR applies to entities within a place to which the GDPR otherwise applies by virtue of public international law. This primarily relates to diplomatic missions.

This section has highlighted how the GDPR is applicable to the space sector, under the current legal regime. The GDPR is applicable, in accordance with the above, to the majority of entities both public and private; however, European Union institutions, international organisations, and public and national security entities have different data protection laws applicable to them. Given the role of these entities within the European Union space sector, the following sections shall discuss what European Union data protection law is applicable *vis a vis* those entities.

4 The Space Sector and Data Protection Law within EU Institutions and International Organisations

The previous section drew attention to the broad definition of personal data, along with the wide territorial scope of the GDPR, cumulatively emphasising the fact that the GDPR is applicable to various entities within the space sector. Below shall detail key considerations where personal data is processed by or

48 *See* Guidelines 3/2018 on the territorial scope of the GDPR (Article 3) Version 2.1 (7 January 2020) 17.

49 See the work and resources of the Interplanetary Networking Special Interest Group at http://ipnsig.org/.

in cooperation with European Union institutions and international organisations, such as ESA.

4.1 *EU Institutions*

Article 189 of the Treaty on the Functioning of the European Union (TFEU) provides that the European Union shall draw up a European space policy and to this end "may promote joint initiatives, support research and technological development and coordinate the efforts needed for the exploration and exploitation of space." The European Union subsequently passed the European Space Policy in 2007.[50] Article 189 of the TFEU established the commitment of European Union institutions to the advancement of the European Union space sector. Indeed, European Union institutions encompass an important role in the European Union space sector. For example, the Galileo global navigation satellite system (GNSS), that went live in 2016, was created by the European Union through the European GNSS Agency. Furthermore, Copernicus is the European system for monitoring the Earth and is managed by the European Commission.

In line with the essence of the GDPR, a new data protection framework specifically for European Union institutions, bodies, offices and agencies (EUIs) was established via Regulation (EU) 2018/1725. This regulation governs the processing of personal data by EUIs (rather than the GDPR). Mirroring the GDPR, it sets out similar data protection obligations for EUIs when processing personal data and developing new policies, including similar requirements for transparency and security. Both the European GNSS Agency and the European Commission (for the purposes of Copernicus) are EUIs and are thus subject to Regulation (EU) 2018/1725 when personal data is processed. Personal data within Regulation (EU) 2018/1725 has the same definition as in the GDPR, which was discussed in detail in the previous section.

If an entity (private or otherwise) is contracted by an EUI to carry out an activity, then Regulation (EU) 2018/1725 applies to any personal data processing that occurs within the scope of that activity.[51] Thus, Regulation (EU) 2018/

---

50 Resolution on the European Space Policy as adopted by the Council on 22 May 2007, COM(2007) 212 final.

51 *See* Regulation (EU) 2018/1725, Art. 29; Regulation (EU) 2016/794 of the European Parliament and of the Council of 11 May 2016 on the European Union Agency for Law Enforcement Cooperation (Europol) and replacing and repealing Council Decisions 2009/371/JHA, 2009/934/JHA, 2009/935/JHA, 2009/936/JHA and 2009/968/JHA (OJ L 135, 24.5.2016): 53; and Council Regulation (EU) 2017/1939 of 12 October 2017 implementing enhanced cooperation on the establishment of the European Public Prosecutor's Office ('the EPPO') (OJ L 283, 31.10.2017): 1.

1725 can be applicable to private entities or other international organisations within specific contexts. For example, to the extent that remote sensing satellite operators are processing personal data on behalf of EU institutions, then Regulation (EU) 2018/1725 applies to that processing activity.

As with the GDPR, Regulation (EU) 2018/1725 has a defined scope, which provides that it has limited applicability to criminal justice issues, including *vis a vis* Europol and the European Public Prosecutor's Office.[52] In addition, regarding security and defence, Article 2(4) of Regulation (EU) 2018/1725 provides that the Regulation shall not apply to the processing of personal data by missions referred to in Articles 42(1), 43 and 44 of the Treaty on European Union (TEU), which implement the common EU security and defence policy. Recital 15 states: "Where appropriate, relevant proposals should be put forward to further regulate the processing of personal data in the field of the common security and defence policy." Thus, while entities such as the European Defence Agency (EDA), and the European Union Satellite Centre (EUSC), which support the European Union in the field of the Common Foreign and Security Policy, state on their website that they process personal data subject to Regulation (EU) 2018/1725 – this is limited by Article 2(4) of Regulation (EU) 2018/1725 in the context of particular missions. Thus, there is a gap as to when and what, if any data protection laws, are applicable to EU security and defence missions, which may include space missions. Further legal discussion is warranted on this topic but goes beyond the scope of this chapter.

4.2 *International Organisations*

There are no explicit references as to whether European Union data protection law is directly applicable to international organisations. However, European Union data protection law (via the GDPR and Regulation (EU) 2018/1725) extensively regulates the transfer of personal data to international organisations and requires entities to provide transparency when transferring data to international organisations.[53] There are several international organisations that play a significant part in the EU space sector, such as the European Organisation for the Exploitation of Meteorological Satellites (EUMETSAT),[54] the European

52 *See* Regulation (EU) 2018/1725, Art. 2.

53 GDPR, Arts. 13(1)(f),14(1)(f), 15(1)(c) and Regulation (EU) 2018/1725, Arts. 15(1)(e), 16(1)(f), 17(1)(c).

54 Convention for the Establishment of a European Organization for the Exploitation of Meteorological Satellites (EUMETSAT), Geneva, done 24 May 1983, entered into force 19 June 1986; 1434 UNTS 3.

Southern Observatory (ESO),[55] and the European Space Agency (ESA).[56] This section shall focus on ESA, as ESA plays a major role in the EU space sector, epitomised by the reference to cooperation with ESA in the primary law of the European Union via Article 189(3) of the TFEU: the European Union "shall establish any appropriate relations with the European Space Agency." Furthermore, the 2004 ESA/EU Framework Agreement provides the basis for cooperation between ESA and the European Union.[57] ESA is an international intergovernmental organization. In accordance with the Convention for the establishment of the European Space Agency,[58] ESA enjoys legal personality, privileges, and immunities.[59] ESA falls within the category of an 'international organisation,'[60] which is broadly defined within EU data protection law as "an organisation and its subordinate bodies governed by public international law, or any other body which is set up by, or on the basis of, an agreement between two or more countries."

Personal data may only be transferred to countries outside of the European Union or to international organisations (whether within or outside the European Union) where certain safeguards are in place that ensure the protection of personal data. The focus here is on the transfer to international organisations; however, similar considerations apply *vis a vis* transfers to countries outside the European Union. The safeguards and rules governing the transfer of personal data to international organisations are detailed in Chapter 5 of the GDPR and Chapter 5 of Regulation (EU) 2018/1725. Regarding these Chapter 5 requirements, the European Court of Justice clarified that regular transfers of personal data to international organisations must provide a level of data protection that is 'essentially equivalent' to that guaranteed under EU law.[61]

55 Convention for the establishment of a European Organization for Astronomical Research in the Southern Hemisphere, Paris, done 5 October 1962, entered into force 17 January 1964; 502 UNTS 225.

56 Convention for the Establishment of a European Space Agency, Paris, done 30 May 1975, entered into force 30 October 1980; 1297 UNTS 161.

57 Council Decision of 29 April 2004 on the conclusion of the Framework Agreement between the European Community and the European Space Agency (2004/578/EC).

58 Convention for the establishment of the European Space Agency (1975).

59 *Id.* at Art. XV.

60 GDPR, Art. 4(26) and Regulation (EU) 2018/1725, Art. 3(21).

61 Case C-362/14, Maximillian Schrems v Data Protection Commissioner (ECLI:EU:C:2015:650): para. 52, 73 (detailed requirement for "essential equivalence" under Article 45 GDPR); and developed in Case C-311/18, Data Protection Commissioner v Facebook Ireland and Maximillian Schrems, para. 105, 203 (detailed requirement for "essential equivalence" under Article 46 GDPR); European Data Protection Board, Frequently Asked Questions on the Judgment of the Court of Justice of the European Union in Case C-311/18 – Data

WP29 provided a set of "core data protection principles that have to be present in an international organization in order to ensure essential equivalence with the EU framework."[62] The principles detailed by WP29 directly reflect the core GDPR requirements, including those of transparency and security. For occasional, or one-off data transfers, a list of alternative transfer mechanisms is provided that arguably do not require the 'essential equivalence' assessment, such as the gathering of consent;[63] however, these would not be very practical to international organisations that regularly engage in personal data transfer practices.

While EU data protection law (via the GDPR and Regulation (EU) 2018/1725) does not explicitly reference the privileges and immunities of international organisations, there is independent commentary by the EDPB clarifying that the application of the GDPR is "without prejudice" to the provisions of international law, such as laws on privileges and immunities.[64] Thus, regardless of whether EU data protection law is applicable, international organisations nevertheless typically have privilege against legal enforcement.[65] This has created a tension in which international organisations may not need to comply with EU data protection law, but, due to the Chapter 5 requirements, other entities cannot engage with international organisations unless they provide a level of protection that is 'essentially equivalent' to that under EU law.[66] In other words, while international organisations may be immune from enforcement, entities that work with international organisations may not be immune, and therefore, need to be compliant with Chapter 5 requirements when working with and transferring personal data to international organisations. This has led to certain international organisations adopting their own internal data protection rules as a "halfway house."

Protection Commissioner v Facebook Ireland Ltd and Maximillian Schrems, adopted 23 July 2020. Note that these decisions were made *vis a vis* data transfers to countries outside of the EU, but equally apply to transfers to international organisations.

62 Article 29 Working Party, 'Adequacy referential (updated)' (WP 254, 28 November 2017): 2.

63 GDPR, Recital 111, Art. 49; European Data Protection Board, Guidelines 2/2018 on derogations of Article 49 under Regulation 2016/679, Adopted on 25 May 2018; and Regulation (EU) 2018/1725, Recital 68, Art. 50.

64 European Data Protection Board, Guidelines 3/2018 on the territorial scope of the GDPR (Article 3), Version 2.1 (7 January 2020).

65 Christopher Kuner, "International Organizations and the EU General Data Protection Regulation: Exploring the Interaction between EU Law and International Law," 16 International Organizations Law Review 158–191 (2019): 13–15.

66 Christopher Kuner, "The GDPR and International Organizations." AJIL Unbound 114 (2020): 15–19; Kuner, "International Organizations and the EU General Data Protection Regulation," 24–26.

ESA did this and established their own data protection framework.[67] However, this still leaves the issue of whether these frameworks can be considered a sufficient solution to satisfy Chapter 5 obligations when transferring data to international organisations, in particular the requirement for 'essential equivalence'. Unfortunately, this is an unsettled area of law that needs to be determined via legislation or the courts.[68] As such, entities are left in an ambiguous situation as to whether they need to enforce additional measures via contracts when working with international organisations, in order to comply with Chapter 5. However, international organisations are unlikely to accept additional contractual measures as this may be considered a waiver of their privileges and immunities.[69] As a solution, Kuner proposes that EU institutions should consider the possibility of providing alternative data transfer mechanisms within EU data protection law to cover the special situation of international organisations.[70]

While the EDPB has provided recent guidance as to the meaning of 'essential equivalence,'[71] the criteria for 'essential equivalence' as provided by the WP29 offers a more useful method for the purposes of this chapter to assess whether 'essential equivalence' is achieved in situations,[72] such as with international organisations, where entities are not relying on standard GDPR transfer contracts due to privileges and immunities. The ESA framework largely reflects the requirements under the GDPR and on its face appears to tick the majority of boxes for 'essential equivalence' detailed by WP29. This places ESA, and the entities that work with ESA, in a good position to face any European Union data protection obligations that may emerge. A breakdown of the core European Union data protection principles required to achieve "essential

67 The framework has three parts (1) The Principles of Personal Data Protection, as adopted by ESA Council Resolution (ESA/C/CCLXVIII/Res.2 (Final)) adopted on 13 June 2017, (2) The Rules of Procedure for the Data Protection Supervisory Authority, as adopted by ESA Council Resolution (ESA/C/CCLXVIII/Res.2 (Final)) adopted on 13 June 2017 and (3) The Policy on Personal Data Protection adopted by Director General of ESA on 5 February 2018 and effective on 1 March 2018.

68 This was to be considered, but the court declined to assess the question due to irrelevance to the main proceedings in Case C-505/19 WS v. Federal Republic of Germany, which was to address the question "Does an international organisation such as the International Criminal Police Organisation – Interpol – have an adequate data protection level ...?"

69 Kuner, "The GDPR and International Organizations." 18.

70 *Id.* at 19.

71 European Data Protection Board, Recommendations 01/2020 on measures that supplement transfer tools to ensure compliance with the EU level of protection of personal data, Version 2.0 (18 June 2021).

72 Article 29 Working Party, 'Adequacy referential (updated)' (WP 254, 28 November 2017).

equivalence" are provided below, along with how each principle is provided for within ESA's Policy on Personal Data Protection,[73] and the associated article within the GDPR, for reference purposes see Table 10.1:

This section highlighted the applicable European Union data protection laws and key considerations when dealing with EUIs and international organisations, many of which are key European Union space sector stakeholders. Next, the applicable data protection laws when dealing with space activities involving security and defence, shall be discussed.

5 The Space Sector and Data Protection Law within EU Defence and Security

As with EUIs and international organisations, this section shall address another area where the traditional GDPR does not strictly apply. The European Space Policy recognises the common use of space technologies for both civilian and defence purposes.[74] In light of the role defence plays in the space sector, this section shall detail the extent European Union data protection law is applicable in the context of both a public security and national security perspective, also taking into consideration dual use activities.

5.1 *Public Security*

The processing of personal data for the purposes of law enforcement falls outside the scope of the GDPR.[75] The Data Protection Law Enforcement Directive applies where personal data is processed for the purposes of law enforcement, which primarily includes preventing, investigating, and prosecuting a criminal offence by the relevant authority.[76] As this is a Directive, as opposed to a Regulation, it is binding as to the results to be achieved and European Union

73 The Policy on Personal Data Protection adopted by Director General of ESA on 5 February 2018 and effective on 1 March 2018.

74 Resolution on the European Space Policy as adopted by the Council on 22 May 2007, COM(2007) 212 final, sect. B, para. 8.

75 GDPR, Art. 2(d).

76 Directive (EU) 2016/680 of the European Parliament and of the Council of 27 April 2016 on the protection of natural persons with regard to the processing of personal data by competent authorities for the purposes of the prevention, investigation, detection or prosecution of criminal offences or the execution of criminal penalties, and on the free movement of such data, and repealing Council Framework Decision 2008/977/JHA.

TABLE 10.1 A breakdown of (I) the core EU data protection principles required to achieve "essential equivalence," (II) corresponding section in the ESA policy on personal data protection and (III) the corresponding GDPR provision

	Core EU data protection principles: Requirements to achieve "essential equivalence" (as detailed by WP29)	**Reference in ESA's policy on personal data protection**	**Main equivalent provision in the GDPR (for reference purposes)**
1	Basic data protection concepts should be provided for	Section 3 provides definitions using similar terminology to the GDPR	Article 4 GDPR
2	Personal data must be processed in a lawful, fair and legitimate manner	Section 5.2.1 details fair and legitimate processing obligations	Articles 5(1)(a)-(b) GDPR
3	Personal data may only be processed for a specified purpose and subsequently only used for that purpose	Section 5.2.1 details the purpose limitation principle	Article 5(1)(b) GDPR
4	Personal data should be kept accurate, and personal data should only be processed to the extent that is justifiable needed for the specific purpose	Section 5.1 provides for the principles of personal data quality, accuracy, and proportionality (necessity)	Articles 5(1)(c)-(d) GDPR
5	Personal data should be retained for no longer than is necessary for the specified purpose	Not specifically addressed but implied via section 5.2.1 which states that the necessity of the data processing must be considered	Article 5(1)(c) GDPR
6	Personal data should be processed in a secure manner	Section 5.5 details security obligations	Article 5(1)(f) GDPR

TABLE 10.1 A breakdown of (1) the core EU data protection principles (*cont.*)

	Core EU data protection principles: Requirements to achieve "essential equivalence" (as detailed by WP29)	**Reference in ESA's policy on personal data protection**	**Main equivalent provision in the GDPR (for reference purposes)**
7	There should be transparency provided *vis a vis* the personal data processing	Section 5.4 details transparency requirements as part of individual's rights	Article 5(1)(a), Articles 12–15 GDPR
8	Individuals should be provided with rights *vis a vis* their personal data (including access, rectification, erasure, and objection)	Section 5.4 details individual's rights, including access, erasure, and rectification	Chapter 3 GDPR
9	There should be safeguards concerning the transfer of personal data	Section 5.5 (paragraph 2) and section 5.7 detail requirements when contracting, working with and transferring personal data to another entity	Chapter IV-V GDPR
10	There should be specific consideration for special categories of data, direct marketing and automated decision making and profiling	Section 5.2.2 details provisions on sensitive personal data; there is no reference to direct marketing and automated decision making	Article 9. Article 21, Article 22 GDPR
11	There should be a competent, independent supervisory authority	Section 6 details a governance structure, including a data protection supervisory authority (which is governed by the Rules of Procedure for the Data Protection Supervisory Authority and includes the requirement for independence)	Chapter 6 GDPR

TABLE 10.1 A breakdown of (I) the core EU data protection principles (*cont.*)

	Core EU data protection principles: Requirements to achieve "essential equivalence" (as detailed by WP29)	Reference in ESA's policy on personal data protection	Main equivalent provision in the GDPR (for reference purposes)
12	There should be a system in place to ensure and track compliance	Section 5.6 details measures to ensure effective compliance with personal data protection measures, section 7.1 also details the role of the Data Protection Officer, who can ensure compliance	Article 32, Article 39 GDPR
13	There should be accountability requirements whereby compliance can be verified	Section 6 and the associated Annex provides the Governance Scheme of the Agency's Personal Data Protection, of which Part I includes the duty to keep and update personal data records, as defined in Section 3 thereof	Article 5(2), 30 GDPR
14	There should be mechanisms via which individuals can ask for assistance *vis a vis* their personal data rights and concerns	Section 5.4.1(IV) provides the right for individuals to lodge a complaint before the ESA Supervisory Authority	Article 12 GDPR

Note: The Rules of Procedure for the Data Protection Supervisory Authority, as adopted by ESA Council Resolution (ESA/C/CCLXVIII/Res.2 (Final)) (13 June 2017).

Member States must decide how best to implement it into national law.[77] This Directive does not apply to EUIs[78] (see Section 4.1 on EUIs).

The Law Enforcement Directive is similar to the GDPR in terms of the rights and obligations it gives rise to, including security requirements. It also includes the Chapter 5 requirements on the transfer of personal data to countries outside the European Union and to international organisations, as detailed in the previous section, which is important for entities such as the International Criminal Police Organization (INTERPOL).[79] Within the Law Enforcement Directive certain obligations, such as the obligation for transparency, are lower than in the GDPR in order to avoid prejudicing the prevention, investigation, or prosecution of a criminal offence.[80] For other elements within the Directive, there remains a high requirement for security mirroring the GDPR. Therefore, there is not a considerable difference in the EU data protection law *vis a vis* public security. Thus, if a criminal offence was to take place in space, where an EU Member State law applies by virtue of Article VIII of the Outer Space Treaty, the Law Enforcement Directive would apply.

Taking the International Space Station (ISS) as an example where criminal activity could take place, the ISS is governed by the Intergovernmental Agreement (IGA) on Space Station Cooperation.[81] The European member states of ESA signed this agreement, known within the IGA as the "European Partner." Article 5.2 of the IGA refers to Article VIII of the Outer Space Treaty and reiterates that each partner "shall retain jurisdiction and control over the elements it registers ... and over personnel in or on the Space Station who are its nationals." The nation refers to the IGA signatory State of which the astronaut is a national. Article 22 of the IGA governs criminal jurisdiction and states, in the first instance, that the State of the alleged criminal offender has jurisdiction. Thus, for example, if a French astronaut committed a criminal offence under French law, the French government would have jurisdiction and would be required to treat the astronaut's personal data in line with the Law Enforcement Directive. Note that within Article 22 of the IGA there is an alternative for criminal jurisdiction in certain instances, including if the alleged

77 TFEU, Art. 288.

78 Directive (EU) 2016/680, Art. 2(3).

79 Directive (EU) 2016/680, Chap. V.

80 Law Enforcement Directive, Recital 44, Art. 13.

81 Agreement among the Government of Canada, Governments of the member states of the European Space Agency, the Government of Japan, the Government of the Russian Federation and the Government of the United States of America Concerning Cooperation on the Civil International Space Station, done 29 January 1998, entered into force 27 March 2001, A/AC.105/C.2/2013/CRP. 24 (16 April 2013).

offender's State does not investigate the alleged incident, the victim's State may claim jurisdiction, in which case the Law Enforcement Directive would not apply *vis a vis* the victim's State.

5.2 *National Security*

While public security is treated in a very similar manner to the GDPR, national security is very different because it is outside the scope of European Union law. Article 4(2) of the TEU states that matters of national security are not regulated by the European Union and remain the sole competence of the individual European Union Member State. Thus, the GDPR does not apply to the processing of personal data for the purposes of safeguarding national security and defence.[82] However, European Union Member States may implement national laws to address the processing of personal data in the defence and security sphere. For the avoidance of doubt, the definition of what constitutes "national security" is a matter for the national law of individual European Union Member States.[83]

While European Union data protection law via the GDPR, or otherwise, is not applicable to national security, other international instruments are applicable to national security. For instance, the original data protection law and the first legally binding international instrument in the data protection field is the Council of Europe's 1981 "Convention 108" (as amended in 2018),[84] which is applicable to national security issues. This Convention is outside European Union law; the Council of Europe is a human rights international organisation that all European Union Member States are members of. The Convention essentially contains the key principles that are seen in the GDPR, including rights and requirements for transparency and security. Article 11 details exemptions to the data protection requirements on the basis of national security (among other things). It provides that such exemptions may only be provided for national security purposes if "it constitutes a necessary and proportionate measure in a democratic society," known as the democratic necessity test.[85] Essentially, a State needs to be able to demonstrate why the exemption

82 GDPR, Recital 16.

83 Case T-26/01 Fiocchi Munizioni v Commission [2003] ECR II-03951, para 58.

84 Convention for the Protection of Individuals with regard to Automatic Processing of Personal Data, European Treaty Series No 108, as modernised by Amending Protocol (CETS: 223).

85 Democratic necessity test discussed in relation to the European Convention of Human Rights: Handyside v. the United Kingdom judgment of 7 December 1976, A 24; Silver v. the United Kingdom, report of 11 October 1981, B 51 judgment of 25 March 1983, A 61; and Lingens v. Austria judgment of 8 July 1986, A 103.

is needed in a certain instance. For example, a State should not provide the exemption to all employees working in their national defence office as this would not be necessary – fulfilling employees data protection rights would not hinder security interests. Thus, any exemption must be proportionate and measured in light of the purpose for which the national security exemption is needed.

Due to Convention 108, it is likely that claims to 'national security' will not serve as a blanket exemption to European Union Member States data protection laws. For example, in the United Kingdom an individual (pre-Brexit) asked MI5 whether MI5 had any of their personal data. MI5 did not confirm or deny whether they held the individual's personal data on the basis of a national security exemption.[86] The national court ruled that there should not be a blanket exemption and any exemption should not be "wider than is necessary to protect national security." The court stated that any determination must take into consideration "the consequence for national security if the data is released or even its existence is acknowledged at the time of the request."[87] Ultimately each situation will need to be determined on its own merits as to whether necessity can be demonstrated, with any disputes in this regard ultimately needing to be determined by the courts.

Therefore, if personal data is processed in the context of space activities that fall within the scope of "national security" for a European Union Member State, the GDPR will not be applicable. However, national law may provide additional laws that are applicable in those contexts due to Convention 108 requirements. Thereafter, any exemption to data protection law should be taken in light of the 'democratic necessity' test and be pressure tested to ensure that the processing activity is indeed a necessity on the basis of national security.

Regarding dual use space activities, meaning that the activity may be both for civilian and military purposes, there is no significant academic discussion surrounding data protection law and dual use activities. Article 346 of the TFEU is the key article to consider for dual activities; Article 346(1)(a) of the TFEU clarifies that European Union Member States are not obliged "to supply information the disclosure of which it considers contrary to the essential interests of its security." Thus, notwithstanding Article 4(2) of the TEU, described above, this can be read to mean that no European Union law (GDPR or otherwise) can oblige European Union Member States to disclose personal information if it

86 Baker v Secretary of State for the Home Department [2001] UKHRR 1275.

87 [2001] UKHRR 1275, [113], see description in Scott, Paul F, National Security, Data Protection, and Data Sharing after the Data Protection Act 2018 (February 23, 2019), at 3–4.

would impact the European Union Member State's 'essential' security interests. In determining whether something is 'essential' the European Union Member State needs to take into account whether it is necessary in light of the security interest and whether it is a proportionate approach in light of the security interest.[88] Thus, whether data protection law applies to dual use space activities will need to be assessed on a case-by-case basis in light of the purpose for the personal data processing. For example, consider a remote sensing project that gathers satellite imagery and geographical location data about individuals for civilian humanitarian aid, and this project is also being conducted for defence surveillance purposes to track terrorists. The information about the individuals remains the same, but the individual would be entitled to the protections under data protection law regarding the civilian purpose, and would likely not be entitled to that protection under the defence purpose. Thus, if the individual requested to receive information about what information was collected and why, the individual would only receive information back regarding the civilian purpose.

This section covered the final group, for the purposes of this chapter, with distinct European Union data protection laws, namely space activities involving security and defence. This section showed that the core tenants of European Union data protection law provided in Section 3 (transparency and security) are even considered within the security and defence sphere.

6 Conclusion

This chapter provided a tour of the European Union data protection law that is applicable to the space sector, and will become more relevant with further advancements in this area. This chapter covered the spectrum of European Union data protection law, from how privacy laws are applicable in space via Article VIII of the Outer Space Treaty to the GDPR and ESA's Data Policy. The future of space is very exciting, but the future of space will inevitably involve more personal data, just as the space sector touches on a plethora of other legal areas. The key principles of European Union data protection law, being transparency and security, were touched on throughout this chapter and it will be interesting to see how the space sector implements these principles going forward, in particular, considering remote sensing advancements. One of the

88 What is an 'essential' security interest is determined via a necessity and proportionality test, see discussion by Vincenzo Randazzo, Art. 346 and the qualified application of EU law to defence, European Union Institute for Security Studies, Brief 22, July 2014, at 3.

requirements of European Union data protection law to ensure data protection principles, are built into the lifecycle of systems, is privacy by design,[89] which requires that items are designed with privacy principles in mind. The space sector can take advantage of their position and already begin designing future space architecture with privacy principles accounted for, as the future of space will certainly involve personal data.

89 GDPR, Art. 25.

CHAPTER 11

The Regulation of the 'Open Data' Policy and Its Elements: The Legal Perspective of the EU Copernicus Programme

Sandra Cabrera Alvarado

1 Introduction

Satellite 'open data' is not a new term in the space sector. In fact, in the Earth observation (EO) sector, the United States EO program Landsat introduced the use of EO open data to the scientific community after its launch in the early 70's and enshrined it by law in the Land Remote Sensing Policy Act of 1992.[1] By doing so, the US Congress recognized the open data practice as crucial guaranteeing it a position as long-term practice in the Landsat programme.

More countries have decided to emulate this initiative and adopted an open data policy for their EO national programmes due to the economic and social benefits this practice brings to the society. Nevertheless, despite the fact that legal frameworks and policies have been issued to regulate EO open data distribution, none have precisely defined the term EO 'open data'. As a consequence, different interpretations, expectations, and understandings of the open data policy occur among the legislators and diplomats. For example, just the question of 'how far open is open?' can generate debate.

Although the international legal and political practice shows convergence on some open data elements, there is still a need of mapping and identifying them to achieve some clarity, mainly regarding its level of regulation. Some organisations, such as the Group on Earth Observation (GEO)[2] and the Committee on Earth Observation Satellites (CEOS)[3] strived to shed some light in this matter by defining the term EO open data, yet the level of regulation of its elements needs to be further analysed for a coherent implementation. Most importantly, it is critical to clarify which elements should be preserved by law on a long-term basis, while others should remain in a policy shape with

1 Land Remote Sensing Policy Act of 1992, 102 Pub. L. 555 (1992), codified at 51 U.S.C. 6010.

2 GEO Secretariat, *The Value of Open Data Sharing* (Paris 2015): 43.

3 Joint ICSU/CODATA ad hoc Group on Data and Information, 'Data Access Policies,' (accessed 25 June 2019), www.codata.info/data_access/policies.html.

 DOI:10.1163/9789004527270_012

a guideline character to have an accurate understanding of expectations, risks and limitations of the open access activity.

This chapter contributes to the discourse on open data in the EO context by proposing a 3x3 Model, based on the Copernicus programme regulatory framework's experience in defining openness. This model aims to explain the main elements and itslevels of regulation seen from a regional perspective, by being one of the first legal texts to define open data with an initial step of using the terms of full, free, and open. Although the law does not go further and leaves these terms undefined, the practice of openness in the EU programme Copernicus leads us the way to identify several elements that comprehensibly explain the terms of full, free, and open, which shall be explained and analysed in this chapter.

2 Convergent Elements of Openness in the EO Data

The common needs and interests of several actors worldwide led to the establishment of national open data policies in EO programmes aimed to provide broader access to data from different sources and to overcome existing legal limitations. For example, high prices and restrictive licenses on sharing data and information hindered the development of value-added products for environmental purposes and meteorology.

The adoption of the open data policy for the United States' Landsat programme in the 90's enshrined in law the most prominent elements of "non-discriminatory access"[4] and the limitation of charging the data flow only at a "cost of fulfilling user requests."[5] Other national EO programmes followed the US example when adopting their EO data policies. The adoption of the open data policies did not come in isolation from national interpretations. Analysing these data policies, the existence of some convergent elements on their data distribution and access regulation can be noted. These legislations have converged on the key aspects of openness when regulating the access and distribution of EO data and information.

Although in practice, open data policy implementation has convergent elements with similar interpretations, these policies can still differ in their wording and importantly, in the level of regulation from hard to soft law. It is

4 The non-discriminatory principle is present in the Land Remote Sensing Policy Act of 1992, Chap. V, § 5651(a).

5 Land Remote Sensing Policy Act of 1992, Chap. V, § 5651(d). For further information, see, *infra*, 2.3).

precisely the level of regulation that impacts the interpretations and expectations of open data policy execution. As a consequence, the definition of 'open data' is critical to understanding the scope, limitations, and efficiency of the implemented policy. But this must be understood in light of the lack of a legal definition in statutory law in many cases which leaves room for interpretation in its implementation.

To understand further the legal meaning of an 'open data,'[6] this chapter develops a representation of the open data policy depicting its key convergent elements and its levels of regulations based on the Copernicus' open data policy by developing a 3x3 Model.[7] Most importantly, these basic elements should guarantee the expected benefits of openness and clarify its limitations on access.

The Model is divided in the main three pillars of open, full, and free that are established in the current Copernicus legislations – Regulation 377/2014 and Delegated Regulation 1159/2013.[8] Each pillar counts with several elements that conform it, along with its regulation. There are three regulatory levels: 1) the binding legal acts for authorities; 2) the contracts defining the relationship between the authority and the user; and 3) the policy documents. The analysis of these levels and the identification of their elements brings us to the formation of the 3×3 Model (Figure 11.1).

Based on the Copernicus example which follows the same trend as other national EO programmes, it can be said that these elements – including their legal effect, validity, and enforceability – must be maintained in order to guarantee the idea of an open data policy. In particular, these elements should be considered as a set of specific requirements necessary for open data policy implementation to provide and deliver the openness of any regional EO

6 Christophe Venet, *Key Trends in the European Earth Observation Sector* (IFRI 2011): 4.

7 This trend for open data policy implementation is visible across developing and developed countries, with the Brazilian-Sino satellite CBERS-2 granting a free access to the satellite and the ground stations data; France with Spot World Heritage Archive Licence Agreement between SPOT and the End User which provides a "Non-Exclusive Licence to Use Spot Archive Product for Non-Commercial Purpose Only"; Germany with Earth Observation on the WEB (EOWEB GeoPortal) released in 2018 which shares on an online platform satellite data and products of the DLR satellites TerraSAR-X data, TanDEM-X products, amongst others; India with Bhuvan Indian Geo-Platform of ISRO, 'Open Data Archive'; and Japan with JAXA's ALOS-2 satellite and its Science Project initiative, among many others.

8 These legislations have been replaced by the Regulation of the European Parliament and of the Council establishing the space programme of the Union and the European Union Agency for the Space Programme. See Proposal for a Regulation of the European Parliament and of the Council establishing the space programme of the Union and the European Union Agency for the Space Programme, COM/2018/447 final – 2018/0236 (COD).

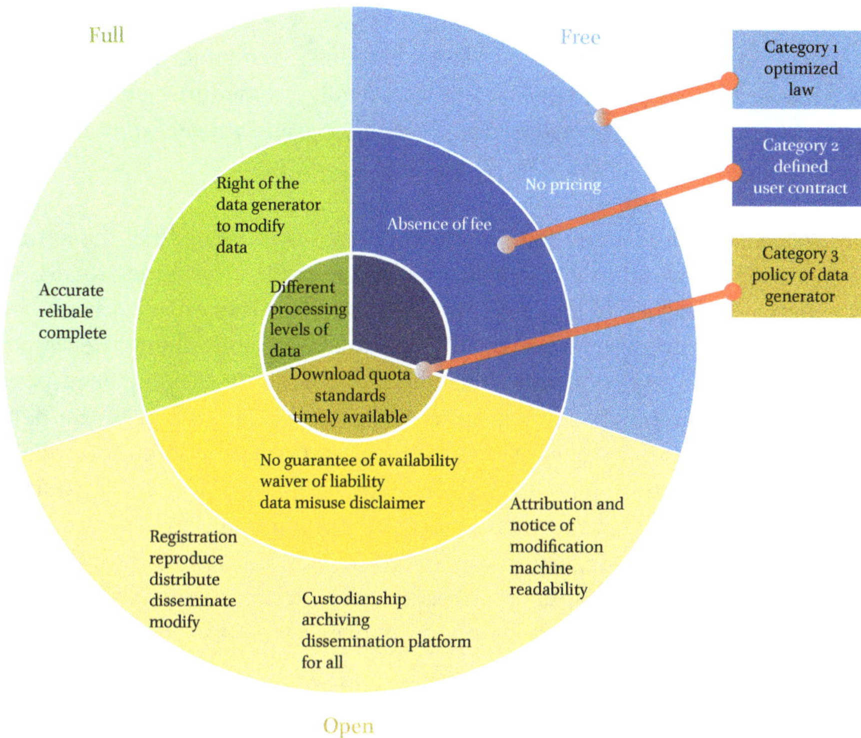

FIGURE 11.1 The 3×3 Model: Core elements defining openness
SOURCE: AUTHOR, TAKEN FROM HER DOCTORAL THESIS "THE PURSUIT OF OPENNESS"

programme. The next section will deconstruct the legal definition of these elements and their level of regulation.

2.1 *'Open' Pillar*

Different from the pillars of 'free' and 'full', what distinguishes the 'open' pillar is the heavy influence of technical aspects that shape its elements. Some of these elements have been already identified under the Harris and Browning Model.[9] The main contribution of Copernicus programme is the inclusion of these elements in the law, thereby assuring the highest level of commitment; consequently, long-term preservation is left outside of the discretion of the data provider.

---

9 Ray Harris and Richard Browning, *Global Monitoring: The Challenges of Access to Data* (Routledge 2005): 72.

2.1.1 First Level: Essential Elements in Law

The elements enshrined in the hard law to be considered under the open pillar are: 1) ownership or custodianship, 2) access to all, 3) dissemination platforms, 4) machine readability, 5) registration, 6) archiving, and 7) users' digital rights.

2.1.1.1 *Ownership*

Although some could argue that open data has no owner due to of the nature of openness allowing everyone to use the data, it must be understood that indeed data, regardless of its openness, does have an owner or, as explained by Harris and Browning, a custodianship.[10] A custodian appointment is necessary to implement the tasks of data management and handling. Among its responsibilities, the custodian has the competence to leverage legal barriers for data sharing and distribution. In case where several parties are involved in a collaborative regime to develop an EO system, a clear distribution of responsibility is paramount for the management and handling of open data. For example, Article 28 of the Copernicus Regulation 377/2014 identifies the Commission as the owner of tangible and intangible assets and with this the main responsible entity of management and distribution of data under an open data policy.

2.1.1.2 *Access to All*

Open data policies provide access to EU data to all users worldwide. This approach is also defined as 'non-discriminatory access'. In the Copernicus case, the legal term used is 'access to all' under Article 3 of Delegated Regulation 1159/2013[11] and Article 23.2 of Regulation 377/2014.[12] Copernicus shall grant access to EO data without establishing any exception, legal restriction, or technical limitation on the basis of nationality or user type and provide the same terms and conditions for all.[13] Any violation or absence of these characteristics would alter the legal intent of the open pillar and the 'access to all' principle.

Nevertheless, as in other international practices, this principle is subject to general limitations based on political and economic protection of the custodian and its international relations. Currently, the main limitation on access to

10 *Id.*

11 Delegated Regulation 1159/2013, Art. 3 ("Users shall have free, full and open access to GMES dedicated data and GMES service information").

12 Regulation (EU) 377/2014 of the European Parliament and of the Council of 3 April 2014 Establishing the Copernicus Programme, 122 O.J. L (2014), Art. 23.2 ("Dedicated mission data and Copernicus information shall be made available through Copernicus dissemination platforms, under pre-defined technical conditions, on a full, open and free-of-charge basis …").

13 "GEO13," *Data Science Journal*, v. 8 (7 October 2009).

EO data and information are constraints linked to the protection of national security interests, foreign policy, and international obligations, as well as overlaps with military interests regarding critical areas and privacy violations.[14]

2.1.1.3 *Dissemination Platforms*

The Copernicus programme went forward in the implementation of the 'openness' element by introducing in law for the first time the establishment of data dissemination platforms, requiring the data custodian to employ specific technical efforts. Article 23 of Copernicus Regulation 377/2014 mentiones the existence of such dissemination platforms, ensuring under pre-defined technical conditions the practice of disseminating data as widely as possible.

2.1.1.4 *Machine Readability*

Ensuring by law the machine readability of the EO data through a unified format diminishes the risk of theincompatibility of datadue to the variety of formats and enhancing data usage. As Copernicus is a regional programme based on data sharing enshrined in the European INSPIRE Directive,[15] this element has been included in the legal instrument on Copernicus. In such regional programme with open data policy, the envisaged machine readability assures the homologation of data formats to ensure interoperability among users located in different locations and using different dataset formats. Even if data are available and easily findable, the lack of machine readability could easily lead to the non-access to data and thus a failure of the open data policy.

2.1.1.5 *Registration of Users*

Although this specific feature of the approach to EO data is not a constitutive element of all open data policies, it can be important in ensuring better administration and control of the data and information, especially for security and metrics purposes. Its instruments are i.e., the measurement of data downloads, monitoring of geographic regions of users, and the types of demanded usage.[16] The requirement of registration is not always regulated by law. For example, the US Landsat regulation does not require the custodian to impose a registration to the user; therefore, the US National Oceanic and Atmospheric

---

14 Matxalen Sánchez Aranzamendi, Rainer Sandau, and Kai-Uwe Schrogl, 'Current Legal Issues for Satellite Earth Observation' (Vienna: ESPI, August 2010): 48.

15 Directive 2007/2/EC of the European Parliament and of the Council of 14 March 2007 establishing an Infrastructure for Spatial Information in the European Community (INSPIRE), O.J. L 108.

16 Serco, *ESA Sentinel Data Access Annual Report 2018* (5 June 2019).

Administration (NOAA) who disseminates Landsat data does not have a specific registration procedure.[17] This absence of registration of the users of the EO data can impact tracking of their behaviour, needs, and origin, while at the same time it provides freedom. Contrary to the US legislation, Article 17 of Copernicus Delegated Regulation 1159/2013 establishes a registration process for users who want to download and modify data.[18]

2.1.1.6 *Archiving of Data*

This element can be defined as a reflection of forward thinking. The importance of this element is linked to data preservation as a long-term practice in spite of the high costs of data storage. Copernicus law includes this element and obliges the custodianship to bear the costs of archiving to preserve Copernicus data under its Article 6[19] of Regulation 377/2014. To compare, due to its costly nature, other EO open data policy systems do not regulate this element by law, but as a best practice. The remaining question is the accessibility of EO data archives: Limitations of access to such archives are legally possible as the EU law remains silent on the request or access to such archives, but covers only the question of the storage of data. Consequently, the response to a request for access to EO data archives raised by foreign companies could be delayed or even restricted.

2.1.2 Second Level: User's Contract

In implementing the legal framework, the custodian or data provider communicates these rights to the Copernicus users in the form of a user's contract. In case of Copernicus, Article 7 of the Delegated Regulation 1159/2013 allows the reproduction, distribution, dissemination, adaptation, and modification of Copernicus data and information. As a result, the Copernicus user contract, issued through the dissemination platforms, governs the end-users' handling with the data and grants them the authorisation to "redistribute, disseminate *any* Copernicus (…) product in their original form via *any* media, modify, adapt, develop, create and distribute Value Added Products or Derivate Work (…) for

---

17 NOAA, 'GOES Imagery Viewer – NOAA / NESDIS / STAR' (accessed 15 February 2020) https://www.star.nesdis.noaa.gov/GOES/index.php.

18 Delegated Regulation (EU) No 1159/2013, Art. 17.

19 Regulation 377/2014, art. 6 ("(a) provision of spaceborne observations, including: (I) completion, maintenance and operation of dedicated missions, including tasking of the satellites, monitoring and control of the satellites, reception, processing, archiving and dissemination of data, permanent calibration and validation").

any purpose."[20] Hence, in an open data policy, these user rights should not be exchangeable or altered, but be preserved to achieve the goal of the openness.

2.1.2.1 *Reproduction, Distribution, Dissemination, Adaptation and Modification*

To preserve these rights in the user's contract, ESA, as the main responsible entity for the data dissemination and management,[21] issues an open data licence in the form of the CC BY-SA 3.0[22] IGO (Attribution-ShareAlike) Creative Commons (CC).[23] The type of or even the use of the license are not specified in the framework of Copernicus law, thus a margin of manoeuvre exists as long as the users' digital rights are respected. ESA found that the CC open licence fits the Copernicus' open data principles stated in Copernicus legislation.

In addition, the data provider should also communicate the reaches or limitations of the open data policy. A disclaimer in the user contract establishes the conditions of no warranty and a waiver of liability stating that "express or implied warranty, including as regards quality and suitability for any purpose" of the service[24] are excluded. These disclaimers represent a protection of the data generator *vis a vis* the user in cases of misuse of the data or faulty information provision.

Although the responsibility of the data supplier is to provide accurate and quality data, disclaimers are permissible under the premise that the data supplier is executing its responsibility under its best efforts in the processing, management, and distribution of data and information. Also, as this technology is in a constant evolution, such disclaimers of non-warranty and waiver of liability should be considered permissible. Moreover, in the case of Copernicus,

20 Copernicus, "Marine," (accessed 12 December 2021) https://www.copernicus.eu/en/copernicus-services/marine.

21 *See* ESA – EC GMES Agreement on the Implementation of the Space Component of GMES of 28 February 2008 [ESA/LEG/382], which establishes the basis of the GMES Space Component, including infrastructure in space (space segment) and on the ground, delivering Sentinel data with quality standards to end users.

22 'Conditions of Use & FAQ for ESA Images, Videos and Other Content Licenced under Creative Commons' (Accessed 6 December 2021) http://open.esa.int/image-usage-creative-commons/.

23 Creative Commons developed its licenses based in part on the Free Software Foundation's GNU General Public License (GNU GPL), alongside a web application platform to help to license works freely for certain uses, on certain conditions, or dedicate the works to the public domain. *See* www.creativecommons.org.

24 European Commission, "Legal notice on the use of Copernicus Sentinel Data and Service Information" (n.d.) https://sentinel.esa.int/documents/247904/690755/Sentinel_Data_Legal_Notice.

ESA includes a condition in its Term of Data Supply, not established in the legal texts, stating that the user "shall act in good faith and shall not misuse or interfere with the service of the portals."[25] These terms and conditions are essential in the open data policy practice to enhance the benefits of the open data policy, while also protecting the data distributor.

2.1.3 Third Level: Policy of the Data Generator

There are certain elements of the open data policy that are not governed by law, but instead by the data generator in its own data policies that represent guidelines more suitable for change any time. These elements are download quotas and data processing standards.

2.1.3.1 *Download Quotas*

In EO programmes with open data policies, the numbers of users might increase exponentially. To face this challenge, the data supplier needs to develop the most adequate data policies or measures to efficiently handle and distribute data to the users preserving their expectations. How the data supplier handles the data in terms of download rates, quality, and technical standards is not defined by law, and the data supplier is left with wide discretion to adopt the best measures that fit the EO reception system. In the case of Copernicus, the only valid policy would be the one that imposes certain download quota by arguing that a heavy traffic in download could jeopardize the integrity of the system. This measure is not intended to limit the access to data, but it does constitute a certain limitation of the data flow that finds its place in the silence of the law. For example, in relation to the Copernicus programme, ESA makes a distinction between two concurrent data downloads for the scientific community, and ten concurrent downloads for the EU Member States and the European institutions.[26]

Regarding data processing standards, neither the European Union nor the US Landsat establish any specific standards of the data processing phase on the data generators, and thus leave the processing quota to their discretion.[27] For example, a degradation of service response times and occasional downtime[28]

25 ESA, 'Terms of the Copernicus Data Hub Portals and Data Supply Conditions' (n.d.) §9, https://scihub.copernicus.eu/twiki/do/view/SciHubWebPortal/TermsConditions.

26 Serco, 'ESA Sentinel Data Access Annual Report 2018' p.11.

27 ESA, 'Sentinel-2 MSI Document Library – User Guides – Sentinel Online' (accessed 6 December 2021) https://sentinels.copernicus.eu/web/sentinel/user-guides/sentinel-2-msi/document-library.

28 ESA, 'Open Access Hub.'

are the elements of the processing standards that can take place without breaching the open data policy legal principles. A system maintenance is also an element crucial for the efficiency of an EO system that is not necessarily regulated by law, yet important in regional programmes where several actors are responsible in the handling and management of data.

2.1.3.2 *Timely Delivery*

Another element of the efficient open data policy is the timely delivery of data. Harris highlights the delivery of data in a timely manner as a key contribution to maximizing the benefit of the data yet not defined by law. In the Copernicus case, Article 4 of the Regulation 377/2014 requires the provision of *accurate, timely,* and *reliable* information. Thus, the EU Commission is bound to provide complete datasets with the widest access possible and with as little disruption as possible. However, there is no definition of how timely is 'timely'. The interpretation of this term is left to the discretion of the data supplier. Taking into consideration ESA's interpretation of this notion in relation to the Copernicus satellites, with respect to the Sentinels, information from Sentinel 2A and 2B is made available online via the online platform Copernicus Open Access Hub, on average 5 hours after being gathered via remote sensing (the full range is 2 to 12 hours)[29] whereas Sentinel 1 SAR data are accessible after 24 hours. Some products are even available within 1 hour after reception. However, a distinction is made in terms of delivery. For critical Copernicus services and Member States' national services, notably maritime surveillance, data are transmitted in real-time for reception by local collaborative ground stations.[30] As a result, delays are permissible for certain services, in order to provide reliable and quality information, depending on the type of data and user typology.

Although this feature has been subject to specific recommendations, by the EO data policy advocates – such as the GEOSS Data Sharing Principles,[31] there are only few traces of attempts to adopt binding legal rules in this area.[32] Should

29 ESA, 'FAQ – Sentinel Online' (accessed 26 August 2019) https://sentinel.esa.int/web/sentinel/faq.

30 ESA, 'Sentinel Online, Data Distribution Schedule,' (accessed 26 August 2019) https://sentinels.copernicus.eu/web/sentinel/missions/sentinel-1/data-distribution-schedule.

31 Group on Earth Observations, *Implementation Guidelines for the GEOSS Data Sharing Principles* (GEO, 17 November 2009).

32 According to international political documents, such as the CEOS principles, "real time" is defined as "making data available by direct broadcast or immediately after acquisition and/or initial processing." However, the time of reception and dissemination of the data depends on the type of data and the quality control applied to processing the data into reliable information.

the law specify these conditions, or should they remain broadly drafted? We argue that as a minimum, some guidelines defining the time period within which the data and information must be released is desirable when there is no a binding provision.

All these elements are indispensable for the open data policy programmes. They find their place in the policy sphere and are subject to easier modification as they are not governed by formal law. In other words, the technicalities of data management and handling are eligible for modification, but not the legal principles such as the non-discriminatory principle[33] or the users' rights. In some cases, the terms used by the legislators such as the "free access" is the same, but in others the selected notion is different, such as the "access for all" in case of the EU programmes, or "non-discriminatory access" in the US Landsat progamme where any kind of end user, either citizen, organisation or State can access EO data and information.

In the international arena, however, although the UN Remote Sensing Principles, following the US example, also worded this principle as 'non-discriminatory access,' the aim is the same, but its scope is different. These principles are applicable to sovereign nations' access to data from their territories, rather than to the civil society. In addition, the origin of this legal principle is different. While the US and EU cases aim – among other reasons – to foster innovation through the development of EO value-added products worldwide,[34] in the UN case this principlewas intended to mitigate the use of EO technologies without prior authorization of the sensed State. Thus, the background of the 'non-discriminatory access' can differ, yet its purpose is the same, to provide access to data with a minimum of economic and political barriers possible.

The other two pillars of 'full' and 'open' have several elements which are equally important as the 'open' pillar.

2.2 *'Full' Pillar*

The reader might have the tendency to exchange the terms of full and open in their substance. This approach would be inaccurate. To shed some light on the definition of the notion 'full', it is useful to take as a basis the etymological explanation, which is 'ample' or 'complete'.[35] In other words, 'full' relates to the characteristics of the data or the information, implicating the access to

33 Nextspace, *Study on the Copernicus Data Policy Post-2020* (2019): 55.

34 Radiant Earth, 'Open Satellite Data Downloads' (n.d.) https://geospatialmedia.s3.amazonaws.com.

35 The Law Dictionary (accessed 22 January 2019) https://thelawdictionary.org/letter/f/.

integral and complete data, and it is not related to the means of how the users acquire the data or through which mechanism – these fall under the 'open' pillar's access feature.

The term 'full' refers to the presentation and handling of information in its authentic form without any abrogation or alteration of datasets or information, unless it is duly justified under the protection of national security, international relations, or privacy. In case of open data systems, data generators strive to provide EO data to users as complete as possible and with minimal errors; nevertheless, there is no law that binds them to fulfill certain expectations of users. Under the view that open data is free of charge and the users should be pleased and grateful, the Copernicus programme raises the bar by binding the data provider with key elements that raise users' expectations regarding the level of quality of data.

2.2.1 First Level: Essential Elements in Law

In its aim to establish a legal definition of the term 'full,' the European legislator mentions three key elements the provision of data must correspond under an open data policy: accurate, reliable, and comprehensive.

2.2.1.1 *Accuracy, Reliability and Comprehensiveness*

According to Article 4.2 of Regulation 377/2014, the data provider – in this case the Commission through ESA – should provide *accurate and reliable* Copernicus data, information and services.[36] To achieve these legal expectations, the Regulation obliges the data generator to take necessary technical measures to ensure minimal disruption in the processing of data.[37] As a consequence, the data generator must follow high standards of data and information management to achieve consistency, continuity, reliability, and quality in the provision and distribution of data.[38] Corrupted datasets, missing areas of the image, blurriness, or poor quality resolution would contravene the intent to ensure integrity and comprehensive data and information. A margin of error is permitted based on the best efforts of the data provider's technical capacity;

36 Regulation 377/2014, Art. 4.2 ("Copernicus shall have the following specific objectives: a) delivering accurate and reliable data and information to Copernicus users, supplied on a long-term and sustainable basis enabling the services referred to in Article 5(1) and responding to the requirements of Copernicus core users …").

37 European Parliament, 'European Parliament Legislative Resolution of 4 April 2019 on the Proposal for a Directive of the European Parliament and of the Council on Open Data and the Re-Use of Public Sector Information,' P8_TC1-COD(2018)0111 (2019): preamb. 54.

38 *Id.* at preamb. 56.

yet, failure to meet users' expectations could diminish the value of the EO data with negative consequences for users, and impact the sustainability and credibility of the EO programmes and its open data policy.

On the other hand, it is well known that full access to EO data does not mean an unconditional total access. Legal limitations to the 'full' principle and its elements could be invoked based on the protection of public interests, such as security. Data can be lawfully downgraded, delayed, or provided partially. However, in open data policies the fewest disruptions or alterations should be preserved, taking into consideration both technological developments and public interest protection. The right to these limitations handled by the data provider are further specified in the user's terms and conditions.

2.2.2 Second Level: User's Contract

2.2.2.1 *Right of the Data Provider to Terminate or Modify Data*

It is well known that in open data policies, where data is available to all with no fee, the provider cannot guarantee their total delivery. Although the data provider acknowledges and endeavours to make complete or near-complete data available to users, a failure of delivery could be caused either by technological circumstances or the protection of public interests. These must be notified to the user though the user's terms and conditions.

2.2.2.2 *'Different Levels of Processing' Provision*

The Copernicus programme has introduced a further element of the open data policies in the user contracts. It deals with the level of processing of the data to be provided to the user. It is well known there are several types of data processing and several expectations of users depending on the type of data (that is, optical or radar satellite data). For example, Copernicus users can access either raw data or a high-level processed data; these specificities are not included in the law but are formulated in the internal policies of the entity. The data provider can decide any time whether the users outside a region would get data with the maximum level of processing (that is Level 3) or raw data (which could be of high interest of researchers in the SAR [radar] data). For example, in the case of the Copernicus ESA Hub, raw SAR data from Sentinel-1 are available to the public, whereas raw optical data from Sentinel 2 are not.[39] These availabilities are usually conditioned onthe users' needs, skills and interests. Consequently, a restriction based on the level of processing of data under this element is in line with the effective law.

39 ESA, 'Open Access Hub' (accessed 12 July 2019) https://scihub.copernicus.eu/userguide/.

Our last pillar is the 'free pillar' with only few elements, as its explanation is based on its economic nature.

2.3 'Free'

Some readers might understand the notion of 'free access' as using data without any legal barriers. However, 'free' should be understood in the economic sense and not be confused with the freedom of access formulated by the 'open pillar'. This nuance and difference is crucial when drafting an open data policy and its terms and conditions. This economic meaning is also used in international practice and the case of Copernicus is not anexception.

It is reflected in the two main legal conditions formulated by the 'free' pillar. Either 1) the public institutions assume the costs and provide the information and data without charge,[40] or 2) they allow a marginal cost pricing, which ideally covers the costs of collection, production, reproduction, and dissemination of the data and information, that is, digitalization operations.[41] For the Copernicus programme, the European Union chose the establishment of a no-fee system instead of the cost recovery required for Landsat data.

2.3.1 First Level: Provision without Any User's Fee

To guarantee this 'free of cost' provision to the user, the European Union embedded this 'gratuity' into Articles 3[42] and 4[43] of Delegated Regulation 1159/2013. Article 3 states that "[u]sers shall have free, full and open access to

40 Article 6 of the Open Data Directive allows to charge for information, establishing a threshold to avoid public service institutions to charge higher costs and any profit. The main principle is that this charge aims to recover the costs of the handle and management of information only. The same principle of the marginal cost is included in the INSPIRE Directive in its preamble, Article 17 promoting the sharing of geo-spatial data, as well as the Aarhus Convention, Article 3, which, in order to leverage all possible stopovers to the right of information, allows public bodies to charge the data under the condition that the charge "shall not exceed a reasonable amount." Regarding the space data and information, Landsat, ESA, and EUMETSAT allow for charging a marginal cost for the data under open data policies from their space missions in order to shift some part of the economic burden from the institutions.

41 Heiko Richter, 'Open Science and Public Sector Information – Reconsidering the Exemption for Educational and Research Establishments under the Directive on Re-Use of Public Sector Information,' *Journal of Intellectual Property, Information Technology and E-Commerce Law* v. 9(1) (2018) https://www.jipitec.eu/issues/jipitec-9-1-2018/4679.

42 Regulation (EU) No. 1159/2013, Arti. 3 ("Users shall have free, full and open access to GMES dedicated data and GMES service information ...").

43 Regulation (EU) No. 1159/2013, Article 4 ("Free access shall be given to GMES dedicated data and GMES service information made available through GMES dissemination platforms ...").

GMES dedicated data and GMES service information";[44] this principle is also replicated in Article 52 of the new regulation of the EU space programme by reaffirming the 'free' term in the provision related to Copernicus data and information.[45] These legal foundations can be explained by the hypothesis that the most fundamental principle on which the free access principle rests, is the existence of a common interest by all members of the EU region, followed by bearing of the costs by the European citizens.

In case that a regional programme intends to implement an open data policy, it is paramount that all members of the region share the same interests and agree upon the adoption of the 'free pillar' when achieving the open data promise. Otherwise, the open data policy would not have the expected effect and reach.

2.3.2 Second Level: User's Contract Notification of Gratuity

The data provider should notify to the user in its terms and conditions, that the data and information is not subject to a fee, and that also no licence fee is required. Based on the Copernicus programme, this notification corresponds to the Copernicus' legal framework. In case this legal framework is modified and a recovery fee is required, or in case of any other change in the legal texts, this step will impact the drafting of the user's contract. In other words, the user's contract shall reflect the modifications of the legal texts of the EO programme.

3 Conclusion

This contribution proposes a 3x3 Model explaining the core elements of the full, free, and open pillars that leads to a comprehensive open data policy and its divergent levels of regulation. An understanding of the general expectations of the open data policy, its legal intent and its purpose could dissipate myths, fears, and misunderstandings.[46] The three levels of regulation are classified

---

44 Delegated Regulation (EU) No 1159/2013, Art. 3.

45 Proposal for a Regulation of the European Parliament and of the Council establishing the space programme of the Union and the European Union Agency, Art. 52.1 ("Copernicus data and Copernicus information shall be provided to users under the following free, full and open data policy: (a) Copernicus users may, on a free and worldwide basis, reproduce, distribute, communicate to the public, adapt, modify all Copernicus data and Copernicus information and combine them with other data and information ...").

46 *See also* Marijn Janssen, Yannis Charalabidis, and Anneke Zuiderwijk, "Benefits, Adoption Barriers and Myths of Open Data and Open Government," *Information Systems Management* v. 29(4) (2012): 258–268.

from hard to soft law: 1) binding legal acts for authorities guaranteeing their long-term implementation; 2) contracts defining the relationship between the authority and the user; and 3) policy documents which serve as guidelines haveing lower legal value and being susceptible to modifications at any time. As the model shows, some of theseelements found in the model's 'Category 3' understood as a soft law may suffer from the lack of enforcement as they are not dependent on the level of regulation but at the discretion of the data provider. As a result, these elements are suitable for modifications.

In addition to the law making process, another element to consider in the open data policies implementation is the technological aspect. How technology advances will indirectly affect both the application of legal norms and the wording of the law. This effect is clearly seen in the elements of the 'open' pillar with considerable broad wording of legal provisions and thus subject to interpretation. Whereas quality and completeness of the data are the main characteristics in the provision of 'full' pillar, these are also linked to technology but not so heavily impacted. The 'free' pillar on the other hand could be considered to have no room for interpretation at any level, based on its economic nature that rules it.

In conclusion, it is mainly the technological factor which affects the drafting and interpretation of the open data policy and its pillars. All their elements are important to know as they give some clarity on the users expectations, and their coherent implementation. What is most important is to know that the key elements of the open data policy cannot be set aside to achieve the promise that it seeks. Finally, the Copernicus open data policy definition can be perceived as three musketeers. Its three pillars – full, free, and open – can be equated with the famous sentence: "All for one and one for all, united we stand divided we fall."[47]

47 Alexandre Dumas, *The Three Musketeers* (1844).

Index

www.ingramcontent.com/pod-product-compliance
Lightning Source LLC
Chambersburg PA
CBHW071228230926
51849CB00001B/57
9789004527263